THE SPIRIT OF '68

The Spirit of '68

*Rebellion in Western Europe and
North America, 1956–1976*

GERD-RAINER HORN

OXFORD

UNIVERSITY PRESS

*This book has been printed digitally and produced in a standard specification
in order to ensure its continuing availability*

OXFORD
UNIVERSITY PRESS

Great Clarendon Street, Oxford OX2 6DP
Oxford University Press is a department of the University of Oxford.
It furthers the University's objective of excellence in research, scholarship,
and education by publishing worldwide in

Oxford New York

Auckland   Cape Town Dar es Salaam   Hong Kong   Karachi
Kuala Lumpur Madrid Melbourne Mexico City   Nairobi
New Delhi Shanghai   Taipei Toronto
With offices in
Argentina Austria Brazil Chile Czech Republic France Greece
Guatemala Hungary Italy Japan South Korea Poland Portugal
Singapore Switzerland Thailand Turkey Ukraine Vietnam

Oxford is a registered trade mark of Oxford University Press
in the UK and in certain other countries

Published in the United States
by Oxford University Press Inc., New York

ISBN 978-0-19-927666-0

Acknowledgements

This book is above all the product of several decades of involvement in—and study of—social movement practice on both sides of the Atlantic. Without a six month period of study leave, however, it would never have been written. I thank the University of Warwick for one term of Study Leave, matched by a second term of Study Leave supported by the Arts and Humanities Research Council. Without the competent assistance of the staff of the University of Warwick's Interlibrary Loan service—recently ominously rebranded 'Document Supply'—the source base for this volume would have been significantly reduced. Various individuals in a number of countries furnished me with additional hard-to-find documentation. I have tried to name these benefactors when referring to the information with which I was supplied.

Several friends and colleagues read a number of chapters of earlier manuscript versions of this text: Rik Hemmerijckx, Jan Kurz, and Reiner Tosstorff. If the number of embarrassing mistakes and misinterpretations has been reduced to a tolerable minimum, then this is in good measure a result of these critics' scrutiny. Michael Kazin served as the 'anonymous' reader of the first final draft. His insightful and straightforward critique helped tremendously in the preparation of the final manuscript. It is a sign of his generosity and confidence in my project that he instructed my editor to lift the veil of anonymity. The final portion of the published text, my Conclusion, is entirely due to his urgent suggestion *not* to end with Chapter 5. Whether the substance of what I have to say in my concluding pages would meet with his approval remains to be seen, but I hope that he would agree with the spirit of this text as well.

Last but not least, a major word of thanks to Hendrik Ollivier and the support staff in the Audiovisual Department of the Institute for Social History (AMSAB) in Ghent. Hendrik Ollivier greatly facilitated access to the photo collection deposited in the AMSAB by Frans Pans. Rik Hemmerijckx first alerted me to the value and, indeed, the existence of this collection. Hendrik Ollivier then put me in touch with Frans Pans, and a first meeting with Frans Pans took place in the AMSAB in September 2004. I gratefully acknowledge the authorization by Frans Pans and the AMSAB to utilize the pictorial materials included in this book. Pans' artistic œuvre chronicles virtually the entirety of the milieux at the centre of my present study, and I chose to include a photo essay on the Belgian manifestation of '1968'—placed between Chapters 4 and 5—to illustrate the processes, people and events this book is all about. Frans Pans died on 30 July 2005. I partially dedicate this book to his memory. But I also wish to dedicate this book to my parents, Christel and Erwin Horn, who taught me to appreciate the seemingly unimportant smaller things in life, without ever losing sight of the larger picture.

 Arts & Humanities
Research Council

Contents

List of Illustrations

Introduction

This is a study of the spirit of '1968'. Pride of place is given to the dynamic towards personal and collective liberation unleashed in '1968' and the rise of social movements at that time. Written at a time of widespread pessimism experienced by social movement activists in the age of Blair and Bush, it appeared important to recall a very recent period in modern and contemporary history when, to paraphrase one of the ubiquitous Situationist graffiti gracing the walls of Paris in 1968, it was considered realistic to demand the impossible.

In November 1967, student leaders from across Catholic Europe gathered in Paris to air their worries about what they considered as the most important problem facing their cohort: generalized student apathy. As happened to Lenin, who, in January 1917, predicted that a Russian Revolution would be unlikely to occur during his lifetime, fast-paced events soon proved dour predictions to be wrong. Within a few months, if not weeks, students around the world—to once again paraphrase imaginative Parisian graffiti—began to take their desires for reality, inspired by the sudden recognition of the reality of their desires. Then workers joined up in the forward march of societal revolt. And other previously subordinate population groups began to smell that spring was in the air. 'Let us open the gates of nurseries, universities, and other prisons' read a slogan daubed on the walls of a concert hall in a Parisian suburb. Radicalizing women, activists within the student new left, were some amongst many who interpreted this injunction as a call to action, and they embarked on the long and winding road towards a feminist society of the future precisely in the years of greatest contestation on university and factory floors. 'Run forward Comrade, the old world is behind you' was yet another slogan capturing the mood of that era. It is the reconstruction of the simultaneously radicalizing and liberating dynamic of those years which lies at the heart of this transnational study.

This book is expressly *not* intended as a treatise to dissect the multiple reasons for the *failure* of this period of popular unrest to give free rein to utopian longings. To understand why this remarkable sequence of turbulent upheavals failed to usher in fundamental socio-economic and political changes is an enormously important task. But a serious account of not just the rise but also the fall of '1968' would have required an additional volume, for many of the factors influencing the ultimate fate of this promising cycle of popular revolts were often only vaguely related to the factors responsible for the flowering of the emancipatory initiatives in '1968'. Almost forty years later, the most important task remains to rescue these experiments in 'participatory democracy' and the corresponding social struggles from the historical distortion and condescension to which much recent historiography appears to condemn that promising era of revolt. The journalistic and historical literature on 1968 is increasingly concerned, or so it seems, to point out the limitations of this period of rapid and transnational change. The most well-intentioned representatives of this genre 'merely' concentrate on divesting 'global 1968' of its radical edge. A cultural—not a political and most definitely not a socio-economic—revolution is seen as heading the agenda, and any deeper challenges to the late capitalist status quo are safely interpreted as youthful follies devoid of major consequences or larger meanings. Less benign observers reinterpret '1968' as the beginning of all evil in the modern world today. In their eyes, family values, community cohesion, and the stabilizing factors of tradition were shattered under the onslaught of insurgent rebels constituting the 'generation of 1968' to make room for nihilism, hedonism, destructive cynicism, and—of course!—terrorism.

This monograph is designed to contradict such arguments. Idealism was far more universal than nihilism and cynicism at the time. What establishment pundits today proclaim as destructive criticism turns out to have been above all else a ceaseless effort to construct a different and more egalitarian social order, a world where company and university paternalism were to make way for workers' control, student power, and generalized self-management in all walks of life. What today's apologists for the past and present status quo misinterpret as a frontal attack on community cohesion turns out to have been a transnational effort not only to imagine but also to construct the contours of community—but a community stripped of hypocrisies, power hierarchies, and the marginalization and suppression of imagination and revolt.

Of course, like all concrete social phenomena, the reality of radical social movements was contradictory from the start. Student movements and worker revolts were not only ever so many open rebellions against the forces of tradition, but they were simultaneously also products of an alienating cultural and socio-economic environment. The heavy weight of tradition left an indelible birthmark on the forces seeking change. Thus, what deserves to be prominently underscored is not so much the persistence of authoritarian characteristics which were to be found all too easily in social movements of any kind and in any national context. Instead, it is the extent to which social movement activists felt empowered to begin to construct a viable alternative, to evolve away from the authoritarian, elitist, and paternalist traditions weighing down on them like demons from the past, which deserves to be highlighted. The following pages are an attempt to understand precisely those elements which were redemptive and cathartic in the social movements of '1968'. The limitations of such efforts to construct a better world will emerge in the process of analysis and description soon and clear enough.

The calendar year '1968' is a frequent reference point in the ensuing pages. '1968', henceforth in most cases used without inverted commas, stands primarily as a symbol for a far larger moment in time. Several chapters indeed repeatedly stray back into the 1950s to prepare the terrain. Chapters 1 and 4 both open with a narrative of—rather disparate—events occurring in 1956. That year may thus be considered as the opening moment of a story unfolding in the subsequent twenty years. The calendar year of 1976 constitutes the other extreme chronological limit of the movement culminating in 1968. For 1976 was the last year when Italian workers lived through their unprecedented experience of wide-ranging control over their workplaces in a buoyant mood; and it was in the course of 1976 that the definitive defeat of the Portuguese Revolution in November of the preceding year became obvious for anyone who cared to look. The geographic limits of this study are far more easily defined. Western Europe—notably including Mediterranean countries but leaving Scandinavia aside—and the United States of America are at the centre of this investigation. Eastern Europe, for all practical purposes, has been excluded from this study, despite the conjunctural importance of the Prague Spring. The reconstruction of the turbulent events occurring at that time in the Soviet sphere of influence would have required a significant enlargement of this text.

Last but not least, a note on the guiding principles behind the construction of the individual chapters. This book is no encyclopedia of '1968'. It reflects a conscious decision to highlight certain central features of this period. Even with such a 'limited' focus, however, choices had to be made. Cultural rebellion and youth revolt, student radicalism, worker protest, the permutations of the left and, finally, the realities and meanings of 'participatory democracy'; each and every one of these topics constitutes a vast investigatory terrain in and of itself. To capture the spirit of that era, it was deemed most evocative and persuasive to select a limited but representative sample of countries, locations, movements, and cultural trends to pinpoint the dynamic operating behind this transnational series of events. Such a selection mechanism will probably be most apparent in Chapter 2, as the literature on student unrest has thus far generated by far the largest collection of non-academic and academic studies of any single feature constituting '1968'. Finally, a word of warning to those readers in search of easy answers to explain the phenomena described below. As I suggest in my Conclusion, I do not believe in structural answers for the various features explored in this text. My explanations are far more tentative and contingent, but precisely for this very reason they may also be far closer to historical reality and historical truth.

Chapter 1, then, traces some prominent instances of cultural rebellion and youth revolt, two distinct features of the post-Second World War era which eventually merged in the creative universe constructed by the Amsterdam Provos, a media-conscious movement combining the 'best' of both forms of rebellion. Chapter 2 targets the world of the university student. The crucial role of US students is an important, if uncontroversial feature of this study. By contrast, the deeds of West German and French student rebels are consciously not a focus, though French students briefly make a cameo appearance in Chapter 3. Instead of the relatively well-known cases of Germany and France, this chapter concentrates on the lesser known cases of Belgium and Italy. For, in Europe, Belgian students were the first to question authority on a mass scale. And it was in Italy that student unrest shut down an entire system of higher education, long before French students began to dream of occupying the Sorbonne. Chapter 3 gives equal space and attention to a much-neglected but potentially far more powerful social player than university students could ever hope to become. Worker protest is oftentimes missing from standard accounts of '1968'. As the reader will discover, for Romance-language Europe such an omission is inexcusable. (And Romance-language Europe constitutes, after all, more than half of continental Western Europe!) The same cavalier ignorance of much of 'Mediterranean' Europe has partially blocked the vision of several generations of interpreters of the 1960s' new left. By contrast to the northern European and Anglo-Saxon, student-oriented variants of the new left, the pre-1968 'Mediterranean' new left remains understudied and ignored. Chapter 4 is designed to rectify this 'omission,' at the same time that it suggests a clear delineation of the new from the far left, for the post-1968 North American and Western European far left, though much maligned, has found few historians and is ill-understood. Chapter 4 may thus serve not only to cast some new light on the old left and the new, but it will hopefully also serve to stimulate more detailed investigations of the most numerous and influential component of the post-1956 radical left: the insurgent far left.

Chapter 5 casts light on concrete manifestations of the striving for a new type of society and a new spirit of community at the centre of this book. Efforts to construct qualitatively distinct and novel forms of interpersonal communications, counter-institutions, and alternative distribution mechanisms of power and knowledge on factory and university floors are the subject of this final section. The examples chosen for closer attention will underscore the experimental and unusual nature of this moment, for the years at the centre of this study constituted a prolonged period of ceaseless efforts to facilitate individual and collective liberation from the constraints of everyday life, politics as usual, and the manifold unwanted and superfluous hierarchies, bureaucracies, and authorities. '1968' was what I like to call a transnational moment of crisis and opportunity, a period of contemporary history when hundreds of thousands, and at times even millions, of individuals, deprived of the usual avenues of political and social power, firmly believed that under the cobblestones lay the beach. The Conclusion attempts to place the events of this period in the larger context of world-historical space and time.

1

Outcasts, Dropouts, and Provocateurs: Nonconformists Prepare the Terrain

1. THE FIRST WORLD CONGRESS OF FREE ARTISTS

It was the very beginning of September 1956. The setting? A provincial town in Piedmont, Italy, located 35 kilometres south-east of Turin: Alba. The administrative centre of the bucolic, wine-growing Langhe region, Alba's most famous son is Beppe Fenoglio, a partisan in the Second World War, author of *Johnny the Partisan*, a semi-autobiographical account of antifascist guerrilla warfare in the Langhe, including the temporary liberation of his native Alba in October 1944.[1] The second most famous son of Alba is Pinot Gallizio. The local pharmacist had likewise taken part in the antifascist underground and had been a member of the Langhe area National Liberation Committee (CLN). Immediately after liberation he became a municipal councillor on the CLN ticket; subsequently he was elected to the municipal government of Alba on an independent ticket linked to Christian Democracy. From 1951 to 1960 he served as a municipal councillor as an independent running on various left-wing tickets. A gregarious, vivacious man with a distinct sense of humour and a penchant for the unusual, Pinot Gallizio by the mid-1950s began to make a name for himself as a modernist, experimental painter.[2] Connections to other artists were quickly established, including to Asger Jorn.

Jorn, like many other Danish artists, had been a member of the Danish Communist Party in the Second World War underground, and he was one of the activists responsible for the printing of the illegal party newspaper. In the immediate post-war years, he became a leading member of the avant-garde art movement COBRA, together with Constant Nieuwenhuys, Christian Dotremont, and others. By the mid-1950s, Jorn had moved to Albisola on the Ligurian coast, a bit more than a hundred kilometres from Alba. In August 1955, in Albisola, Gallizio and Jorn met by chance.[3] Further connections were made to like-minded artists and intellectuals, and plans got under way to gather the handful of interested parties around one table to discuss their ideas, share their experiences and to map out future endeavours. Alba soon emerged as the most convenient venue for this meeting of unusual minds, for Gallizio offered his home town as the meeting place where, as a town councillor, he was well-placed to facilitate the provision of the necessary infrastructure. Negotiations were entered into with the municipal administration for financial and logistical support to what was billed as the First World Congress of Free Artists. Panels and speeches were planned to be held over a period of seven days, from 2 to 8 September 1956. Two exhibitions were announced, one of futurist ceramics, the other of contemporary works by the visiting artists themselves. The town fathers looked forward to this extraordinary event, a unique chance for this sleepy provincial town to bask in the limelight of an unexpected international gathering.[4]

The day of the arrival of the high-calibre international conference team arrived. The city arranged for musicians to greet the dignitaries upon arrival at the Alba train station. The atmosphere was dignified but relaxed. Maurizio Corgnati describes the scene:

Musicians wearing the ceremonial galloon hats stand in formation in two rows inside the station building. Three municipal councillors; the secretary responsible for tourism; the chief accountant of the *Banca Popolare* as the official delegate from the school for viticulture; the director of the local post office, the correspondent of the provincial newspaper; together with Pinot Gallizio, they all chat about the progress of the vintage. Three flags are leaning against the wall; the flag of Saint Cecilia, the flag of the merchant guild, and the flag of the Alba Sports Association. The welcoming committee is prepared.

The assembled crowd expects that honourable gentlemen would step from the train— the first class carriage, of course—serious, their temples marked with the symbol of wisdom, sprinkled with grey, orderly clothing, perhaps not exactly in dress-coats, but in darkly colored attire. When the moment comes, in fact only one person steps out of the first class carriage whose comportment comes close to the idealized portrait in the minds of the waiting small crowd. If the band did not begin to play the chosen march, that was solely because there was only one such gentleman. This was most fortunate, as it turned out that he was a traveling salesman of chocolate and other sweets. . . .

Maurizio Corgnati continues:

While standing there with disappointment written on their faces, pensively, suddenly their gaze caught hold of a group of young people, dressed in impossible outfits, who were probably imagining Alba to be a giant campground. The committee was beginning to think of a mix-up, that this was after all not the appointed date, that the conference participants were perhaps sitting in the wrong train, or that they had accidentally left the train too early, in Fossano or Cuneo, this would be the most likely possibility. . . , but then the realization suddenly dawned on them that the international conference delegates were precisely this colorful, odd assortment of campers.

'Furious, the town council elder read his welcoming speech, paused when he shouldn't have, and reading rapidly without a pause when he should have stopped.' When he had finished, one member of the motley group of visitors 'stepped forward in order to make a speech in reply, then changed his mind and limited himself to the single word—in Italian—of *grazie*'.[5] Apparently, however, the council members' anger soon abated, as a photograph of the subsequent conference proceedings in the Alba City Hall shows some of the 'Free Artists' gathered around a varnished rectangular table, together with three councillors, snacks, half-empty glasses and bottles in front of them, everyone appearing rather laid back and good-humoured.[6]

The members of the Alba City Council could be forgiven for their guarded initial reaction to this 'handful of desperados' invading their town.[7] None of them were well-known figures then to anyone but a tiny group of aficionados in European art circles. Some of them would later on gain a certain notoriety and even a degree of fame. All of them, however, by virtue of being present at this act of civic generosity put on by the Alba political elite, participated in the launch of an intellectual, artistic, and political movement which exemplified the spirit of 1968 better than any other grouping, leaving their imprint on the radical decade at the centre of this book. For the First World Congress of Free Artists turned out to be the preparatory conference, the launching pad for the Situationist International.

2. FROM LETTRISM TO SITUATIONISM

Officially, this movement got under way at a gathering in an even smaller Italian provincial location, the village of Cosio d'Arroscio, located on the edge of the Italian Alps, in a hillside village not too far from the Ligurian coast. But it was the Alba gathering which set in motion this talented, iconoclastic group. The actual founding of the International in late July 1957 merely ratified the existence of this association of free-thinking revolutionaries.[8] Who were some other figures in this group? All three figureheads of the short-lived COBRA current (1948–51) were officially invited to the Alba gathering. The Belgian Christian Dotremont had been chosen to preside over the proceedings, but he had to cancel for health reasons.[9] The Dutch Constant Nieuwenhuys made it to Alba and soon became a leading light within the organization. It was Asger Jorn, the Danish co-founder of COBRA, however, who had made the necessary connections with Italian co-thinkers, and by the time of the festivities in Alba he, together with the Milanese Enrico Baj and others, had founded a successor organization to COBRA, the Movement for an Imaginist Bauhaus.[10] Baj, in turn, put Jorn in touch with the small group of young activists in the Lettrist International.[11]

There is no need to detail the chronology of the lifespan of the Lettrist International, another tiny group of intellectual bohemians, which, to make things worse, in turn emerged from a split of the original Lettrists, around Isidore Isou. A few hints may suffice at the genealogy and spirit of these Lettrist groups. Isou, of Jewish descent, precisely (and therefore symptomatically) in the darkest moment of the Second World War, in 1942, living in Bucharest, had begun work on a manuscript which he brought along to Paris in 1945 and which was published by Gallimard, entitled *Introduction to a New Poetry and a New Music*. In some respects not too dissimilar from Dadaist precepts emerging out of the horrors of an earlier world war, Lettrist performance art soon became a regular feature of certain existentialist jazz cellars and hang-outs in Paris. Designed to confuse, shock, and create hilarity and outrage, Isou attracted a group of followers.[12] Prescient publications, like the 1949 *Manifesto for an Uprising of Young People*, make clear that Isou meant to revolutionize more than just the Parisian Left Bank coffee-house culture.[13] Prefiguring the events of 1968, almost twenty years earlier Lettrist activists covered the walls of the Paris Latin Quarter with posters proclaiming '12,000,000 Young People Will Take to the Streets to Make the Lettrist Revolution.'[14]

Outrageous public happenings *avant la lettre* soon catapulted this tiny handful of cultural rebels into the public's view. On 9 April 1950, during High Mass on Easter Sunday, four young Lettrists, one dressed as a Dominican monk, rushed onto the pulpit of Notre Dame in Paris and proclaimed the death of God. Their action netted them front page headlines in Paris dailies and, predictably, solidarity statements by Surrealist intellectuals, such as André Breton and Maurice Nadeau.[15] When not impersonating others, young Lettrists behaved in equally controversial and unusual ways. They dyed their hair, wrote slogans on their pants, got drunk, accosted passers-by in the street, and generally behaved as a precocious mixture of what later on became known as bohemians and 'delinquent gangs'.[16] Their networks of sociability converged on a pub in Saint-Germain-des-Prés, Chez Moineau. Frequent visitors there included Henri de Béarn, eventually changing his career pattern to become a leading figure in the Gaullist movement, Fritz Hundertwasser, later on to become one of Austria's most notorious nonconformist artists and architects, and Guy Debord.[17]

The Italian historian Bruno Buongiovanni aptly describes Debord as a 'unique figure within the radical critique of the second half of the twentieth century'.[18] And, indeed, Guy Debord indisputably took centre stage within the colourful history and evolution of the Situationist International until it dissolved itself in 1972. The ideas and practices of Situationism are inextricably linked to this enigmatic personality who preferred to act behind the scenes and who, eventually, became the author of Situationism's keynote theoretical treatise: *The Society of the Spectacle*. The Situationist International, an intensely transnational avant-garde brain trust which had a minuscule cumulative membership of no more than seventy individuals,[19] evolved in a process of constant interaction and the creative development and adaptation of other individuals' ideas. It it thus best presented by a brief explanation of its keynote propositions with limited references to individual authorship.

Central to Situationist endeavours is the analysis of the contemporary world as plagued by an all-encompassing impoverishment of everyday life. Whether at work or at home, human beings living in the modern world are experiencing permanent alienation on virtually every level of their existence. To make everyday life ostensibly more bearable, contemporary capitalism has fostered a culture of consumption, serving simultaneously as safety valve and pacifier to millions of frustrated and alienated individuals. Instead of living a creative and fulfilled life, men and women in the modern age are encouraged to possess the objects of their longing. Rather than having their desires fulfilled in daily life, the mental and physical universe of today's citizens is preoccupied with consuming rather than living life. Worse yet, given the obvious impossibility of even the advanced stage of capitalism to procure limitless numbers of objects to all of its subjects, a culture of vicarious enjoyment increasingly displaces consumption as the central mechanism ensuring the perpetuation of alienated life. While still relying on the provision of objects to satisfy the subaltern masses, a growing industry providing images of objects, rather than the objects themselves, is increasingly taking on the role of popular entertainment. 'Popular entertainment' in this totalizing sense encompasses all aspects of everyday life, far exceeding the realm of cinema, public relations, spectator sports, or high politics. The cult of celebrities may stand as just one of many lucid examples of the mechanism employed to present the alienated person in the contemporary world with an identification mechanism satisfying the craving for individual expression and creativity by the adoration and worship of stars who appear to incorporate 'precisely what is missing from the actual lives of all other individuals, trapped as they are in vapid roles'.[20]

Yet the truly inspiring dimension of Situationist thought lies not in this razor-sharp dissection[21] of the mechanisms undergirding an increasingly dysfunctional and hypertrophied society and the operational principles fostering its apparent strength and survival. What made Situationism into a movement prefiguring the thoughts and deeds of an entire generation of political activists was its refusal to accept this dystopian status quo as an inevitable, if perhaps deplorable, feature of modern existence. Unlike postmodernists, who subsequently developed similar trenchant critiques of contemporary society, Situationists refused to regard the society of the spectacle as an immovable condition of (post)modernity.[22] Situationists were authors of passionate cultural critiques, but they understood their primary occupation to be that of a certain type of revolutionary. In the spirit of Dadaism, Surrealism, and its immediate precursor, Lettrism, Situationists never abandoned their 'conviction that the whole world must be torn down then rebuilt not under the sign of the economy but instead under that of a generalized creativity'.[23] What was different from preceding waves of cultural iconoclasts was the Situationists' enduring belief in the liberating powers of certain features of everyday life as lived by those countless, alienated human beings filling homes, offices, factories, and streets. Or, in the words of the Belgian theorist Raoul Vaneigem: 'People who talk about revolution and class struggle without referring explicitly to everyday life, without understanding what is subversive about love and what is positive in the refusal of constraints—such people have a corpse in their mouth.'[24]

This tiny handful of marginalized intellectuals never gave up their firm belief in the self-emancipation of humanity from the seemingly all-encompassing tentacles of the society of the spectacle. Like the radical fringes in the era of popular fronts a generation or two earlier, the Situationists were uncompromising: 'What do we demand in backing the power of everyday life against hierarchical power? We demand *everything*.' But they did not postulate their own role as that of a substitutionist vanguard, as some sort of enlightened leaders who would lead their flock to the promised land. They 'merely' saw themselves as interpreters of a widespread, if often painfully suppressed, *volonté générale* to turn society upside down. 'The vast majority of people', wrote Vaneigem in 1963, 'have always devoted all their energy to survival, thereby denying themselves any chance to live.' But in their daily attempts to cope with an alienating environment, ordinary individuals engage in countless acts of defiance. Therefore Situationists, Vaneigem argued paraphrasing Friedrich Engels and Karl Marx, have no interests separate and apart from those of other ordinary members of contemporary society. In fact, Vaneigem reasoned, 'all situationist ideas are nothing other than faithful developments of acts attempted constantly by thousands of people to try and prevent another day from being no more than twenty-four hours of wasted time'.[25]

3. SITUATIONIST PRACTICE

In their single-minded libertarian quest for a better world organized along radically different lines or, as they poetically put it in 1963, 'in setting autonomous people loose in the world',[26] Situationism engaged in a number of fascinating enterprises. For the first years of their existence, their efforts were primarily geared towards the artistic and creative sphere. Given their conviction that 'all the elements needed for a free life are already at hand, both culturally and technologically speaking, [and that] they have merely to be modified as to their meanings, and organized differently',[27] Situationists began literally to roam the cities they inhabited in the search for hidden meanings and landmarks on the way to (re)discover the possibilities of non-alienated life. Many of their literary meanderings should be read as poetic blueprints in their search for revolutionary strategies:

All cities are geological; you cannot take three steps without encountering ghosts bearing all the prestige of their legends. We move within a closed landscape whose landmarks constantly draw us toward the past. Certain shifting angles, certain receding perspectives, allow us to glimpse original conceptions of space, but this vision remains fragmentary. It must be sought in the magical locales of fairy tales and surrealist writings: castles, endless walls, little forgotten bars, mammoth caverns, casino mirrors.[28]

Others in the movement were not content with the accidental discovery of promising pathways towards a non-alienated life. The former COBRA painter Constant Nieuwenhuys, for instance, in the mid-1950s set aside paintbrush and easel and began to design immensely detailed and evocative imaginary cities where the free citizens of the future could wander about, engaging in creative and playful activities of their choosing, liberated from the chores of everyday life.[29] Constant's New Babylon was a visionary attempt to give concrete architectural expression to Karl Marx's famous call for the construction of a society

where nobody has one exclusive sphere of activity but each person can become accomplished in any branch one wishes to pursue, where society regulates general production and thus makes it possible for anyone to do one thing today and another tomorrow, to hunt in the morning, fish in the afternoon, rear cattle in the evening, be a critic after dinner, just as one pleases, without ever having to become a hunter, a fisherman, a shepherd or a critic.[30]

For the moment, however, Situationists and their sympathizers were far from having any noticeable effect on their environment. And, realizing that change would not come about by itself, by spontaneous generation, Situationists set about to help things along. They began to create situations, brief moments in time and space, which pointed out to anyone willing to look and listen the absurdity of life as currently organized and the possibility of a radical shake-up, if only people were willing to jump out of their own shadows. 'So far philosophers and artists have only interpreted situations; the point now is to transform them. Since man is the product of the situations he goes through, it is essential to create human situations.'[31] And so they did. If the 1950 Easter Mass provocation in Notre Dame was a particularly eye-catching demonstration of Lettrists' propensity to shock their audiences into a reassessment of their values and to prod them towards critical thinking and actions of their own, Situationists did not lag far behind. One such occasion was the famous 1958 World Exposition in Brussels, a city home to many nonconformist movements and artists for many decades. Here Situationists pursued a two-pronged tactic. Asger Jorn and Constant Nieuwenhuys, for instance, showed some of their works—in the case of Constant, his architectural designs—in the Danish and Dutch pavillions. At the same time, for instance, a Situationist leaflet was distributed to participants at the Convention of Art Critics, which met on location as part of the World Expo. The text, such as it was, insulted the assembled crowd, demanding: 'Disappear, you art critics, idiots of detail, incoherence and disunity!'[32]

In the late 1950s and early 1960s, however, often Situationist-induced 'situations' took the form of more or less outrageous artistic creations. 'Industrial art', sometimes produced on endless rolls of painted canvas, sometimes presented on live female models covered with bits of painted canvas, a specialty of Pinot Gallizio's Laboratorio Sperimentale in Alba, soon became a hit from Turin to Paris.[33] In one sense, of course, such activities or creations merely placed the Situationist network within the vanguard of wider changes in the contemporaneous artistic sphere. Happenings and similar cutting edge innovations soon became the rage on street corners and in art galleries from Wuppertal to New York.[34] Provocative experimentations were never a monopoly of Situationist tacticians. But the Situationists not only operated on the cutting edge of this increasingly popular artistic terrain but they soon, once again, turned out to march to an altogether different drummer. By the early 1960s, some of the leading Situationists, most prominently Guy Debord, began to grow increasingly disenchanted with the International's primary orientation towards the artistic world. Once again freely adapting the most famous of Marx's *Theses on Feuerbach*, in 1963 they proudly announced: 'Our era no longer has to write out poetic orders; it has to carry them out.' The translation of this statement into concrete action did not lead Situationists altogether to renege on their earlier forms of cultural critique. Quite the contrary! Indeed, the very same article announcing a shift from cultural practices to the culture of practice in its opening lines once again underscored: 'The problem of language is at the heart of all struggles between the forces striving to abolish present alienation and those striving to maintain it.... We live within language as within polluted air.'[35] But a distinct shift of emphasis began to affect the Situationist critique.

In terms of personal politics, this paradigm shift from cultural to political action engendered the increasing distance of several leading Situationist artists from the International's project, most notably Asger Jorn and Constant Nieuwenhuys. Their central role in the Situationist universe was taken over by Raoul Vaneigem instead, a student of the poetry of Lautréamont, introduced to Debord by their mutual acquaintance, the Marxist sociologist of everyday life and urban encounters, Henri Lefebvre.[36] In terms of their publications, new topics gained the upper hand, even if at first announced by traditional titles. Under the heading 'The Decline and Fall of the "Spectacular" Commodity Economy', in December 1965 Guy Debord penned a passionate analysis of the Watts riot in Los Angeles, interpreted as 'a protest by men against the inhuman life', the beginning of 'the positive transcendence of the spectacle'.[37] As Sadie Plant rightfully underscores, 'artistic intervention continued to characterize the practices of the movement, with a number of situationists developing their own cultural adventures and avant-garde tactics continuing to inform the situationists' subversive response to the recuperative powers of the spectacle'.[38] Nonetheless, a new stage in the life of the Situationist movement can be clearly discerned, 'transforming the most political of all artistic movements into the most artistic of all political movements'.[39]

Still, until 1966, the Situationist International remained a well-kept secret. Few radicals, let alone the general public, had heard of this group of esoteric individuals. All this began to change on 14 May 1966, when the executive committee of the Student Union at the University of Strasbourg voted into power six individuals known for their extremist ideas. Close friends of this gang of six soon thereafter visited members of the Situationist brains trust in Paris. The election result of 14 May had been largely a result of the widespread apathy of *strasbourgeois* students. But handed this precious opportunity to influence campus life, the Situationist International's Mustapha Khayati soon penned a brochure which was destined for fame: *On the Poverty of Student Life: Considered in its Economic, Political, Psychological, Sexual, and Particularly Intellectual Aspects, and a Modest Proposal for its Remedy.*[40] One may get a sense of the 'modest proposal' for the improvement of student life from the closing passage of this incendiary brochure: 'Proletarian revolutions will be festivals or nothing, for festivity is the very keynote of the life they announce. Play is the ultimate principle of this festival, and the only rules it can recognize are to live without dead time and to indulge untrammeled desire.'[41] But the real scandal broke when the Strasbourg University Student Union used official funds to print 10,000 copies of the brochure and then chose to distribute it free of charge at a solemn occasion. During the official opening ceremonies of the academic season in the main assembly hall of the Palais Universitaire, members of the Strasbourg Student Union passed out their pamphlet: 'All representatives of the Strasbourg elite, from the bishop to the prefect, from the general to University President Maurice Beyen, taking their seats in the hall, thus become the first to read a brochure which is, starting the next day, also distributed at the doors of university cafeterias and all over campus.'[42]

'To create at last a situation that goes beyond the point of no return' was one of the headings in Mustapha Khayati's brochure. No one knew better than the Situationists how to stage such an event. Indeed, at last a situation had been created that went beyond the point of no return. Keen cultural critics and long-standing analysts of the media and the information industry, the student activists poured oil on the flames by holding a carefully prepared press conference the following day, an occasion the Student Union representatives utilized to announce, in true Situationist style, their plan to dissolve the University of Strasbourg Student Union as soon as possible. A storm of indignation now broke. National dailies gave the Strasbourg events front-page coverage. The further away the commentators, the more wildly exaggerated the story became. When news swept across the Alps, the Turin daily *Gazetta del Popolo* informed its readers: 'In Paris and other university cities in France, the Situationist International, galvanized by the triumph of its adherents in Strasbourg, is preparing to launch a major offensive to take control of the student organizations.'[43] Meanwhile, some moderate members of the Strasbourg Student Union had woken up to this latest challenge to their moral and organizational universe and, together with civic leaders of Strasbourg, took action in the courts. True to form, the courts almost immediately shut down the Situationist-inspired Student Union executive, denying the duly elected representatives access to their campus offices, sequestering their remaining finances, and imposing a judicial administrator. All legal challenges to this autocratic move were consistently denied. The Strasbourg authorities thus made clear that students, as soon as they decided to break through the crust of 'business-as-usual' student unionism, could expect to be treated precisely as Mustapha Khayati had explained in his pamphlet *On the Poverty of Student Life*.

But the promotion of the Situationist agenda went beyond the free publicity by newspaper commentators in Alsace, in France as a whole, and even elsewhere in Europe. When the judge presiding over the complaint filed by the Strasbourg notables rendered his verdict on 13 December 1966, he formulated his concerns in most evocative terms. It is a pleasure to cite him at length. Referring to Khayati's text and 'other literature inspired by the Situationist International', the legal expert continued:

These publications express ideas and aspirations which, to put it mildly, have nothing to do with the aims of a student union. One has only to read what the accused have written, for it is obvious that these . . . students, scarcely more than adolescents, lacking all experience of real life, their minds confused by ill-digested philosophical, social, political and economic theories, and perplexed by the drab monotony of their everyday life, make the empty, arrogant and pathetic claim to pass definitive judgements, sinking to outright abuse, on their fellow students, their teachers, God, religion, the clergy, the governments and political systems of the whole world. Rejecting all morality and restraint, these cynics do not hesitate to commend theft, the destruction of scholarship, the abolition of work, total subversion, and a worldwide proletarian revolution with 'unlicensed pleasure' as its only goal.[44]

An unconsciously Situationist text. The International made good use of it.

Notoriety preceded fame. A second edition of Khayati's pamphlet was printed in March 1967. And, indeed, *On the Poverty of Student Life* became 'the most widely circulated situationist text' with about a dozen translations and a combined print-run of close to half a million copies worldwide.[45] Situationist publications were now highly sought-after texts. In the autumn of 1967, the two most famous Situationist books, Raoul Vaneigem's *The Revolution of Everyday Life* and Guy Debord's *The Society of the Spectacle* were published within weeks of each other[46]—just in time for the campus explosions, followed by a three-week long general strike which changed the face of France—and much of the rest of Western Europe—in wholly unexpected and unprecedented ways.

4. THE MEANING OF CULTURAL REVOLT

How many contemporaries were aware of the Situationist critique? Prior to the Strasbourg revolt, probably not very many. How many of the leading activists in 'global 1968' were consciously striving to create 'situations' in accordance with the Situationist model? Probably even fewer, although in actual fact, as we will see in later chapters, grass-roots rebels often applied 'situationist' tactics in their everyday pursuits. Situationist luminaries, including Guy Debord, were active in the Paris May 1968 events. In his daily political routine, the internationally most famous Paris-based student rebel, Daniel Cohn-Bendit, often worked with René Riesel, an activist hailing from the Situationist milieu.[47] The chronicler of the Situationist spirit, Laurent Chollet, claims that the majority of the imaginative graffiti gracing the walls of the Sorbonne, the Odéon National Theatre and other high temples of the student revolt—for example, 'All Power to the Imagination' or 'Under the Cobblestones Lies the Beach'—were the product of a little-known Situationist activist by the name of Christian Sébastiani.[48] Whether this claim is correct may never be ascertained with anything approaching certainty. In fact, this assertion should probably be best interpreted as yet another example of characteristic Situationist hyperbole. The case of the Situationist-influenced radicalization of West German student politics in the 1960s is likely to prove the exception rather than the rule.[49] On the whole, then, Situationism's direct political impact on the events of '1968' must be regarded as rather limited. Instead, its legacy for contemporaneous activist movements lay elsewhere.

It would be misguided and misleading to judge the political impact of cultural rebellion solely by direct, verifiable, and quantifiable echoes within the milieu of social movement activists. To begin with, such concrete links are rather difficult to reconstruct. It is, of course, quite feasible to trace certain lines of communication by means of, for instance, the limited number of memoirs that pay attention to such cultural countercurrents and dynamic impulses from outside the sphere of politics as customarily defined. But the impact of cultural critique on political activism remains for all practical purposes off-limits to social scientific efforts striving for neat compartmentalization and a tightly differentiated succession of distinct and verifiable accumulations of hard data. Yet it is one of the two central arguments of this chapter that the social and political explosions of '1968' built on earlier manifestations of societal discontent, the latter initially finding its expression in various forms of cultural iconoclasm, rejections of the social order by way of individual rebellion rather than openly conducted political revolt. How did this mechanism work?

In times of political quiescence, nonconformity most frequently takes on artistic form or finds expression in unusual lifestyle choices. In turn, pioneering examples of cultural nonconformity may become fluid points of reference for subsequent generations of outcasts and rebels searching for an outlet for their frustrations with everyday life, though still not necessarily striving for overtly political revolt. Of course, some cultural cross-currents lend themselves more easily towards stimulating political action than others. We may recall that Situationism's express purpose was precisely to create 'situations' in which powerless individuals could begin to exercise control over their daily life, situations in which previously silent members of subaltern social groups and classes would begin to express their desires, to exercise free will. Not unlike some other cultural iconoclasts, Situationists, then, developed a subversive model of a deep cultural critique of modern-day industrial society, together with a recipe for concrete action. There exists, however, no mechanism by which even the most well-intentioned cultural rebellions will lead to subsequent political revolts. But, crucially, if circumstances eventually generate the potential for more overtly political forms of rebellion, earlier forms of cultural critique may take on great relevance as inspirations to transgress social norms in matters of politics as well. The radical years under investigation in this study constitute one of the most remarkable recent demonstrations of the feasibility of such transnational and transgressive moments of change. The first half of this chapter, then, is devoted to the analysis and description of several important variants of cultural and artistic challenges to the pre-1968 status quo.

5. BEAT POETS

If, with some degree of arbitrary choice, Situationism can be traced to the darkest days of the Second World War in 1942 Bucharest, a second strand of cultural non-conformity emerging in the 1950s can likewise be traced to the wartime years. When, in the course of the first half of 1944, William Burroughs, Jack Kerouac, and Allen Ginsberg were introduced to each other by mutual friends in New York, a process of creative tension was set loose which eventually changed the face of American culture for several decades. And, given the cultural hegemony of the English language in the post-Second World War Western world, by extension the words and images created by the Beat Generation poets also affected several generations of (not only) Western European youth in fundamental ways. Unlike the Situationists who, until the late 1960s, for practical purposes remained unknown, the Beat poets, after a dozen restless years, hit fame by 1957 with the publication of Jack Kerouac's *On the Road*. Largely written within less than three weeks in April 1951, *On the Road* can easily be regarded as the literary expression of the Situationists' search for meaning in seemingly random ramblings through the streets of Paris at the very same time. But *On the Road*, conforming to American-style dimensions, covers vastly larger geographic terrain, criss-crossing 'America' from east to west. Likewise, whereas the Situationists mostly travelled between places like Alba, Munich, Amsterdam, and Paris, Beat poets moved effortlessly not only between New York and San Francisco, but to Tangiers, Morocco, and Paris, France, as well.

If the Strasbourg scandal made Situationism into a concept outside of narrow circles of the esoteric few, an event on 7 October 1955 performed a similarly catalytic function for the American literary geniuses who had, by then, shifted the geographic centre of their energies from Manhattan to the San Francisco Bay Area. When Allen Ginsberg delivered his first public twelve-minute long performance of *Howl* to a select crowd of 'anarchists, college professors, poets, carpenters',[50] and others, the audience was electrified and all present realized that they had witnessed the birth of something grand—which was eventually given the name of San Francisco Renaissance. *Howl* was simultaneously the opening salvo for a generational, philosophical, cultural, and political revolt. Though few, if anyone, present at the extraordinarily emotional rendition of such lines as 'Moloch! Solitude! Filth! Ugliness! Ashcans and unobtainable dollars! Children screaming under the stairways! Boys sobbing in armies! Old men weeping in the parks!',[51] would have believed that this author, who became the United States' most influential unconventional individual in the third quarter of the twentieth century, when preparing to study at Columbia University twelve years earlier, had taken a vow to 'study labor law and [to] devote his life to helping the working class'.[52] From the mid-1950s onwards, the Beat poets at the epicentre of the San Francisco Renaissance became the quintessential American prototype of the spirit animating the radical decade at the centre of this book. And their American origins simultaneously limited their analysis but broadened their reach. For, as anyone familiar with American culture and possessing a reasonably open mind will second: 'In the U.S. you have to be a deviant or die of boredom.'[53] And, reflecting this astute poetic insight into the pathologies of American culture, Ginsberg's opening and closing lines of the first sentence of his desperate *Howl*, a single sentence running on for no less than twelve pages, goes like this: 'I saw the best minds of my generation destroyed by madness, starving hysterical naked . . . with the absolute heart of the poem of life butchered out of their own bodies so good to eat a thousand years.'[54]

Unlike Lettrists and Situationists, the Beat poets were oblivious to the finer points of Marxist cultural critique and the latest insights of the sociological imagination. But, in part for this very reason, the architects of the San Francisco Renaissance could give expression to the suppressed desires of a far wider generation of young rebels than was possible for Guy Debord and his circle of friends in the stultifying socio-political context of the 1950s. Jack Kerouac once defined the Beat generation's socio-cultural origins in the following apposite terms: 'Members of the generation that came of age after World War II, who, supposedly as a result of disillusionment stemming from the Cold War, espouse mystical detachment and relaxation of social and sexual tensions.'[55] Beat poets 'withdrew from society into an anti-social subculture, instead of challenging and trying to change the society. But with the traditional voices of dissent mute, the Beat Generation became the only option for those in opposition. The Beats may have been rebels without a cause, but theirs was the only rebellion in town.'[56] As had other American writers before them, Beat poets set out on the long road to discover 'the highest spirituality among the marginal and the dispossessed, establishing the links between art and pathology, and seeking truth in visions, dreams, and other non-rational states'.[57] Yet, in this process of self-discovery, they gave voice to a growing sentiment of cultural malaise and existential revolt. 'More than anything else, the Beat generation was a portent, the first wind of a new storm, a coded signal that America's youth was starting to gag on conformity, materialism, and silence.'[58]

The ripples of this new wind blowing from the west soon hit European shores. Acknowledgements of the impact of Beat poetry on another, subsequent generation of cultural and political rebels in Europe are legion. For the moment, two such references may suffice, both symptomatic of the growing unease of European youth and the beginnings of new trends in European cultural expression. As early as 1959, three students at the Liverpool College of Art would frequently meet at the local student pub, discussing for hours 'Kerouac and the "beat" poets, Corso and Ferlinghetti whose works stirred up in them vague restlessness and yearning for open roads.'[59] The three were Stuart Sutcliffe, perhaps the most unusual and creative mind within the circle of individuals eventually forming 'The Beatles', Bill Harry, soon to become the founding editor and guiding spirit of *Mersey Beat*, the prototype for all subsequent British youth-oriented music magazines, and John Lennon. The latter, ten years later, evolved into the most politicized Beatle.[60] But Paul McCartney, too, the Beatle closest to the counterculture and rarely a political rebel, when reminiscing about the early 1960s, asserted as a matter of course: 'We were all reading Ginsberg and that stuff, everyone was. It's a point that people often miss.'[61]

And, beyond doubt, it was Allen Ginsberg who best personified the link between Beat rebellion and the subsequent mutation into political revolt. Most Beat poets generally stayed in the political shadows—or worse. Kerouac, for instance, was left fundamentally untouched even by the widespread expressions of sympathy and hopeful expectations placed in John F. Kennedy at the time of the presidential elections in 1960, not because Kennedy was merely the modernizer of the unobtainable American dream, but on account of Kerouac's penchant for the comforts of a certain type of familial conservatism: 'Though he had, on principle, never voted—"avoid the authorities"—had he done so Jack Kerouac would have chosen Richard Nixon.'[62] Ginsberg's private, public, and political persona was of a rather different kind. Though he did not attend his first political protest rally until October 1963,[63] he subsequently became a frequent, if consistently idiosyncratic participant in such events. Allen Ginsberg emerged as a public figure 'wonderfully symbolic of the energies, traditions, and heresies for which the prevailing culture had no use'.[64] He did so by using 'his life as an exhibitionistic and apocalyptic platform for the revolution of the word, the politics of sex, the mind-expanding potential of drugs, and the evils of capitalism'.[65] To cite Morris Dickstein once again: 'What made Ginsberg especially important to the youth culture of the sixties was less his mantic ecstasies, than the complex generosity of his presence and his values.'[66] Another brilliant analyst of the 1960s explains: 'At poetry readings and teach-ins, he need not even read his verses: he need only appear in order to make his compelling statement of what young dissent is all about. The hair, the beard, the costume, the mischievous grin, the total absence of formality, pretense, or defensive posturing'[67] sufficed to carry the message. In part because of the radiant presence of Ginsberg, Beat poetry became the music of social movements in the 1960s, especially, but not only, in the English-speaking world.

Constant Nieuwenhuys and Guy Debord, in an eleven-point manifesto of the Situationist International, self-confidently proclaimed in their opening line: 'The situationists must take every opportunity to oppose retrograde forces and ideologies, in culture and wherever the question of the meaning of life arises.'[68] For good reasons, initially at the very least, the Situationists limited their interventions primarily to the artistic sphere. For the creative arts, since ancient times, have provided a free space, an oasis of sorts, for a great many nonconformists of varying stripes, who, alienated from their surroundings and often in particular from the political process, sought outlets for their strivings to prefigure or to help usher in a non-alienated world. The Beat poets squarely fit into this particular niche.

6. LITERATURE AND THEATRE OF REVOLT

Paris and San Francisco were not the only laboratories of cultural dissent, and poetry and painting were not the only media for the anticipation of 'the good life'. The world of literature in the larger sense of that term, that is, not just poetry, was likewise increasingly affected by creative unrest. The story remains to be written of how certain literary journals, such as the *Kursbuch* in West Germany or the *Quaderni Piacentini* in Italy, began to harden their critical edge, eventually mutating into leading publications of radical social and political critique within their respective national operational terrain.[69] In hinting at this process, it is of crucial importance to differentiate between at least two stages in the politicization of cultural critique. The more famous one is surely the moment when the world of literature, music, painting, poetry, and sculpting becomes profoundly affected and jolted into action by radical moves already under way in their respective societies. The less well-known but all the more important aspect of the relationship between art, artistic production, and social action is the moment when creative intellectuals *anticipate* subsequent societal debates prior to the eruption of social movements on a grand scale or, perhaps more adequately expressed, when intellectual debates prefigure and inspire growing waves of social protest, for in this earlier stage of cultural critique, intellectuals and artists could and did serve in the role of instigator or at least as motivator for social activism.

The precise moment when cultural revolts, initially performing a vanguard role in fostering—or giving voice to—wide-ranging socio-political critique, no longer primarily propel social movements but increasingly *react* to ongoing societal polarization differs from country to country and case to case. For West Germany, in the specific case of literature, a convincing case has been made for 1967 as the crucial turning point.[70] Here, possibly, the October 1967 four-day gathering of the most influential avant-garde literary association in the cold war frontier state, the Gruppe 47, may have been the real and symbolic moment when the two phases briefly overlapped. The crème de la crème of German literary intellectuals—and their periphery of literary critics—had gathered in rural Franconia only to find their proceedings disturbed by uninvited provocateurs hailing from the milieu of radical students from the nearby University of Erlangen, arriving in 'happening-style war paint' and mini-skirts; worse yet, the Gruppe 47 encountered militant opposition from certain well-prepared circles *within* the Gruppe 47 as well.[71] A comparative study of similar moments elsewhere in the Western world would surely make a fascinating read. Short of more such detailed investigations, it remains difficult to judge how autonomous or exemplary, rather than derivative, artistic radicalizations were in the respective manifestations of existential discontent. Pride of place, in any case, would have to be given to the role of theatre. Unlike most other forms of artistic production, theatre by definition thrives on its existence at the cutting edge, or at the literal point of contact between art and audience, and—conceptually at the very least—it is far more difficult for theatre to remain unaffected by ongoing social revolt than it might be for poetry or the plastic arts. Consequently, the history—and the prehistory!—of 1968 is inconceivable without reference to theatrical revolt in the various senses of that expression.

The 15 May 1968 occupation of the Paris Odéon Théâtre de France, played a central role in the generalization of the Paris student revolt.[72] Inspired by the creative abuse of the Odéon's facilities, ten days later the unsuspecting audience of a production of Bertold Brecht's *The Life of Galileo* in the Brussels National Theatre found themselves in the middle of a similar takeover event.[73] In Paris, central 'ringleaders' behind the takeover of the Odéon were two artistic figures with a long history of radical provocations: Jean-Jacques Lebel and Julian Beck. Lebel had been the leading proponent of happening-style art in France since the 1950s, having learnt the tricks of his trade in earlier creative encounters with André Breton, Marcel Duchamp, Benjamin Péret, as well as William Burroughs, Allen Ginsberg, and Gregory Corso.[74] Julian Beck was the animator of the Living Theater, the prototype of radical theatre companies blossoming before, during and after 1968. Coming of age in the same atmosphere and location as the Beat poets, the Manhattan of the late Second World War years and the immediate post-war period, Julian and Judith Beck, on the day of the Odéon takeover, 'led the insurrectionary crowd of insurgent students, workers, and actors singing the "Internationale" and waving black anarchist flags'.[75]

In Italy, the personal, political, and artistic itineraries of Dario Fo, already at the time of the 1964–5 season the most-performed living author in Italy and all of Europe, and that of his companion, Franca Rame, are inextricably intertwined with the forward march of extraparliamentary social movements between 1966 and 1976. In the case of Fo and Rame, it is beyond the shadow of a doubt that their plays, performances, and reconceptualizations of cultural productions *tout court* were simultaneously cause and consequence of the wider societal upheaval then attempting to liberate Italy from the gridlock of Christian Democratic conservatism.[76] The history of radical developments in the world of theatre before, during, and after 1968 can be extended at will.[77]

7. THE PLACE OF CULTURAL CRITIQUE

Was cultural critique as important as more overtly political forms of dissent? This question is difficult to answer, but it is an important one. It seems that cultural nonconformity, where present, had the most impact in those countries where generalized societal revolt was least developed or, looked at over a period of years, at those moments in the history of respective states, when students and workers or other activist population groups were least visibly engaged. To compare the events of 1968 in Brussels and Paris is instructive in that regard. Paris, the capital city of a country experiencing a student insurrection and a three-week long general strike, witnessed a manifold flowering of initiatives in the cultural sphere, of which the occupation of the Odéon was only one amongst many. Still, in all accounts of May/June 1968 in Paris not specifically geared to the role of the arts, the story of the revolution in the realm of cultural production is just one amongst many and generally pales in significance to the space devoted to radical ferment in many other sectors of social life. By contrast in Brussels, during the calendar year 1968, the role of artists is second only to that of university students.[78]

The prominence of artistic rebellion in Belgium, of course, should not be mistaken to suggest that their counterparts in France were more quiescent. Quite the contrary![79] But two symbolic facts may nonetheless underscore the far greater centrality of the role of artists in Belgium. The main assembly halls of, respectively, the University of Paris–Sorbonne and the Free University of Brussels served as the revolutionary headquarters and main arenas of the two university student revolts. But, whereas the Sorbonne was draped with revolutionary slogans, the Brussels equivalent was festooned with an immense canvas, painted by one of the most well-known contemporary Belgian painters, Roger Somville, in a marathon session in his studio, delivering a finished section every morning for almost ten days in a row, each piece immediately hoisted onto the walls by enthusiastic students. To be sure, the huge banner painted by Somville prominently included insurrectionary slogans, but these 'texts' were integrated into the overall work of art rather than free-standing demands.[80]

The second symptomatic act refers to the occupation of the Palais des Beaux-Arts. The central temple of the Belgian arts establishment contained space for multiple exhibitions, a large concert hall, a theatre, a cinema, and a café, and it became a natural target for the insurgents. Indeed, it seems that on the night of 28 May two separate groups of Belgian artists were preparing to take the Beaux-Arts by storm. A team of Flemish writers and artists, amongst them the most famous contemporary Belgian novelist, Hugo Claus, were hedging plans to capture the palace when another group pre-empted them by taking over the art nouveau building designed by Victor Horta, draping two banners across its façade, reading 'General Assembly' and 'Occupation—Everyone Welcome.' This act of hands-on cultural critique, the functional equivalent of the French assault on the Odéon, however, far outlasted the occupation of the French National Theatre. The Odéon remained in the hands of the rebels from 15 May to 14 June. The 'misappropriation' of the Palais des Beaux-Arts continued until the very end of August.[81]

Ultimately, it seems, the prominence and longevity of certain features of the Belgian artistic revolt in and after 1968 may be partially explained by the relative weakness of the revolutionary challenge of the Belgian '1968' as such, certainly when compared with its southern neighbours. Perhaps the unusual vitality of Belgian artistic movements throughout the twentieth century, disproportionately present and exceptionally vibrant in all exemplary artistic avant-garde movements from the 1930s to the 1960s—Surrealism, especially after the Second World War,

COBRA, and Situationism—played a role.[82] And, of course, the centrality or relative marginality of the cultural critique at the height of radical activism need not cast a light on the function of artistic critique in the medium-to-long term preparation of such events. Still, for the moment, the hypothesis of an inversely proportional relationship between the prominence of cultural revolt and generalized societal rebellion may be posited. The deeper and more all-encompassing the socio-political challenge, the less outstanding and exceptional appears the revolt in the arts. Nonetheless, read in reverse, this provisory conclusion pinpoints the vanguard nature of the world of creative intellectuals and artistic talents. In times and locations of relative quiet, artists may turn out to be the revolutionaries par excellence.

There is no better confirmation of this point than a set of brilliant studies on the antecedents of 1968 in one of the few locations in Western Europe no one would ever suspect as the seat of fervent nonconformist, let alone rebellious, acts: Switzerland's capital city of Bern. Yet, perhaps this is the time to draw attention, first, to the frequently extraordinary role of 'the lands between', the smaller countries usually in the shadows of their larger and militarily more powerful neighbours. Belgium, Switzerland, and—as we will discover at the very end of this chapter—the Netherlands turned out to be locations where certain catalytic or symbolic developments of great importance in this book were found earlier and/or in more unadulterated fashion compared with similar tendencies in more well-known states. In larger states, similar developments occurred sometimes only later and often mixed in with competing trends and tendencies, thus sometimes blurring the analytic gaze. In Chapters 3 and 5, I devote some space to yet another 'marginal' European state, whose modern history today is solely known to area studies specialists: Portugal. But the Portuguese Revolution of 1974–5 must surely count as a highpoint of the story line at the centre of this book. For the moment, however, let us return to the city of Bern, the conservative capital city of a peculiar country, which takes great pride in its uninterrupted seven hundred years-long history without foreign occupations or domestic monarchs.[83]

In his two-volume masterpiece *Begerts letzte Lektion* and *Muellers Weg ins Paradies*, Fredi Lerch describes in sublime language and fascinating detail the way in which the staid and traditionalist city of Bern slowly began to spawn a nonconformist subculture which, however, well into the 1960s, was barely noticed by the average Bernese notable city fathers and their disenfranchised wives.[84] The centrality of artistic endeavours was crucial to this marginal milieu 'which, bit by bit, began to take shape, nourished by the oblique, the bizarre, the maladjusted, the recalcitrant and the unruly—creating culture beyond convention and ready-made production, beyond respectable arts and crafts or commerce'.[85] Initially led by the guiding spirit of the elementary school teacher and amateur philosopher of life Fritz Jean Begert, basement theatres and underground performance venues soon began to emerge, allowing the young nonconformists to share their intellectual pursuits which were, in the 1950s, most decidedly outside the mental horizon of academic literary studies. Folk tales, myths, pulp fiction, and other manifestations of popular culture were analysed at length in a manner not too dissimilar from the way the Situationists or Beat poets were hunting for signifiers indicating trace elements of a non-alienated life in Parisian alleyways or on American highways.

Initially agnostic about politics, slowly but unmistakably the relentless and often provocative cultural critique began to take on a distinct political colouration. By the early 1960s, these young literary rebels began to reinterpret their perceptions of a cultural void as a manifestation of a wider societal malaise. The collectors of legends and fairy-tales turned into nuclear weapons protestors and organizers of anti-Vietnam War demonstrations. Crucially, in the canton and the region of Bern, these literary nonconformists cum political rebels were at the forefront of the creeping politicization of their Bernese subculture. Without relinquishing explicitly cultural critiques, this circle of literary bohemians for much of the 1960s performed the combined role of literary and political avant-garde before, towards the very end of the decade, ultimately giving way to more standard forms of new left activism to be covered in Chapter 4. The case of the Bernese prophets of the possibility of a different life—some of them, like other nonconformists elsewhere, 'carrying out a precarious balancing act between ingenious unconventional lateral thinking and mental imbalance'[86]—is yet another convincing case study underscoring the role of cultural critique in preparing the terrain for the socio-cultural and political rebellion toward the end of the 1960s and in the first half of the 1970s.

8. THE FIRST TRANSNATIONAL YOUTH REVOLT

Culture rebels were not necessarily by definition young. By the time of the San Francisco Renaissance, for instance, William Burroughs was in his forties. So was Julian Beck when he led the charge on the Odéon and then turned the Avignon Festival upside down. Still, the radical decade after 1965 is remarkable also for the prominence of youth. The second strand of this chapter's investigation will aim to cast a light on the prehistory of the radical period's generational revolt. In comparison with the role of cultural protest as precursor to the turmoil of '1968', the ubiquity of 'youth' in the wave of protest movements in the rebellious decade under investigation stands uncontested. But, for all the universal recognition of the centrality of youthful revolt, the actual sequence of events often remains shrouded in obscurity. The remaining pages of this chapter will therefore attempt to sort through the various stages of this rebellion. For, as the decade of the 1960s opened, generational revolt, such as it was, still remained overshadowed by social class division. Then, partially under the impact of certain forms of cultural experimentation, a cross-class generational consciousness began to be formed.

In the post-Second World War era, most observers tend to agree, youth as such became an object of attention and concern, equally reflected in newspaper headlines and a wave of sociological treatises in the second half of the 1950s. From the end of the Second World War until the mid-1950s, most interested observers of youth culture in the Western world had been mostly worried about the manifestation of widespread apathy and lack of interest in societal concerns. Yet in the context of post-war American hegemony, such disengagements were of little serious concern, above all since most youth proved only too willing to integrate themselves within the mounting consumerist paradigm. The second half of the 1950s, however, shook up much of this academic sociological complacency.[87] Gilles Perrault, always a perspicacious chronicler of contemporary socio-cultural and political trends, in 1961 drew attention to a new, unexpected, and, for most, unwanted social role for industrial society's young generation:

In Stockholm, in January 1961, five thousand youth between fifteen and twenty years of age invade the city center, ransack department stores and attack a hundred police officers. In Poznań (Poland) the police is forced to use tear gas to keep thousands of hooligans under control. In New York, the forces of order have launched a veritable offensive against the revolt of the teenagers. In all western capital cities, the most problematic neighborhoods for the police . . . are precisely those where gangs of adolescents freely roam. . . . Stealing, raping, injuring, killing. [They are called] in England Teddy boys, *Halbstarke* in Germany, *teppisti* in Italy, *hooligans* in Poland, *raggare* in Sweden, *blousons noirs* in France, *nozems* in the Netherlands, *taizo zoku* in Japan, *naderumper* in Denmark.[88]

A recent student of this phenomenon in West Germany, Thomas Grotum, adds the Spanish *gamberros*, the Viennese *Plattenbrüder*, and the Soviet Union's *hooligans* to the list. Once again drawing attention to the worldwide sweep of this phenomenon, Grotum concludes: 'Whether emanating from the United States, Greece, Sweden, Norway, Poland or Czechoslovakia, even from Japan and South Africa news of rioting adolescents spread like wildfire.'[89]

What was happening in the United States, Europe, and other parts of the industrial world? What caused significant minorities within an entire generation of young people benefiting from an unprecedented economic boom period to become 'deviants', 'hoodlums', and 'hooligans'? In many ways we still do not know, and it is a remarkable and challenging fact to recognize that, fifty years after the event, there still exists not a single serious study which attempts to draw some cross-cultural conclusions. A number of important single-country case studies, however, permit some preliminary observations to be made. With the recent burgeoning of cultural studies, much fine-tuned attention has been paid to the way in which this cohort of young people began to develop a distinctive dress, style, and personal comportment. This theme will be elaborated further below. But some of the more astute analysts of youth 'delinquency' of the second half of the 1950s are the first ones to point to similar manifestations of youthful rebellion in earlier generations, complete with equally separate and distinct modes of dress, leisure time habits, and even musical repertoires. The important question, then, it seems, is to uncover what made the mid to late 1950s wave of youth revolt unique.

Several observers make a claim that precisely this generation of youth was the first one to transcend constricting demarcations of social class or status. Youth subcultures as such were no innovation of the 1950s, they argue, but earlier manifestations were usually able to be ascribed to youth belonging to one specific social class. Here the relevant discussion for the West German case is particularly detailed and attempts to portray the *Halbstarken* phenomenon as the moment when class-based behaviours and styles began to be tendentially superseded by modes of interaction, dress, and public comportment characteristic of a generation rather than a class. This debate is important, and it is regrettable that most authors engaging in this discussion exclusively rely on the findings of sociologists writing in the immediate aftermath of the events. Some contemporary observers had indeed noted the incontrovertible fact that police arrests had netted young people hailing from a variety of social classes, leading one recent commentator to proclaim that 'in the street fights and performance venue altercations in the years 1956 to 1958 increasing numbers of youth from the middle classes took part' as well.[90] But, upon closer examination of the evidence reported in contemporaneous academic analyses, Detlev Peukert, a notable authority on youth subcultures in twentieth-century Germany, concludes that the active hardcore engaging in street brawls were clearly to be found amongst classic blue-collar working-class youth.[91] And the sole detailed recent sociological survey of the German youth riots, Thomas Grotum's careful analysis of police statistics for the state of Lower Saxony, further undermines the thesis of the *Halbstarkenkrawalle* as the first manifestation of the growing importance of generation over class. The working class, and most specifically the blue-collar working-class nature of arrested suspects emerges crystal clear from the evidence. And the sole documented case of an arrested university student only serves to highlight the exceptional nature of this particular case.[92] Short of further detailed investigations, then, it seems that the tendency to proclaim the youth revolts of the second half of the 1950s as the first cross-class generation-specific youth revolt is likely to remain a wishful reinterpretation of actual events coloured by actually existing experiences of that particular kind in succeeding decades. What then does make the 'youth delinquency' of the 1950s into a phenomenon *sui generis*?

The most stimulating studies generally address that cohort's inventions of characteristic styles, and Stanley Cohen is only one amongst many—though he may very well have been one of the first—to draw attention to 'their symbolic innovation'[93] as their particular contribution to the cultural history of the twentieth century. In his brief discussion of the British variant, the Teddy boys, Cohen stresses that 'style' should not be given a narrow reading: 'The stylistic innovations were seen—and quite rightly so—as being not just ones of dress, but as heralding a new cultural contour to be taken into account in society's normative mapmaking.'[94] Where Cohen goes astray in his assessment of Teddy boys' inventiveness is in his ascription of original creativity to the Teddy boy critique: 'They were the first group whose style was self-created', Cohen writes. Acutely aware of the influence of American role models, Cohen points to the Teddy boys' various Britain-specific mutations and adaptations of American style or, in his own words, to 'all the proliferation, confusion and sorting out in the [British] youth scene during the subsequent few years'.[95] Was the Teddy boy style truly *sui generis*?

Here it seems that the laudable desire of the Birmingham Cultural Studies school to ascribe creativity, autonomy, and independent thinking to the subjects of their studies goes one step too far. It is of course plainly undeniable that Teddy boy culture developed certain stylistic differences from the American prototype, just like the Dutch *nozems* were no exact carbon copies of US 'delinquent gangs'. Likewise, it would have been wholly astounding if the German *Halbstarken* had developed in ways identical to the Italian *teppisti* or the francophone *blousons noirs*. But, in the case of style and cultural comportment of this phenomenon of youthful rebels, to focus on relatively minor differences would be to miss the forest for all the trees. The penchant for black leather jackets or similar 'proletarian' gear, the preference for jeans over more elegant leg-wear, the carefully crafted 'careless' look, the Elvis-style coiffed hair, were all part of the quasi-universal language of this particular generation of nonconforming working-class youth. Bill Haley, Elvis Presley, Marlon Brando, and James Dean were their idols, equally admired and partially copied from Manchester to Milan.

What truly made these 'angry young men' into an unprecedented phenomenon and a portent of things to come was not their supposed cross-class social composition or their much-acclaimed stylistic inventiveness. The differences between the symbolic languages 'spoken' by the respective national groups resembled related dialects much more than different language groups. It was precisely the similarity between the various behaviours of these unruly crowds which points to the important feature of this phenomenon, for it was the first instance of a truly transnational, if class-based, youth rebellion. Utilizing the mechanisms placed at their disposal by the culture industry of 'the society of the spectacle' (Guy Debord), the young rebels adapted a suitable juxtaposition of images emanating from North American dream factories to stake their claims on society. And, in doing so, they affected subsequent generations of youthful rebels, influencing, as Kaspar Maase suggests for the West German case, 'their consumer wishes; their hedonistic attitudes of "having fun while you're young"; their way of spending leisure time in the public sphere and at commercial places such as cinemas, concerts, cafes, and dance halls instead of in the intimate space of the family . . .'.[96] In short, a genie was let out of the bottle.

1968, however, was still a long way away. For the most part, in the late 1950s the spirit of rebellion remained unfocused, diffuse, and non-specific. Symptomatic for this state of affairs was the following exchange in the cult film *The Wild One*. When Marlon Brando, the leader of a biker gang, was asked: 'What are you rebelling against?', he answered: 'What have you got?'[97] There was, however, at least one important exception to the non-political direction of this working-class youth revolt in the second half of the 1960s.

9. MARLON BRANDO TURNS COMMUNIST

In Italy, delinquent gangs first caught the headlines of newspapers in late 1957 and early 1958, when a string of car thefts, random assaults, and general acts of gratuitous vandalism, carried out not by individuals but by groups of youth, suddenly were reported from cities across the country,[98] although the crest of the wave of disorderly conduct was yet to come: '1959 was the year of the Italian *teppisti*.'[99] A series of public altercations unremittingly brought into the Italian public consciousness the reality of the moral panic which was beginning to abate north of the Alps by that time. Yet the destructive energies of young *teppisti* soon found outlets unheard of further north.

In the late 1950s, the Christian Democratic stranglehold over Italian politics seemed to be briefly loosening its grip, and in the spring of 1960 it appeared to survive a cabinet reshuffle solely thanks to a vote of parliamentary support by the monarchists and the neofascist Movimento Sociale Italiano (MSI), thereby indirectly giving a boost to the direct descendants of Mussolini's Blackshirts. When the MSI soon thereafter announced that they would hold their annual convention in the city of Genoa, there was a public outcry. For Genoa had been a traditional stronghold of the left. Genoa had been the site of particularly bloody confrontations between the antifascist underground and the Nazi occupation forces. In the closing days of the Second World War, faced with a determined insurrectionary offensive by the Ligurian underground, the German regional commander was finally humiliated into signing an unconditional surrender document—capitulating not to the advancing Allied armies but to the solidly implanted Genoese guerrilla forces. The MSI's decision to stage its congress in Genoa was thus meant as a provocation, and it was responded to in kind.[100]

The entire Genoese trade union movement and political left mobilized in a quickly ascending cycle of public expressions of disgust. On 28 June, in front of a crowd of 30,000 demonstrators in the Piazza della Vittoria, Sandro Pertini, a prominent antifascist socialist in the Second World War and a future President of the Republic, proclaimed a general strike for 30 June. The strike paralysed the city, but what struck observers most about this event was a series of unplanned and unprecedentedly violent confrontations between demonstrators and police. In wave after wave of relentless attacks unknown young demonstrators went on the offensive, not shying away from using makeshift weaponry to intimidate the forces of law and order, though ultimately losing their battle against superior force.[101] Newspaper columnists and media commentators immediately seized upon this novelty of the battle of Genoa, for most of those arrested were young street kids—*ragazzi di strada*—often hailing from Italy's impoverished south, who had come north with or without their families in search of employment, only to find themselves stuck in substandard housing and in menial jobs with little hope left for fulfilment of their dreams. Having adopted the dress code and comportment of the *teppisti* they were searching for an outlet for their frustrations. Given the politicized culture and condition of the Italian state, their targets this time were not random victims but the defenders of the MSI's right to indulge in public provocations of Italians' antifascist sentiments.

At the time, the *teppisti* of Genoa found few defenders, including on the organized left. Old left commentators, but initially also the figurehead theoretician of the emerging new left, Raniero Panzieri, denounced the fearless streetfighting men as provocateurs or, at best, unwitting dupes playing into the hands of the state as well as the conservative and radical right. Only later did published opinion on the Italian left begin to reassess their initial reactions, for it soon became apparent that the *moto di Genova* was not an isolated fluke. When the Tambroni government responded by toughening its public stance, a wave of similar protest actions affected almost the entire Italian state. From Bari to Bologna, up and down the Italian boot, the images of Genoa were replayed over and over again, with a similar line-up of forces. Protest demonstrations organized by the mainstream old left became battlegrounds of young rebels with open collars, striped jackets—*magliette a strisce*, the specialty outerwear preferred by the politicized *teppisti* in Genoa and elsewhere—and Marlon Brando haircuts versus the Italian police.[102] Crucially, the dividing line between old left peaceful protestors and youthful rebels became increasingly blurred. When, on 7 July 1960, police opened fire on demonstrators in Reggio Emilia, killing five and injuring nineteen, one of the victims exemplified the new trend: 19-year-old Ovidio Franchi, son of antifascist activist parents, was the secretary of the local branch of the Communist Youth Federation (FGC) but, his friends recounted after his death, he had grown increasingly disenchanted with old-style old left politics as usual. His cohort of FGC friends sought other outlets for their alienation, including the pleasures of rock'n'roll.[103]

It should be noted here that the July 1960 altercations gave rise to bitter recriminations and accusations within high politics in Italy primarily *not* on account of the sudden prominence of young militant streetfighters. The protest demonstrations and strikes having been organized by the mainstream forces of the old left, the conservative spectrum of Italian published opinion and their closely allied political elites most prominently used this occasion to cast aspersions on the political project above all of the Italian Communist Party (PCI), depicted as the instigator of the street battles and as harbouring violent revolutionaries. In short, the disturbances of the summer of 1960 must be regarded as multilayered experiences, leading to a series of sometimes contradictory observations and consequences. For, while being accused by the Italian right of fomenting an insurrectionary atmosphere, the leadership of the old left organizations—parties and trade unions alike—were engaged in a containment battle of their own. It appears from the available evidence that the youth groups associated with the old left—and, amongst others, also of the Catholic left—were indeed in the forefront of activism in July 1960, becoming increasingly difficult to control by their elders.[104] In turn, the dividing lines between the radical initiatives by political youth organizations and the underground violence by young *teppisti* became increasingly blurred.[105] Given the absence of detailed sociological studies of the July 1960 disturbances, the precise distribution of roles and responsibilities between radicalized political youth groups and spontaneous violence by *teppisti* must for the moment remain unclear. Certainly, the unsubstantiated assertion of Ilaria Del Biondo that the youthful protagonists of July 1960 had nothing in common with the *teppisti* appears more than doubtful.[106] It is far more realistic to view the July 1960 altercations as an unplanned and unexpected fusion of youthful energies simultaneously originating in a variety of political and ostensibly non-political corners of Italy's urban youth milieu.

The cycle of politicized revolts ebbed out later on in the summer of 1960 but flared up again during the July 1962 revolt of the Piazza Statuto in the heart of Turin, another landmark altercation in the history of the post-war Italian Republic. Again, for a number of days, protesters battled with the police, a battle once again spearheaded by young men defying authority, 'i capelli alla Marlon Brando'.[107] Perhaps one particularly noteworthy and symptomatic—certainly symbolic—indicator of a close identification between young left-wing activists and the Teddy boy phenomenon of Italian *teppisti* that bears mention in this context is the emergence of political protest songs sung in the aftermath of the 1960 *moto di Genova* and the July 1962 *rivolta di Piazza Statuto*, which clearly established at the very least a spiritual link: *E poi poi poi ci chiamavano teddy boy* (And Then they Called us Teddy Boys, 1960), adapting the music of a song popular in the Italian *risorgimento*, and the *Inno dei teppisti* (Hymn of the Youthful Delinquent Gangs, 1962), the latter sung to the tune of the traditional Italian labour movement song, the *Inno dei lavoratori* (Hymn of the Workers).[108]

By the mid-1960s, it was beginning to dawn on a growing number of observers that, far from being a mindless rebellion of young delinquents that merely gave excuses to the authoritarian state, the battles of Genoa, Turin, and elsewhere were the opening shots in a new era. Prior to 1960, Italian youth had frequently been at the forefront of societal revolts. But their earlier activism had been part and parcel of more established political traditions, dominated by adults, which provided the organizational structure and ideological points of reference. The mass movement phase of Italian antifascist underground resistance between 1943 and 1945 was clearly a phenomenon of youthful revolt, though guided and inspired by long-established political traditions. July 1960 opened up a growing gulf between generations, young activists no longer content to follow the directives emanating from old left adults. We will return to the consequences of this particular generation gap in subsequent chapters.[109]

For the moment, the lesson of the *teppisti* battles of 1960–2 which needs to be retained is that, in Italy at the very least, in the apt expression coined by Marco Grispigni, 'Marlon Brando turns communist'.[110] In this specific instance, of course, the term 'communist' should be interpreted to mean 'radical', 'unorthodox', 'anti-authoritarian', or 'uncompromisingly oppositional', rather than denoting a particular proclivity towards Communist Party politics. For, as we shall see in greater detail in Chapter 4, the PCI engaged in its own vicious defamation campaign of the *teppisti* with their trademark *magliette a strisce*. At any rate, the 1960 and 1962 *teppisti* revolts were living testimony to the universality of a growing youth revolt, coupled with the particular confrontational vitality of Italian civil society.[111] We will have frequent occasion to return to this theme, which gave the Italian radical decade a most peculiar and, for some, appealing twist.

10. BEATNIKS, HIPSTERS, EXISTENTIALISTS

The culture of delinquent gangs[112] was of course not the only youth culture prominent in the 1950s. There existed other expressions of cultural non-conformity and rebellion, though none of them came close to the transnational significance of the working-class subculture described in preceding pages. Those which existed, if on a smaller scale, were, however, equally class-specific or, at the very least, not at all expressions of a generation-specific rather than class-based alienation. The San Francisco Renaissance, for instance, spawned a bohemian subculture all of its own, combining public poetry readings with interest in jazz and folk music, creating a sufficient economic base for bars, clubs, and coffee-houses to flourish. The appeal of such eclectic venues gave rise to the eventual fame of certain neighbourhoods as centres of experimentation in all sorts of ways. Haight-Ashbury in San Francisco or, on a smaller scale, the subcultural oases created by eccentric minds in cities such as Minneapolis, where Dinkytown, Stadium Village, and the West Bank helped shape the creative genius of Bob Dylan, were mostly havens for middle-class dissenters, initially of a non-political kind.[113]

There exist very many colourful descriptions of the beatnik scene. One of the most famous chroniclers is Norman Mailer, whose insights into American culture of the 1950s and 1960s are probably without parallel—at least from a literary perspective. Like most observers, Mailer includes both 'hipsters' and 'beatniks' under the generic label 'Beat Generation', and he asserts that both hipsters and beatniks 'share the following general characteristics: marijuana, jazz, not much money, and a community of feeling that society is the prison of the nervous system'.[114] For Mailer, however, the hipster is the more proletarian of the two, and consequently he devotes most of his attention to highlighting the 'psychopathic brilliance' of this 'new breed of adventurers, urban adventurers who drifted out at night', approvingly quoting a contemporaneous psychologist for whom 'the psychopath is a rebel without cause, an agitator without a slogan, a revolutionary without a program',[115] something Mailer, but not only Mailer, could identify with. Mailer's labelling of the hipster as an expression of 'a muted rebellion of the proletariat'[116] is best taken as a literary device to denote closer proximity in style and comportment to the lumpen element of society, rather than as a sociological insight. Most observers of the Beat Generation would include most hipsters—and not just beatniks—as hailing from the American middle classes. Compare, for instance, Steve Watson's definitions of hipster style—'likes jazz, specifically bebop, especially Charlie Parker; beret; goatee'; 'smokes marijuana; drinks strong espresso coffee'; 'knows existentialism'; 'jeans, black turtleneck, black sweater'—with his illustrations of beatnik style which includes 'goatees; berets; smokes marijuana; jeans'; 'dark glasses'; 'chants poetry to jazz back-up'; 'appreciates Method acting'; or, for the female beatnik, 'jeans; black leotards; waxy eye make-up; Morticia-like complexion; svelte; drinks dark espresso coffee; cooks with garlic; dates black jazz players'.[117] The similarities here probably outweigh the differences in style.[118] Be that as it may, the Beat Generation took (small portions of) American society by storm.

A closely related and equally famous subcultural middle-class milieu existed in Saint-Germain-des-Prés on the left bank in Paris roughly ten years earlier. Already notorious in the decades prior to the Second World War as a venue where artists, bohemians, and assorted nonconformists could gather, the neighbourhood experienced its last—though not the least consequential—bout of creative synergy in the post-liberation 1940s, when the presence of Boris Vian, Jacques Prévert, Juliette Gréco, Maurice Merleau-Ponty, Jean-Paul Sartre, and Simone de Beauvoir gave it an increasingly distinct existentialist flavour.[119] Not all existentialist authors were necessarily very young by the time they achieved a certain fame, but their following was definitely most pronounced in the nonconformist middle-class or university milieu. As did Beat poetry later on, existentialism swept across national borders. In West Germany, for instance, the so-called existentialist milieu, a phenomenon appearing in the course of the 1950s, constituted 'the first association of middle class youth in the postwar era which opposed the silent consensus on the [German] political past and challenged the dominant paradigm of performance and consumption, be it only via their retreat into the ghettoes of jazz cellars, ice cream parlors or art schools'.[120] Their colour of choice was, once again, black, but black turtleneck sweaters were their stock in trade, no leather jackets and unkempt Elvis haircuts here; instead men preferred the short and layered look (*Cäsarenschnitt*) and women opted for masculine styles. Cool jazz was their music of choice.

No country may serve better as an example of the vast gulf separating such middle-class subcultures from working-class milieux than Britain, a country where even today the realities of social class cut across society more deeply, visibly, and painfully than almost anywhere else. So much the more in the late 1950s. Here is what a British expert has to say about the class-based nature of British style:

The [respective] subcultures were in fact literally worlds apart. The college campuses and dimly lit coffee bars and pubs of Soho and Chelsea were bus rides away from the teddy boy haunts deep in the traditional working-class areas of south and east London. While the beatnik grew out of a literate, verbal culture, professed an interest in the avant-garde (abstract painting, poetry, French existentialism) and affected a bemused cosmopolitan air of bohemian tolerance, the ted was uncompromisingly proletarian and xenophobic. The styles were incompatible, and when 'trad' jazz emerged as the focus for a major [middle-class] British subculture in the late 50s, these differences were even more heavily underlined.[121]

Nonetheless, the British context, in a peculiar twist of fate, soon produced a musical style and a corresponding set of cultural markers which, for the first time on a major scale, managed to transcend the boundaries of social class.

11. BRITISH ROCK

At the beginning of the 1960s, it seemed as if styles would change but class divisions would merely be replicated and perpetuated in new forms. The Teddy boy subculture began to fade but was soon replaced by not just one but two competing working-class subcultures: mods and rockers. ' "Mod" meant effeminate, stuck-up, emulating the middle classes, aspiring to a competitive sophistication, snobbish, phony. "Rocker" meant hopelessly naïve, loutish, scruffy . . .'.[122] Middle-class existentialism eventually faded, ultimately replaced by hippy culture as the middle-class nonconformity of choice. In northern and north-western Europe—and, of course, the United States—in the 1960s long hair and the trappings of 'flower power' remained markers of middle-class dissent, just as the existentialist or beatnik look had done a few years earlier.[123]

It was the quintessentially working-class port city of Liverpool which spawned a musical tradition which soon became the cultural glue to unify a young generation beyond long-established and obviously continuing class divides. Countless elements undoubtedly contributed to create the Mersey Beat sound and, ultimately, British rock, and this is not a history of popular music. Two elements, however, need to be highlighted. It has already been noted that some of the most creative minds at work in Liverpool were keenly interested in vanguard cultural trends elsewhere. A close personal friend of Stuart Sutcliffe and John Lennon in their art college days, later on the mastermind and editor of *Mersey Beat* magazine, Bill Harry, confirms: 'The American Beat Generation poets were the "thing" at the time',[124] but Sutcliffe, Lennon, and their circle of friends still dressed and acted in the best tradition of the Teddy boy craze well into their Hamburg period.[125] Did their syncretism of style assist in their creation of a new sound?

The second element which needs stressing is closely related to the essence of the first: the syncretism of music venues. The club most closely associated with Beatle fame, the Cavern Club, occupied a well-established slot in Merseyside's music subculture long before the Beatles gave their first performance there in January 1961. 'The Cavern had skiffle evenings on Wednesdays, modern jazz on Thursdays and trad at the weekends.'[126] When Ray McFall took over as new owner in October 1959, he soon realized that the short-lived popularity of 'trad' was rapidly waning and modern jazz 'attracted only the earnest, intellectual few'. Although himself 'a passionate jazz fan', McFall soon opened the doors of the Cavern Club to pop. A keen businessman, he also took advantage of another largely unsatisfied niche market and opened his club not only for the usual evening crowd but also for a lunchtime audience of mostly white-collar office workers taking their midday break. It was to this audience that the Beatles first played at the Cavern Club.[127]

Club culture could be varied, and another Liverpool club employing the future Fab Four was the Jacaranda coffee club, whose owner, Allan Williams, was also known 'to open Liverpool's first strip club'.[128] This connection between cultural 'deviance' of a certain kind and beat music was likewise the hallmark of the second music club famous in the history of the rise of British pop: Hamburg's Star-Club. Its impresario, Manfred Weißleder, had made a name for himself as the owner of about a dozen St Pauli establishments in the second half of the 1950s, notably several striptease clubs. In April 1962, Weißleder switched from selling the spectacle of sex to promoting rock. Next to an 'Erotic Film-Night-Club', Weißleder's new venue soon became the leading rock venue in all of Germany, contributing to shaping Hamburg into the cradle of British rock.[129] We will return to other forms of cultural and political nonconformity, as expressed in programme offerings of both the Cavern and the Star-Club, later on.

For the moment, it is imperative to draw attention to the changing sociology of the audience of British pop. For the most part a somewhat softer, less abrasive reconfiguration of American rock'n'roll, it was sufficiently palatable to appeal to a variety of listeners without losing its grip over its original proletarian crowd. The Star-Club audience also initially attracted working-class youth, with only a small sprinkling of existentialist 'cross-overs' hailing from the middle classes. Astrid Kirchherr was one such erstwhile frequenter of the existentialist milieu; another one was the photographer Günter Zint.[130] But soon the popularity of rock accelerated, in the process spreading not only geographically but ignoring most social class boundaries in the process of topping the charts. In West Germany, the Star-Club soon became 'a small piece of freedom inmidst of a hostile world dominated by authorities, prohibitions and coercions, opposing or attempting to suppress everything connected with pleasure'.[131] Accordingly, it increasingly attracted 'high school and university students, and it turned into a social crucible of the new youth culture'.[132] But in other countries, too, exemplified by the rhythm of beat, 'a new appreciation of life, transcending all social strata, fueled by a desire to experience pleasure and adventure', affected young people.[133] In the 1950s, rock'n' roll was by far most popular amongst working-class youth. 'In the 1960s a changing pattern is recognizable. More and more middle class kids felt inspired by beat.'[134] The diversifying sociology of the rock audience was of course mostly a reflection of more general changes in patterns of social mobility rather than a mystical effect of beat rhythms themselves. Still, it is not easy to imagine another music style which could have similarly fashioned an audience which, ten years earlier, would rarely have been listening to identical tunes.

In England itself, the tide was turning by late 1963: 'Never again would Pop music be considered the prerogative only of working-class boys and girls. The Beatles were now played not only in Council houses but in West London flats, in young ladies' finishing schools and in the blow-heated barns where landowners' daughters held their Christmas dances.'[135] Or, as the archetypal historian of this musical genre, Nik Cohn, writes in a passage on the rather more aggressive Rolling Stones, 'they were liked by Aldermaston marchers and hitch-hikers, beards and freaks and pre-Neanderthal Mods everywhere'.[136] An Italian observer notes that 'within few years, first in England and the United States, then in a number of European countries, a new and diverse face of youth culture can be discerned: these are the years in which beat culture conquers the means of mass communication, exclusively targeting the youth market, spreading its symbols amongst ever wider strata of youth'.[137] Or, in the words of a Swiss analyst: 'Pop turned into the first fully operational universal language, and via music which could be commercially exploited, a wholly unprecedented global communication via signs and symbols began to function.'[138] What message did these symbols carry?

Beat became the universal language of this first cross-class generational youth culture. Its most effective signifiers were the mini-skirt and long hair; the transgressive implications of shoulder-length hair on men far outdistanced receding hem lines on women which, on one level, did little to challenge traditional gender roles. Not all members of this generation, obviously, conformed to this code. But even a superficial perusal of the mainstream newspaper press establishes beyond the shadow of a doubt that beat, long hair, and other trappings of that era were perceived as threats to the social order by the older generation and treated as such. Yet how truly subversive were these trends? The answer to this important query depends on the definition of the categories of analysis. Inasmuch as the new forms of interpersonal communication constituted the opening wedge in a loosening of dominant forms of uptight moral regimentation, the challenge was not only subversive but ultimately successful. We will return to the 'cultural revolution' effected in the course of the 1960s in Chapter 5.[139] But was there also a corresponding in-built political challenge? Was there a direct link between the youth counterculture of the 1960s and the challenges symbolized by the explosions of 1968?

Some well-known observers of the British scene are rather scathing in their critique of the ultimately non-political dimensions of key stylistic features of the British youth revolt. 'At all events the political upheaval of 1968 proved that pop music, in the revolutionary sense, was a non-starter, a fake revolt with no programme much beyond the legalization of pot'; and the same author elsewhere dots most of the remaining 'i's: 'Pop, anti-authoritarian when its own interests are threatened, played no part in the events of those months.'[140] Other participant-observers are less dismissive in their remarks. The historian of the British counterculture, Jonathon Green, for instance, has assembled a monograph and a corresponding collection of interview transcripts on the kaleidoscope of features belonging to what he calls the English Underground, in the process leaving no doubt of its distinct impact on the politics of that time. Still, stimulating and encyclopedic as his materials are, his data ultimately leave the question strangely unanswered.[141] Beat promoters, however, did not shy away from linking music and radical politics, even at a time when such explicit connections did not necessarily guarantee certain financial benefits. Once again highlighting the syncretism of beat culture, in December 1964, for instance, the Liverpudlian Cavern Club organized a happening of sorts, called 'Bomb', bringing together two rock bands, pop artists, and poets in a condemnation of nuclear weapons proliferation around the world.[142] The Hamburg Star-Club likewise served as a platform not only for British rock but for radical writers and poets as well, such as Reinhard Baumgart, Peter O. Chotjewitz, Hubert Fichte, and Gabriele Wohmann.[143]

In the English-speaking world, the hippy crowd was perhaps most closely identified with the youth counterculture of the 1960s and, certainly in the United States, the evidence points to their frequent involvement in political protests, though rarely playing a decisive role. An active promoter of countercultural identities at that time, Theodore Roszak, commented approvingly: 'So it is that when New Left groups organize their demonstrations, the misty-minded hippies are certain to join in, though they may tune out on the heavy political speechifying in favor of launching a yellow submarine or exorcizing the Pentagon.'[144] Norman Mailer likewise remarked on the astounding mix of participants at the October 1967 March on Washington he chronicled so well:

They came walking up in all sizes, a citizen's army not ranked yet by height, an army of both sexes in numbers almost equal, and of all ages, although most were young. Some were well-dressed, some were poor, many were conventional in appearance as often were not. The hippies were there in great number, perambulating down the hill . . .[145]

No obvious and apparent link, then, can be detected between this first cross-class generational youth culture and the holding of leadership roles in ongoing and newly emerging social movement protest in the 1960s. Certainly, the anti-authoritarian and anti-hierarchical underpinnings of this youth rebellion predisposed the members of this generation to take up political causes with greater ease than preceding generations of young people, the latter, even when revolting, still following the precepts, ideologies, and organizational models provided by their elders. Having learnt to question authority, the beat generation of the 1960s had fewer barriers, psychological and others, to overcome when pressed to take radical political stances. It is unlikely that the years 1965–75 would have taken on such radical contours if it had not been for the groundwork laid by earlier cultural and other forms of societal critique which helped open up the floodgates of revolt. Still, without additional factors, the generational revolt alone would likely not have made a major difference in shaking up politics as usual.

12. BEAT CULTURE IN ITALY

One country where a variety of influences helped to elevate the beat revolt into a certain degree of prominence within an emerging, more all-encompassing social rebellion was, once again, the Italian state. From all available evidence, it was in Italy where the transgressive dimension of long hair, mini-skirts, and related components of 1960s youth culture became most closely, indeed inextricably, interlinked with far-reaching political challenges to the status quo. Some of the reasons for the volatility of Italian society will be addressed in later chapters. For the moment it may suffice to describe some of its manifestations.

The emerging cross-class youth culture of the 1960s had given rise to a host of magazines, some officially launched and supported by 'respectable' publishing houses aiming to take advantage of a market niche, others operating—at least initially—as independent ventures from below, some laying claim to the honourable mantle of 'underground' magazines. The history of these youth magazines remains to be written, and the few existing serious studies of this genre merely reinforce the urgent need to develop an understanding of their role as transnational transmitters of youth culture.[146] But no other country produced a youth-oriented magazine quite like the Milanese *Mondo Beat*. Whereas many other youth magazines served, above all, the role of fanzines, with politics relegated to, most frequently, a rather secondary role, *Mondo Beat* combined the generational, lifestyle, sexual, cultural, and political revolt like no other conduit in Italy or elsewhere.[147] An early editorial in *Mondo Beat* included the following exhaustive programmatic line: 'We've had enough of authority, family, sexual repression, consumer economy, war, police, priests, culture, pedagogues, and demagogues.'[148]

The Italian 'underground' and hippy community, the real backdrop to *Mondo Beat*, was a sociological microcosm of the Italian boot. There were upper- and upper-middle-class 'dropouts' involved, but likewise runaway adolescents from the impoverished south, many of them converging on Milan, a city with a long and vital radical tradition but, above all else, the biggest metropolis of Italy, thus allowing a significant amount of personal anonymity. An article in the March 1967 edition of *Mondo Beat* described how 'every day dozens of kids (*ragazzi*) emerge out of the escalator from the Cordusio metro station with their sleeping bags and backpacks on their shoulders, kids who have fled from their homes, from factories, prisons, political parties, from the morass of an existence they do not know how to accept'.[149] Similar communities existed in other Italian towns, but Milan became their organizational and ideological centre. In the Porta Romana section of Milan they briefly created the very first autonomous youth centre, a forerunner of the subsequently rather more long-lived and widespread *centri sociali*.[150] The underground activists behind *Mondo Beat* soon began to practise what they preached. Pacifism was one of their defining characteristics, so it was only natural that they organized and participated in anti-Vietnam War events.

Here they soon encountered a number of obstacles. If not hampered in their movements by police, the marshals provided by the mass organizations of the old left increasingly locked horns with young *capelloni* and other dissident youth, who often refused to comply with officially agreed-upon police requests for the protest marches to stay safely out of sight of some of the most hated symbols of militarism, such as the American Embassy. Some antiwar demonstrations bypassed the traditional channels of the old left, and certain events were jointly organized by the emerging far left and the hippy crowd, such as a small April 1967 action targeting both American policies in Vietnam and the military coup in Greece, a demonstration which led the flagship national daily *Corriere della Sera* to draw up a headline reading: 'China Lovers and Long Haired United in Renewed Turmoil in the City Centre Streets.'[151]

Elsewhere in Europe long hair also made inroads into the more politicized youth milieu and gradually became a signifier of political dissent. Che Guevara, the quintessential icon of the increasingly restless youthful left, certainly fits this image. So did, to name but one other, Rudi Dutschke, the most well-known exponent of the West German student left. Outside of Italy, the existing hippy communities may have given certain sartorial impulses to their more politicized cohort of generational rebels, but nowhere did they form a distinctly left-wing current of their own. In Italy, as the editors of *Corriere della Sera* recognized, until 1969 the distinction between the various unorthodox currents increasingly challenging the authority and hegemony of the old left was not always that easily made. And it is symptomatic of the particular volatility of the Italian public sphere that, in the summer of 1969, the provincial town of Novara, not quite halfway between Turin and Milan, became the site of a five-day running battle between hippies (*capelloni*), army draftees stationed in or near Novara, and the law enforcement community. Until 1969 the Novarese hippy community had not been particularly noted for its political engagements. But in late June of that year, small-scale provocations between hippies and soldiers, the latter wearing the near-skinhead look usually mandated by army regulations in Italy as elsewhere, had begun to evolve into regular hit-and-run attacks. The authorities decided on an unprecedented show of force. Setting up road blocks on all major arteries leading into town, five hundred armed representatives of the Italian state, originating from the entire kaleidoscope of Italy's multiple and competing police agencies, stopped and searched all vehicles entering or leaving Novara, in search of refractory *capelloni*. Citizens of Novara, initially bemused by the skirmishes between hippies and army recruits, both equally disliked by most locals, soon realized that Novara was beginning to resemble a militarized police state. Delegations of all mainstream parties except for the radical right soon felt compelled to seek out the local prefect to demand a return to normal peacetime measures for the maintenance of public order rather than the ostentatious display of armed might reminding Novarese of the state of siege in Greece, then under the rule of the colonels. The battle of Novara was, for many, living proof that, if the hippy community itself was reluctant to enter the path of politicization, the repressive Italian state would be more than willing to promote such an evolution for reasons all of their own.[152]

The link between beat music, the counterculture and radical politics was made most explicit by Giangiacomo Feltrinelli, head of a major publishing empire and proprietor of a growing chain of bookshops across Italy, catering to the entire spectrum of nonconformist Italians moving, just like Feltrinelli himself, ever more rapidly further to the political left. Personally cultivating the unkempt, long-haired look, Feltrinelli, for instance, stocked his Roman bookstore, then conveniently located near the Spanish Steps, the internationally most well-known mecca of hippies, runaway youth, and assorted youthful tourists south of the Alps—Amsterdam performed a similar magnet role north of the Alps—with more than just books. A juke box and a pinball machine were prominent features, next to stacks of books covering the entire spectrum of old, new, and far left concerns. A sales clerk later reminisced:

They took the pinball into the backroom, but even the distributor couldn't believe his eyes. In 1965, pinball was at best something you found in a few bars patronised by really young people. . . . The high school kids would come in and start dancing; the Feltrinelli bookshop was the first discotheque in Rome. It was a scandal, these fourteen- or fifteen-year-old kids dancing in the store to the music from the jukebox.[153]

On the walls, an eclectic mix of 'photos of James Dean, Bogart, Valentino, Toscanini, Marlon Brando, the Rolling Stones, Bob Dylan and Mao Tse Tung' greeted the customer. In Florence, in 1966, the Feltrinelli store invited one of the regular bands at the Piper Club in Rome, the Italian equivalent to the Cavern or Star-Club, to perform for a string of afternoon engagements. The gigs played by The Primitives, a British band, were a success. On the second day, all pedestrian traffic outside the store on the Via Cavour, a major artery in the city centre, was blocked by 'hundreds of young listeners occupying the sidewalks in front of the store'.[154] Italy, then, once again provided a melting pot *sui generis* within the larger outlines of this emerging transnational cross-class generational youth culture. Yet the association of youthful rebels that best exemplified the multi-coloured, experimental, and visionary milieu described so far did not emerge from the grimy streets of proletarian Milan, nor from the haunting grounds of existentialist cum Situationist Left Bank Paris, nor the marijuana-saturated café culture of Haight-Ashbury.

13. THE AMSTERDAM PROVOS

The most provocative and media-savvy critics of society to emerge in those years were the products of an urban environment few would have suspected could produce a troupe of cultural subversives with impact far exceeding the narrow limits of their native land. The Dutch Provos best exemplify the multiple strands of cultural and political critique which, to underscore the thesis of this chapter, prepared the spiritual and political terrain on which the explosion of 1968 and thereafter could develop, prosper, and grow. The Provos were either inspired by or actively inspired every single one of the various subcultural or proto-political milieux described thus far. The young men and women around Roel van Duijn, Rob Stolk, and Robert Jasper Grootveld provided the creative spark which fused the various artistic traditions and creative aspirations into a powerful and innovative weapon taken over or adapted by rebels elsewhere.

Virginie Mamadouh, in the most comprehensive description of the various waves of social movement activism spawned by the creative genius of Provo, which fundamentally changed the image and the reality of the erstwhile rather prim and proper Dutch state, opens her chapter on the Provos by noting: 'The genesis of Provo is usually described as the encounter between art and politics',[155] a more than apt description of the key influences on this milieu. A decidedly non-academic writer, Mustapha Khayati, in his incendiary brochure which spread the message of Situationism far beyond the limits of Strasbourg, that most German of all French cities, devotes a central paragraph to the experience of the Provos. Its opening sentences proclaim: 'The Provos are the first form of supercession of the experience of the *blousons noirs*, the organization of its first political expression.' With characteristic Situationist hyperbole but also more than a measure of respect, Khayati continued: 'They were born out of an encounter between a few leftovers from the world of decomposed art in search of a career and a mass of young rebels in search of self-expression. Their organization [i.e. the Provos] enabled both sides to advance toward and achieve a new type of contestation.'[156] Provo fame soon spread across the European continent. In his 1991 foreword to a new edition of his *The Revolution of Everyday Life*, Raoul Vaneigem reports that this polemical treatise, originally published in late 1967, had been written 'between 1963 and 1965' but for a long time had not found a publisher. Then, soon after Gallimard had become the latest publishing house to reject his manuscript, the literary supplement of *Le Figaro* 'published an article decrying the influence of situationists on the Provos in Amsterdam. That same evening Queneau [a Gallimard editor] sent me a telegram requesting that the manuscript be resubmitted.'[157] When, in November 1966, the month the Strasbourg scandal hit the news, three groups of countercultural rebels in Milan resolved to henceforth join their efforts to destabilize the Christian Democratic ruling consensus, one of these three associations was a namesake of the Amsterdam Provos. The other two were *Onda Verde* and *Mondo Beat*.[158] Daniel Cohn-Bendit, the quintessential student revolutionary in 1968, operating across the borders of several European states, devotes an important chapter in his reminiscences to the influence of the Provos on himself and his generation of young rebels.[159] What lies behind the spectacular national and international success of Provo?

The Dutch Calvinist tradition would appear to be an unlikely breeding ground for a novel admixture of drugs, youth revolt, street theatre, and smoke bombs, yet prior to the sudden impact of the Provos in their two short years of existence (May 1965 to May 1967) Amsterdam had already attracted a fair sprinkling of experimental philosophers and small-time, off-beat entrepreneurs, such as Nicolaas Kroese and his Magisch Centrum Amsterdam, or the Dutch answer to the San Francisco Renaissance, Simon Vinkenoog. In the apt description of the most comprehensive chronicler of the Dutch Provos to date, Niek Pas, 'a climate of mild insanity' already marked the atmosphere in certain parts of Amsterdam.[160] The Provos, however, took this potent admixture, added some ingredients of their own, and soared to new heights.

Disenchanted with traditional old left forms of activism, the Dutch Provos aimed to change society not by legal mass demonstrations or non-violent civil disobedience and the like, but by openly staging spectacles, happenings, and other media-oriented activities which, after a long hiatus, brought the ludic element back into the service of the progressive cause. If, in the late nineteenth century, such inspired pieces of cultural inversion as Paul Lafargue's *The Right to be Lazy* had been standard reading for the European left, the subsequent creeping accommodation of social democracy to the status quo and the Stalinization of the Communist line had left little room for irony, cultural experimentation, and playfulness within the left. In an age still largely untroubled by most forms of real and imagined terrorism, the Provos harkened back to the real and imagined world of anarchist individual terrorism of the late nineteenth century, and they stepped into the limelight of the Dutch media with outlandish (in reality non-existent) plans to set off bombs and otherwise destroy the complacent Dutch petty-bourgeois public sphere on a variety of occasions. Street theatre, countercultural happenings, and theatrical self-dramatizations made it clear to anyone watching that the Provos were different—and that they meant business. In a stroke of (largely accidental) genius, they, for instance, devised and popularized an ecological action plan *avant la lettre*, the closure of Amsterdam's city centre to all forms of traffic propelled by combustion engines and the corresponding free availability of 20,000 bicycles—all painted white! In reality, anticipating the fate of virtually all other Provo-inspired 'white plans', few white bicycles ever graced the narrow streets of central Amsterdam. But out of this idea emerged the concept and the reality of the colour 'white' as the quintessential 'color of provocation'.[161] Soon white jeans and jeans jackets became the unofficial uniform of Provos and their rapidly growing periphery of sympathizers.

One factor which probably helped place ludic and other non-traditional methods of activism centre stage was, paradoxically, an underlying current of profound pessimism in Provo circles, but a pessimism of the Gramscian kind, a pessimism of the intellect coupled with an optimism of the will. Full well realizing the likely impossibility of carrying out a real social revolution in their native land, Provos nonetheless consciously set out—at the very least—to do their level best to turn Dutch society upside down while they could. And so they did. Already by March 1966 all forms of 'trouble' and unrest in Amsterdam were blamed by the authorities on the Provos, regardless of the real perpetrators—a sure sign of name recognition. Indeed, the strategic deployment of smoke bombs at the occasion of the 10 March 1966 Dutch royal wedding, celebrated with appropriate pomp and circumstance with, amongst other highlights, a royal cortège winding through Amsterdam's streets, catapulted the Provos to national and international fame—even though only a portion of the various smoke bombs thrown in the path of the royal carriage had been manufactured by the Provos themselves. Riding the growing wave of popularity, on 1 June 1966, the Provos even managed to have one of their leading spokespersons, Bernhard de Vries, elected onto the Amsterdam municipal council. Provo groupings were now founded across the country and in the Flemish part of Belgium. Soon letters arrived from all over Europe in bundles, then sackloads, written by young nonconformists fascinated by Provomania in the Dutch state. By the early summer of 1966, newspaper coverage and television interviews and documentaries had made Provo activism a watchword far beyond the borders of the Netherlands.[162]

Soon, however, and for good reason, this most image-conscious group of nonconformists began to feel uncomfortable with their success. Even before Guy Debord published his seminal *The Society of the Spectacle* in 1967, the masters of image building, the organizers of the most spectacular and popular happenings in the 1960s, began to realize that they no longer furnished spectacles but that they had become one. Already in the course of 1966, for instance, the Dutch Milk Council had jumped on the 'white' bandwagon and promoted a 'white glasses plan', thus taking advantage of the Provo idea. The public burial of Provo in the Vondelpark on 13 May 1967 was only the last, but perhaps the most consequential theatrical staging of this remarkable group of young Dutch activists.[163]

Clearly, in a movement celebrating individualism and thriving on idiosyncrasies, different spokespersons personified a wide variety of political and/or cultural interests. Perhaps Roel van Duijn, whose first hero as an adolescent growing up in The Hague was the Algerian freedom fighter Ahmed Ben Bella, was indeed the most openly political member of the Provos' Amsterdam brains trust. But it is obviously of more than marginal significance that this most well-known representative of Provo repeatedly and insistently emphasized, in practice and in writing, the necessity of forging a creative union 'between avantgarde-type culture and left politics', a link that, van Duijn underscored, had been severed in earlier decades, 'leading to a significant weakening of the revolutionary power of both'. Van Duijn continued: 'We are [now] attempting to reconstitute this link; between, on the one hand, happenings, beat, pop-art, protest songs and, on the other, anarchism, *provotariaat* [and] anti-militarism . . .'.[164] Significantly, Provo regularly and enthusiastically engaged in joint political action campaigns with other parties of the Dutch old and new left. Clearly, Provo must be regarded as a constituent part of precisely this Dutch left. Rather than remaining wholly anchored in the 'countercultural development phase' of the Dutch 1960s, as Niek Pas maintains,[165] the significance of Provo was precisely that it constituted the spiritual and organizational bridge—that missing link—between the countercultural and the openly political phase of the 1960s. The Provos personified more than any other grouping described in this chapter the creative unity of art and politics, the moment when the combined explosive forces of these cultural and generational revolts turned into an openly political revolt. Long after the Provos had disappeared from Amsterdam's lively cultural and political map, their radiance continued to brighten up even some of the more remote corners of the European world.[166]

NOTES

1. Beppe Fenoglio, *Johnny the Partisan* (London: Quartet, 1985) is one of the few Italian novels of the Second World War resistance experience to have been translated into English. Alba may, of course, be best known to some English speakers as the location for the detective novel by Michael Dibdin, *A Long Finish* (London: Faber & Faber, 1998).

2. The information on Pinot Gallizio is taken from Roberto Ohrt, *Phantom Avantgarde: Eine Geschichte der Situationistischen Internationale und der modernen Kunst* (Hamburg: Nautilus, 1990), 145 and 152, and the unsigned and undated 'Pinot Gallizio: L'uomo, l'artista e la città', http://www.fondazione-ferrero.it/EVE/GALLIZIO/gallizio.htm (24 Nov. 2004). The 'ranking' of Alba's most famous citizens is adapted from other website information provided by the Fondazione Ferrero in Alba.

3. Relevant information on Asger Jorn is taken from Ohrt, *Phantom Avantgarde*, 99–117 and 145.

4. Ibid. 146.

5. The playful tongue-in-cheek description of the train station scene is taken from the unpaginated Maurizio Corgnati, 'L'uomo di Alba', in Pinot Gallizio, *La Gibigianna* (Turin: Edizioni d'Arte Fratelli Pozzo, 1960). I thank Roberto Ohrt for sending me a copy of this chapter of this rare book.

6. For the photo, see Ohrt, *Phantom Avantgarde*, 150.

7. Citation taken from Corgnati, 'L'uomo di Alba'.

8. Ohrt, *Phantom Avantgarde*, 169.

9. Ibid. 151. On COBRA, see Willemijn Stokvis, *Cobra: 3 Dimensions* (London: Lund Humphries, 1999), but above all Jean-Clarence Lambert, *COBRA* (London: Sotheby, 1983).

10. Ohrt, *Phantom Avantgarde*, 140–3.

11. Ibid. 143–5, on the initial contacts between Jorn and the Lettrists.

12. Isidore Isou, *Introduction à une nouvelle poësie et à une nouvelle musique* (Paris: Gallimard, 1947). See, once again, Ohrt, *Phantom Avantgarde*, 15–49, for a stimulating discussion of Isidore Isou and the Lettrist movements. Roberto Ohrt has drawn attention to the origins of Lettrism (and thus, subsequently, Situationism) in the depths of the Second World War, at the time of the Battle of Stalingrad, on pp. 9–10. Lettrism, of course, is also a major focus of attention for Greil Marcus in his *Lipstick Traces: A Secret History of the Twentieth Century* (London: Faber & Faber, 2001). The most extensive history of Lettrism, however, including countless Lettrist 'poems', remains Jean-Paul Courtay, *La Poésie lettriste* (Paris: Seghers, 1974). The dating of the

Manifesto is taken from Jean-Louis Brau, *Cours, camarade, le vieux monde est derrière toi! Histoire du mouvement révolutionnaire étudiant en Europe* (Paris: Albin Michel, 1968), 61.

13. Laurent Chollet, *L'Insurrection Situationniste* (Paris: Dagorno, 2000), 25.

14. Marcus, *Lipstick Traces*, 269. I have slightly adapted the translation.

15. An entertaining rendition of the misappropriation of Notre Dame can be found in Marcus, *Lipstick Traces*, 279–86.

16. This is the term given to this phenomenon a few years later by American sociologists when confronted with this phenomenon on a mass scale; see, for instance, the classic Richard A. Cloward, *Delinquency and Opportunity: A Theory of Delinquent Gangs* (London: Routledge & Kegan Paul, 1961).

17. See Ohrt, *Phantom Avantgarde*, 51–6, for textual and pictorial information on this group and its activities. Chollet, *L'Insurrection*, 49, draws attention to Henri de Béarn's personal and political itinerary.

18. Bruno Buongiovanni, 'Situazionismo', in Aldo Agosti (ed.), *Enciclopedia della sinistra europea nel XX secolo* (Rome: Riuniti, 2000), 584–5.

19. Chollet, *L'Insurrection*, 12.

20. Citation taken from Anselm Jappe, *Guy Debord* (Berkeley, Calif.: University of California Press, 1999), 6–7.

21. Anyone familiar with Situationist texts may be puzzled at this ascription of 'razor-sharp dissection' to the Situationist critique. In truth, Situationist texts are often filled with rather diffuse and open-ended passages, whose meaning must remain elusive to most readers. Yet, as a rule, such painfully long and obscure ramblings are usually interspersed with frequently brilliant insights, pithy observations that make the study of Situationist texts an exercise in discovering hidden delights.

22. The juxtaposition of Situationist and postmodernist critiques of contemporary societies is most trenchantly developed in Sadie Plant, *The Most Radical Gesture: The Situationist International in a Postmodern Age* (London: Routledge, 1992). Note, for instance, the following passage: 'The postmodern condition is like Dada without the war or surrealism without the revolution; postmodern philosophers are the sold-out situationists who wander without purpose . . . enjoying the superficial glitter of a spectacular life. Naïvely offering an uncritical home to the notion of the spectacle, postmodern discourse is filled with chatterings about a concept it never imagines was once saturated with revolutionary intent' (p. 150).

23. Jappe, *Debord*, 47.

24. Raoul Vaneigem, *The Revolution of Everyday Life* (London: Rebel Press, 2003), 26.

25. The citations in this paragraph are from Raoul Vaneigem, 'Basic Banalities (II)', in Ken Knabb (ed.), *Situationist International Anthology* (Berkeley, Calif.: Bureau of Public Secrets, 1981), 122, 123, and 118; emphasis in the original.

26. 'Questionnaire', in Knabb (ed.), *Anthology*, 140.

27. Jappe, *Debord*, 61.

28. Ivan Chtcheglov, 'Formulary for a New Urbanism', in Knabb (ed.), *Anthology*, 1–2. This 1953 document properly belongs to the intellectual heritage of the Lettrist movement, but it became a founding statement of the Situationist movement and was indeed first published in the very first issue of their journal, *Internationale Situationniste*, in 1958; on the location of Ivan Chtcheglov's piece within the intellectual map of Situationism, see Ohrt, *Phantom Avantgarde*, 74–6.

29. See, above all, Mark Wigley, *Constant's New Babylon: The Hyper-Architecture of Desire* (Rotterdam: 010 Publishers, 1998), but also Simon Sadler, *The Situationist City* (Cambridge, Mass.: MIT Press, 1998), and the illuminating discussion in Ohrt, *Phantom Avantgarde*, 117–38.

30. The Marx quote is from Karl Marx, *The German Ideology* (London: Lawrence & Wishart, 1965), 44–5, translation slightly altered.

31. 'Questionnaire', 138.

32. For this episode, see Ohrt, *Phantom Avantgarde*, 187–8.

33. Two representative pictures of such 'industrial art' are reproduced in Ohrt, *Phantom Avantgarde*, 192.

34. Wolf Vostell, one of the premier European artists popularizing 'happenings', had studied in Wuppertal, an old textile town on the southern edges of the industrial Ruhrgebiet. From 1954 onwards Vostell contributed to expanding the cultural boundaries of this city marked by a strong pietist tradition by choosing to stage many of his happenings in this unlikely location. Two excellent volumes showcasing a cross-section of such wider artistic avantgarde productions, both in words and pictures, Jürgen Becker and Wolf Vostell, *Happenings, Fluxus, Pop Art, Nouveau Réalisme* (Reinbek: Rowohlt, 1965), and Wolf Vostell, *Dé-coll/agen 1954–69* (n.pl.: Edition 17, 1969), exemplify the self-evident political dimension of many such avant-garde artistic productions at that time.

35. 'All the King's Men', in Knabb (ed.), *Anthology*, 114–17; citations on pp. 117 and 114.

36. The role of Lefebvre in hooking up Debord and Vaneigem is mentioned in Chollet, *L'Insurrection*, 51.

37. The most accessible English translation can be found in Dark Star (ed.), *Beneath the Paving Stones: Situationists and the Beach: May 1968* (Edinburgh: AK Press, 2001), 98–103, citation on p. 103.

38. Plant, *Radical Gesture*, 84–5.

39. Chollet, *L'Insurrection*, 84.

40. This remarkable document is accessible in English in Dark Star (ed.), *Paving Stones*, 9–27, and in Knabb (ed.), *Anthology*, 319–37. The 'Strasbourg scandal' is presented in relative detail in Pascal Dumontier, *Les Situationnistes et Mai 68: Théorie et pratique de la révolution (1966–1972)* (Paris: Ivrea, 1995), 80–97.

41. I have taken over elements of both translations referred to in the preceding note. For the original French text, I have relied on the reproduction of this document in René Viénet, *Enragés et situationnistes dans le mouvement des occupations* (Paris: Gallimard, 1968), 219–43. The relevant passages in the two English-language translations can be consulted in Dark Star (ed.), *Paving Stones*, 23–4, and Knabb (ed.), *Anthology*, 337.

42. Dumontier, *Les Situationnistes*, 87.

43. Reported in 'Our Goals and Methods in the Strasbourg Scandal', Knabb (ed.), *Anthology*, 207; also in Dark Star (ed.), *Paving Stones*, 9.

44. Cited in the editorial introduction to the reproduction of Khayati's brochure in Dark Star (ed.), *Paving Stones*, 9.

45. On the initial reprint, see Dumontier, *Les Situationnistes*, 93. The other claims and the citation are from an editorial footnote in Knabb (ed.), *Anthology*, 377. Michael Seidman suggests that *On the Poverty of Student Life* 'was probably (and may continue to be) the most widely read and translated French tract produced in the 1960s'; see his

The Imaginary Revolution: Parisian Students and Workers in 1968 (New York: Berghahn, 2004), 29. The suggested total press-run of 500,000 copies should nonetheless be taken with a grain of salt.

46. Chollet, *L'Insurrection*, 16.

47. A photo of both contestants sitting side-by-side in a protest action at the Sorbonne can be found in Viénet, *Enragés et situationnistes*, 51.

48. Chollet, *L'Insurrection*, 51.

49. For an elegant effort to highlight the contributions of Situationist-inspired transgressions in revolutionizing the West Berlin student milieu, see Bernd Rabehl, 'Die Provokationselite: Aufbruch und Scheitern der subversiven Rebellion in den sechziger Jahren', in Siegward Lönnendonker, Bernd Rabehl, and Jochen Staadt, *Die antiautoritäre Revolte: Der Sozialistische Deutsche Studentenbund nach der Trennung von der SPD*, i. *1960–1967* (Wiesbaden: Westdeutscher Verlag, 2002), 400–512.

50. Steven Watson, *The Birth of the Beat Generation: Visionaries, Rebels, and Hipsters, 1944–1960* (New York: Pantheon, 1995), 186.

51. Allen Ginsberg, *Howl and Other Poems* (San Francisco: City Lights Books, 1959), 21.

52. Andrew Jamison and Ron Eyerman, *Seeds of the Sixties* (Berkeley, Calif.: University of California Press, 1994), 141.

53. William S. Burroughs, *The Letters of William S. Burroughs 1945–1959* (London: Picador, 1993), 185.

54. Ginsberg, *Howl*, 9 and 20.

55. Citation taken from Watson, *Beat Generation*, 5.

56. Jack Newfield, *A Prophetic Minority: The American New Left* (London: Anthony Black, 1967), 44.

57. Watson, *Beat Generation*, 6.

58. Newfield, *Prophetic Minority*, 47.

59. Philip Norman, *Shout! The True Story of the Beatles* (London: Elm Tree Books, 1981), 52.

60. On this 'political' phase of John Lennon's life in the late 1960s and early 1970s, itself a reflection of larger generational and political processes part and parcel of the radical decade under investigation in this book, the quintessential study remains Jon Wiener, *Come Together: John Lennon in his Time* (London: Faber, 1985).

61. Paul McCartney, in Jonathon Green (ed.), *Days in the Life: Voices from the English Underground 1961–1971* (London: Pimlico, 1988), 46.

62. Dennis McNally, *Desolate Angel: Jack Kerouac, the Beat Generation, and America* (New York: McGraw-Hill, 1979), 280.

63. Barry Miles, *Ginsberg: A Biography* (London: Viking, 1990), 330.

64. Morris Dickstein, *Gates of Eden: American Culture in the Sixties* (Cambridge, Mass.: Harvard University Press, 1997), 5.

65. Watson, *Beat Generation*, 230.

66. Dickstein, *Gates of Eden*, 21.

67. Theodore Roszak, *The Making of a Counter Culture: Reflections on the Technocratic Society and Its Youthful Opposition* (London: Faber & Faber, 1971), 129.

68. 'The Amsterdam Declaration', in Wigley, *New Babylon*, 87.

69. But see some preliminary comments in this regard in Vibeke Rützou Petersen, *'Kursbuch' 1965–1975: Social, Political and Literary Perspectives of West Germany* (New York: Peter Lang, 1988), 139, and in Attilio Mangano and Antonio Schina, *Le culture del Sessantotto: Gli anni sessante, le riviste, il movimento* (Bolsena: Massari, 1998), 59.

70. Martin Hubert, *Politisierung der Literatur: Ästhetisierung der Politik* (Frankfurt: Peter Lang, 1992), 98.

71. The event is playfully—and sardonically—reconstructed in the stimulating book-length essay by Klaus Briegleb, *1968: Literatur in der antiautoritären Bewegung* (Frankfurt: Suhrkamp, 1993), 122–30. For an insightful overview concerning the place of the Gruppe 47 in the post-war West German public sphere, see the article by Ingrid Gilcher-Holtey, ' "Askese schreiben, schreib: Askese": Zur Rolle der Gruppe 47 in der politischen Kultur der Nachkriegszeit', *Internationales Archiv für Sozialgeschichte der deutschen Literatur*, 25/2 (2000), 134–67.

72. Some wonderfully evocative snapshots of the atmosphere within this Valhalla of the French cultural establishment during the month-long occupation can be found in Christiane Fauré, *Mai 68 jour et nuit* (Paris: Gallimard, 1998), 64–5.

73. Serge Govaert, *Mai 68: C'était au temps où Bruxelles contestait* (Brussels: Pol-His, 1990), 133.

74. For the life and art of Jean-Jacques Lebel, see the brief survey, with some illustrations, in Chollet, *L'Insurrection*, 38–43.

75. John Tytell, *The Living Theatre: Art, Exile and Outrage* (London: Methuen Drama, 1995), 232. A most stimulating source of information is the wealth of documentary evidence contained in Jean-Jacques Lebel, *Entretiens avec le Living Theater* (Paris: Pierre Belfond, 1969). At the end of May 1968, the Living Theater company went to take part in the annual Theatre Festival in Avignon, contributing to a series of *éclats* at this most important and famous theatre festival in Europe. For a recent creative adaptation of the Avignon revolt, see the text (and, better yet, the performance) of the brilliant one-man show, written, produced, and singularly acted by Philippe Caubère, *68 selon Ferdinand* (Paris: Joëlle Losfeld, 2002), in particular the second part, 'Avignon', and here especially the subsection 'Le jeu de Jean Vilar', pp. 173–214.

76. Amongst the wealth of literature on Europe's leading radical theatre producer, director, and actor, note esp., in English, Tony Mitchell, *Dario Fo: The People's Court Jester* (London: Methuen Drama, 1999), and Tom Behan, *Dario Fo: Revolutionary Theatre* (London: Pluto, 2000); the reference to Fo's overwhelming popularity as early as the mid-1960s is taken from Behan, *Dario Fo*, 21.

77. Two interesting snapshots emanating from the West German theatre scene are Wolfgang Matthias Schwiedrzik, 'Theater als "Aktion" ', in Ingrid Gilcher-Holthey (ed.), *1968: Vom Ereignis zum Gegenstand der Geschichtswissenschaft* (Göttingen: Vandenhoeck & Ruprecht, 1998), 225–38, and the illustrative statement by Botho Strauß, 'Versuch, ästhetische und politische Ereignisse zusammenzudenken: Neues Theater 1967–70', *Theater heute* (Oct. 1970), 61–8. For one of the countless offshoots of the spirit of 1968, the hope to create a truly 'popular theatre', the little-known case of the Brussels Théâtre du Parvis is symptomatic of similar efforts elsewhere at that time; see Michèle Seutin, 'A propos de l'ex-Théâtre du Parvis', *Cahiers de la production théâtrale*, 9 (Sept. 1974), 55–94.

78. Serge Govaert, the author of the standard history of 1968 in Brussels, devotes 20 per cent of his pages to the effervescence of the cultural critique and the spirit of rebellion in the domain of theatre, cinema, and the fine arts; see Govaert, *Mai 68*, 119–43 and 155–62.

79. Two short essays may serve to remind the interested reader that France's cultural sphere made equally profound contributions to the revolution of everyday life in

May 1968: Laurence Bertrand Dorléac, 'Les artistes et la révolution', and Marie-Ange Rauch, 'Le théâtre public, lieu de contestation', both in Geneviève Dreyfus-Armand, Robert Frank, Marie-Françoise Lévy, and Michelle Zancarini-Fournel (eds.), *Les Années 68: Le Temps de la contestation* (Brussels: Complexe, 2000), 225–38 and 259–71.

80. For a photo of a central section of Somville's contribution to the students' cause, see Govaert, *Mai 68*, 12–13.

81. On the contestations focusing on the Brussels Palais des Beaux-Arts, see Govaert, *Mai 68*, 155–62; the dating of the Odéon affair is taken from Fauré, *Mai 68*, 65. I thank Rik Hemmerijckx for providing some of the factual details of the facilities at the Beaux-Arts.

82. For more detail on the Belgian art scene during '1968', see Gerd-Rainer Horn, 'The Belgian Contribution to Global 1968', *Revue belge d'histoire contemporaine/Belgisch Tijdschrift voor Nieuwste Geschiedenis*, 35 (2005), 597–635.

83. There exist plenty of literary approximations of the phenomenon of 'Switzerland'. Two such essays by leading Swiss novelists are Peter Bichsel, *Des Schweizers Schweiz* (Frankfurt: Suhrkamp, 1997), and Hugo Loetscher, *Der Waschküchenschlüssel oder Was Wenn Gott Schweizer Wäre* (Zurich: Diogenes, 1988). For a historian's view, note Jonathan Steinberg, *Why Switzerland?* (Cambridge: Cambridge University Press, 1996).

84. Bernese women only obtained the right to vote in cantonal elections in 1968; for the right to cast a ballot in national elections, all Swiss women had to wait until 1971. I thank Beat Kümin for this information.

85. Fredi Lerch, *Begerts letzte Lektion: Ein subkultureller Aufbruch* (Zurich: Rotpunkt, 1996), 134.

86. Fredi Lerch, *Muellers Weg ins Paradies: Nonkonformismus im Bern der sechziger Jahre* (Zurich: Rotpunkt, 2001), 593.

87. The picture of the 1950s as a decade deeply split in terms of youth attitudes and corresponding scholarly concern is non-controversial. A particularly clear definition of this paradigm shift in the middle of that decade can be found in Franco Rositi, 'La cultura giovanile', in Alberto Martinelli (ed.), *Socializzazione e cultura giovanile* (Milan: ISEDI, 1978), 109.

88. Gilles Perrault, *Les Parachutistes* (Paris: Seuil, 1961), 87–8. For the French case, note the recent reprint of a 1962 study, Émile Copfermann, *La génération des blousons noirs: Problèmes de la jeunesse française* (Paris: La Découverte, 2003). Copfermann worked as an editor for the new left publisher François Maspero, in whose series 'Cahiers libres' the volume originally appeared. Unsurprisingly, his study differed from most contemporaneous sociological studies of the *blousons noirs*, which mostly regarded this phenomenon as a manifestation of criminal deviance.

89. Thomas Grotum, *Die Halbstarken: Zur Geschichte einer Jugendkultur der 50er Jahren* (Frankfurt: Campus, 1994), 84–5.

90. Heinz-Hermann Krüger, ' "Es war wie ein Rausch, wenn alle Gas gaben": Die "Halbstarken" der 50er Jahre', in Willi Bucher and Klaus Pohl (eds.), *Schock und Schöpfung: Jugendästhetik im 20. Jahrhundert* (Darmstadt: Luchterhand, 1986), 274. This hypothesis is most pronounced in Marina Fischer-Kowalski, 'Halbstarke 1958, Studenten 1968: Eine Generation und zwei Rebellionen', in Ulf Preuss-Lausitz, Peter Büchner, and Marina Fischer-Kowalski, *Kriegskinder, Konsumkinder, Krisenkinder: Zur Sozialisationsgeschichte seit dem Zweiten Weltkrieg* (Weinheim: Beltz, 1983), 53–70.

91. Detlev Peukert, 'Die "Halbstarken": Protestverhalten von Arbeiterjugendlichen zwischen Wilhelminischem Kaiserreich und Ära Adenauer', *Zeitschrift für Pädagogik*, 30 (1984), 543–4.

92. Grotum, *Halbstarken*, 110–19. For a straightforward and informative recent survey article of the *Halbstarken* phenomenon, see Jürgen Zinnecker, ' "Halbstarke": Die andere Seite der 68er-Generation', in Ulrich Herrmann (ed.), *Protestierende Jugend: Jugendopposition und politischer Protest in der deutschen Nachkriegsgeschichte* (Weinheim: Juventa, 2002), 461–84.

93. Stanley Cohen, *Folk Devils and Moral Panics* (London: Routledge, 2002), 151. This product of the now defunct Birmingham Centre for Contemporary Cultural Studies was first published in 1972.

94. Ibid. 154.

95. Ibid. 154 and 155.

96. Kaspar Maase, 'Establishing Cultural Democracy: Youth, "Americanisation" and the Irresistible Rise of Popular Culture', in Hanna Schissler (ed.), *The Miracle Years: A Cultural History of West Germany, 1949–1968* (Princeton: Princeton University Press, 2001), 439.

97. Laszlo Benedek, *The Wild One* (Columbia Pictures, 1954), 22nd minute.

98. Simonetta Piccone Stella, ' "Rebel Without a Cause": Teppisti e giovani negli anni del boom', in *La prima generazione: Ragazze e ragazzi nel miracolo economico italiano* (Milan: FrancoAngeli, 1993), 45–180.

99. Marco Grispigni, 'Combattenti di strada: La nascità delle culture giovanili in Italia', in Massimo Canevacci *et al.*, *Ragazzi senza tempo: Immagini, musica, conflitti delle culture giovanili* (Genoa: Costa & Nolan, 1993), 23.

100. The context leading to the Christian Democratic Tambroni government's reliance on parliamentary support from the fascist MSI are laid out in Paul Ginsborg, *A History of Contemporary Italy: Society and Politics 1943–1988* (London: Penguin, 1990), 254–8. The story of the liberation of Genoa is briefly highlighted in the classic narrative of the Italian underground by Giorgio Bocca, *Storia dell'Italia partigiana: Settembre 1943–maggio 1945* (Milan: Mondadori, 1995), 513–16.

101. For the reconstruction of the battle of Genoa, I have relied upon, amongst other sources, Diego Giachetti, *Anni sessanta comincia la danza: Giovani, capelloni, studenti ed estremisti negli anni della contestazione* (Pisa: BFS, 2002), 15–17; Nanni Balestrini and Primo Moroni, *L'orda d'oro 1968–1977: La grande ondata rivoluzionaria e creativa, politica e esistenziale* (Milan: Feltrinelli, 1997), 20–7; and Cesare Bermani, *Il nemico interno: Guerra civile e lotta di classe in Italia (1943–1976)* (Rome: Odradek, 2003), 168–80.

102. On the generalized replication of the battle of Genoa throughout the Italian state, see above all Bermani, 'L'antifascismo del luglio sessanta', in *Nemico interno*, 141–263. A recent monograph on the events surrounding the Tambroni scandal is Philip Cooke, *Luglio 1960: Tambroni e la repressione fallita* (Milan: Teti, 2000).

103. On the case of Ovidio Franchi and his circle of friends, see Giachetti, *Anni sessanta*, 18–19.

104. Note, for instance, the autonomous initiatives by an array of youth groups of varying political persuasions during the July crisis in Turin; on this see Fabrizio Loreto, '1960: La "lunga" crisi', in Luca Baldissara *et al.*, *Un territorio e la grande storia del '900: Il conflitto, il sindacato e Reggio Emilia*, ii. *Dal secondo dopoguerra ai primi anni '70* (Roma: Ediesse, 2002), 157–58.

105. In this context Andrea Rapini's side-by-side discussion of mainstream journalistic discussions of *teppismo* in Reggio Emilia and a closely related debate about generational conflicts of interest held in Communist trade union organizations and party gatherings, again in Reggio Emilia, is most suggestive in this regard. See Andrea Rapini, 'Modernizzazione e conflitto: alle origini del luglio '60 reggiano', in Baldissara *et al.*, *Dal secondo dopoguerra*, 215–32.

106. See Ilaria Del Biondo, 'Il PCI, i giovani e il luglio '60', in Baldissara *et al.*, *Dal secondo dopoguerra*, 113.

107. On the *rivolta di Piazza Statuto*, see Dario Lanzardo, *La rivolta di Piazza Statuto* (Milan: Feltrinelli, 1979); citation taken from Grispigni, 'Combattenti di strada', 35; (*capelli* = hair).

108. These suggestive comments, including the full-length text of the two songs, can be found in Cesare Bermani, 'Il nuovo canzoniere italiano: Vent'anni della "nostra" storia', in Pier Paolo Poggio (ed.), *Il Sessantotto: L'evento e la storia* (Brescia: Fondazione 'Luigi Micheletti', 1988–9), 350–1.

109. Many commentators have pointed out the implications of the revolt of the Genoese *teppisti*. The most evocative and convincing discussions of this paradigm shift are Paola Ghione, 'L'emergere della conflittualità giovanile: Da Piazza Statuto a Paolo Rossi', and, specifically on the revelations of July 1960, Giovanni De Luna, 'Genova 1960: L'antifascismo dei giovani come diritto alla disobbedienza', both included in the excellent anthology edited by Paola Ghione and Marco Grispigni, *Giovani prima della rivolta* (Rome: Manifestolibri, 1998), 115–31 (Ghione) and 105–14 (De Luna).

110. The title of a subheading in Grispigni, 'Combattenti di strada', 32.

111. An interesting, brief discussion of some continuities between various strands of Italian youth revolt in the 1960s can be consulted in Andrea Rapini, 'Dai "teddy boys" ai "cinesi": Antifascismo e giovani generazioni', in Diego Melegari and Ilaria La Fata (eds.), *La resistenza contesa: Memoria e rappresentazione dell'antifascismo nei manifesti politici degli anni settanta* (Milan: Punto rosso, 2004), 29–45.

112. Here, finally, an important note on the gender of these youthful delinquents, given a different name in each national context, must be inserted. Though a highly masculine phenomenon—there was e.g. no female idol comparable to James Dean or Elvis Presley—young women did not stand on the sidelines, though arrest records point to males as the hardcore in news-making altercations. It is one of the pathbreaking contributions of Uta Poiger to have combined not only experiences from both parts of Germany, but those of both genders on either side of the wall as well; see her *Jazz, Rock and Rebels: Cold War Politics and American Culture in a Divided Germany* (Berkeley, Calif.: University of California Press, 2000), particularly pp. 71–105 and 168–206.

113. For the Minneapolis alternative scene, note Robert Shelton, *No Direction Home: The Life and Music of Bob Dylan* (New York: Beech Tree Books, 1986), 62–86.

114. Norman Mailer, 'Hipster and Beatnik: A Footnote to "The White Negro" ', in *Advertisement for Myself* (London: Andre Deutsch, 1961), 316.

115. Norman Mailer, 'The White Negro: Superficial Reflections on the Hipster', *Advertisement*, citations on pp. 284, 285, and 288. For a useful partial corrective to Mailer's polemical insights expressed in this particular essay, see Nat Hentoff, 'A Brief Note on the Romance of "The White Negro" ', in *Jazz Life* (London: Panther, 1964), 118–21.

116. Mailer, 'Hipster and Beatnik', 316.

117. Watson, *Beat Generation*, 121 ('symptoms of the hipster') and 259 ('the "archetypal" beatnik').

118. A final citation from Norman Mailer should not be withheld from the bemused reader, as it once again underscores Mailer's talent to pinpoint the essence of a phenomenon by the creative fusion of exaggeration, sarcasm, and historical analogy: 'The beatnik—often Jewish—comes from the middle class and [Mailer wrote in the late 1950s] twenty-five years ago would have joined the YCL [Young Communist League];' see 'Hipster and Beatnik', 316.

119. An accessible and brief snapshot of this post-1944 atmosphere is contained in the chapter on 'The Great Boom of Saint-Germain-des-Prés', in Antony Beevor and Artemis Cooper, *Paris After the Liberation, 1944–1949* (London: Penguin, 1995), 376–87.

120. Heinz-Hermann Krüger, 'Viel Lärm um Nichts? Jugendliche "Existentialisten" in den 50er Jahren: Spurensuche', in Bucher and Pohl (eds.), *Schock und Schöpfung*, 268.

121. Dick Hebdige, *Subculture: The Meaning of Style* (London: Methuen, 1979), 51.

122. Jeff Nuttall, *Bomb Culture* (London: Paladin, 1970), 33.

123. This point may be self-evident to many readers. For authoritative confirmation, see, for the USA, Timothy Miller, *The Hippies and American Values* (Knoxville, Tenn.: University of Tennessee Press, 1991), 15: 'The hippies were mainly children of privilege, and their outlook reflected their heritage'; and, for the English context, Paul E. Willis, *Profane Culture* (London: Routledge & Kegan Paul, 1978), 8: 'The hippies were exploring and broadening a middle-class tradition of the bohemian intelligentsia . . .'

124. Untitled introduction to Bill Harry (ed.), *Mersey Beat: The Beginnings of the Beatles* (New York: Quick Fox, 1977), 6.

125. Rather than one or several of the legions of often rather fanciful, free-flowing, and superficial essays on the genesis of the Beatles' stylistic choices, interested readers may consult as striking evidence the photos taken by Astrid Kirchherr, Stuart Sutcliffe's German girlfriend, 'Fotografien 1960–1965', in Rüdiger Articus *et al.*, *Die Beatles in Harburg* (Hamburg: Christians, 1996), 36–66.

126. Spencer Leigh, *Let's Go Down to the Cavern* (London: Vermilion, 1984), 26.

127. Norman, *Shout!*, 98–103, citations on p. 99.

128. Leigh, *Let's Go Down*, 34–7, citation on p. 36.

129. This expression is, of course, taken from a book with a wonderfully mean title: Alan Clayson, *Hamburg: The Cradle of British Rock* (London: Sanctuary, 1997). The presence of the immediately adjoining 'adult' establishment can be ascertained in the full-page photo of the Star-Club's front entrance in Dieter Beckmann and Klaus Martens, *Star-Club* (Reinbek: Rowohlt, 1980), 17. I thank Detlef Siegfried for supplying me with a photocopy of this collector's item.

130. Beckmann and Martens, *Star-Club*, 132, is the source of much of the information in this passage. The reference to the personal itinerary of Günter Zint is taken from Detlef Siegfried, 'Vom Teenager zur Pop-Revolution: Politisierungstendenzen in der westdeutschen Jugendkultur 1959 bis 1968', in Axel Schildt, Detlef Siegfried, and Karl Christian Lammers (eds.), *Dynamische Zeiten: Die 60er Jahre in den beiden deutschen Gesellschaften* (Hamburg: Christians, 2000), 601. Günter Zint's œuvre largely parallels the themes and topics of the Flemish Frans Pans, a selection of whose photographs are included elsewhere in this volume.

131. Beckmann and Martens, *Star-Club*, 139.

132. Siegfried, 'Pop-Revolution', 601.

133. Wolfgang Kraushaar, 'Time is on my Side: Die Beat-Ära', in Bucher and Pohl (eds.), *Schock und Schöpfung*, 220.

134. Peter Zimmermann, 'Aufwachsen mit Rockmusik: Rockgeschichte und Sozialisation', in Preuss-Lausitz *et al.*, *Kriegskinder*, 117.

135. Norman, *Shout!*, 194; I have slightly altered small portions of this text, whose original version suffers from grammatical and composition errors.

136. Nik Cohn, *Awopbopaloobop Alopbamboom: Pop from the Beginning* (London: Pimlico, 2004), 159.

137. Rositi, 'Cultura giovanile', 107.

138. Jakob Tanner, ' "The Times they are A-Changin" ': Zur subkulturellen Dynamik der 68er Bewegungen', in Gilcher-Holtey (ed.), *1968*, 211.

139. The most persuasive and voluminous study emphasizing the importance of this cultural paradigm shift is Arthur Marwick, *The Sixties: Cultural Revolution in Britain, France, Italy, and the United States, c.1958–c.1974* (Oxford: Oxford University Press, 1998).

140. George Melly, *Revolt into Style: The Pop Arts in Britain* (London: Allen Lane, 1970), 120–1 and 119.

141. Jonathon Green, *All Dressed Up: The Sixties and the Counterculture* (London: Pimlico, 1998), and Green, *Days in the Life*. A classic, colourful account of the British Underground is Richard Neville, *Play Power* (St Albans: Paladin, 1971).

142. Dieter Baake, *Beat: Die sprachlose Opposition* (Munich: Juventa, 1970), 35.

143. Siegfried, 'Pop-Revolution', 618. Bachmann and Martens, *Star-Club*, 208, note that Fichte read portions of his latest work between songs played by Ian and the Zodiacs.

144. Roszak, *Counterculture*, 65.

145. Norman Mailer, *The Armies of the Night: History as a Novel—The Novel as History* (New York: Plume, 1994), 91. A richly detailed description of the heyday of US hippy culture in the Bay Area in 1965–7 is Charles Perry, *The Haight-Ashbury: A History* (New York: Vintage, 1985).

146. An early harbinger of a future trend was the West German BRAVO; see Kaspar Maase, *BRAVO Amerika: Erkundungen zur Jugendkultur der Bundesrepublik in den fünfziger Jahren* (Hamburg: Junius, 1992), 104–75. For good insights on the prototype of ostensibly non-commercial, financially 'autonomous' youth magazines emerging in the 1960s, Daniel Filipacchi's *Salut les Copaines*, see Marwick, *The Sixties*, 95–109. On Italy's burgeoning world of youth magazines, see Marco Grispigni, 'S'avanza uno strano lettore: La stampa giovanile prima del'68', in Ghione and Grispigni (eds.), *Prima della rivolta*, 55–72.

147. In this context it should be noted that Arthur Marwick quite correctly underscores the far wider geographic reach of radio, compared with the youth-oriented magazine press; see Marwick, *The Sixties*, 109. But serious research on the role of radiophonic contributions to the youth revolt of the 1960s are, as of yet, completely absent for any national context. Here perhaps the wave of primarily Dutch and British pirate stations operating from North Sea ships may turn out to be the most promising terrain for innovative investigations. Though, for some cautionary remarks about the ultimately limited political message emanating from such pirate ships, see Melly, *Revolt into Style*, 192–4.

148. Cited in Roberto De Angelis, 'Il beat italiano', in Ghione and Grispigni (eds.), *Prima della rivolta*, 76. De Angelis suggests that this text appeared in the first issue of *Mondo Beat* which he dates to Sept. 1966. An extensive reprint of the seven issues of *Mondo Beat* which saw the light of day makes clear that the very first issue of this journal was actually published on 15 Nov. 1966. The citation is nowhere to be found in any of the texts of this first issue of *Mondo Beat* included in Gianni De Martino and Marco Grispigni (eds.), *I Capelloni: Mondo Beat, 1966–1967: Storia, immagini, documenti* (Rome: Castelvecchi, 1997).

149. De Martino and Grispigni (eds.), *I Capelloni*, 106–7. The largest such community in the world was centred on the Haight-Ashbury in central San Francisco where, Charles Perry suggests, by late 1967 'probably 75,000 people' had at one point called it their home, but Haight-Ashbury became almost exclusively identified with the burgeoning soft drug culture rather than the political left.

150. Perhaps most famous because of their close association with Italy's vibrant anti-globalization movement starting in the late 1990s, *centri sociali* became permanent institutions in the wake of the 1977 youth rebellions shaking up Italian cities, a revolt beyond the purview of this study. For information about the extensive network of *centri sociali* in Italy today, see 'Centri Sociali Autogestiti', http://www.tmcrew.org/csa/csa.htm (24 Nov 2004).

151. Cited in Giachetti, *Anni sessanta*, 147. The original headline reads: 'Alleati filocinesi e capelloni in una nuova chiassata per le vie del centro.' *Filocinesi* was the prefered derogatory expression for the rapidly growing Maoist crowd.

152. This incident is best described in Bermani, 'Novara, estate 1969: Capelloni contra militari', in *Nemico interno*, 265–88.

153. Franca Fortini, cited in Carlo Feltrinelli, *Senior Service* (London: Granta, 2001), 279–80.

154. Giachetti, *Anni sessanta*, 131–2.

155. Virginie Mamadouh, *De stad in eigen hand: Provo's kabouters en krakers als stedelijke sociale beweging* (Amsterdam: Sua, 1992), 54. I thank the author for supplying me with a copy of this important book.

156. Khayati, 'Poverty of Student Life', in Knabb (ed.), *Anthology*, p. 327. I have slightly amended the translation based on the original passage in 'De la misère', 230. Most notably I have left the term *blousons noirs* in its original French, as it makes clear the link to the tradition of the *Halbstarken, teppisti, nozems*, or 'delinquent gangs', a purposeful link in Khayati's text which the English translation 'delinquents' completely obliterates. The other readily available English translation omits portions and further distorts the French original; see 'Poverty of Student Life', in Dark Star (ed.), *Paving Stones*, 16.

157. Vaneigem, *Everyday Life*, 14.

158. When *Onda Verde* published a manifesto in the Mar. 1967 *Mondo Beat*, it was for more than one reason that the statement was entitled: 'The <u>Provo</u>cative Method of *Onda Verde*'. The author signed off as 'Marco Daniele, *Onda Verde Provo*'. The document is reproduced in De Martino and Grispigni (eds.), *I Capelloni*, 102–6, partial underlining added. *Onda Verde, Mondo Beat*, and the Milanese Provos began to operate in common in late Nov 1966; on this see Balestrini and Moroni, *L'orda d'oro*, 116–17. The fusion of *Onda Verde* and *Mondo Beat* was announced in the second issue of *Mondo Beat*, issue no. 00 (Dec. 1966), reprinted in De Martino and Grispigni (eds.), *I Capelloni*, 95.

159. Dany Cohn-Bendit, *Nous l'avons tant aimée, la révolution* (Paris: Bernard Barrault, 1986), 49–58.
160. Niek Pas, *Imaazje! De verbeelding van Provo 1965–1967* (Amsterdam: Wereldbibliotheek, 2003), 90.
161. Ibid. 115.
162. Niek Pas describes the Provomania outside of the Netherlands, ibid. 301–34. The most important non-Dutch spin-off from the Amsterdam original arose in the Belgian state, particularly Flanders and Brussels. Niek Pas devotes pp. 263–99 to his discussion of the Belgian Provo movement. However, the indispensable references for the Belgian case of Provomania are two unpublished history theses: Bart Coenen, 'Provo in Vlaanderen', Vrije Universiteit Brussel, 2000–1, and Joris Verschuren, 'Plaats voor de Homo Ludens! Vlaamse Provo's als nieuwe sociale beweging in een ruimtelijk wereld-systeem-analytisch perspectief', Rijksuniversiteit Gent, 2002–3. Coenen provides much detailed information on Provo activities; Verschuren is best at reconstituting the networks of sociability informing the Provo presence in Antwerp, Brussels, and Ghent in particular.
163. A few months later, on 6 Oct. 1967, the San Francisco hippy community performed a similarly theatrical and symbolic public burial of the hippy movement; on this see Perry, *Haight-Ashbury*, 242–4.
164. Pas, *Imaazje!*, 377–8. For Roel van Duijn's personal view of the history of Provo, see his *Provo: De geschiedenis van de provotarische beweging 1965–1967* (Amsterdam: Meulenhoff, 1985).
165. Pas, *Imaazje!*, 341.
166. On 3 May 1979, the French flagship daily, *Le Monde*, reported on a new initiative in the Swiss capital of Bern: 'Since May Day, the citizens of Bern can partake of a new means of public transportation: the bicycle. A group of Bernese residents, Young Bern, which obtained 10 per cent of the votes in the most recent municipal elections, is at the origins of this initiative. Seventy-five bicycles, all painted in green [the preferred colour of contestation in the late seventies and much of the eighties], have been provided free of charge to all residents and visitors in the medieval city centre.' The fascimile of this article from *Le Monde*, entitled 'Bernois à Vélo', is reproduced in Yves Frémion, *Provo, la tornade blanche* (Brussels: Cahiers JEB, 1982), 80. Attentive readers of this chapter will not be surprised that such copycat initiatives flourished in—of all places—Bern.

2

Under the Cobblestones Lies
the Beach: Student Activism in the 1960s

1. SIT-INS, SNCC, AND FREEDOM RIDES

It was the first day of February 1960. The setting? A provincial town in the Piedmont area of North Carolina: Greensboro. Apart from its textile and furniture industry, Greensboro was above all known as the home of the predominantly black Agricultural and Technical College. In the late afternoon of that Monday, four young black college students decided to go to the downtown Woolworth store and to sit down at the lunch counter reserved for white customers only. This provocation was not carefully prepared; indeed they had come up with this scenario during conversations the previous evening. None of the four students was particularly radical or even unconventional. Certainly, none was a known civil rights activist.

As expected, the four black students were not served. The black waitress behind the counter instead berated them for their brazen move, which she deemed rather naïve and counterproductive. The manager told his employees to ignore the four men, who remained sitting until the store closed. They then returned to their campus, emboldened by the lack of retaliation. They immediately contacted student government representatives and returned to the Woolworth lunch counter the next day. This time more than thirty black students sat down at the 'whites only' counter for two hours. Again they were not served but likewise encountered no effort at forced removal. On this second day, however, news teams covered the event. The segregated Woolworth lunch counter had sixty-six seats. On the third day of the sit-in almost all of them were occupied by black protesters, with three white students joining them in solidarity in the course of the afternoon. Thursday saw hundreds of black students, with a fair crowd of hostile white students taunting them. By the end of the week the manager shut down the Woolworth store in an attempt to defuse the situation. Over the weekend Greensboro students decided on a moratorium.

But by then the genie had been let out of the bottle. Monday morning, 8 February, sit-ins took place in nearby Winston-Salem and Durham. By Wednesday the first arrests occurred in Raleigh, North Carolina. Wednesday, 10 February 1960, was also the day when sit-ins spread beyond state borders, first to neighbouring Virginia. By mid-February, sit-ins had occurred in fifteen communities in five states. By the end of February thirty cities in seven states had been affected, and this was still only the beginning.[1] The participant-observer and historian, Howard Zinn, reports that, ultimately, more than 50,000 individuals participated in one or more sit-in protests throughout the American South, with more than 3,600 protestors spending some time in jail. By the end of 1961, the movement had succeeded in desegregating hundreds of lunch counters in a swath of southern borderstates reaching from Texas and Oklahoma all the way to Virginia and North Carolina. Yet, in an ominous portent of things to come, the Deep South, that is, South Carolina, Alabama, Georgia (with the exception of the Atlanta conurbation), Louisiana, and Mississippi, remained impervious to the efforts of mostly youthful sit-in protestors.[2]

From the very beginning, college students were in the forefront of this rapidly advancing social movement. Soon various efforts got under way to coordinate this loose, amorphous, but immensely inspirational cohort of sit-in activists. The ultimately most successful of these gatherings took place on the campus of Shaw University in Raleigh, North Carolina. Financially supported by the Southern Christian Leadership Conference (SCLC), the guiding spirit behind this event was the long-time civil rights activist Ella Baker. She had hoped to attract about one hundred students. When the meeting took place on Easter weekend, 15–17 April 1960, more than twice as many showed up: 126 delegates arrived from fifty-six southern colleges and high schools. Nineteen northern colleges had sent representatives as well, as did the national civil rights organizations, the Congress of Racial Equality (CORE), the umbrella organization of American students, the National Student Organization (NSA), the recently renamed Students for a Democratic Society (SDS), and others.[3] Some SCLC officials present at the Raleigh Easter conference pushed for the incorporation of the young student activists within the structures of the SCLC. Finding a strong defender of a distinctly more independent role in Ella Baker, the conference, however, voted to launch a new organization instead: the Student Nonviolent Coordinating Committee (SNCC). No one present could have realized that this was to be merely the first page of the first chapter of what eventually became an international student revolt. For the moment the assembled activists had their hands full with the organization of the sit-in revolt. At a mid-October gathering in Atlanta, Georgia, SNCC gave itself a formal structure and adopted a mission statement.[4]

The next big wave of civil rights activism did not emerge from the deliberations of SNCC members. Though undoubtedly partially inspired by the lunch counter sit-in tactic which had given birth to SNCC, the decision to target interstate travel segregation by a series of well-planned and publicized 'freedom rides' was the brainchild of CORE. The trouble with civil rights in the United States had rarely been a lack of adequate legislation or appropriate Supreme Court decisions. Thus, desegregation of interstate travel buses or trains, that is, public transportation, had technically become the law of the land soon after the end of the Second World War.

In December 1960 the Supreme Court extended this mandate for desegregation to include facilities at bus and train terminals which, in a peculiar twist of the American mind, had been spared from earlier legislation. In the heady atmosphere of the growing popularity and success of lunch counter sit-ins, CORE decided that the time was ripe to test the waters. For the important judicial orders had rarely been followed up by effective measures to ensure their smooth operation in reality, a curious state of executive paralysis common to both Republican and Democratic administrations.[5]

The first freedom riders left Washington, DC, as an interracial group of seven blacks and six whites, headed for New Orleans. With long lay-overs en route, they made it safely through Virginia, North Carolina, and even Georgia. On Mothers' Day, 14 May 1961, in Anniston, Alabama, the journey came to a sudden end. A mob attacked the Greyhound bus in the Anniston terminal, breaking windows and slashing tyres. Somehow the driver managed to get the bus out of town, but then a roadblock forced it to come to its final unscheduled stop. More windows were smashed, and finally a firebomb was thrown into the bus, which burst into flames. The freedom riders narrowly escaped and had to be treated in a local hospital for smoke inhalation. As was to become a pattern, the police had arrived fashionably late at the scene of the crime. Then, Alabama law enforcement officials refused to provide protection from the bloodthirsty white mob which had followed the injured freedom riders and awaited them outside the hospital. A convoy of cars sent by Birmingham civil rights groups was able to rescue the intercepted freedom riders from the clutches of police-sanctioned mob rule in Alabama. The CORE freedom riders then took an aeroplane for the remainder of their journey to their original destination, New Orleans.[6]

This was the moment when SNCC activists entered the scene. Unwilling to see the CORE initiative defeated by frenzied white crowds, on 17 May 1961 a group of SNCC activists set off on a public bus from Nashville, Tennessee, to Birmingham, Alabama, where they intended to set off for New Orleans—again by bus! For good measure, the group was arrested upon arrival in Birmingham and spent a night in jail. Police deported them the next day to the Alabama–Tennessee state border, where they were left to fend for themselves in the middle of nowhere on the open road. Back in Nashville, they immediately turned around and, this time, made it safely to Birmingham. On Saturday, 20 May, they entered a bus headed for Montgomery. The numerous police cars providing 'safe passage' suddenly vanished when the bus crossed the Montgomery city limits. When the bus turned into the terminal, the waiting white mob began to pummel the freedom riders with sticks, fists, baseball bats, and other makeshift weaponry. Within minutes not only the freedom riders but also media representatives were beaten to a bloody pulp, some lying on the sidewalk bleeding profusely and/or unconscious.

The federal government had, true to form, once again limited its involvement to sending observers who were busy taking notes. This time around, however, even they were not spared the fury of the righteous crowd. President Kennedy's personal emissary, John Siegenthaler, when offering to protect a white freedom rider in the safety of his car, was knocked unconscious and lay on the pavement for almost a half hour before police condescended to drive him to a hospital. When a newspaper reporter asked the Montgomery Police Commissioner, present on the scene, why no ambulance was called for any of the injured, he received the standard reply: 'Every white ambulance in town reports their vehicles have broken down.'[7] Now President Kennedy realized that more needed to be done than careful notetaking. One of the measures was the dispatch of a sizeable contingent of US federal marshals. Despite the presence of armed federal officials, the siege was far from over. The next day, Sunday, 21 May 1961, Martin Luther King Jr. flew in to address a crowd of more than a thousand supporters in Ralph Abernathy's First Baptist Church. That night the densely packed crowd were imprisoned in the church, as the southern white mob hurled rocks through shattering windows, battering against the door and at one point gaining entry, only to be pushed out by intervening federal marshals.

Yet the freedom ride, incredibly enough, continued. On Wednesday, 24 May 1961, eleven black and one white freedom rider left Montgomery for Jackson, Mississippi, to continue the journey towards New Orleans abandoned by the battered CORE activists. But Jackson was as far as the second freedom ride ever got. For, unbeknownst to the freedom riders, President Kennedy and his brother Robert, the Attorney General, had entered a tacit agreement with Alabama and Mississippi state officials. Desperately trying to retain electability while not losing face internationally at a moment of heightened crisis in the cold war, 'Kennedy agreed to let state officials defend segregation by making forcible, unconstitutional arrests of the Freedom Riders so long as those officials did not let mobs accomplish the same purpose by violence.' It was the quintessential equivocation of American liberalism. Thus, an army of police cars, helicopters, and aeroplanes accompanied the freedom riders safely to Jackson. But, upon arrival, every single one of the riders was promptly arrested and put in jail.[8]

2. MISSISSIPPI FREEDOM SUMMER

Although the freedom riders included activists from other backgrounds, SNCC was once again propelled into the limelight, and it would remain a key point of attraction for both activists and the media for quite some time. After an acrimonious debate whether to continue with direct action tactics or to switch towards voter registration campaigns, a compromise allowed SNCC members to engage in both. 'As matters turned out, there really was no conflict, because both the students who favored direct action and those who favored voter registration encountered such repression in the South that any distinction became meaningless.' The Kennedy administration had pulled out all stops in the remainder of the turbulent spring of 1961 and the following summer in order to convince the civil rights community to discontinue the troublesome freedom rides and to concentrate on supposedly more wholesome voter registration instead. But its victory turned out to be a Pyrrhic one. For, once again, the Kennedy brothers had not entered SNCC into the equation. SNCC did spend most of its energies up to 1964 on voter registration in the Deep South, but took this new assignment seriously.[9]

SNCC's tireless voter registration drive in the Deep South was as dangerous as their engagement in freedom rides. Indeed, a number of local activists were murdered in cold blood. Federal protection was equally sporadic, and the going was tough and exceedingly slow. Several specifically targeted campaigns brought mixed success, a disappointment which did not exactly come unexpected. For the freedom rides, largely successful in the Upper South, had also been ground to a halt in the Deep South. It was once again time for SNCC to take stock. The lunch counter sit-ins had shown SNCC activists and anyone else who cared about civil rights that extraparliamentary action could achieve spectacular results. The freedom rides had made activists 'aware of their collective ability to provoke a crisis that would attract international publicity and compel federal intervention'. It was time to try out another innovative initiative.[10]

From 1960 onwards, the innovative, extraparliamentary, direct action-oriented social movement activism of SNCC had become a magnet for white student radicals. SNCC, from its inception, had included white students on its staff, though never losing its predominantly black membership. The voter registration drive attracted many visiting supporters as well. In July 1963, for instance, Bob Dylan, whose girlfriend at the time, Suze Rotolo, the woman on the cover of Dylan's *Freewheelin'* album, was a full-time secretary for CORE, spent some time with SNCC workers in Greenwood, Mississippi.[11] Tom Hayden, later on to become the most famous spokesperson of SDS, spent seven months in 1961 working with SNCC as a southern field secretary for his Ann Arbor, Michigan, based fledgling group, getting beaten up and jailed in the process.[12]

In late 1963, the guiding spirit of the militant voter registration campaign, Robert Moses, proposed that SNCC embark on a coordinated campaign to attract a significant number of white northern student volunteers for what soon became billed as the Mississippi Freedom Summer campaign. It was part of a conscious design by the SNCC leadership to up the ante in their (lack of) inter-actions with the federal government. If a serious and sometimes deadly campaign by mostly black SNCC activists in the Deep South was insufficient to galvanize the nation into solid backing for the voter registration campaign, perhaps a sudden influx of large numbers of northern white students might do the trick. After overcoming a series of doubts, SNCC voted to go ahead with their bold plan.[13] Technically sponsored by the umbrella organization representing the array of civil rights organizations in the streets of Mississippi, the Council of Federated Organizations, the summer months of June through August 1964 saw more than a thousand northern volunteers arrive in Mississippi to play prominent roles in forty-four community projects spread throughout the Delta state. In practice run and supported by SNCC, the volunteers, the vast majority hailing from elite northern universities and including sons and daughters of well-known families, took part in voter registration activities, the setting up and running of 'freedom schools', voluntary schools set up for black children kept in near-total ignorance by the racist official school system, and similar engagements. The plan was to make it impossible for the white power structure in Mississippi to apply the same brutal methods of repression as was customary when dealing with mostly black SNCC activists. That hope was only partially met.[14]

The following account by one of the black lawyers aiding SNCC efforts in the Deep South, Len Holt, graphically depicts the limits of protection enjoyed in Mississippi even by offspring of the northern white elite. Present at the arrival of a group of nine northern volunteers at the Jackson, Mississippi, train station, here is what Len Holt and others witnessed:

One of the nine incoming persons, Stephen Smith, 19, of Marion, Iowa, went to retrieve his bag, which had been placed in the street by persons unknown. Unsuspectingly, he bent over to pick up the bag. A foot slammed into him. His assailant, not satisfied yet, pursued his course. Smith was subjected to smashing blows to the face with fists. Gleefully watching the beating were three, baby-blue-uniform-shirt-wearing members of the Jackson 400-man police force. Taking notes was an FBI agent.[15]

Little seemed to have changed since 1961. Another volunteer, Andrew Goodman, as soon as he arrived from the north, was murdered in cold blood in Neshoba County on 21 June 1964, along with two SNCC staff members one black and one white.[16]

Nonetheless, part of the calculations of the SNCC brains trust ultimately did work out. For the Freedom Summer not only—once again—brought out the worst in southern white segregationist culture, but along with the northern volunteers arrived generally sympathetic media representatives. By the time most Freedom Summer volunteers returned to their home base or universities up north, the tide of popular opinion in the United States at large began to shift in favour of broad support for the extension of civil rights. Along with the parallel flourishing of other campaigns—the famous 1963 March on Washington may stand as symbol for this renewed wave of social movement activism—SNCC activism and in particular the Freedom Summer campaign must be credited with a fair share of civil rights breakthroughs in the early to mid 1960s. Yet these achievements constitute only a portion of the actual accomplishments and changes stirred up by SNCC. In June 1964, while undergoing preparatory training exercises in Oxford, Ohio, before the trip heading south, a northern student presciently wrote to a friend: 'The organisation here is a real student movement. And it looks like it will be around a long time. I would not be surprised if it really does, with time, influence the course of American history through the leaders it produces and develops.'[17] Len Holt in 1965 made a further shrewd observation: 'It appeared that the black college student came closest to fulfilling the role of catalyst for meaningful social reform (and sometimes revolution) that is played by students in Africa, Europe, Asia and Latin America.'[18] Parts of the Asian and Latin American student population were already on the move, but in 1965 European students were still relatively quiescent. And we will see that their social movement activities did not begin to pick up unusual speed until, at the earliest, 1966. Yet both the student volunteer jotting down his reflections in June 1964 and the black lawyer anticipating global reform if not revolution turned out to be dead right.

For the northern volunteers underwent a tremendous process of lifelong radicalization in less than three months, and when they returned to the north they began to serve as well-placed and influential multipliers of the lessons learnt in the Deep South. From the spring of 1965 onwards, anti-Vietnam War activity provided the most important catalyst for the rapidly growing student movement in the north. Teach-ins, the organization of alternative lecture series on topics of particular interest to student activists outside of the regular university curriculum, became one of the most popular and innovative tactics within the antiwar camp. Not only in the conception of the very first prototype of university teach-ins, the 24–5 March 1965 teach-in at the University of Michigan in Ann Arbor, but also in most subsequent events throughout the nation, civil rights activists and specifically former Freedom Summer volunteers played central roles, combining the lessons learnt from the sit-in movement earlier in the decade with the strategy of Freedom Schools that formed a core of Freedom Summer activities in 1964.[19] Indeed, some of the most insightful and observant histories of Freedom Summer and the subsequent rise of social movements in the US have made a convincing case to pinpoint Freedom Summer as the key turning point and launching pad not only for the subsequent antiwar movement but for the women's movement, student movement, and the new left in general.[20] Anticipating arguments reserved for later chapters in this book, one can only add that, therefore, via the US student and women's movements as well as the influence of the American new left, indirectly at the very least, Freedom Summer and the forces organized in SNCC can be held 'accountable' for much of the initial inspiration behind the rise to prominence of Western European radical social movements in the decade after the Greensboro sit-ins on 1 February 1960.

3. THE BERKELEY FREE SPEECH MOVEMENT

To return to 1964. One of the northern campuses with a sizeable contingent of Freedom Summer volunteers was the University of California at Berkeley. It was at Berkeley where the creative spark set free by SNCC and Freedom Summer activists first ignited on northern soil. Six months before the growing opposition to America's involvement in the Vietnam War exploded across American universities after April 1965, an issue arose in Berkeley which served to polarize the campus, focused national and international media attention, and served as a prototype for northern campus revolts elsewhere for the remainder of that decade. Predictably, the issue was closely linked to the southern students' activist focus on the centrality of civil rights. The Berkeley Free Speech Movement resembled the Freedom Rides and Freedom Summer in more than just its name.

The most prominent sociologist of the American student movement, Seymour Martin Lipset, looking back in 1971, straightforwardly asserted: 'The Berkeley Revolt was the prototype event of the student movement.'[21] Another contemporary sociologist, Edward Shils, wrote that 'when the Berkeley students ... began their "revolution," the radiation from the center outward began. It was like the radiation of the revolution of February from Paris in 1848, when all of Europe felt the repercussions.'[22] And the transnational dimension alluded to here was a feature highlighted by others as well:

It is indicative of Berkeley's importance in setting the pace for the wider movement that the two International Days of Protest of the 1965–1966 school year involving demonstrations around the world from Montevideo to Tokyo were determined by the Berkeley academic calendar. The first protests, October 15 and 16, coincided with Berkeley's Family Day, the occasion on which thousands of parents of students visit the campus. It is inherently the day on which radical political demonstrations are most embarrassing to the University. The second set, March 24 to 26, included Berkeley's Charter Day, the celebration of the University's founding . . . .[23]

What then happened in this most famous of all West Coast universities?

For some time, a narrow strip of the sidewalk on Bancroft Way, at the very edge of the campus, had served student political activists as a safehaven for all types of campaigning operations. Located in the strategic spot where the main campus mall ended and where—on the other side of Bancroft—a major commercial artery, Telegraph Avenue, began, activist groups traditionally set up their tables, soliciting for contributions to their respective causes, and generally behaving as if this part of Bancroft was theirs. On 16 September 1964 this right to free expression was suddenly taken away with the notification of all student organizations that, starting 21 September 1964, all tables, posters, fund-raising activities, membership drives, and speeches were henceforth forbidden on Bancroft Way. A far more restrictive set of activities would henceforth be tolerated solely in specifically designated portions of the campus, in areas, student activists were quick to point out, far less centrally located and mostly off the beaten track of most of Berkeley's students. What tarnished the liberal image of Berkeley's administration, however, was not only these sudden restrictive measures but the fact that these decisions had been reached without any consultation with any student representatives, including the generally rather docile student government.[24]

The university administration made a few concessions in the second half of September but, when they were announced, they were too little too late to stem the tide of student activism. Apart from the student organizations that served as student wings of established political parties or individual candidates for political office, much of Berkeley's activist student population had been engaged in civil rights support work for quite some time. As far back as the 1959–60 school year most student protests on the Berkeley campus revolved 'around the issues of civil rights',[25] and this orientation persisted throughout the early 1960s. In late 1963, 'Berkeley CORE, under Jack Weinberg's leadership, organized up to 150 pickets nightly for three weeks in front of 180 of the 200 businesses on Shattuck Avenue in downtown Berkeley'[26] in an effort to change segregationist hiring practices. Seymour Martin Lipset was not the only one who noted that 'the protests that attracted the most sympathy' were those linking up two particular strands of activism: 'civil rights as the object of the original protest, and then the civil liberties of the students taking part'.[27]

With hindsight, it was thus not a particularly brilliant move on the part of the university administration to restrict the civil liberties of Berkeley's students, as many of the tables along Bancroft were manned by individuals aiming to support the efforts of groups such as SNCC and CORE. As could be expected Berkeley students responded in kind. By 17 September 1964 a United Front of all political student organizations, some twenty groups spanning the entire spectrum of political forces from socialist groups to the University Young Republicans, was created from scratch. Having learnt the lessons of the civil rights movement, civil disobedience became the name of the game, manifesting itself initially in purposeful violations of the new rules. Jo Freeman recalls 'that each group would make its own decisions as to whether and which rules to violate, but none would denounce any other for making a different decision'.[28] On 4 October the United Front rebranded itself as the Free Speech Movement (FSM), under which name it entered the annals of social movement history.

When the administration ban went into effect, a first picket line attracted 200 demonstrators—out of a total student enrolment of 27,500 at that time. Two days later, 300 participated in a similar event. On 28 September yet more students attended a protest rally. 'The most eloquent speaker at the rally turned out to be a junior in philosophy, a hitherto unknown student named Mario Savio.' Afterwards, close to a thousand picketers walked to the Student Union Plaza, where an official convocation ceremony was held, 'and circled in a serpentine pattern through the aisles that had been set up'.[29] Two students, including SNCC member Mario Savio, who had returned from Mississippi Freedom Summer a few weeks earlier, 'were threatened with disciplinary actions; some of the clubs were given warnings'.[30] On Wednesday, 30 September, the administration escalated the conflict. Five students manning 'illegal' tables advertising SNCC and CORE issues were told to appear at the dean's office. At the appointed time, the five made a punctual appearance, but they were accompanied by 500 others, who had all signed statements that they, too, had manned the contentious tables. In the course of that evening the administration's refusal to acknowledge the self-incriminations led to the very first sit-in on Berkeley's campus, with several hundred students refusing to leave the administration building, Sproul Hall, until the wee hours of the morning of 1 October 1964. At midnight, Chancellor Strong announced that eight students had been indefinitely suspended from the university. 'It was characteristic of the panicky virulence with which Strong and [university president] Kerr moved to strike that they fixed on a penalty which did not even exist in the very university regulations which they were presumably defending.'[31]

Less than eight hours after the last sit-in demonstrator left Sproul Hall, tables went up in central locations, openly flouting the new university rules. When, just before noon, administration representatives, joined by a university police officer, approached the table set up by CORE a further escalation in the unfolding drama occurred. When one of the CORE staffers, Jack Weinberg, refused to comply with demands to remove the table and then to identify himself, he was promptly led to a waiting police car. Then the unthinkable happened. Spontaneously—no one could later reconstruct who initiated the move—students standing next to the police car sat down on all sides of the vehicle, effectively blocking its departure to book the arrested Weinberg, who sat in the car. Jo Freeman recalls her impressions when she left a meeting elsewhere and happened to walk 'to Sproul Plaza where I saw several thousand people sitting around a police car parked in the middle. My jaw dropped open and my blood raced.'[32] For the next thirty-two hours an extraordinary spectacle unfolded in the most central location on campus with thousands present and administrators looking on from adjoining Sproul Hall. When Mario Savio stepped onto the roof of the blockaded car, having carefully removed his shoes to avoid unnecessary damage, and then began to address the assembled crowd, he was only the first in a long line of speakers to do the same. In the course of the blockade numerous students, some faculty members, the university community's Catholic priest, and even a university dean all took off their shoes, stepped onto the car's roof and used this platform to address the crowd: a remarkable demonstration of the powers of free speech. At the same time this bold and spontaneous action galvanized media attention: 'From this point on, both local and national news media followed events at Berkeley.'[33]

It would far exceed the limits of space to provide a more detailed narrative of the course of subsequent events. A compromise agreement led to the ending of the police car blockade in the early evening of 2 October 1964, but the battle of Berkeley was far from over. Two highlights must be mentioned in brief. When, over Thanksgiving weekend, the university administration informed four student activists that they had been singled out for expulsion, the managerial elite had apparently forgotten that such vindictive, arbitrary actions were precisely what had previously incensed student opinion. On Wednesday, 2 December, a crowd of roughly 5,000 demonstrators assembled in front of Sproul Hall. Mario Savio gave his most poetic and eloquent speech to date. With Joan Baez singing to the huge crowd the anthem of the civil rights movement, *We Shall Overcome*, a steady stream of demonstrators once again illegally entered the inner sanctum of the administration, Sproul Hall. At one point up to 1,500 people occupied Sproul Hall. Against the advice of President Kerr, California's liberal governor, Pat Brown, then called in the police. Shortly after 3.00 a.m. on the morning of 3 December 1964, the arrests began. It took California police twelve hours to book the sit-in demonstrators who refused to leave.[34] On the evening of 2 December the University Young Republicans officially withdrew from the Free Speech Movement, stating: 'What the FSM is asking, in effect, is that the administration cease to be an administration.'[35] But they did not represent campus public opinion. While uniformed law officers still carried out Sproul Hall sit-in demonstrators, on the morning of Thursday, 3 December, a student strike erupted which changed the face of Berkeley politics. According to the best available estimate, 'an estimated 10,500 students probably took part in the strike'.[36] Hal Draper put it in a larger perspective. Writing in July 1965, he called it

undoubtedly the longest and most massive student strike in this country, and it demanded nothing less than a backdown by the administration of the largest campus of the largest state university in the country. It was instrumental in winning a great deal for students, and there were no reprisals. It was probably the mightiest and most successful single effort of any kind ever made by an American student body in conflict with authority.[37]

Soon, of course, much larger campus struggles broke out in almost every single state of the union.

Undoubtedly, Berkeley students were aided by supporting moves on the part of the faculty. Former Berkeley University president Clark Kerr is quite correct when, in a recent reflection on the events of 1964, he wrote: 'The events of the fall of 1964 can be properly understood only as a student–faculty uprising.'[38] But the driving force behind the campus rebellion was clearly located in the FSM. There was one more decisive moment which helped turn the tide. The ultimate administrative blunder occurred in the late morning of 7 December, when the university community, faculty, staff, and students, were called to assemble in an extraordinary convocation in the Greek Theater. At 11.00 a.m. President Kerr, flanked by representatives of all academic departments, addressed the estimated crowd of 16,000 people, announcing a series of concessions in the effort to calm the agitation that had been tearing apart the campus for more than two months. The ceremonial and diplomatic move badly backfired, however, when, after Clark Kerr had finished his speech, Mario Savio walked onto the podium to address the assembled crowd. In front of 16,000 disbelieving onlookers, many of them supporters of the FSM, many others undecided, they gazed at a lesson in the denial of free speech. To cite a moderate campus supporter of the FSM: 'As [Savio] reached for the mike, three campus cops emerged from behind a curtain draping the entrance to backstage. Two grabbed his arms and another his tie, and they dragged him through that door. All hell broke loose.'[39] The drama at the Greek Theater became a formative moment for many present. Though, obviously, not everyone was yet convinced of the FSM's demands and tactics, on that very same day regular elections to Berkeley's student government were held. All seven contested positions fell to pro-FSM candidates by a wide margin of victory. The tide had turned. In early January 1965 the university administration agreed to a series of concessions, correctly interpreted by the students as a victory.

4. US STUDENT MOVEMENTS AFTER BERKELEY

The Berkeley student revolt, as we have seen, not only captured the imagination of California students but inspired US students around the country in subsequent years. Indeed, as mentioned before, the Berkeley student revolt has rightfully been regarded as the prototype for subsequent campus revolts in other countries of the Western world. Within the US—and indeed elsewhere—soon the issue of Vietnam began to rival and outpace the topic of civil rights as a mobilizing agent. By the high point of antiwar activity in the aftermath of the invasion of Cambodia and the 4 May 1970 killings on the campus of Kent State, Ohio—followed by the murder of two black students in, once again, Jackson, Mississippi, on 14 May— few activists were primarily motivated by civil rights. Indeed, cogent observers have noted the discrepancy between the massive wave of student strikes across the country in the immediate aftermath of the Kent State shootings compared with the more subdued response to the Jackson State killings, the latter mostly limited to predominantly black colleges. But the combined total number of student activists involved in the crucial two-month period of 1 May to 30 June 1970 speaks for itself: 32.4 per cent of all US college campuses witnessed 'incidents which resulted in the disruption of the normal functioning of the institution'. Adding 'non-disruptive' protests, 57 per cent of all campuses were affected.[40] 'Strikes broke out at about 30 percent of the nation's twenty-five hundred campuses', reports Todd Gitlin, who goes on to suggest that 'at least a million students probably demonstrated for the first times in their lives during that month of May'.[41] 'In addition, uncounted high school, junior high school, and even elementary school students participated. By all accounts it was the biggest student strike in world history.'[42] In the fall of 1964, none of the FSM activists would have ever even dreamt of such events.

Still, social movements are rarely totally spontaneous campaigns created from scratch. They also build upon the perceived lessons learnt from victories and defeats elsewhere. In the San Francisco Bay Area, FSM veterans were amongst the leaders behind one of the very first major national anti-Vietnam War demonstration in US history in October 1965.[43] More generally, two astute observers of American campus politics remarked already in 1969 that all across the United States the battle of Berkeley had provided 'psychological strength to the dissenting academics (students and teachers) in their next great struggle: the national campaign against the war in Vietnam'.[44] A similar mechanism of cross-fertilization had occurred, as has repeatedly been suggested before, between the civil rights movement—and in particular the SNCC campaign—and the revolt at Berkeley. The academic authority on the Mississippi Freedom Summer campaign, Doug McAdam, makes clear 'that for most of the leaders of the Berkeley revolt, the movement was seen as an extension of the civil rights struggle and the Summer Project in particular'. Of the half dozen central leaders of the Berkeley FSM, two, Mario Savio and Steven Weissman, had just returned from the Mississippi Summer when the Berkeley revolt got under way. Of the twenty-one Freedom Summer volunteers who re-enrolled at Berkeley in that fall, twelve were amongst the arrested sit-in protesters on 2–3 December in Sproul Hall. The language of civil rights was ubiquitous on the Berkeley campus in those months. Civil rights songs were common fare during the Berkeley protests. The fact that the FSM adopted SNCC's tactic par excellence, sit-ins, as their own trademark feature was surely no pure coincidence.[45]

No one, of course, would want to make the claim that, without the civil rights movement and in particular SNCC, Berkeley's FSM would never have got off the ground. But it is also clear and present from all available data that a prior history of social movement activism was more likely to motivate individual Berkeley students to demonstrate than any other explanatory factor. An on-the-spot sociological survey of the police car blockade on 1–2 October 1964 identified that more than half of the participants had already taken part in other demonstrations.[46] As most campus action then was focused on civil rights, there clearly was a link between earlier engagement for civil rights and active participation in Berkeley's FSM. Seymour Martin Lipset, no friend of students at the time of the FSM when he taught in Berkeley's Sociology Department, suggests an obvious, more general pattern along similar lines. In his monograph on student activism in the United States, Lipset avers 'that as in Berkeley during 1964–65 the best predictor of reaction to the confrontations [later on in the decade] was the general political ideology of the students',[47] in many ways not a surprising conclusion but worth noting nonetheless. The more to the left a person's political outlook, the more likely that person was to take to the streets. One of the distinguishing features of social movement activism, be it Freedom Summer or FSM, was its unleashing of a slow but steady process of gradual radicalization of many—though obviously not all—participants in such events, continuously feeding an open-ended learning process in an ascending spiral ever further towards the political left.

For the moment, however, it is most crucial to note the self-evident influence of earlier social movements on subsequent events elsewhere. This is, of course, a pattern by no means unique to American politics. But significant attention has been bestowed on US student movement activism in the early 1960s not only because SNCC and FSM activities displayed many near-universal features of the inner workings of social movements in laboratory-like conditions in the Deep South and the San Francisco Bay Area, but also because American student activism was far more developed at that time than anywhere else in the geographic regions at the centre of this study. Looking back from the vantage point of the early twenty-first century, it is perhaps not easy to believe that the United States did serve as an inspiration for social movements around the world, including in particular Western Europe. In the course of the 1960s, this was simultaneously an incontrovertible and non-controversial aspect of social reality. Just as SNCC tactics inspired FSM methods, and both SNCC and FSM energized the fledgling US anti-Vietnam War movement, American students served as role models for their European counterparts. It is time to turn to the origins of the student movement in Western Europe.

5. THE PECULIARITIES OF BELGIUM

The first Western European university town to witness running battles between demonstrators and police was the Flemish town of Leuven. The first Western European university to become the centre of a national controversy in the course of the 1960s was not one of the branch campuses of the University of Paris or the Free University of Berlin. The very Catholic University of Leuven, founded in 1425, holds the honour of having sparked a major controversy leading to militant altercations in the city's streets and the polarization of public opinion in the country at large. This feat, however, was initially by no means due to particularly radical action on the part of its student body, but instead a result of some peculiarities of Western Europe's least well-known territorial state.

The country of Belgium emerged out of the turmoil of the 1830–1 revolutions affecting several European states.[48] Split into two roughly equal halves along linguistic lines, initially one of the unifying mechanisms was provided by the Catholic religion, practised in both Dutch- and French-speaking areas at the expense of virtually all other faiths. The first continental European country to industrialize, its early industrial development was concentrated in the French-speaking Walloon half; the Dutch-speaking Flemish provinces, with the exception of Antwerp's shipping-related industry and the textile trade in Ghent, remained a rural backwater, providing cheap industrial migrant labour for the French-speaking Belgian bourgeois elite. This pattern of Flanders serving as an internal colony for the rapidly modernizing Walloon south persisted until the middle of the twentieth century. With the emergence of a (mostly) secular labour movement as an inherent by-product of the industrial revolution, the Walloon provinces, where most industries were located, quickly underwent a process of secularization, whereas the Flemish Dutch-speaking half, benefiting little from any of the advantages of industrialization, remained solidly attached to the Catholic Church. By the early twentieth century at the latest, Belgium consisted of a dynamic, bourgeois-run, increasingly secular Wallonia in the south and a traditional, rural, heavily Catholic, Dutch-speaking north. The economic dominance of the francophone elite translated into a similar near-total dominance of the French-speaking bourgeoisie in national politics and all other matters of national relevance, including the army. The First World War, which was played out to a significant extent in the fields and meadows of West Flanders, served to highlight French linguistic chauvinism in a particularly acute way. Stories abound of Belgian army units composed of Dutch-speaking rural recruits being sent into battle by an almost exclusively French-speaking officer corps, dying in merciless battles unable to make sense of their superiors' Gallic sounds.

Part of the total package of francophone superiority and elitism was the design and implementation of the Belgian system of higher education as an exclusively francophone assembly of institutions. Four flagship campuses dominate the terrain until the present day: two state institutions, one in Ghent and one in Liège, an institution founded by the free-thinking liberal Belgian bourgeoisie, the Free University of Brussels (the term 'free' harkens back to the central role of freemasons in its founding), and the Catholic University of Leuven. Of these four institutions, only Liège's campus was located in an incontrovertibly French-speaking town, though Brussels too, despite its location at the linguistic divide, was predominantly francophone. Ghent and Leuven lay squarely in Dutch-speaking terrain. Nonetheless, all four universities operated as exclusively francophone centres of higher education for much of the nineteenth century.[49] Efforts to accommodate the Dutch-speaking half of Belgium in this linguistically hostile environment proceeded in a painfully slow manner, and even the state-run University of Ghent, the first to effect this switch, did not become an exclusively Dutch-language institution until 1930! Meanwhile, in Leuven, the Catholic bishops in charge of the famed Catholic centre of learning, in the course of the 1930s conceded the provision of courses at the university in both languages, French and Dutch, in most subjects, though not all of them, exempting, for instance, the all-important Faculty of Theology from such attempts at linguistic democratization. And this remained the situation, with no major changes, until the late 1950s and early 1960s when the 'language question' as such began to make waves in Belgium, soon concentrating on the fate of the Catholic University of Leuven.

Complicating the situation in the country as a whole were two additional conjunctural factors. One was the fact that Flemish resistance to francophone arrogance had rarely been dominated by 'progressive' forces, an inherent difficulty given the socio-economic backwardness of the Dutch-speaking provinces. Certain forms of intellectual and other forms of cooperation between ultra-conservative Flemish nationalists and the Nazi occupation forces in the Second World War only reinforced this peculiar development of a viable Flemish radical right with a substantial periphery of fair-weather sympathizers. The second important development setting the stage for the confrontations of the 1960s was a historic reversal of the traditional gulf between a prosperous and dynamic francophone south and a poverty-stricken Dutch-speaking north. In the course of the second half of the twentieth century, a complete role reversal was effected. As heavy industry declined in the francophone Walloon provinces, the industrial and post-industrial take-off concentrated in the Dutch-speaking provinces. Though only becoming obvious for everyone to see in the last quarter of the twentieth century, the process was already recognizable by the time the Flemish community mobilized to make the Catholic University of Leuven an entirely Flemish institution.

6. LEUVEN VLAAMS

Religious cleavages, economic turmoil, linguistic colonialism, and corresponding political divides thus combined to fashion Belgium into a powderkeg of sorts. By the early 1960s, this whirlwind of contradictory and shifting allegiances happened to concentrate on the fate of the oldest Catholic university in north-western Europe. Initially, almost the entire array of Flemish political and cultural organizations engaged in this battle, and the students of Leuven played an important but generally subordinate role. In 1962 the decision was reached to split all Leuven faculties into separately administered Dutch- and French-language institutions, though preserving the unity of the campus as a whole by a centralized top hierarchy, unchanged from the past. By 1963 the official language boundary between francophone and Flemish Belgium was drawn on the map. Seeing that Belgium, along with virtually all other developed nations in the Western world, was then actively contemplating and planning a major expansion of overall university capacity, entailing huge expenditures for campus extensions or brand new greenfield campuses to be built, the question soon arose whether the French section of the Catholic University of Leuven would be best accommodated on the edge of the medieval Flemish town—or whether it should undergo a wholesale move to a new location south of the linguistic border.

With few significant exceptions, francophone opinion opted to stay. Flemish activists, by contrast, saw little reason why the French-speaking portion of the university community should not be removed in an effort to make linguistic equity irreversible. In the course of the first half of the 1960s, various mobilizations of the Flemish community occurred in Leuven and elsewhere, and a distinct type of counter-chauvinism began to mark the effort of most Flemish protestors who, faced with what they regarded as francophone arrogance, in a quasi-spontaneous fashion elected as their central organizing slogan the battlecry *Walen buiten* (French Speakers Out Now). Often present in full force, the Flemish radical right thus found fertile terrain to sow its seeds of extremism and gratuitous violence. Not exactly a situation likely to foster a radical left-wing student movement characteristic of the 1960s elsewhere! Or so it seemed . . . For one of the reasons why not inconsiderable space has been devoted to setting the stage for the events in Belgium in general and Leuven in particular is that out of this peculiar type of Flemish nationalist agitation which, for good reason, appears most unlikely to be able to spawn a radical student left, within very little time emerged an increasingly independently operating and agitating student movement which polarized the town of Leuven, helped shake up the Belgian state, and eventually served as an inspiration for French students getting ready to occupy the Sorbonne. The case of the Leuven student revolt is testimony par excellence to the radicalizing dynamic of social movement activism, a hallmark of the spirit of 1968.

In the city on the River Dijle, 'May 1968' began two years earlier. The birth of Leuven student radicalism can be traced back all the way to May 1966, more specifically 15 May 1966, when the Belgian episcopacy made public a decision they had arrived at two days earlier. The pastoral letter took most everyone by surprise, as it unequivocally reconfirmed the unitary nature of the Leuven campus, brushing aside all efforts to split the university in two. Up to this moment, most Dutch-speaking Belgians had regarded the Catholic Church— rock solid in the Flemish half, but weak and far more powerless in the Walloon portion of the Belgian state—as part of the Flemish community and supportive of that community's social and political concerns. To be sure, with the post-war modernization of the Flemish half of Belgium proceeding apace, a certain loosening of the umbilical cord linking many Flemish to the Catholic Church could be noticed here and there already prior to the mid-1960s. With hindsight the secularization process affecting many European societies at that time was beginning to affect Belgium as well. But few contemporary observers were prepared for the sudden and unprecedented response by the hitherto rather docile Leuven student body to the pastoral letter arriving from Mechelen.[50]

In the course of Sunday, 15 May, students began to assemble in pubs and cafés in ever-increasing numbers to express their furious disagreement with this official edict, planning for an organized response the next day, Monday, 16 May, including a rally in front of city hall. Paul Goossens, the undisputed leader of the subsequent student revolt, recalls how, thus far rather uninterested in the finer points of the language issue and the modalities of a solution to the crisis of the Catholic University, he suddenly found himself on top of the flight of outside stairs leading up to the entry of the magnificent city hall with a microphone shoved in front of his face. Later on an accomplished, charismatic speaker, but for the moment nervous and uncertain what to say, he limited his first speech to three short sentences. 'Tomorrow, out of protest, we shall go on strike.' This spontaneous, unplanned announcement fell on open ears. The second announcement was even more outrageous: 'The academic year will therefore be ending tomorrow.' Paul Goossens records 'immense joy' as his audience response.[51] The third sentence amplified in front of the growing crowd filling the Grote Markt in front of city hall warrants a brief explanatory digression onto the text of the 13 May pastoral letter. In their closing sentence, the Belgian bishops solemnly declared: 'May the Holy Ghost let us share in its light and its strength, so that the University of Leuven, in the future as in the past, may faithfully fulfil its important and indispensable mission.'[52] Here is what Paul Goossens said after calling for a student strike and the unscheduled early ending of the academic year: 'And upon special request from the Holy Ghost, the Catholic University of Leuven shall from now on become pluralist.' Goossens records in his memoirs: 'That was a direct hit.'[53] The crowd became delirious, though quickly brought back to planet earth as the police were then beginning to clear the square with the aid of billy clubs and more.

Anger towards the church hierarchy ran so high that Goossens's impromptu strike call was effortlessly heeded the very next day. Three days later, on 20 May, the university authorities, to avoid further altercations, unexpectedly fulfilled Goossens' second point and officially declared the academic year to have prematurely ended. From, Monday, 16 May, student and police had been engaged in running battles in the city's streets. Despite the mayor's proclamation of a mini-state of siege—outlawing all gatherings of more than five people— evening after evening, as soon as nightfall provided the semblance of protective cover, students turned out in full force. Paul Goossens's three-sentence maiden speech became a declaration of independence for Leuven students from the tight embrace of their elders in various organizations and institutions, who had also agitated for the Catholic University to be transformed into a purely Flemish school, but who were generally quite unwilling to question the university's Catholic orientation, let alone to support some of the more radical slogans that could suddenly be heard. For Paul Goossens records that, in response to his icono- clastic speech, the traditional unifying slogan, *Walen buiten*, was not be heard that evening and instead students shouted *Bischoppen buiten* (bishops out now!) and *Revolutie* (revolution).[54] A learning process began, which initially mani- fested itself in what the flagship Flemish daily, *De Standaard*, called a 'wave of anticlericalism'.[55] To cite Paul Goossens once again: 'Almost everyone present in Leuven at that time came from Catholic high schools and had experienced at least eighteen years of Catholic upbringing. There were people present who, at this particular moment, settled their accounts with that past and who shouted words which, earlier on, they had barely been permitted to think.' 'With this revolt Flanders, which had thus far lived in fright of Rome and Mechelen, lost its fear of the bishop's crozier.'[56]

Clearly, this process of breaking away from the tutelage of the Catholic Church became most pronounced amongst Leuven students, although the process affected this prime constituency in an uneven manner. In their common efforts for the removal of all French-language teaching from the university, on the whole, though with diminishing frequency, the slogan *Walen buiten* remained quite central.[57] But something had begun to snap. 'Flanders, which—leaving aside several Antwerp neighborhoods and meeting places—seemed to remain immune to the spirit of the Provo movement, now began also to display Amsterdam-like symptoms. You could smell, see and hear it.'[58] But foreign inspirations were by no means limited to the smoke-filled happenings, the political message of the colour 'white' and the ludic energies entering Belgium from its immediate neighbour to the north.

7. MISSISSIPPI ON THE DIJLE

The traditional battlesong of Flemish nationalism, *Vlaams Leeuw* (The Flemish Lion), had been part of the standard repertoire of the growing agitation around *Leuven Vlaams* (A Flemish Leuven). In the late spring of 1966, a song never sung on Flemish fields before began to be heard: *We Shall Overcome*, the classic civil rights anthem symbolizing the religious heritage and inspiration but also the determination to change fate on the part of black activists in the American South. And this turned out to be only the beginning of a growing identification with black activists—many of them students as well—in the Deep South. In March 1965, one of the quintessential turning points in the black civil rights struggle in the US occurred with the now famous march from Selma to Montgomery, Alabama. On Tuesday, 4 October 1966, Leuven students and supporters embarked on a march across more than half of Flanders: from Ostend to Leuven. To dot all the 'i's, they named it the James Meredith March. James Meredith was a black activist whose attempt to enrol as the first black student ever at the lily-white University of Mississippi in Oxford, Mississippi, in 1962 had been met with extensive mob violence. On 5 June 1966, James Meredith, on a march across the state of Mississippi to prove the point that black citizens could exercise their rights without fear, was seriously injured by three shotgun blasts. The Leuven students' choice of name did not exactly fall on receptive ears. For the mostly rather more conservative—if not worse—adult Flemish leaders of the movement to make *Leuven Vlaams* certain questions began to take on a sudden relevance. Who were these students who used to regularly attend coalition meetings—but who, since mid-May 1966, had begun to skip important joint planning sessions? 'Were these Flemish students or were these perhaps American or, worse yet, South African blacks who were sitting around the same round table?' At the end of each day's itinerary, public meetings with invited speakers addressed the marchers and local supporters. In the planning stages for these events, the first dissensions, 'even rows', broke out between adult and student representatives. The unholy alliance on the issue of *Leuven Vlaams*, ranging from the radical right to the student left was beginning to disintegrate.[59] Shortly after the conclusion of the trek across Flanders, Paul Goossens was elected president of the Leuven student association, the local branch of the Catholic Flemish University League (KVHV).

For the remainder of 1966 and throughout all of 1967, activism continued to smoulder, and various guerrilla tactics were employed, some once again directly inspired by SNCC and the Berkeley FSM. On 20 October 1966 several hundred Flemish students walked into the imposing wood-panelled main reading room of the main university library to stop the university machinery from functioning as usual. Pictorial evidence shows the large hall filled with idle students packing the aisles, while their Walloon colleagues kept working at their shiny wooden desks. Goossens claims in his memoirs that this was the first of many creative adaptations of the sit-in idea. Other photographs suggest that his memory failed him in this case. One picture taken on 11 October 1966 in Leuven's main city centre traffic artery, the Bondgenootenlaan, resembles certain features of the October 1964 Berkeley police car blockade. A crowd of students was sitting in the street, making all car traffic impossible, a public bus stuck behind the crowd, with plentiful onlookers taking in the spectacle.[60] Within the Leuven student milieu the cry for *Walen buiten* increasingly made way for specific demands for the complete democratization of the university and the equally uncompromising demand for the separation of the university from the Catholic Church. Anticlericalism obviously remained a standard feature of Leuven students' political outlook but, as the year 1968 approached, the slogan *Bischoppen buiten* or *A bas la calotte* (Down With the *Calotte! Calotte* = skull-cap, clergy) began, in turn, to be replaced by another expression symbolizing the further evolution of the Leuven Zeitgeist: *Bourgeois buiten*! This particular catchphrase had the advantage of simultaneously joining traditional dislike of francophone students in Leuven, seen as disproportionately hailing from the upper-middle or upper classes, with growing anti-capitalist sentiments. It would be a most stimulating project to chronicle the rapid succession of unifying slogans in the Leuven student revolt, with particular attention to probable shifts of meaning of ambiguous catchphrases used for lengthy periods of time.

By January 1968 it seemed that *Bourgeois buiten* may very well have lost its tendentially chauvinist meaning, becoming the general anti-elite slogan par excellence. When the francophone section of the university community on 15 January 1968 announced their decision, arrived at the previous day, to keep the Leuven campus bi-lingual, the dyke burst once again. Far surpassing the turbulent events of May 1966, the city turned into a battlefield. The administrative offices were invaded, furniture thrown out onto the adjoining Old Market and set on fire. 'Even the most staid types continuously shouted with clenched fists: "Revolution"; and individuals who, two weeks earlier still personified moderation and tranquillity turned out to be frightful agitators. The entire Leuven student body seemed to have been infected by a rebellious virus and had become propagators of the most radical points of view.'[61] Or, in the words of Christian Laporte: 'An insurrectionary climate of revolutionary inspiration took over the old centre of the Brabant town: black flags were raised and one began to see wall newspapers, directly inspired by the Chinese dazibaos, while a journal with the explicit title *Revolte* explained in scientific terms how to manufacture Molotov cocktails.'[62] On 16 January, 325 students were arrested. But the battle had hardly begun, with masses of students defying orders to stay clear of city streets. During the night of 20–1 January, an auditorium went up in flames; on 24 January another 675 persons were arrested by the police. Most worrisome for the authorities, the virus began to spread beyond Leuven.[63] Students at the University of Ghent expressed their solidarity with the Leuven students in no uncertain terms. And on 23 January 1968 a most extraordinary process of trickle-down activism began to affect the Catholic high school student milieu. Between 23 January and 6 February, with universities in Flanders in turmoil, tens of thousands of high school students grabbed this window of opportunity to express their solidarity with the Leuven students and to press for democratization at their own institutions, usually far more dicatorially run than any of the universities. Sometimes encouraged by emissaries from Leuven, often alumni returning to their high school alma mater to stir up the crowd, the numbers of demonstrators and the locations of such rallies speak for themselves. Small provincial towns witnessed extraordinary assemblies of angry young students. Here are some figures for towns most non-Belgians will have never heard of: Mol (1,500), Lommel (1,500), Bilzen (3,000), Diest (3,500), Izegem (1,500), Tielt (1,500), Puurs (1,000), Eeklo (1,500), Waregem (2,000), Maaseik (1,000), Menen (800), Veurne (700); not to mention the even larger crowds in more prominent towns.[64] On 7 February 1968 the Belgian government stepped down. The road to *Leuven Vlaams* was now irreversibly cleared.

At the end of March 1968, Paul Goossens recollects, a packed bus of Leuven radicals drove to Paris for an international conference to plan activist campaigns. Paris students were just then beginning to stir. The Nanterre campus, far to the west of the city centre, had already moved, but the Sorbonne itself was still eerily quiet. Arriving in the courtyard of the Sorbonne, the Leuven students joined others standing around. It turned out that the organizers had yet to find an adequate meeting hall, as the authorities had refused to sanction the use of university property for the purposes of this event. Goossens reports that the Leuven delegates had been warmly received as battle-hardened, experienced fighters. It was thus only natural that 'we removed the impasse with Flemish methods (*Vlaams alaam*) and resolve. A window broke into pieces and everyone clambered through the empty frame into the building.' In the ensuing debates on the way to proceed for students, Daniel Cohn-Bendit, fresh from his victory at Nanterre, implored his comrades to emulate their Belgian co-thinkers: 'We have to prepare actions just like the Flemish comrades have shown us here and in Leuven.'[65] Five weeks later the Sorbonne became simultaneously an occupied and a liberated zone.

8. SOCIOLOGY IN TRENTO

Yet long before France became a hotbed of student activism, Italian students mobilized for a variety of goals and, by the time Leuven radicals showed their French colleagues in late March 1968 how to gain access to blocked meeting rooms in the Sorbonne, the entire Italian university system had ground to a halt— and this already for a number of weeks! What was happening on the sunny side of the Alps?

As is the case with any massive social movement, any reference to specific locations and precise dates as the point of origin is, to some extent, an arbitrary choice, perhaps most of all in a country with a vibrant and multifaceted tradition of political activism such as Italy. Two US student radicals on a grand tour of European campuses in 1968 put it like this: 'Occupations—even fights with fascists and police—were about as much a part of the Italian university scene as beer brawls on American campuses.'[66] Though undoubtedly a somewhat romanticized depiction of Italian realities, the Ehrenreichs' observation contains more than a kernel of truth. Still, the movement of strikes, building occupations, and assorted other strategies and tactics ultimately shutting down business as usual on all Italian campuses in the late winter of 1967 and spring of 1968 is most frequently traced back, with some degree of accuracy, to 1966. Here the small provincial town of Trento, deep down in the valley of the Adige, on the western edge of the Dolomites, is often given pride of place.

This conservative Alpine town counting little more than 60,000 souls in the mid-1960s had last obtained a certain amount of notoriety as the location chosen by the Catholic Church to deliberate effective measures to stem the tide of European Protestant revolt. The Council of Trent put an end to centuries of lax morality and obvious venality within the Catholic Church. The Catholic Counter-reformation codified its major reforms in three extended working sessions of this council between 1545 and 1563. The second time Trento made major headlines was a result of three extended university occupations between 1966 and 1968 which ushered in the most sustained series of protest movements any Western European country experienced in the period under discussion in this book. The first occupation, which lasted eighteen days, took on all the characteristics of a genuine popular festival with support to occupying students emanating from all social strata and political camps, including the benevolent tacit support of the university administration. This first Trento occupation had been decided on almost unanimously in the course of a general assembly of all university students on 24 January 1966.[67] What had brought about this most unusual, broad-based popular and elite support for protesting students?

The idea to place a university in this small Alpine town had been the brainchild of progressive Catholic social theorists who had managed to convince their conservative party colleagues in the regionally dominant Christian Democracy (DC) that the founding of a university would not only bring the region an institution which would boost the region's image but could eventually perhaps begin to stem the tide of constant outmigration to the industrialized cities further south. In 1962 the decisive step was taken to approve the founding of a new university in a vote of the regional assembly where the conservative DC held an absolute majority. The few parliamentarians of the Italian Communist Party (PCI) voted against the proposal, claiming that the establishment of an institute of higher education would close off for many prospective students the possibility of escaping the suffocating political climate of their native provincial administrative centre.[68] Indeed, Catholic politicians and academics had chosen Trento precisely because they deemed it safe territory—politically and culturally—for experiments in Catholic social theory. And, in some very important respects, the new University of Trento was designed to be truly innovatory. Paradoxically, in a country with a long history of attempts at social engineering, up to 1962 not a single university counted sociology as an officially approved and sanctioned course of study. The new Higher Institute of Social Studies was thus explicitly designed to be the very first Department of Sociology in all of Italy. Throughout the 1960s, sociology was the sole subject a student could take in Trento. But this proved to be an attraction and not a deterrent—in more ways than one.

The Trento DC interest in sociology was partially inspired by their admiration of the United States, its beacon in the cold war—and the spawning ground for much of academic sociology in the preceding decades. The curriculum closely followed American models. Genuine reforming efforts on the part of the university's founding fathers were also reflected in a new didactic approach which was to guide teacher–student interactions. The Italian tradition of a particularly pronounced gulf between frequently absent and almost always inaccessible professors and a passively notetaking and likewise frequently absent student body was to be replaced by open channels of two-way communication. In addition, admissions criteria were adjusted to allow the inscription of graduates from technical institutes and not just the holders of a diploma from the traditional, more elite-oriented *liceo classico* (classical high school) or *liceo scientifico*. Up to the summer of 1966, less than a thousand students attended classes at the newly founded University of Trento. In the academic year 1966–7 the number rose to 1,207, and in 1968–9, 2,813 students were officially inscribed. Yet, despite its small student numbers, Trento University soon gained a certain notoriety far beyond the region itself, because news spread that, at Trento, you could encounter a threefold innovation: the possibility of studying sociology, the utilization of student-friendly didactic methods, and the possibility for graduates from 'inferior' technical institutes to study a subject other than the two fields of study—economics and agricultural sciences—which the academic powers had deemed appropriate for holders of such 'proletarian' degrees at all other universities.

The immediate cause of the first of the three Trento university occupations between 1966 and 1968 had been a decision by the Italian legislature in Rome. In large part due to the obstructionism of the Italian left, engaged in a parliamentary guerrilla tactic à la Don Camillo and Peppone, the legal status of the diploma in sociology, the result of intensive years of study in the Alpine valley to the north, had remained in doubt. Finally, with the first graduating class nearing the end of their course of study, the legislative body chose what they regarded as a compromise. There was to be no sociology degree but a degree in 'political and social sciences with an emphasis in sociology'.[69] It was this compromise solution which galvanized not only student opinion but public opinion in Trento at large. Students regarded this decree as a devaluation of their cherished degree; residents of Trento resented this Roman move as yet another slap in the face of an impoverished and disadvantaged region. The Senate denial of equal status to the new sociology degree had occurred in May 1965. Various diplomatic manoeuvres of

Trento DC politicians and university administrators appeared to have led nowhere fast. This is when Trento students took the initiative to dramatize their case. On 24 January 1966 they decided in a near-unanimous vote to occupy their institute. And in the course of the ensuing intense negotiations, it came to a truly all-encompassing popular front. Student radicals, including Renato Curcio, a few years later to become one of the guiding spirits of the terrorist Red Brigades, together with Flaminio Piccioli, a leading DC and publisher of the Trento daily paper *L'Adige*, went to Rome jointly to lobby members of parliament.[70]

But the ultimate trump card was the immensely popular and media-savvy takeover of the small campus in the middle of a conservative Catholic small town. The relevant authorities quickly backpedalled and decided to allow a 'diploma in sociology'. For the Trento students it became an important lesson in applied sociology. What traditional behind-the-scenes diplomatic manœuvres had been unable to achieve, the (technically) illegal action of a unified student body, organized as an (at this point small-scale and exclusively local) social movement, was able to obtain. Non-traditional forms of political action had scored a victory over politics as usual. A victory for the reform-minded founders of the first department of sociology on Italian soil?

9. MOBILIZATIONS AND REFLECTIONS: TRENTO (AND ITALY), 1966–1967

The precise circumstances of the murder of Paolo Rossi on 27 April 1966 in Rome have never been determined. But what is certain is that this student activist at the University of Rome had suffered a beating by neofascist student storm troopers who were trying to disrupt student elections taking place on this day. Moments after the assault, Paolo Rossi either lost consciousness or his balance or was pushed by one of the fascist students; he fell off the veranda of the building housing the department of philosophy and onto the stone floor four metres below. He never regained consciousness, and his death was pronounced in the course of the following night.[71] The murder of Paolo Rossi is sometimes seen as the opening shot in the ascending cycle of Italian student activism for the remainder of that decade, for a series of protest demonstrations, student strikes, and building occupations followed his violent death on the campus of the largest university in Italy. What may be of particular interest in the wake of the preceding discussion of the Trento events is the fact that, in all the various cases of student unrest in late April and early May 1966, only one location witnessed violent clashes between demonstrators and police: Trento. On the morning of 30 April 1966, 5,000 demonstrators had marched through the city centre to express their rage and anger. When the official rally had ended, a group of students separated from the main group and moved towards the local headquarters of the neofascist Italian Social Movement (MSI). As they refused to disperse, police began to bludgeon students away from the MSI's offices, leading to minor injuries and a handful of arrests.[72] The beginnings of the radicalization of the sociological approach?

The national solidarity actions to protest against the murder of Paolo Rossi subsided after approximately one week and left few lasting traces behind. The brief altercations in Trento were the sole exception to the rule of a peaceful response to the violent death of their 'comrade' in Rome. Thus, it is with greater accuracy and justification that the second of the Trento occupations has usually been chosen as the true opening shot in the rapid spread and national rise to prominence of the *movimento studentesco*. The second occupation of Trento University took place between 22 October and 7 November 1966.[73] Unlike the festival atmosphere surrounding the first occupation, the second takeover was far more contentious. Small wonder, for this time around the students clamoured for a goal which few non-student residents of Trento, certainly not the university top management, could easily identify with: the demand for democratization of the university. The university administration immediately declared this second occupation to be illegal, a total contrast with the community-wide and virtually unanimous popular support for the first student occupation of the Sociology Institute at the beginning of the year. As a matter of fact, however, the goals and victories achieved during the first occupation had in a very real sense prepared the terrain for the far more contentious occupation in the autumn. What lay behind this remarkable transformation of the dynamic of university politics in the space of less than one year?

Once the future of the Sociology Institute had been assured in the wake of the first occupation, the key task became the fine-tuning and consolidation of the Institute's statutes and the corresponding curriculum. And here the popular front reaching from top-level university administrators down to the undergraduate student body started to unravel. Administrators, trained to regard themselves as not only the ultimate experts but also the final arbiters in all matters of import-ance to the university community, now busily devised various blueprints with little regard for student interest and concerns. Operating in secrecy with little attempt at meaningful public consultation, most fundamental decisions had already been taken by the time the various draft documents became available to the public. Students in particular were rather upset when they began to realize that administrative goals and curricular means widely differed from student wishes for what the latter regarded an enlightened and modern course of study. Students now began to put their own ideas on paper. It is likely that, having engaged in militant actions to save the Institute earlier the same year, students felt particularly justified and empowered to have their say in these vital matters of the Institute's operations. At any rate, it is from these irate responses to the officially sanctioned curriculum that various plans and counterplans were devised by students which eventually crystallized into the idea and praxis of countercurricula as such.[74]

In the short term, the unsatisfactory response by university authorities to student insistence on elements of co-participation led to the second occupation of

22 October to 7 November 1966. Renato Curcio recalls that the occupation itself was characterized by a 'considerable chaos. In any case, we organized rallies, discussions, votes.' And, along with the first tentative gropings towards counter-curricula, while occupying the Institute students organized an alternative lecture and performance circuit. They 'invited prominent figures who were far removed from the academic environment: for instance Lelio Basso, who had been to Vietnam and showed us fragmentation bombs that had been used to combat the Vietcong; or Julian Beck's Living Theater Company, which stayed in town for fifteen days and created a great scandal and much excitement'.[75] The idea of countercurricula, alternative education courses, and 'critical' or 'free' universities, of course, as we shall see in Chapter 5, had first been mooted and then practised in the United States which in the 1960s pioneered many crucial innovations of social movement activism later on adopted and adapted elsewhere. It is surely wholly unsurprising that the first Italian practice of such alternative education schemes saw the light of day precisely in this Alpine town whose fledgling sociology department had been created to introduce American social sciences into the Italian public sphere. When doing so, Trento University's founding fathers, of course, did not exactly have in mind the transfer onto Italian soil of the radical dimension within the rich American sociological imagination. Quite the contrary! But, given the context of international politics and social action in the decade of the 1960s, and in particular the rapid development of insurgent sociological alternatives to the dominant paradigm of status-quo-oriented American sociology prominent in the 1950s and early 1960s, it only stood to reason that Trento students, encouraged to strike out on their own by progressive Catholic social theorists, began to employ their own imagination and their language skills and thus indeed embarked on a journey all on their own.[76]

When ideas and practices developed in 'foreign' national contexts take root in other cultural environments, then prosper and develop features of their own, it is difficult, if not impossible, to pinpoint the degree to which such transfers of models across geographic and cultural frontiers are due to inspiration from abroad or whether local adaptations are primarily the result of socio-cultural and political preconditions in the respective locations being 'just right' for the implementation of similar or related experiments. In Trento, in the second half of the 1960s, undoubtedly a combination of these factors was at play. For, not only did Trento students undergo a process of increasing radicalization, but their copious attempts to give analytical expression to their concrete experiences were replete with explicit references to the works of leading American social theorists and in particular sociologists. In January 1966, Trento students had mobilized to obtain equality of treatment for their host institution and the discipline of sociology, a laudable goal which, in Trento itself, found few detractors. Trento students certainly did not set out to challenge the university hierarchy; in many ways they instead aimed for greater institutional security for their chosen alma mater. Towards the end of 1966, Trento students not only openly defied their university's administration, but went one step further. In a November 1966 document, the Trento activists postulated that the desirable and necessary changes in the internal organization of their alma mater could only become a concrete possibility if radical changes brought about an entirely novel society which would permit such institutional reorganization to become reality. In short, by November 1966, Trento students not only had begun to challenge their university, but were beginning to demand radical changes of Italian society as such.[77]

The Trento students' increasing radicalization is also highlighted by another document produced in the same period, in which new forms of 'direct democracy' (to be discussed in greater detail in Chapter 5), in contrast to reliance on traditional student organizations structured along party-political lines, are emphasized and recommended as vehicles for student concerns. Such new forms of representation were not yet theorized as permanent acquisitions in the arsenal of student demands but regarded as tactical innovations generated in the heat of battle and not yet counterposed in principle to established channels of political activism.[78] The most famous and influential product of this second occupation, however, turned out to be the 'Manifesto for a Negative University', a first version of which was completed in the spring of 1967, published in June 1967, then reissued in a second, revised edition in November 1967. It is this theoretical elaboration which is often justifiedly interpreted as the first major programmatic document to emerge from the Italian student movement.[79] Most individual elements of the analysis were further developments of specific points already formulated and published in the course and during the aftermath of the second occupation in the autumn of 1966. Thus its novelty was essentially due to its synthesis of various conclusions Trento students had arrived at earlier on. The necessity to radically reshape the university, the latter understood as an instrument of class domination in society; the impossibility of doing so without revolutionizing society as such; even the propagation of counterseminars and counterlectures to rival and compete with the standard fare of university curricula had been anticipated in various documents directly emanating from the autumn occupation of Trento University.[80] The combination of these features in a concise document furnished the explosive content helping to stimulate debate on Italian university campuses across the land from 1967 onwards.

As was the case with many features of the student movement, the 'Manifesto for a Negative University' was the product of collective efforts as much as individual endeavours. For the most part shaped into its final form by another great independent thinker of the Italian nonconformist left, Mauro Rostagno, a first draft was penned by Renato Curcio at the beginning of the second occupation in October 1966. Curcio recalls that, when writing that draft, he had been inspired by 'what the students at Berkeley had managed to create'.[81] And, clearly, American social theory played a crucial role in the elaboration of the Manifesto and related Trento documents. Both the German-American philosopher Herbert Marcuse and the American sociologist and intellectual godfather of the early new left, C. Wright

Mills, served as essential intellectual signposts for the authors of the various Trento student movement publications. From Marcuse they adopted the biting critique of the tendency of modern civilization to integrate potential oppositions into the repressive structures of the contemporary liberal but nonetheless authoritarian state. C. Wright Mills inspired Trento students to break free from the constraints of mainstream academic sociology, which served above all else to justify and reinforce existing power structures in society, and instead to engage in the construction of a critical sociology, designed to expose the pathologies of present-day societies.[82]

10. RADICALIZATION: TRENTO (AND ITALY), 1967–1968

One of the particular points of aggravation on the part of students and other sections of the Italian academic community in the years 1964–8 was a plan for university reform associated with the Minister of Education, Luigi Gui. On 31 March 1964 Gui had presented the first of several variants of a proposal to restructure university education in Italy, entailing a closer alignment of university curricula with the demands of the business community and the labour market, including the imposition of access restrictions based on performance of prospective students in high school, as measured by grade point averages or degree classifications. The various Gui plans became clear and present targets for student protests in this period. But in early 1967, for the first time, such anti-Gui mobilizations merged with a growing awareness of and revulsion at American intervention in Vietnam to form a particularly volatile combination of grievances.[83] In the first five months of 1967, a massive wave of student protests erupted from Bari to Turin and from Venice to Palermo, all across the Italian state, leading to major altercations with law enforcement officers and culminating in several building occupations, the most notorious instances occurring in Pisa and Turin. In Trento, a week of solidarity actions with Vietnam in March 1967 ended in a two-day student strike and a brief occupation of the sociology institute.[84] But the final tidal wave of student protest which was to change the face of Italian politics began in November 1967.

Fifteen minutes after midnight on 18 November 1967, after seven hours of heated debate approximately 1,000 to 1,200 students gathered in a general assembly voted to occupy their university to protest an imminent 50 per cent increase in student fees. What was unusual about this decision was not necessarily the act of militant insurgency but the fact that it occurred at the flagship private Catholic University in Italy, the Catholic University of the Sacred Heart, in Milan, home to 20,000 students at that particular time. What propelled the Catholic University into the forefront of Italian student politics was, however, not so much the act of insubordination by the students there as the decision by the university president to have police clear the occupied building at 3.20 a.m. on that same morning of 18 November 1967. For, since its founding as a private university sponsored by the Vatican, including the twenty years of Mussolini's rule, not a single policeman or soldier had ever set foot on the *Cattolica*'s soil. This proud tradition at *La Cattolica* was now abandoned by open invitation of the Vice Chancellor. From this point on and for the remainder of the decade and into the 1970s, the Catholic University of Milan would stay on the cutting edge of student politics in Italy, and it would produce a host of national student leaders, perhaps the most well-known spokesperson being Mario Capanna.[85] In the autumn of 1967, however, the Catholic University was only one amongst many Italian university campuses in open revolt, though for a while it remained the most unusual—and therefore prominent—case. Events in Trento may, once again, exemplify the larger national trends.

By the time the Milanese *Cattolica* joined the fray, Trento students had already resumed their struggle. A general assembly on 1 November 1967 had proclaimed an 'active strike', which initially lasted more than twenty days, and which applied mobilization strategies already practised in Trento for quite some time. An active strike was to go far beyond the more or less passive refusal of students to participate in regular lectures and seminars. It called for the engagement of students in a series of general assemblies to deliberate policy, but it also actively promoted the proliferation of committees and subcommittees, which were to tackle particular issues and problems of student concern, providing a decentralized framework for student activism where individuals who tended to remain silent in the often huge general assemblies could develop their leadership skills in a less intimidating context and atmosphere. Last but not least, an active strike was to liberally employ the sit-in tactic to respond to a variety of conjunctural issues or to highlight more structural, ongoing concerns.[86]

Not strangers to occupations, as we have seen, Trento students this time refrained from recourse to this ultimate weapon until 31 January 1968, when one of the seemingly never-ending series of general assemblies decreed the third and longest occupation of the Sociology Institute, which survived various reprisals and lasted for a period of sixty-seven days. Already in November 1967, however, Trento students had set new standards in their ascending spiral of radicalization engendered by quasi-permanent activist pursuits. A November 1967 document clearly spells out the end of all attempts to utilize traditional venues of student politics, such as established structures of student government, in their quest to construct organs of student power *vis-à-vis* all forms of academic authoritarianism. A subsequent statement, serving as the basis for the 31 January 1968 decision to commence the third occupation, ratified the Trento students' resolve to break with all forms of co-determination and participation in the running of the university's affairs, and it extended the total opposition to authoritarian structures beyond the resolute attack on university authorities to target also the powers of the police and the entire repressive apparatus of the state.[87]

Within the space of less than two years, then, Trento students had undergone an evolution from organizers of protest actions designed to strengthen their home institution to radical activists who stood in total opposition not only to their university but to all forms of authoritarianism including notably the arsenal of repressive mechanisms in the hands of the Italian state. A comparison of Trento students' autumn 1966 design of an alternative sociology curriculum with the structures of their counteruniversity curriculum in early 1968 speaks volumes in this regard. The late 1966 blueprint constituted a fine-tuned suggestion for the improvement of the existing sociology degree. The various study groups set up in early 1968 certainly targeted specific issues of concern to university and specifically sociology students, but it also included in its remit far wider reaching topics, such as 'factories', 'imperialism', 'society and repression', or 'authoritarianism', issues which were then still largely absent from the sociological imagination of the shapers of official curriculum design.[88]

Two other early hotspots of youthful activism, Turin and Pisa, experienced similar truly incredibly rapid learning processes amongst students on a massive scale.[89] And, instead of focusing on the Alpine valley community of Trento, the story of the blossoming of the Italian student revolt in the second half of the 1960s could have just as easily been told by concentrating on university affairs in either the city of FIAT or the home town of Galileo Galilei, where local student movements developed early on in a similarly autonomous fashion. Yet, curiously enough, thus far the Sociology Faculty struggles at Trento have received less systematic exposure than related campaigns at the much larger and older campuses further south. In addition, Trento also appeared to be a more promising investigatory terrain, as here the novelty and the Catholic nature of the institution as a whole ensured the absence of long-established radical political traditions on Trento campus soil. In short, in Trento, just as in Berkeley and in Leuven, if under a rather different set of historical circumstances, radical ferment was largely home-grown. In all three cases, students were exploring largely uncharted terrain. Lacking pre-existing models to emulate, Trento, Leuven, and Berkeley became laboratory experiments. By contrast, student activists in later campus struggles constantly operated with the perceived lessons of such pioneering flagship campus movements preoccupying their minds and influencing their actions.

11. THE SHUT-DOWN OF HIGHER EDUCATION IN ITALY: 1968

The process of seemingly unstoppable and permanent radicalization did not limit itself to these early centres of student power which, indeed, Trento, Turin, and Pisa had become. Starting in November 1967, the wave of student insubordination developing into a confrontation not only with university hierarchies but with the structures of the Italian state began to affect the vast majority of Italian campuses, large or small. Not only good-sized cities such as Florence, Genoa, Rome, or Naples witnessed building occupations and the spread of the 'active strike', but much smaller towns with some university departments, such as Sassari, Lucca, Lecce, Macerata, Urbino, or Carrara, became host to identical events. By late February 1968,

tens of thousands of students were on strike, hundreds of thousands of students saw no further possibilities to continue their studies in a regular fashion. The universities were blocked up, besieged or occupied; professors faced locked or empty lecture halls; regular instruction only took place on an irregular basis; exams were postponed or cancelled altogether; for all practical purposes there was no more contact between students and teaching staff. Countercourses, general assemblies and commissions, discussions, occupations and demonstrations had replaced the daily study routine of activists. And in the various protest actions ideological divisions made way for common action which targeted a common enemy in authoritarianism.[90]

And then it happened. On 1 March 1968, Roman students, when confronted by heavily armed police blocking their demonstration winding through the park of the Villa Borghese on the way to their destination, the Faculty of Architecture of the University of Rome, in the ensuing mêlée with the armed representatives of the Italian state, for the first time did not scatter in the face of superior might but spontaneously began to fight back, venting their rage with their bare hands, pieces of wood, rocks, empty bottles, and books. They managed to force their way into the architecture building, then defending their fortress with all means at their disposal, above all the various pieces of furniture readily at hand, before eventually being flushed out by an equally furious police. The Battle of Valle Giulia changed the dynamics of Italian politics for the ensuing ten years.[91]

In the immediate aftermath of this landmark event, student movement activism in Italy reached an absolute crescendo. A new wave of building occupations broke out in solidarity protest actions with their Roman comrades across the country.[92] 'Measured by participation rates and geographic breadth of protest, the student movement reached its summit in March 1968, when every day thousands of demonstrators marched through large and small university towns alike. Likewise, in the first weeks of March, occupations of faculties, institutes and entire universities occurred in the hundreds.' But then a reflux could be noted, and the tide began to turn.[93] The increasing brutality of encounters between police and demonstrating crowds, combined with the growing realization on the part of the student protestors that the conquest of universities alone would not usher in any significant radical changes, led to the gradual decline of student actions. Also, a majority of students was unwilling to follow a minority of activists into the spiral of opposing the violence of the police with counterforce.[94] Symptomatically, national gatherings of the *movimento studentesco*—a first meeting took place in Turin on 8 January 1968—ended in September 1968.[95]

Indeed, by March 1968 the Italian student movement had gone as far as it could. It had managed to paralyse the entire system of higher education in the

Italian state under the banner of total opposition to the existing structures of society and the state. The sole further courses of action open to students consisted in shifting attention from the universities to other sectors of social life. One such terrain for subversive activism beyond the higher education system as such was the vast network of Italian high schools which reached even further down the capillaries of Italian civil society into countless small provincial towns devoid of university campuses but often well-supplied with secondary schools. Guido Crainz highlights that 'for several more years the latter constituted above all else the centres for further agitation' in the scholastic field.[96] But student movement activists, buoyed by success yet frustrated by their apparent inability to change the system despite their total sway over campus life, were not content merely to influence the next generation of university students. 'At this point commences the grand diaspora of the Italian student movement, in search of the forces necessary to exert influence over far wider circles, an extension of its range of actions rendered indispensable by the centrality of the question of power relations and the confrontation with the state.' From the spring 1968 until the spring 1969 Italian student activists were in constant hot pursuit of a new social agent which could complete the project begun only two years earlier but which, students now realized, they could not complete on their own. Thus they engaged with various artistic and cultural movements of revolt; they devoted full-time attention to neighbourhood organizing; they ardently campaigned for the rights of the mentally ill.[97] They eventually settled for an encounter with the blue- (and white-)collar working class.

NOTES

1. The preceding information is taken from Clayborne Carson, *In Struggle: SNCC and the Black Awakening of the 1960s* (Cambridge, Mass.: Harvard University Press, 1995), 9–12, and Howard Zinn, *SNCC: The New Abolitionists* (Cambridge, Mass.: South End Press, 2002), 16.
2. Zinn, *SNCC*, 16–17. Carson, *In Struggle*, 11, reports that the 50,000 mark with regard to demonstrators had already been reached in mid-Apr. 1960.
3. For the Easter gathering in Raleigh, see Carson, *In Struggle*, 19–24. Zinn, *SNCC*, 33, reports that fifty-eight (not fifty-six) southern schools were represented. On the rebranding of the Student League for Industrial Democracy into SDS in January 1960, see Kirkpatrick Sale, *SDS* (New York: Random, 1973), 17. In early 1960, SDS was still a largely unknown entity with only three local chapters and 'at best a few hundred members, most of whom were once-a-year activists and many of whom were well past their undergraduate years'; ibid. 15.
4. On the behind-the-scenes manœuvring at the Easter conference, see Zinn, *SNCC*, 33–4, and Carson, *In Struggle*, 24. For the 14–16 Oct. 1960 conference, see Carson, *In Struggle*, 27–9.
5. For the relevant Supreme Court legislation in the immediate post-war era, see Zinn, *SNCC*, 41. Zinn's remarkable account first published in 1964 is also an excellent source on the legal history of civil rights and the astounding near-total refusal of both the Eisenhower and Kennedy administrations to back up the law of the land with

effective measures; see Zinn, *SNCC*, 190–215. On CORE's key role in the freedom rides, see August Meier and Elliott Rudwick, *CORE: A Study in the Civil Rights Movement* (New York: Oxford University Press, 1973), 135–44.

6. For the vagaries of this first freedom ride, see Meier and Rudwick, *CORE*, 136–7; Zinn, *SNCC*, 42–4; but above all Taylor Branch, *Parting the Waters: Martin Luther King and the Civil Rights Movement 1954–1963* (London: Macmillan, 1990), 412–50.

7. The itinerary of SNCC freedom riders on their way from Nashville to Montgomery is best portrayed in Zinn, *SNCC*, 44–50, citation on p. 48.

8. The story of the siege of Montgomery's First Baptist Church and the final leg of the second freedom ride with guaranteed safe passage into Mississippi's jails is best portrayed with colourful detail in Branch, *Parting the Waters*, 451–77, citation on p. 469.

9. On the pressure to abandon freedom rides, see Branch, *Parting the Waters*, 477–91. On the specific debate within SNCC, see Zinn, *SNCC*, 58–9; Carson, *In Struggle*, 38–42; and James Forman, *The Making of Black Revolutionaries* (Seattle: University of Washington Press, 1997), 221–2, citation on p. 222. Forman had just then become SNCC's new executive secretary.

10. For SNCC's ceaseless voter registration drives, see above all Zinn, *SNCC*, 62–166; Carson, *In Struggle*, 45–82; and Forman, *Black Revolutionaries*, 28–9. For the citation on the overall message of the freedom rides, see Carson, *In Struggle*, 37.

11. On Suze Rotolo as full-time employee of CORE, see Jon Wiener, *Come Together: John Lennon and his Time* (Urbana: University of Illinois Press, 1991), 218. On Dylan's visit to Greenwood, Miss., see Mike Marqusee, *Chimes of Freedom: The Politics of Bob Dylan's Art* (New York: New Press, 2003), 73–8.

12. Sale, *SDS*, 35–6.

13. On SNCC discussion of the Mississippi Freedom Summer plans, see Carson, *In Struggle*, 96–100.

14. The most thorough account of Freedom Summer is Doug McAdam, *Freedom Summer* (New York: Oxford University Press, 1988). A powerful collection of excerpts from letters to family and friends, written by northern volunteers from the Deep South, is Elizabeth Sutherland (ed.), *Letters from Mississippi* (New York: McGraw-Hill, 1965). A recent useful collection of documents surrounding the Freedom Summer campaign is John F. McClymer (ed.), *Mississippi Freedom Summer* (Belmont, Calif.: Wadsworth, 2004). Mary Aicking Rothschild, *A Case of Black and White: Northern Volunteers and the Southern Freedom Summers, 1964–1965* (Westport, Conn.: Greenwood, 1983), is a joint discussion of the 1964 Freedom Summer and the 1965 efforts at voter registration in the Deep South. An excellent, insightful autobiographical account is Mary King, *Freedom Song: A Personal Story of the 1960s Civil Rights Movement* (New York: William Morrow, 1987), 301–436.

15. Len Holt, *The Summer that Didn't End* (London: Heinemann, 1966), 101.

16. McAdam, *Freedom Summer*, 69–70.

17. Sutherland (ed.), *Letters*, 16.

18. Holt, *Summer*, 52.

19. McAdam, *Freedom Summer*, 173–4.

20. The most convincing and eloquent proponents of this thesis are McAdam, *Freedom Summer*, and Sara Evans, *Personal Politics: The Roots of Women's Liberation in the Civil Rights Movement and the New Left* (New York: Vintage, 1980).

21. Seymour Martin Lipset, *Rebellion in the University: A History of Student Activism in America* (London: Routledge & Kegan Paul, 1972), p. xix.

22. Edward Shils, 'Dreams of Plenitude, Nightmares of Scarcity', in Seymour Martin Lipset and Philip G. Altbach (eds.), *Students in Revolt* (Boston: Houghton Mifflin, 1969), 25.

23. Seymour Martin Lipset and Philip G. Altbach, 'Student Politics and Higher Education in the United States', in Seymour Martin Lipset (ed.), *Student Politics* (New York: Basic Books, 1967), 204.

24. Unless specifically referenced, the ensuing narrative is based on a number of texts which recount the turbulent fall semester 1964 with varying degrees of detail: Hal Draper, *Berkeley: The New Student Revolt* (New York: Grove Press, 1965); Seymour Martin Lipset and Sheldon S. Wolin (eds.), *The Berkeley Student Revolt: Facts and Interpretations* (New York: Anchor, 1965); and Max Heirich, *The Spiral of Conflict: Berkeley 1964* (New York: Columbia University Press, 1971), who provides the most detailed day-to-day chronicle of events. Most recently, Robert Cohen and Reginald E. Zelnik (eds.), *The Free Speech Movement: Reflections on Berkeley in the 1960s* (Berkeley, Calif.: University of California Press, 2002), and the memoirs of the then-leading activist within the Berkeley campus Young Democrats and later feminist Jo Freeman, *At Berkeley in the Sixties: The Education of an Activist, 1961–1965* (Bloomington: Indiana University Press, 2004), provide some interesting nuances. W. J. Rorabaugh, *Berkeley at War: The 1960s* (New York: Oxford University Press, 1989), a solid overall study, is not particularly insightful on the Free Speech Movement.

25. Seymour Martin Lipset, 'Students and Politics', in Lipset and Wolin (eds.), *Berkeley*, 22.

26. Rorabaugh, *Berkeley at War*, 72.

27. Lipset, 'Students and Politics', 22.

28. Freeman, *At Berkeley*, 147.

29. Heirich, *Spiral of Conflict*, 116.

30. Draper, *Berkeley*, 33.

31. Ibid. 35.

32. Freeman, *At Berkeley*, 153.

33. Heirich, *Spiral of Conflict*, 463.

34. On the various claims and counterclaims as to the total number of arrested, see 'Chronology of Events: Three Months of Crisis', in Lipset and Wolin (eds.), *Berkeley Student Revolt*, 175. They range from 761 to 814 arrested individuals.

35. Heirich, *Spiral of Conflict*, 274.

36. Ibid. 287.

37. Draper, *Berkeley*, 116–17.

38. Clark Kerr, 'Fall of 1964 at Berkeley: Confrontation Yields to Reconciliation', in Cohen and Zelnik (eds.), *Free Speech Movement*, 375. For a detailed history of faculty engagements in the contestations at Berkeley, see Reginald E. Zelnik, 'On the Side of the Angels: The Berkeley Faculty and the FSM', in Cohen and Zelnik (eds.), *Free Speech Movement*, 264–338.

39. Freeman, *At Berkeley*, 218–19. President Kerr, in his 2002 reminiscence, uses the identical expression: 'All hell broke loose.' He also suggests that he had personally 'explicitly asked' the campus police to be excluded from the Greek Theater; see Kerr, 'Fall of 1964', 384.

40. Lipset, *Rebellion*, 46; the first quotation was the wording of a central passage in the Sept. 1970 report by the President's Commission on Campus Unrest reported by Lipset.

41. Todd Gitlin, *The Sixties: Years of Hope, Days of Rage* (New York: Bantam, 1993), 410.

42. Fred Halstead, *Out Now! A Participant's Account of the American Movement Against the Vietnam War* (New York: Monad, 1978), 561.

43. W. J. Rorabaugh, 'The FSM, Berkeley Politics, and Ronald Reagan', in Cohen and Zelnik (eds.), *Free Speech Movement*, 512. The quintessential innovation of the American antiwar movement on university campuses, the teach-in, was, as mentioned above, likewise an offshoot of Freedom Summer activity. First organized in Ann Arbor, Mich., on 24–5 Mar. 1965, the idea of an alternative lecture and seminar series to compete with the regular university teaching schedule had been the brainchild of a young sociology lecturer, William Gamson. A CORE member in Boston before moving to Michigan, he remembered a successful strategy CORE had employed at the time of a local school boycott. 'As well as asking children to stay away from school, a Freedom School was set up to teach black history and civil rights: this was more positive than just asking kids to stay away from school.' Faculty at the University of Michigan adopted this idea, which then spread across American college campuses and, as we shall see, eventually to Europe in ensuing years. On this anecdote of the origins of the first teach-in in Ann Arbor, see Godfrey Hodgson, *America in our Time* (New York: Vintage, 1978), 285–6.

44. Norman Birnbaum and Marjorie Childers, 'The American Student Movement', in Julian Nagel (ed.), *Student Power* (London: Merlin, 1969), 138.

45. McAdam, *Freedom Summer*, 162–71, citation on p. 162.

46. Glen Lyonns, 'The Police Car Demonstration: A Survey of Participants', in Lipset and Wolin (eds.), *Berkeley Student Revolt*, 522.

47. Lipset, *Rebellion*, 68.

48. For general works on Belgian history, see, amongst many others, the English-language translations of two volumes co-authored by Els Witte, Jan Craeybeckx, and Alain Meynen, *Political History of Belgium from 1830 Onwards* (Brussels: VUB University Press, 2000), and Els Witte and Harry Van Velthoven, *Language and Politics: The Situation in Belgium in an Historical Perspective* (Brussels: VUB University Press, 1999).

49. For the history of the Belgian university system and the role of the language issue, in particular with reference to the itinerary of the Catholic University of Leuven, see the recent comprehensive study by Christian Laporte, *L'Affaire de Louvain: 1960–1968* (Paris: De Boeck Université, 1999), which, despite its subtitle, includes informative chapters on the prehistory of this 'affair'.

50. The archbishop of Mechelen is the traditional *primus inter pares* of Belgian bishops.

51. On the student reaction to the 15 May publication of the pastoral letter including the rally on Monday, 16 May 1966, see Paul Goossens, *Leuven '68 of het geloof in de hemel* (Zellik: Roularta, 1993), 37–40, citations on p. 40.

52. The document is partially reproduced in Ludo Martens and Kris Merckx, *Dat was 1968* (Berchem: EPO, 1978), 10. The full text can be found, entitled 'Verklaring van de Bisschoppen van België betreffende de Katholieke Universiteit van Leuven', in *Dossier Leuven: feiten, cijfers en beschouwingen* (Leuven: De Clauwaert, 1968), 114–24. I thank Patricia Quaghebeur for providing me with a copy of this rare document.

53. Goossens, *Leuven '68*, 40; the demand for pluralism was a frontal attack on the uniquely Catholic orientation of this largest Catholic university outside of Italy.

54. Ibid.

55. Citation in Laporte, *Affaire de Louvain*, 200.

56. Goossens, *Leuven '68*, 43 and 44.

57. This is rightfully underscored by Laporte, *Affaire de Louvain*, 222.

58. Goossens, *Leuven '68*, 47.

59. For the Meredith March, too, Goossens, *Leuven '68*, 51–63, remains the single most important source; citations on p. 60. Goossens was one of the marchers. But see also the relevant pages in ch. 9 in Laporte, *Affaire de Louvain*, entitled 'We shall overcome! Du Mississippi à la Dyle', 221–3.

60. For the claim of the library sit-in as the first such action, see Goossens, *Leuven '68*, 69. The photos of the library sit-in and the street blockade can be studied in Mark Derez, Ingrid Depraetere, and Wivina Van der Steen, 'Kroniek van het studentenprotest' in Louis Vos, Mark Derez, Ingrid Depraetere, and Wivina van der Steen, *De stoute jaren: studentenprotest in de jaren zestig* (Tielt: Lannoo, 1988), 99 (library) and 98 (Bondgenootenlaan).

61. Goossens, *Leuven '68*, 97.

62. Laporte, *Affaire de Louvain*, 286.

63. For the aforementioned (and other) facts and figures, see Derez, Depraetere, and Van der Steen, 'Kroniek', 124–33.

64. On this wholly understudied phenomenon, see Goossens, *Leuven '68*, 105–7. The concrete numbers and locations are taken from Martens and Merckx, *Dat was 1968*, 32–5.

65. Goossens, *Leuven '68*, 110–11.

66. Barbara Ehrenreich and John Ehrenreich, *Long March, Short Spring: The Student Uprising at Home and Abroad* (New York: Monthly Review, 1969), 60.

67. The date of the general assembly is taken from Jan Kurz, *Die Universität auf der Piazza: Entstehung und Zerfall der Studentenbewegung in Italien 1966–1968* (Cologne: SH-Verlag, 2001), 105. The duration of this first occupation is reported in Nanni Balestrini and Primo Moroni, *L'orda d'oro 1968–1977: La grande ondata rivoluzionaria e creativa, politica ed esistenziale* (Milan: Feltrinelli, 1998), 208; its locally non-controversial nature is stressed in Diego Leoni, 'Testimonianza semiseria sul '68', in Aldo Agosti, Luisa Passerini, and Nicola Tranfaglia (eds.), *La cultura e i luoghi del '68* (Milan: Franco Angeli, 1991), 177–8.

68. The information in this—and succeeding—paragraph(s) is taken from Kurz, *Universität*, 104–5; Balestrini and Moroni, *L'orda d'oro*, 204–9; and Leoni, 'Testimonianza', 176–8.

69. Balestrini and Moroni, *L'orda d'oro*, 208, and Kurz, *Universität*, 105–7.

70. The episode of the joint lobbying effort by student radicals and DC heavyweights is recounted in Renato Curcio, *A viso aperto* (Milan: Mondadori, 1993), 33.

71. The events surrounding the death of Paolo Rossi, including the protest demonstrations following his death which occurred until early May, are recounted in Paola Ghione, 'L'emergere della conflittualità giovanile: Da piazza Statuto a Paolo Rossi', in Paola Ghione and Marco Grispigni (eds.), *Giovani prima della rivolta* (Rome: Manifestolibri, 1998), 121–7; Kurz, *Universität*, 97–103; and Guido Crainz, *Il paese mancato: Dal miracolo economico agli anni ottanta* (Rome: Donzelli, 2003), 213–15.

72. For the reconstruction of the events of 30 Apr. 1966 in Trento, see Kurz, *Universität*, 107–9 and 103.

73. See Marco Boato, 'Il movimento studentesco trentino: Origine, storica, esperienze di lotta, prospettive politiche', in *Il '68 è morto: Viva il '68!* (Verona: Bertani, 1979), 325.

74. The most informative brief discussion of the run-up to the second occupation can be found in Boato, 'Il movimento studentesco trentino', 324–5.

75. The citations are taken from Curcio, *Viso aperto*, 34 and 35, where Curcio also explicitly refers to Trento students' efforts 'to create countercourses in accordance with our wishes and on themes we felt passionate about'. In this series of interviews, Curcio and his interviewer, Mario Scajola, repeatedly refer to this particular occupation as having occurred in the autumn of 1967. This is clearly a memory lapse. The biographer of Julian Beck confirms, for instance, that the Living Theater troupe visited Trento in Nov. 1966 (and not 1967). 'Surrounded by rolls of barbed wire and military police, they performed "Street Songs"—with slogans like "Abolish the State," "Open All Jails," "Make Love Not War" '; see John Tytell, *The Living Theater: Art, Exile and Outrage* (London: Methuen, 1997), 218.

76. Not only radical sociologists were godfathers to the Trento student movement, but more activist American traditions had a direct input into Trento affairs as well. John Tytell notes for instance that, when Julian and Judith Beck stayed in Trento that fall, the 'students showed Judith a book about the Berkeley Free Speech Movement, which they regarded as a sort of bible'; see Tytell, *Living Theater*, 218. This book is likely to have been Hal Draper's first-hand account of *Berkeley: The New Student Revolt*, which, in an Italian translation entitled *La rivolta di Berkeley* (Milan: Einaudi, 1966), is prominently listed in an early typewritten draft, signed by Renato Curcio, of the 'Manifesto for a Negative University'. I thank Valentina Marchegiani for sending me a copy of Curcio's draft manifesto. On the 'Manifesto' itself, see below.

77. Major excerpts from this document, 'Osservazioni circa lo statuto e il piano di studi nella diversa elaborazione della direzione dell'Istituto e della Commissione studentesca', are reprinted in Marco Boato, 'Trento: Istituto Universitario di Scienze Sociali', in Movimento studentesco (ed.), *Documenti della rivolta universitaria* (Bari: Laterza, 1968), 8–13. An insightful commentary on the meaning of this document can be found in Balestrini and Moroni, *L'orda d'oro*, 209–10.

78. For this document, 'Bilancio della seconda occupazione', see Boato, 'Trento', 24–39; for Boato's insightful elaborations on the meaning of this document, see pp. 23–4.

79. The most detailed and thoughtful discussion of this 'Manifesto per una università negativa' can be found in Kurz, *Universität*, 109–16.

80. For a detailed scheme of countercourses, a countercurriculum of sorts, published in the fall of 1966, designed to provide a model of what a sociology curriculum in the service of the radical cause should look like, see 'Sul piano di studi per il corso di laurea in sociologia dell'Istituto di Trento', in Boato, 'Trento', 15–22.

81. For the claim of Mauro Rostagno as chief author, see Balestrini and Moroni, *L'orda d'oro*, 214. The citation is from Curcio, *Viso aperto*, 35. A brief synopsis of Mauro Rostagno's personal-political itinerary can be found in Antonio and Giommaria Monti (eds.), *Dizionario del '68* (Rome: Riuniti, 1998), 167.

82. The contributions of Herbert Marcuse, C. Wright Mills, and other theoreticians of the new left will be discussed in Ch. 4. Informative discussions of the legacy of, respectively, Marcuse and Mills on the Trento Manifesto can be found in Kurz, *Universität*,

110–11 and 116, as well as in Balestrini and Moroni, *L'orda d'oro*, 212–13. The influence of Mills and Marcuse, of course, went far beyond the small but influential circle of activists in Trento. On the more general importance of Marcuse in Italy, see Francesca Sidotti, 'Emancipazione e politiche culturali negli anni sessanta: Marcuse in Italia', in *Rassegna Italiana di Sociologia*, 2 (1974), 241–90.

83. On the Gui plans, see Giuseppe Ricuperati, 'La politica scolastica', in Francesco Barbagallo (ed.), *Storia dell'Italia repubblicana*, ii. *La trasformazione dell'Italia: Sviluppi e squilibri*, part 2. *Istituzioni, movimenti, culture* (Turin: Einaudi, 1995), 741–7; Giuseppe Ricuperati, 'La politica scolastica italiana dal centro-sinistra alla contestazione studentesca', in Agosti, Passerini, and Tranfaglia (eds.), *Cultura e i luoghi*, 418–24. On the student response, see also Kurz, *Universität*, 93–6. Kurz, *Universität*, 127–36, is also an excellent source on the role of the Vietnam War in Italian student politics in the late 1960s.

84. A concise chronicle of this protest wave can be found in Crainz, *Paese mancato*, 218–22. But see also Kurz, *Universität*, 117–20, and, for the Trento Vietnam Week affair, pp. 132–3.

85. For the events at *la Cattolica*, see Mario Capanna, 'La lotta all'Università Cattolica', in *L'ipotesi rivoluzionaria*, 205–41; Alberto De Bernardi, 'Le componenti sociali e politiche del Sessantotto a Milano', in Pier Paolo Poggio (ed.), *Il Sessantotto: L'evento e la storia* (Brescia: Fondazione 'Luigi Micheletti', 1988–9), 269–88; Kurz, *Universität*, 148–60; and Robert Lumley, *States of Emergency: Cultures of Revolt in Italy from 1968 to 1978* (London: Verso, 1990), 77–86. Mario Capanna has published an informative and evocative autobiography, *Formidabili quegli anni* (Milan: Rizzoli, 1998).

86. On the meaning of the term 'active strike', first coined by Trento students but then common currency on other Italian campuses for the remainder of the decade, see Boato, 'Lotta a Trento', 29, and in greater analytical detail, Kurz, *Universität*, 142–8. The larger meaning of the extraordinary development and flowering of organs of 'direct' or 'participatory' democracy will be discussed in Ch. 5.

87. On the decision of 31 Jan. 1968 to commence the third occupation which continued until 7 Apr., see Boato, 'Trento', 44. The 7 Nov. 1967 document, 'La nuova fase politica del Movimento Studentesco Trentino', is partially reproduced in Boato, 'Trento', 41–3. The Jan. 1968 text, written by Mauro Rostagno, 'Università come istituto produttivo', can be accessed in Boato, 'Trento', 51–61, and, with small but important additions to the concluding paragraph, in Boato, 'Lotta a Trento', 42–51. Suggestive comments on the ongoing process of radicalization of Trento students can be consulted in Marco Revelli, 'Movimenti sociali e spazio politico', in Barbagallo (ed.), *Storia dell'Italia repubblicana*, ii/2. 405–7. Note, however, that Rossana Rossanda dates the definitive break of Trento student activists with traditional forms of student representation to the events surrounding the Vietnam Week in late Mar. 1967; see her *L'anno degli studenti* (Bari: De Donato, 1968), 69.

88. For the 1966 document, 'Sul piano di studi per il corso di laurea in sociologia dell'Istituto di Trento', see Boato, 'Trento', 15–22. For the early 1968 outline of 'working groups', 'political commissions', and 'self-managed collective seminars', see Boato, 'Lotta a Trento', 52–3.

89. The literature on the *movimento studentesco* in Pisa and, especially, Turin is too vast to list. But for a short and concise assessment of the specifics of student struggles in Turin and Pisa, see, for instance, Revelli, 'Movimenti sociali', 409–11.

90. The rapid spread of the student movement from Nov. 1967 onwards can be best traced in Crainz, *Paese mancato*, 223–31; Kurz, *Universität*, 211–16, citation on p. 213; and Carlo Oliva and Aloisio Rendi, *Il movimento studentesco e le sue lotte* (Milan: Feltrinelli, 1969), 20–7.

91. The most detailed reconstruction of this pivotal event in the history of the Italian student movement is, once again, contained in the most comprehensive overall treatment of Italian student activism between 1966 and 1968, Kurz, *Universität*, 216–30. The fitting musical expression of this symbolic turning point was the fast-paced tune by Paolo Pietrangeli, 'Valle Giulia', included in the collection of Pietrangeli's songs, *Mio caro Padrone/Contessa* (Modena: Dischi del Sole, n.d.). The famous refrain needs no explanation: *Non siam scappati più* (We no longer ran away).

92. Crainz, *Paese mancato*, 264–5.

93. Kurz, *Universität*, 284. On the summit and subsequent decline of the student movement after the Battle of Valle Giulia, see above all Oliva and Rendi, *Movimento studentesco*, 27–46.

94. The reflux and the divisions within the Italian *movimento studentesco* are best analysed in Kurz, *Universität*, 261–3 and 279–81.

95. One listing of the intensive but brief attempts to forge a national structure can be consulted in Walter Franz, *Jugendprotest in Italien: Die lange revolutionäre Welle 1968–1977* (Frankfurt: Haag & Herchen, 1993), 46–8, though he inexplicably ends his chronicle of national student conferences in June. For a more comprehensive treatment of the entire range of national gatherings until Sept. 1968, see Oliva and Rendi, *Movimento studentesco*, 109–17.

96. Crainz, *Paese mancato*, 223. Secondary schools had, of course, been affected by the radical ferment emanating from university towns long before Mar. 1968 and not just in Italy. The activism (and repression of) radicalized high school students remains one of the gaping white spaces in the historiography of 'global 1968'.

97. The approximately one-year period of sounding out the extra-university terrain in search of allies is best conceptualized in Revelli, 'Movimenti sociali', 440–4, citation on p. 440.

3

Vogliamo Tutto: The Working-Class Dimension of '1968'

1. THE VALLEY OF THE TURÓN

It was 7 April 1962. The setting? A provincial town in a mountain valley in Asturias, northern Spain: Mieres. By the 1960s, Mieres, located in the valley of the Turón, was able to look back on a century of mining and industrial activity. Today, the mining industry has virtually shut down, and the area's administration, benefiting from the natural beauty of the Cantabrian mountain ranges and hillsides, is banking on the benefits of a growing tourist industry. In the 1960s, mining and heavy industry was still the mainstay of local employment, though warning signs of impending decline were already clearly visible on the horizon. 'The coal industry was in decline; wages were low; the infrastructure was antique; imported coal was cheaper and of better quality; other forms of energy were highly competitive. The proposed rationalization of the sector—via shut-downs, lay-offs, mergers and so on—was to be carried out at the expense of the workers in benefit of the owners.'[1]

On 7 April 1962, seven miners at the Nicolasa pit in Mieres received their redundancy notice. The rationale? 'Excessively low productivity'. For some time, miners in the area had expected some such move, and talk of possible counter-measures had been in the air. When the seven received their lay-off notice, the response was clear. The workers of the Nicolasa pit downed their tools. The next day the Baltasara pit workers shut down their mine, and then others followed suit. By 16 April 1962 the entire valley of the Turón had shut down in solidarity with the seven arbitrary victims at the Nicolasa pit. Neighbouring industrial and mining communities soon joined the fray, and by 24 April 60,000 Asturian workers, particularly, miners and metalworkers, had joined the protest strike wave. For the first time in over twenty-five years an entire region had gone on strike in Spain.[2]

Spain, of course, since the defeat of the Republican government in the Spanish Civil War (1936–9), had been in the throes of a brutal military dictatorship, closely integrated into the sphere of influence of the fascist Axis powers until the demise of the latter in 1945. Surviving a subsequent short period of relative international diplomatic isolation, with the onset of the cold war Franco's Spain enjoyed a growing acceptance on the part of the Western world. In 1953, the dictatorship entered into an agreement with the United States, providing military bases and other aid for the defence of the 'free world'. The regular exercise of democratic rights remained, of course, illegal and infractions were tightly repressed. The subjugation of all forms of oppositional activity affected not only the fate of political parties but trade unions as well. All existing trade unions were outlawed in Francoist Spain even before the conclusion of the Civil War. In 1947 legislation was passed for the establishment of some form of workplace representation, the *jurados de empresas* (literally, 'factory juries'), to be elected by the workforce with—at least on paper—a relatively significant amount of rights and duties. Given the severe repression of all types of organized opposition in Francoist Spain, in reality these elections usually turned out to be rather less than meaningful affairs. And, lest the *jurados* might at some point take on a life of their own, the government retained disciplinary powers over their operations and their members.[3] Small wonder, then, that, when Asturian workers went on the offensive in the spring of 1962, they largely bypassed the *jurados* and created organizational structures of their own.

In effect, what happened at the Nicolasa pit and then in neighbouring mines, soon in the entire fifty square kilometre Valley of the Turón, and finally in neighbouring portions of Asturias, was a process which in subsequent years spread throughout Spain. Workers at a given mine or factory gathered in a general assembly and freely elected their own leadership. Where such open displays of central challenges to the company management and indeed to the normal functioning of the dictatorial state were not feasible or advisable, certain individuals, benefiting from the confidence of their workmates based on daily interaction over many years, were designated rather than chosen in an open vote. The process of rank-and-file election of workers' delegates in order to democratically represent the entirety of a given workforce was to be repeated, as we shall see, in subsequent years in other European states. On some occasions, Spanish migrant workers seeking employment in other Western European states may have been responsible for introducing this specific tactic into labour struggles hundreds if not thousands of kilometres further north.[4] More often than not, however, and in a variety of national settings, it seems that the option for democratic grass-roots representation emerged as a quasi-spontaneous process emanating from the dynamics of labour struggles. Nonetheless, the fact that Spain, and more specifically Asturias and Euzkadi, saw the first reappropriation of this traditional 'proletarian' tactic after the long night of the cold war 1950s, when such militant tactics had fallen into disuse, more than justifies the choice of Spain for the opening section of this chapter. To be sure, the extraordinary political circumstances of Francoist Spain ensured that Spanish activists were on occasion forced to march to a different drummer. But, on the whole, Spanish politics and society between 1956 and 1976, in its overall outlines, neatly conformed to the dominant patterns elsewhere. The Asturian miners' decision to meet in a general assembly and to choose delegates from amongst themselves differs from similar actions elsewhere only by virtue of its chronological precocity.

On 24 April 1962 delegates from all Asturian mines on strike met in Mieres, chose a committee to negotiate with the authorities, but were immediately rebuffed.[5] Yet the movement continued and began to affect neighbouring and other regions of Spain. In the last week of April the metalworkers in Greater Bilbao in the Basque province of Vizcaya joined the fray, forming picket lines which not only shut down factories but all cinemas, dance halls, and bars in the area as well. By early May virtually all industrial zones and mining areas of the Francoist state were affected by the strike. Galicia, Andalusia, and Catalonia saw elevated strike activity, though the hotbeds of this illegal wildcat strike remained the Asturian region and then the Basque provinces of Vizcaya and Guipúzcoa. Estimates of the total number of Spanish workers on strike vary between 200,000 and 400,000.[6] On 4 May 1962, a state of emergency was declared for Asturias as well as Vizcaya and Guipúzcoa. But the authoritarian government also applied 'the carrot' and not just 'the stick'. The head of the *sindicato vertical*, the sole officially approved and legally operating trade union in Francoist Spain, José Solís Ruiz, arrived in Asturias on 15 May, meeting with mine worker delegates in the main assembly hall of the *casa sindical* in Oviedo, the regional administrative centre, the very same day. Asturian employers were less than enchanted with this paternalistic move by José Solís, but the conflict was resolved when, on 24 May, the centrally determined price of coal was raised by government fiat, with the added stipulation that the accruing benefits should be earmarked to improve miners' wages. On 28 May 1962 Asturian workers began to resume their regular work schedules.[7]

José Antonio Biescas and Manuel Tuñón de Lara conclude: 'The strikes of spring 1962 changed a great variety of things: one can confirm that the general behaviour of the subordinate classes, their manner of organizing themselves, their confrontation with authorities, their self-assurance as social actors henceforward underwent major transformations.'[8] The literature is replete with references to the Asturian general strike of springtime 1962 as the origin of the subsequent rise of the most important underground trade union structure in Francoist Spain: the *Comisiones obreras* (CCOO, workers' commissions). And, in many ways, indeed, the strike wave centred in Asturias ushered in a period of the seemingly unstoppable spread of the CCOO throughout many regions of Spain, initially operating on the grass-roots level in ways quite similar to the mode of operation during the Asturian wildcat strikes. Yet further qualifications should be immediately added.

For one thing, the CCOO as such, especially in Asturias, only began to get organized in the wake of the strikes when the dictatorship resorted once again to the tried and tested mechanism of vicious reprisals, for hundreds of miners were dismissed, many of them jailed or sent into internal exile to remote corners of Spain, soon after the conclusion of the work stoppage. It was amongst these victimized workers made redundant in post-strike reprisals, in addition to pensioners and miners unable to work due to occupational illnesses, that Spanish workers found activists willing and able to construct underground trade union structures.[9] In addition, it is important to recognize that there was a difference between, on the one hand, the quasi-spontaneous movement of workers' committees, springing up in the course of the struggle and—for the duration of the conflict—meeting in bars and cafés and, on the other, 'the organised Workers' Commissions [who often] followed a strategic policy of infiltration and occupation of the official *jurados de empresa*'.[10] Frequently, though not always, the former ad hoc commissions evolved into the CCOO, but these two manifestations of worker discontent should be kept separate not only for analytical purposes. Last but not least, both types of underground worker protest, ad hoc workers' committees and the CCOO, antedate 1962 by a considerable margin. Collective bargaining by illegal means, 'often accompanied by a denunciation of the *jurado de empresa* by the workers in general in illegal assemblies in the plant or outside the gates', had become fairly widespread from 1953 onwards.[11] Officially, the very first example of a functioning workers' commission has been dated back to 1958 and placed firmly in space in the La Camocha mine near Gijón, Asturias.[12] Yet, 'given the spontaneous character of the movement and the ephemeral quality of the [early] commissions, it is impossible to determine definitively where or when the *comisiones obreras* first emerged'.[13]

What makes the Asturian general strike of 1962 pivotal in the history of anti-Franco opposition movements is the indisputable fact that, from then on, despite inevitable ups and downs, working-class opposition, combined with protest movements by allied social forces, including notably university students, underwent an important intensification which, for all practical purposes, only declined a few years after the restoration of democracy in Spain in the wake of Franco's death in November 1975. While the CCOO were not the only underground trade union structure operating in Francoist Spain, much of the success of the working-class opposition after 1962 is closely connected with the evolution of the CCOO. A brief glance at the organizational consolidation and development of the CCOO thus provides solid insights into the growth of the Spanish labour movement *tout court*. Out of the Vizcaya general strike of 1962 emerged the very first provincial network of the CCOO. As was the case in various locations in neighbouring Asturias, victimized workers formed the organizational backbone of the Vizcayan province-wide CCOO. Based on individual factory CCOO structures, a group of twelve representatives—later on reduced to five— was chosen for the provincial council, the first of its kind in all of Spain, mandated to engage in various negotiations with state authorities and employers for the reintegration of the expelled workers and all sorts of other tasks, including the organization of demonstrations and localized strikes.[14] The second provincial CCOO structure, gathering 600 delegates from the all-important Madrid metal industry, met on 2 September 1964. The Barcelona area coordinating body first gathered on 20 November 1964.[15] CCOO organizers in other major metropolitan areas, provinces, and regions followed suit. By the mid-1960s, regular connections were extended for the first time ever across provincial frontiers.[16] In early 1966 a first key national document was published in the name of the CCOO, signed by more than a hundred leading activists.[17] In June 1967 the first national assembly of CCOO delegates met in Madrid, gathering activists from more than thirty provinces.[18] And 1967 was the first high point of working-class opposition in Franco's Spain in more ways than one.

2. MOBILIZATIONS IN UNDERGROUND SPAIN

After the 1962 strike wave which ushered in a period of ascendancy for labour struggles across the Spanish state, the focal point of oppositional activity in the labour movement underground shifted away from the 'declining' industries, such as mining in Asturias or the textile industry in Catalonia, and concentrated in 'the dynamic spheres (Madrid engineering and construction; Barcelona car manufacturing)'. These new centres of labour conflicts could thus take advantage of a profoundly different overall economic context for the pursuit of their demands. Primarily defensive struggles for survival in employment sectors in permanent decline continued to be fought, but workers in booming industries increasingly could profit from the economic opportunities opened up by healthy company balance sheets and the corresponding demands for increasing production, which narrowed the margin of manœuvre for employers faced with an increasingly restless labour force. Sheelagh Ellwood suggests that workers in new and expanding industries 'were in a relatively strong position because of their real ability to threaten key sectors of the economy', and that therefore it became relatively easy to progress from purely economic to openly political demands. The overall strengthening of the anti-Franco opposition undoubtedly played its own part in politicizing the underground revolt.[19]

From approximately 1964 to 1967, the crucial site of class struggles in the Spanish state became the capital city of Madrid. A sensitive location for any political challenge, in the course of the decades of dictatorial rule Madrid had developed into Spain's 'second industrial city', with engineering workers in the forefront of this boom.[20] In the same years, Madrid witnessed the addition of yet another sector to the ranks of militant labour activists: white-collar workers, in particular bank workers. By the late 1960s white-collar underground activism spread into the lower ranks of the civil service.[21] The Basque provinces, long a centre of the important steel and metal industry in the Spanish state, from 1966 onwards showcased the highest incidents of solidarity strikes in all of Spain, a clear sign of the heightened political confrontations in Euzkadi, where the tragedy of political oppression and dictatorship affecting all of Spain was compounded by the realities of national oppression.[22] Yet solidarity strikes became a standard feature not solely in Euzkadi. In the period

from 1963 to 1967 economic demands were predominant (44.2 per cent of 1,676 cases), followed by claims related to collective bargaining (15.2 per cent), while solidarity claims were relatively rare (4.0 per cent). From 1967 onwards [up to 1974] the situation changed: solidarity claims reached 45.4 per cent (of 7,694 cases), demands related to collective bargaining increased to 20.1 per cent, and economic demands dropped to 25.6 per cent.

José Maravall in addition reports a steady radicalization of forms of labour action. He notes 'that strikes and strikes-on-the-job increased as a proportion of the total number of actions [compared to milder and more cautious forms of exerting pressure]: they amounted to 30.3 per cent in the four years between 1963 and 1966, but the percentage increased to 86.6 per cent in the period between 1967 and 1974'.[23] A more fine-tuned analysis of strike data for the years 1963 to 1967 in an earlier work by the same author proves that the degree of intensity and the radical nature of strikes showed a steady increase from year to year.[24]

An early high point was reached, as was alluded to before, in 1967, which in June witnessed the first national assembly of CCOO delegates. In January 1967, the Madrid coordinating body of the CCOO called for a major demonstration in the streets of the capital city, a defiance of the law which the authorities responded to by pre-emptive arrests of leading activists. Nonetheless, workers (and students) assembled at various locations throughout Madrid, boycotting all public transportation for that day. By all accounts, in the course of this action held on 27 January 1967, 'Madrid witnessed the greatest display of working-class protest since the end of the Civil War.' The political challenge of this show of force was further underscored by a strike of 50,000 metalworkers the following day, demanding the release of the arrested union leaders.[25] The 27 October 1967 national day of action brought a further escalation in the unequal tug of war between the Francoist state and the working-class underground. In Madrid alone, 100,000 workers (and, again, students) took to the streets. Catalonia and Asturias also experienced public meetings, despite the fact that, throughout Spain, 'the police occupied the larger towns; their orders were to put down all demonstrations'. A wave of arrests and punitive dismissals resulting from this day of action engendered a relative decline in labour conflict in 1968.[26]

The CCOO emerged organizationally weakened after their bloodletting of October 1967, and up to 1973 they played a notably less central role in the instigation and organization of labour conflicts. Yet, symptomatically, after a brief respite in 1968, labour protest and strikes quickly resumed and far surpassed previous levels in subsequent years. Clearly, labour unrest and ever-rising levels of strike activity were no longer dependent on the fortunes of any particular organizations, such as the CCOO. On 24 January 1969, under the onslaught of joint worker and student protest, the Franco government, for the first time since the end of the Civil War, declared a state of emergency for the entire country. At one point even considering the possibility of declaring a state of war, which would have facilitated the replacement of civilian governors with military governors throughout Spain, the Cabinet did not rescind the state of emergency until 25 March 1969.[27]

Nothing seemed to be able to stop the onslaught of oppositional sentiments. As Sheelagh Ellwood aptly put it, 'the extraordinary circumstances of 1969 [became] the norm in the seventies'.[28] The vicious cycle of ascending levels of protest and repression continued, reaching ever-greater heights. According to official government statistics, 'throughout 1970 there occurred 1,600 labor conflicts. This figure was three times the amount of industrial action in [the already rather turbulent year of] 1969 and equalled the figure for all such actions in the four-year period of 1966–1969.'[29] Sure enough, the next year recorded a renewed drop-off in labour disputes, but even 1971 saw memorable and unprecedented agitation. In October 1971, a bitterly contested battle was fought in and around the factory with the largest number of employees in the entire Spanish state: the SEAT automotive plant in Barcelona, where 28,000 workers attempted to make a living. On 18 October 1971, workers occupied the factory and engaged in a thirteen-hour running battle, hurling tools and pieces of metal at police firing tear gas grenades, gunshots, and launching a cavalry charge against the militant workforce on the company floor. One worker was killed, many were injured, others arrested and beaten while in custody.[30] The SEAT combat action was by far the most militant undertaking engaged in by Spanish workers up to that time, and it symbolized the fact that 'in the seventies Barcelona became the capital of the opposition to the dictatorship'.[31] But, throughout Spain, just as had been the case after the temporary reflux of 1968, the comparative 'lull' of 1971 gave way to a subsequent uninterrupted rise in labour conflicts with no further setbacks, culminating in a crescendo of strikes, demonstrations, and shut-downs following the long-awaited death of Franco in November 1975. From 1972 onwards, local and regional general strikes became a prominent feature of Spanish worker protest, first practised in 1972 in El Ferrol and Vigo, both industrial centres in Galicia in north-western Spain. In 1973 there was a spread of such tactics, with the most famous area general strike of that year paralysing the region around the capital city of Navarre, Pamplona. 'By the end of [1973] these actions had become the most spectacular type of conflict.' They were to remain a standard feature of the socio-economic and political realities of Spain for the remainder of the dictatorship, the latter continuing to mete out massive reprisals.[32]

Catalonia, like Euzkadi, had experienced the double trauma of political repression coupled with national discrimination. In the closing years of Francoist terror, working-class opposition in Catalonia went beyond the organization of clandestine unions and strikes. In 1971 an embryonic form of counter-government was created in the underground, the Assemblea de Catalunya, with CCOO activists propelling such a move, calling for the forging of 'close links between workers and other sections of the population'. Sebastian Balfour cites a former shop steward who operated in this counter-institution functioning from below: 'The *Assemblea* got many people—shopkeepers, small industrialists, and the like— to support us, sometimes giving us money, sometimes hiding us in their houses if the police were searching for us.'[33] Other, closely related counter-institutions of 'direct' or 'participatory' democracy emerged at a grass-roots level in Greater Barcelona. As we will see in Chapter 5, in the early to mid 1970s, residential

associations flourished, and by 1974 ninety such organizations operated in that
port city alone. As is readily apparent with the examples of the *assemblea* or
the neighbourhood associations, anti-dictatorial activism reached far beyond the
working class as such, but the latter formed the backbone and the battering ram in
the eventual destruction of dictatorship in Spain. A final observation, a comparison
with a neighbouring state, may dramatize the truly extraordinary scope of
working-class protests in the Spanish state. Between 1969 and 1973, the Spanish
economy, in each individual year, lost between 4.5 and 8.7 million hours because
of labour unrest. In 1974 and 1975 the number of hours lost hovered around
the 14 million mark. Spain then counted less than 8 million wage earners. Its
neighbour to the north, France, had about 17 million wage earners at that time.
France in the 1970s, as we shall see, was not exactly a haven of labour peace. Here
is what Víctor Pérez Díaz has to say about the ensuing triennium: 'Social conflict
multiplied tremendously. Between 12 and 16 million working days were lost
annually through strikes between 1976 and 1978—three times more than in
France.'[34]

3. FRENCH WORKERS IN THE CALVADOS

France is the country most readily identified with the spirit of '1968'. And
whereas, for most observers, '1968' tends to be almost exclusively identified as 'the
year of the students', the French case is happily regarded as the one exception to
this supposed norm of student insurgency as the chief characteristic of '1968'.
And it would indeed be difficult to ignore the impact of a three-week-long near-
total general strike paralysing an advanced industrial state in the middle of
Western Europe. As this chapter aims to demonstrate, the contestations of '1968'
were by no means limited to radical student activism. Indeed, in a whole range of
European states, most of all but not exclusively in Romance-language areas of the
Old World, the meaning and the dynamics of '1968' cannot possibly be understood without close attention to working-class revolt. The Spanish case described
in preceding pages, of course, can be at least partially explained as a peculiar
response to the anomalies of Iberian politics and society in the era of the long
post-war boom. A rapid though partial industrialization pushed through under
dictatorial rule, one could argue, was bound to erupt in worker revolt. But to the
north of the triumvirate of southern European dictatorships firmly integrated into
the supposed 'free world'—Spain, Portugal, and Greece—surely, in the eyes of
most observers, such working-class rebellion belonged to the increasingly distant
historical past. By the mid to late 1960s, a whole industry of writings pronouncing
if not quite yet 'the end of history' then certainly 'the end of ideology' had
conquered pride of place in academic circles most prominently, but not
exclusively, in the Anglo-Saxon world. But as Raoul Vaneigem, in his prescient
handbook of popular rebellion, wrote in 1967: 'We hear from some quarters that

in the advanced industrial countries the proletariat no longer exists, that it has disappeared forever under an avalanche of sound systems, TVs, small cars and planned communities.' The Belgian Situationist then added in mocking tones: 'Where on earth can it be? Spirited away? Gone underground? Or has it been put in a museum?'[35] Little more than six months after the publication of these lines, the answer arrived loudly and clearly in neighbouring France.

The French labour movement had rarely been quiescent and, even in the cold war years of 1958–62, the number of working days lost through strikes never dropped below the 1 million mark in any of these years. A long and bitterly fought miners' strike in 1963 drove the number of days lost because of labour action almost to the 6 million mark, but this was to be a high point without an immediate sequel. In 1964 and 1966 the strike days were in the region of 2.5 million, but this relatively higher figure was compensated by the unusually low number of days lost through strikes in 1965: just below 1 million. The subsequent rise to approximately 4.2 million in 1967 did, then, not necessarily provide a clue as to what was to happen in the following year.[36] After the explosion of labour conflict in May/June 1968 (about which below), there have been multiple attempts made to (re)discover precursors of this unexpected combativity on the part of a social class presumably doomed to extinction. As is the case when tracing supposed antecedents of major social conflicts in other realms of social life as well, such valiant attempts to point to early warning signs of increasing antagonism must be taken with a healthy dose of scepticism. The precise mechanisms of the transference of social conflicts from one location to another will never be resolved with mathematical precision. But for the French experience of the run-up to May 1968, the case of Caen in late January 1968 may be particularly instructive.

The administrative centre of the rural Calvados, a *département* most famous for its apple-based liquors, Caen counted roughly 100,000 inhabitants in 1968. A university town since 1432, it had been a centre of the textile industry but, by the 1960s, was also home to heavy industries, including a truck assembly plant, the Renault-owned SAVIEM. Located in the Catholic and traditionally anti-communist Normandy, it seemed an unlikely spot for militant action. Nonetheless, within twenty-four hours of the outbreak of a work stoppage by a majority of the 4,800 workers employed by SAVIEM, Caen made national headline news,[37] for on 24 January 1968 the plant gates at the SAVIEM factory were taken over by police, ostensibly to guarantee access for anyone wanting to continue work. And in the city centre itself, on 26 January 1968, police forces charged demonstrating strikers and supporters—a crowd, according to journalists present on the scene, 10,000 strong—liberally dousing them with tear gas. Unwilling to turn the other cheek, protestors responded in kind, using Molotov cocktails and assorted makeshift weaponry to fight a vicious battle lasting until 5 the next morning. When the smoke had cleared, over one hundred had been injured, thirty-six persons were hospitalized, and eighty-five demonstrators had suffered arrest. Shop windows were broken, the chamber of commerce ransacked, and even the prefecture incurred damage. Most amazingly, however, public opinion in Caen was resolutely on the side of the strikers, solidarity strikes breaking out and statements of support flooding into the strike headquarters from throughout the region. How is this to be explained?

Surely, once again the forceful presence of a progressive variant of social Catholicism, already encountered elsewhere in Europe, had helped to prepare the terrain. In Caen itself, for instance, the recently secularized but formerly Catholic Democratic French Trade Union Federation (CFDT) was predominant in virtually all flagship enterprises. By contrast with the Communist-controlled and highly centralized General Labour Confederation (CGT), the CFDT was far less reticent in supporting grass-roots initiatives; it had begun to explore the meaning of workers' self-management (*autogestion*) in 1965; and it was not hesitant to engage in dialogue with the fledgling new and far left in France.[38] In addition, the flagship political organization of the French new left, the Unified Socialist Party (PSU), played a crucial connecting role in linking up various strands of Caen-based nonconforming social movement activism. Having locally obtained an unusually high 6.35 per cent of the popular vote in the 1967 legislative elections, the PSU not only provided a political home to important numbers of local CFDT activists but also counted on a locally firmly implanted cohort of student activists, organized in the Unified Socialist Students (ESU), who had taken over the control of the local branch of the French national student association, the National Union of French Students (UNEF), back in 1965.

The potent cross-fertilization of new left activism, left Catholicism, student protest, and worker unrest, then, was to a large extent what made possible 'this hot week in Caen'.[39] Unusually even for France—prior to May 1968!—traditional social cleavages between working-class communities and middle-class-dominated university student milieux had been overcome in the heat of a concrete struggle, helping to galvanize Caen public opinion against the employers and the state. In total contrast to other locations throughout France, worker–student liaisons in Caen had thus become firmly established months before such encounters became less than exceptional elsewhere in France. And the working-class strike preceded student solidarity and student unrest. Caen thus, clearly, was the exception and not the rule. For, when workers throughout France began to move on a larger scale in mid-May, their actions followed on the coat-tails of a student movement which had, within the space of a precious few weeks, developed from a relatively quiescent constituent part of French civil society into a central challenge to the state.

4. FROM NANTERRE TO THE SORBONNE

This is not the place to describe, except in its briefest of all outlines, the rise of the French student movement up to and including May 1968. Louis Vos, an activist in Leuven at the high point of its student revolt, recalls that, when attending an international conference of Catholic students—not the most passive cohort, as we have repeatedly seen—in Paris in November 1967, the assembled student leaders were still most preoccupied with what they regarded as the key feature of that time: 'the depoliticization of the European student'.[40] Leuven had been an exception, and Italy was far away on the other side of the Alps. In France itself, it was only in November 1967 that a virulent student movement got under way, and then for some months solely on a brand-new but remote branch campus of the far-flung University of Paris. If Trento—along with Pisa and Turin—was the cradle of student power in Italy, Nanterre became the functional equivalent on the north-western side of the Alps. As was the case in Trento, in Nanterre, too, in the words of two English chroniclers of the events in France, 'the sociology department was the nursery of the revolution'. When, on 17 November 1967, Nanterre sociologists went on strike, this action was not the first militant action on the inhospitable campus on the western outskirts of Greater Paris. But it set in motion a sequence of events which eventually led to further actions elsewhere. Unlike Trento University, Nanterre was home to many faculties and the strike soon involved roughly 10,000 students who met in general assemblies in large lecture halls to plan further actions. The first shut-down of the Nanterre campus lasted only ten days, but Nanterre students henceforth remained at the forefront of events. On 22 March 1968, Nanterre witnessed the first student takeover of an administration building in France that year. Traditional forms of student organizations—and divisions between them—began to blur in the course of that particular struggle, and a new Nanterre-based movement of 22 March united an array of new and far left activists, anarchists, Trotskyists, and Maoists, amongst others.[41]

Nanterre remained the focal point of action until the early days of May. On 2 May two decisions taken by the head of the Nanterre campus administration, Pierre Grappin, proved to be the summit and endpoint of Nanterre dominance of the student movement in France. He shut down the campus for an indeterminate amount of time, excluding six student leaders, including the media-savvy Daniel Cohn-Bendit. The next day, Friday, 3 May, a protest gathering called to express solidarity with their Nanterre comrades in the interior courtyard of the venerable Sorbonne on the Left Bank of central Paris assembled several hundred hardcore activists. When University President Jean-Marie Roche decided to have police clear the Sorbonne courtyard, student leaders negotiated a peaceful exit, aiming to avoid needless confrontation with superior force. When they had evacuated the Sorbonne proper, students were confronted by rows of uniformed police, the latter demanding that all evacuees enter police cars for identity checks at police headquarters, and only then did the situation begin to get out of control. A growing throng of student onlookers interpreted the actions as a form of arrest, felt incensed by what they were witnessing, and formed a circle around the police. A sense of Berkeley was in the air.

The ensuing mêlée soon intensified and far exceeded the troubles outside Berkeley's Sproul Hall. The first cobblestone was thrown, smashing a police car windshield and injuring an officer. With sticks and tear gas in plentiful supply, police managed to disperse the crowd, but not without alienating many residents or passers-by in the Latin Quarter who either witnessed or experienced first-hand what they regarded as a blatant display of police brutality. When the last clouds of tear gas cleared the air at 11 p.m., 574 individuals had been arrested. Yet the movement had barely begun. In the next few days various mobilizations got under way, with a first high point of violent altercations on 6 May. A few days later, French student struggles reached the point of no return. The night of 10–11 May has been entered in the annals of social movement activism as 'the night of the barricades', with students constructing makeshift barricades in many streets throughout the Latin Quarter and police counterattacking at precisely 2.12 a.m. The forces of law and order may have temporarily cleared the streets for traffic by the end of that night, but the accompanying orgy of police brutality and the refusal of students to peacefully give in would change the nature of French politics for a number of years. With this spectacular action, the spark of May 1968 in Paris flew far beyond the university terrain and set aflame an unprecedented series of working-class battles to rock the French state.[42]

5. THE GENESIS OF A GENERAL STRIKE

The countdown began at 9 a.m. on the morning after the night of the barricades. At the initiative of the two leading trade union federations, the CGT and the CFDT, actions in solidarity with the repression of the student revolt had been under consideration since 9 May. Initially planned for Tuesday, 14 May, protest demonstrations were called for Paris and provincial France by a united front of virtually all union confederations representing blue- and white-collar workers in addition to students. The bloody night of the barricades precipitated events. UNEF representatives had for some time already pushed for an earlier and more symbolic date: Monday, 13 May, the tenth anniversary of the French Fifth Republic, but had initially been rebuffed by their interlocutors. On the morning of 11 May there was no more hesitation. When the union leadership of the newly created united front met at 9 a.m. in the Bourse du Travail, the stage was set for a further escalation of social conflict in the French state. A twenty-four-hour general strike was called for Monday, 13 May, to be accompanied by massive demonstrations in all of France. This was technically illegal, as French law demanded a five-day advance notice for all strike activities, but no one seemed to care any more about such details. In the course of the afternoon of 11 May, some of the minor union confederations, which had stayed aloof for a while, now also signalled their support and consent.[43]

During the evening of 11 May, Prime Minister Georges Pompidou returned to Paris from a state visit to Central Asia, and at 23.15 he made a live broadcast on French state television. Attempting to defuse the situation he announced that the

Sorbonne, closed since the events of 3 May, would be reopened on Monday, 13 May, and that, with regard to the fighters arrested on the barricades the night before, 'the court of appeal will be able to give a ruling, in keeping with the law, on the requests for release lodged by the condemned students'. Georges Pompidou kept his word. Daniel Singer reports: 'The four demonstrators sentenced to jail obtained their release on parole on Monday; all the others held in custody had been released on Sunday. The land of Montesquieu is not a country with illusions about the separation of powers.'[44] Once again, by the time important concessions were announced, they proved to be too little too late. First, the protest marches were an overwhelming success. A total of 164 demonstrations, some with up to 60,000 participants, took place throughout provincial France. But the mother of them all wound its way through central Paris. 'The weather was on the side of the victors. On Monday afternoon the sun shone on the biggest demonstration Paris had ever known. How many were they? Half a million, a million?—nobody can really say. It was a human sea or, to be more accurate, two huge rivers joining each other rather than merging together.' For labour union supporters and university community activists assembled in separate feeder marches that met on the Place de la République, whence they jointly marched to Denfert-Rochereau on the Left Bank. The first row of the gigantic march leading off from République was given over to university activists, including Daniel Cohn-Bendit. The accompanying strike movement was a corresponding success.[45]

Then, on 14 May, without a grand plan, the initiative for further extension of social movement practices to reach beyond the university terrain was definitively transferred from students to workers. The spark caused a first blaze on the outskirts of Nantes in western France, where workers at the Sud-Aviation aeroplane manufacturing plant had been engaged in small-scale skirmishes with plant managers for several months. Along with other area factories, Sud-Aviation had solidly adhered to the solidarity strike of 13 May. Back at work on Tuesday morning, 14 May, none of the long-standing issues having yet been resolved, the mood remained combative. That afternoon, the decision was taken not only to resume an indefinite strike but to occupy the plant. For good measure, the company director was forbidden to leave company property. 'Towards 4 p.m. the bomb exploded throughout [Nantes]: the rumour circulated from coffee-house to university faculties and from universities to high schools that Sud-Aviation Bouguenais had been taken over by its workforce!'[46]

News quickly spread throughout the country, setting in motion a wave of similar action which was to shut down the entire country within a few days. Workers at the Renault factory in Cléon, not far south of Rouen in Normandy, had learnt of the events in Nantes via the daily newspaper and the radio. On 13 May, only 50 per cent of the Cléon workforce had heeded the call for solidarity actions with university students under government attack. In mid-afternoon on 15 May a group of young workers took the initiative to demand to speak to the company director with regard to satisfaction of an array of grievances. Three times the manager refused even to talk to the delegation. By 6 p.m. production at Cléon had ground to a halt. There was no need to prevent the director from leaving company property. When the delegation had knocked on his door for the third time that afternoon, he had barricaded himself into his office, together with other representatives of the Cléon managerial elite. Renault-Cléon remained on strike until 17 June 1968.[47] Other factories belonging to the state-owned Renault empire could not stay on the sidelines for very long. On 16 May, Renault assembly plants in Flins, Le Mans, Sandouville, and Orléans joined in. By 5 p.m. on 16 May, the biggest factory in all of France, with 36,000 workers, Renault-Billancourt, located on the outskirts of Paris, was shut down. And other factories, not belonging to Renault, joined the fray. On the evening of 16 May, 70,000 workers were on strike. 'On May 17, sit-in strikes spread throughout the engineering industry and on to the chemical industry. Trains all over the country came to a halt, and post offices ceased to function. The area affected by stoppages also increased rapidly.' By 21 May, 5 million workers had downed their tools. The ensuing general strike continued for a number of weeks. When the strike wave finally began slowly to recede in early June, between 6 and 8 million workers had taken part in the largest strike wave ever to occur in the strike-prone French state.[48]

6. THE MEANING OF THE GENERAL STRIKE

Much has been written about the impact and the meaning of the two-to-three-week-long general strike. Predictably, the work stoppage led to the accumulation of piles of garbage in the streets and neighbourhoods of urban and rural France. It also became an experience which left a lasting imprint on the hearts and minds of countless French citizens, caught up in the whirlwind of springtime in France. For some, it may have awakened or reinforced the belief in the possibilities of radical change even in modern-day advanced industrial societies. For many others, the phenomenon of a country turned upside down, with the political and managerial elite on the defensive and in isolated instances even 'sequestered', was experienced as a feeling of physical and psychological liberation from the alienation of everyday life. New forms of sociability and positive interaction were tried and tested for the first time since 1936 on a scale unimagined prior to mid-May. The most important features of newly discovered modes of 'grass-roots' or 'participatory' or 'direct' democracy will be described and analysed in Chapter 5. For the moment, attention will be given to several important aspects of the strike movement which opened up in mid-May.

Many commentators have rightfully underscored, for instance, that the movement, though clearly evolving—and evolving rapidly!—without a grand plan, was ultimately kept under the control of the established trade unions. A recent variant of this interpretation—and there are many—can be found in the richly detailed empirical observations made by Michael Seidman who, after noting that '*gauchistes* [the far left] and their sympathizers have consistently emphasised the spontaneous nature of the strikes as a way of demonstrating the militancy of the base and the CGT's lack of influence on workers', goes on to conclude: 'In fact, in most cases strikes were initiated by unions or their militants.' And, to emphasize his point, Seidman continues: 'Even when the work stoppage began without union sponsorship, union militants ended up interpreting workers' demands and formulating bargaining positions.'[49] In short, spontaneity may have played a certain, limited role at the outset of the work stoppages, but the initiative was quickly regained by union activists in those few cases where events had briefly escaped their control. Unions subsequently channelled the energies of rank-and-file workers into concrete demands, and any danger of grass-roots initiatives bypassing the presumably less radical trade union federations was safely avoided. Indeed, though frequently the unprompted action was triggered by small groups of local activists, in the vast majority of cases strikes were organized in conjunction with concrete assistance by—and not against—local trade union representatives or members. Cases of existing union structures being sidelined by the force of events were exceedingly rare. In contrast, cases where 'the initiative lay in the hands of the unions, whose moves were immediately—and often enthusiastically—supported by the ranks' were rather common. Indeed, Sabine Erbès-Seguin goes on to argue, 'the degree of direct initiative on the part of rank-and-file workers in the launching of a strike is inversely proportional to the capacity for on-the-spot innovation on the part of union militants'. In other words, where union activists operated on the same wavelength as rank-and-file workers, smooth cooperation characterized the organization of the strike. Only in those cases where union representatives were not in tune with the sentiments of their co-workers were union channels initially bypassed.[50]

Difficulties arise not out of the recapitulation of the processes behind the initial launch of the truly massive wave of long-lasting strikes, but with regard to the interpretation of the largely undisputed facts. Seidman, for instance, operates on the assumption that spontaneous action by the ranks is inherently more promising of radical intent, a fallacy which bears correction. His inverse conclusion, the presumption that union-sponsored activity is inherently supportive of the overall status quo, is equally flawed. First, just to take the case of the French May alone, the initiative in calling for solidarity actions on 13 May lay squarely in the hands of the trade union hierarchy. Neither student organizations nor the workers' ranks were primarily responsible for this particular but all-important proposal. Second, particularly in the case of France, it takes some 'courage' to lump all trade union federations in the same bag. Already prior to 1968, but certainly in the course of the May events, the CFDT in particular solidly implanted itself in the vanguard of social movement activity, symbolized by the historic text published by its top leadership on 16 May: 'To civil liberties and rights within universities must correspond the same liberties and rights within enterprises; in this demand the struggles of university students meet up with those which workers have fought for since the origin of the labour movement. We must replace industrial and administrative monarchy with democratic structures based on workers' self-management.'[51] Last but not least, in this discussion of the dynamic of the French strikes, Seidman treats union militants, that is, local rank-and-file activists who were members of a union, as belonging into the same category as the union top brass, when in fact local activists, often on the verge of tearing up their membership cards out of frustration over decisions reached further up their pecking order, cannot readily be identified with federation policy as a whole. But Seidman's dystopian vision has deeper roots. He goes on, for instance, to suggest that

May 1968 fills a void in French social consciousness but may not deserve its prominence. The events did not mark a rupture but instead showed the continuity of social and political trends. No crisis of civilisation suddenly erupted, and no significant attempt at workers' control emerged. On the contrary, the May–June events demonstrated the power of the centralized state and the attractions of a consumer society that had effectively smothered revolution while integrating hedonism.[52]

True enough, after making a number of far-reaching material concessions, the combined forces of the employers and the state presided over the reflux of the strike movement in the course of the first half of the month of June. In two rounds of national elections on 23 and 30 June, Gaullism then emerged not only victorious but further strengthened. Yet did this really mean that May/June 1968 was a colourful but temporary flash in the pan? Did French blue- and white-collar workers return to their workstations as passive and sullen accomplices in their own alienation as if the intervening weeks of experiences and hopes had never happened? Indisputably, a social revolution had evidently not occurred. But, then, the numbers of individuals who had believed in the possibility of such a turn of events had always been rather limited, and their frequency and prominence are persistently exaggerated by hostile or disenchanted observers in need of strawmen that they can then easily and cynically deconstruct. In reality, the importance of France's proletarian May lies elsewhere. In Chapter 5, the process of individual and collective liberation from the yoke of oppressive hierarchies—a feature common to a great variety of social movements prominent in the period under discussion in this book—will be described in ample detail. For the moment, attention will solely be devoted to a handful of specific observations with regard to the strike wave gripping France. They may serve to suggest that those analysts viewing May/June 1968 in France as a short-term diversion are missing the forest for all the trees.

For a movement supposedly bought off by material concessions, the following observation must be difficult to explain. In the majority of cases, at the beginning of each individual strike, no particular concrete demands were put forward by the workforce involved.[53] There exist countless pieces of evidence that individuals, not known for their history of prior activism, got caught up in the maelstrom of events, enthuasiastically joined the movement, while unable to specify the concrete goals they were aiming to achieve.[54] At the Atlantic shipyard in Saint Nazaire on the Atlantic coast near Nantes, workers occupied their plant 'for ten days while staunchly resisting union pressure to draw up a list of demands'.[55] When lists of concrete demands were finally drawn up, they quite often included such vague desires as the wish to obtain greater 'respect at work (*considération au travail*)'. This characteristic example of an ill-defined qualitative demand, which would be rather difficult to quantify in union–management negotiations, was—in the eyes of an on-the-spot investigatory team—a perfect expression of 'everything which wage workers had been able to experience in these weeks of May and June and which enabled them to express' such demands in the first place.[56] The same team of researchers also found that in a majority of the 120 cases studied, the strikes lasted far longer than appeared necessary for the successful conclusion of negotiations around the concrete demands put forth.[57] Did workers really not know what was best for them? Or were they perhaps beginning to express their wish for roses and not just for bread?

It is not known how many factories and workplaces in France witnessed a takeover by its workforce rather than 'just' a weeks-long rock-solid strike. A study of 182 plant sites in the north reports that 86 surveyed factories experienced some form of occupation, although in only 24 cases did at least half the workforce actively participate.[58] The industries located in a swathe of territory along the Belgian border between Maubeuge and Calais, in the north of France, may have been atypically active in the month of May, as Danielle Tartakowsky reports that here the number of medium-sized provincial towns witnessing solidarity demonstrations on 13 May was higher than anywhere else in France.[59] On the other hand, there exists circumstantial evidence that, in general, when looking at all regions of France, the Midi, the parts of France oriented towards the Mediterranean, may have been in the overall lead. Looking at mine workers in particular, in the 1960s this still an important and labour-intensive industry, 'the actions in the South appear more committed when compared to the North'. 'Sometimes more unitarian, often more massive, and in most cases tougher', preferring workplace occupations over 'simple' strikes, mine workers in the south of France took the lead in their particular industry.[60]

Another local initiative generated in the Midi draws attention to another thought-provoking dimension of the French May. A joint communiqué drawn up on 31 May, signed by railway industry representatives of the three most important federations operating in Montpellier, the CGT, CFDT, and FO, began as follows: 'The management of the SNCF [the French national railway company] is at the moment defective with regard to both economic and social affairs. The workforce believes that the administration of this company must be taken over by its personnel, and this is to occur on all levels of the company hierarchy.'[61] May 1968 catapulted discussion of workers' self-management into the limelight. While concrete instances of elements of self-management or even workers' control in the course of the strike wave of May/June 1968 were isolated instances of mostly symbolic significance, the novelty of 1968 was the sudden interest in a thorough discussion of such ideas. The social explosions of 1968 moved debates about the meaning of *autogestion* from conferences organized by the CFDT—the undisputed leader in the promotion of such ideologies and, later, practices—onto factory and office floors. Not everywhere, to be sure, but widespread enough to implant an idea.[62]

7. FRENCH WORKERS AFTER 1968

The fallacy of the view of May and June 1968 as an entertaining but ultimately irrelevant interlude for the world of labour can be gauged in manifold ways when judging post-1968 developments in the field of industrial relations in France. Pierre Dubois, for instance, reports that three important indicators of labour movement activism—the total number of conflicts, the total number of workers involved and the total number of days lost due to strikes—clearly point to enhanced militancy of French workers in the period 1969–73 compared with the years 1958–67.[63] Taking a closer look at the actual content of strike demands, the emerging picture is somewhat more contradictory. The sociologist Serge Mallet reported in 1970 that post-May/June 1968 strikes in France saw a notable increase in qualitative demands affecting work schedules, working conditions, or employment levels.[64] But others note that not only did quantitative, material demands for wage increases remain at the top of union demands, but the relative frequency of qualitative demands actually diminished after the 1968 strike wave compared with the pre-1968 period. Still, the same team of industrial sociologists reports that wage demands in the wake of 1968 'have a more egalitarian tendency than those made before May, and they are directed more towards defending the spending power of underprivileged groups'.[65]

Yet the most telling consequence of '1968' for working-class action in France can be explored in a series of related events which gripped the national (and international) imagination and which began on the morning of 18 June 1973, when workers attached a banner to the entrance to their factory employing 1,200 blue- and white-collar workers: 'It is possible! We are producing by ourselves, we are selling by ourselves, and we are paying ourselves!' The company was a watch factory located in Besançon in eastern France, home town of two of the most famous French promoters of self-management ideas, the nineteenth-century thinkers and practitioners Charles Fourier and Pierre Joseph Proudhon. The company was named after its 1867 founder, Emmanuel Lipmann, and in 1973 managed by Emmanuel's grandson, Fred Lip. The 18 June 1973 decision came on the heels of a months-long conflict that had been gestating for years.[66]

In May 1968 LIP had been occupied by its workforce for fourteen days, gaining a series of concrete improvements in the process. Yet the continuing decline of profitability of the watchmaking industry took its toll. As usual, management attempted to shift the lion's share of the burden onto its workforce. The late winter of 1972 and spring of 1973 witnessed growing confrontations, reaching a first high point with the brief sequestration of some top managers on 12 June. A day later the workers decided to occupy the plant. On 15 June a solidarity demonstration in the city centre attracted 15,000 supporters. When police blocked access to the prefecture, a barricade was built, billy clubs were swung and tear gas used, and by the end of that day close to 200 persons had been arrested. On Sunday, 17 June, a general assembly of all employees in the occupied plant unanimously decided to up the ante and to continue production on their own. For this plan to succeed, of course, LIP workers not only had to produce but also to sell their product. Five subcommittees of the general assembly of the company workforce now running operations assumed responsibilities for the management, production, and distribution of the watches, as well as the protection of self-managed production sites and the popularization of this experiment. Solidarity quickly materialized in the form of countless requests for worker-produced watches from across France and other countries as well. Solidarity strike action and other forms of symbolic and concrete support materialized throughout France. On 14 August a setback occurred when police recaptured the factory grounds, thus temporarily putting an end to self-management practices; but by 30 August production was resumed in secret workshops in the area. On 29 September 1973, 100,000 demonstrators converged on Besançon in an exhilarating and inspiring display of national and international solidarity with a workers' struggle which captured the imagination of an entire generation of activists like no other single industrial dispute.

LIP workers held out until 28 January 1974 when, by a near-unanimous vote, the workforce accepted the relaunch of regular production under new ownership. For ever since the onset of self-managed production, it had been clear to almost everyone concerned that, despite the hopes expressed amongst others by Fourier and Proudhon, self-management in one or several factories would be doomed to fail in the long run, given a hostile overall social, political, and economic climate. Nonetheless, even while underground assembly of LIP watches was still under way, the example of LIP was replicated elsewhere. The phenomenon termed 'the children of LIP' was a direct consequence of the pioneering and inspiring example of the workers at LIP, just as LIP can only be understood as a delayed consequence of 1968. I will discuss 'the children of LIP' in Chapter 5.

8. ITALY'S 'CREEPING MAY'

In France, May 1968 was an explosion which seemingly emerged from nowhere, paralysed (but also energized) an entire country, yet ultimately de-escalated as rapidly as it had begun. In Italy, it never came to such a climax, but the social conflagrations, starting—for workers—at roughly the same moment, springtime

1968, ultimately undermined the status quo far more deeply. What happened in France in a period spanning four to six weeks occurred in Italy over a period of six to eight years! Consequently, the stakes became far higher and the questioning of authority went far deeper, for the learning process proceeded uninterrupted, especially for workers, from 1968 to, roughly, 1976. It is this exceptional experience of Italy's 'creeping May' which accounts for the fact that, even at the beginning of the third millennium, Italy's civil society remains a home to a culture of social movement activism far surpassing similar instances in any other European state.

The catalytic effect of France's student movement on the French workers' upsurge in mid-May is crystal clear. An identical mechanism—though, again, at different speed—was at work in Italy as well. In Chapter 2, we have seen how Italy's student movement evolved in the course of two years from a reform-minded constituency clamouring for improvements in course content and delivery into a frontal challenge to all forms of hierarchies and the powers of the state. By March 1968, we may recall, the entire network of Italian institutions of higher education had been rendered inoperable. Strikes, building occupations, and never-ending series of demonstrations marked the public face of all Italian towns and cities that were home to university departments. It would have been nothing short of miraculous if Italian workers had not taken notice of this chain of events and if they had remained unaffected by this spirit of university discontent. The literature on Italian labour relations and worker unrest is replete with concrete references to the inspirational impact of the student movement's practical conquests and ideological concerns. Perhaps most central for the genesis of the worker revolt was the example of the uncompromising and fearless actions by students who challenged all forms of bureaucracies and thus crucially demystified the supposedly natural superiority and necessity of hierarchical power structures propping up society and economy at large. The lessons of insubordination and revolt in lecture halls were easily transferable to the point of production. As we shall see, institutions of 'participatory' democracy, such as general assemblies open to everyone, or new forms of struggle, such as sit-ins or militant demonstrations, first popularized by activists of the Italian student movement, were rapidly adopted by workplace activists throughout the Italian state.

It is not just a coincidence that, initially, young workers in particular were in the forefront of what became a proletarian revolt. By the mid to late 1960s increasingly sharing elements of a common youth culture with their mostly middle-class generational cohort on university campuses (see Chapter 1), young workers were the primary, though by no means exclusive, conduit for the creative adaptation of radical initiatives, first played out on a grand scale by Italian students, responding to the inhospitable atmosphere of most factory or office floors. When asked whether the Italian workers' movement had been inspired by 'the grand objectives and the grand intuitions of [the student] 1968', one of the key trade union leaders of this period of Italian labour history, Bruno Trentin, responded without hesitation: 'This is certainly the case. I am referring to the antiauthoritarian messages of the student movements, their democratic practices, their attempts to reappropriate the sites of scientific learning and their efforts to construct an autonomous culture, free from the dogmas of the old ruling classes and the old ideologies of the left.' Perhaps the key lesson of the student revolt was a logical consequence of the questioning of all types of authoritarian structures. Inspired by the fearless assault on the powers of the Italian university mandarinate, the students' refusal to accept any longer the distant and unapproachable father figure of the professor, workers began to rediscover the egalitarian roots of the labour movement. And they began to practise what they learnt and liked. They began to question the undisputed authority of the foremen, the seemingly total control of section leaders, and ultimately the managerial elite. A wave of egalitarianism swept across the Italian state, which shook the foundation of the profoundly inegalitarian social order of a late industrial modern state.[67]

Never a haven of industrial peace, Italy had seen labour conflicts undergo a steady intensification ever since the mid-1950s, when the post-war wave of social unrest, begun in March 1943 when Mussolini was still in place, had reached a temporary, cold-war-induced low point. In comparison with other Western European countries—leaving aside the French strike wave of May–June 1968—Italy experienced the highest incidents of industrial unrest in terms of the numbers of conflicts, the numbers of workers involved, and the number of days lost between 1958 and 1968. Yet still the country was ill-prepared for the working-class explosions of the Hot Autumn of 1969, which catapulted Italian workers to the front ranks of social movement activists. For, in Italy, the functional equivalent to the period from mid-May to mid-June 1968 in France were the months between September and December 1969.[68] The symbolic opening shot in the eight-year period of Italian workers' push to centre stage was the 7 March 1968 general strike supported by the largest of the three major Italian trade union federations, the Communist-dominated Italian General Workers' Federation (CGIL), in favour of far-reaching reforms of old age pension provisions for all Italian workers. What was unusual about this particular action was the unexpected turnout of the rank and file, including many members of rival federations which had officially refused to support this day of action. Even the CGIL had initially supported a compromise agreement but changed its tune when faced at its Roman headquarters with an avalanche of protest resolutions emanating from local branches throughout Italy—and similarly militant reactions being voiced in dozens of provincial CGIL bodies. It seems that a grass-roots rebellion was beginning to be felt even within the CGIL which was, in 1968, generally regarded not only as the largest but also the most radical of the union confederations. One should not, of course, forget that 7 March 1968 happened to fall precisely at the high point of 'student power' and one week after the Battle of Valle Giulia in Rome.[69]

On 19 April 1968 in Valdagno, a small provincial town in the Catholic Veneto region of north-eastern Italy, located in the foothills of the Alps, an angry crowd of textile workers toppled the statue of the founder of the local dynasty of textile barons running the company town, Gaetano Marzotto. For some time already a labour conflict had been festering, and a lockout had precipitated running street battles between protestors and the authorities. Valdagno was located roughly halfway between Padua and Trento, and university students from both towns had visited to offer their support. On 19 April 1968 300 demonstrators were arrested, half of them released that very evening, and a hardcore group of 47 transferred to prison cells in Padua. All of the Valdagno 47 called Valdagno their home.[70] Valdagno was a provincial backwater. Mestre is an industrial agglomeration, located across the lagoon from its aristocratic twin, Venice. The Montedison petrochemical complex alone employed 15,000 workers in 1968. Just as had happened in Valdagno, rank-and-file workers bypassed official structures to press their local grievances. In the Porto Marghera section of Mestre, general assemblies open to all workers, whether unionized or not, mobilized the giant workforce into setting up pickets shutting down operations at the entire complex, bypassing official union channels. The July 1968 wildcat strike at Porto Marghera was also the first major instance when student activists, often belonging to the emerging far left, played a major role in influencing the course of the bitter conflict.[71] New forms of action and new organizational structures suddenly became popular in many locations at roughly the same time.

From September 1968 onwards, labour unrest at the Pirelli Bicocca rubber factory in Milan, employing 8,000 manual workers, moved to the centre of attention for labour activists and employers alike. Employing a series of innovative strike tactics, including a coordinated reduction in output (*autoriduzione*), the Pirelli factory became increasingly 'unmanageable', and permanent conflict became a characteristic feature on the factory floor. Once again, traditional union hierarchies and structures had been bypassed, and unitary base committees (CUB), including all workers, whether unionized or not, provided the organizational backbone to the ongoing unrest.[72] I will detail the structure and the functions of the CUB and other organizational innovations of the *biennio rosso* 1968–9 in Chapter 5.[73] The strikes at Marzotto, Montedison, and Pirelli were, of course, merely the tip of the iceberg. Compared with the preceding year, in 1968 the number of strikes rose from 1,016,000 to 3,206,000. The total number of hours lost rose even more dramatically: from 28,619,000 to 49,831,000.

From the spring to early autumn 1969, Turin emerged as the centre of burgeoning unrest, with the giant FIAT automotive works at the epicentre of disturbances. Yet, once again, the spiral of intensifying confrontations was increasing across all of Italy, if usually most visible in the industrial north. Then, from October to the end of 1969, Milan took centre stage again, with Pirelli making headline news. If 1968 had witnessed a massive increase in labour disputes compared with 1967, 1969 upped the ante once again. In the course of 1969 4,734,000 individuals participated in strike activities; yet the most dramatic increase occurred in the total hours lost to labour disputes: 232,881,000! Robert Lumley states that the extent of strike activity concentrated in the Hot Autumn between September and December 1969 'made it the third largest strike movement recorded in history in terms of lost working time (after, that is, the May 1968 general strike in France, and the British 1926 general strike)'.[74]

9. QUESTIONING AUTHORITY ON THE FACTORY FLOOR

Yet the drama of 1969 lay not solely in the skyrocketing of strike statistics. For 'Italian workers not only withdrew their labor on a massive scale, but challenged the organisation of work and the system of authority within the factory.'[75] The year 1969 in particular became known as 'the year of the delegate'.[76] As official trade union structures then often—though not always!—lagged behind the mood of the rank and file, groups of workers took matters into their own hands and, when discontent began to boil over, assembled at their workstations, discussed their grievances and how to pursue them, and then elected delegates to press for further action. These new forms of organization no longer relied on traditional union channels to air their concerns, but shifted decision-making powers onto the factory floor, where assemblies in individual departments—but eventually often encompassing the entire workforce of a factory—discussed and voted on the way to proceed and elected delegates to company-wide strike or unitary base committees (CUB). Given the rapid strengthening of the bargaining power of workers in Italian factories in seemingly permanent conflict at that time, the workplace delegates and related coordinating structures, initially often outside of union control, acquired enormous and unheard of powers.[77] In very many ways, of course, the Italian CUB were replicas of the Spanish CCOO, discussed at the beginning of this chapter.

To what purposes was this new-found influence put? One important objective of worker militancy concerned the equalization of wages—within factories, between neighbouring factories, and between unevenly remunerated workers in different regions of the Italian state. For instance, out of the wave of local agreements emerging from the Hot Autumn, supplementing national accords in the metal industry, an astounding 71 per cent mandated equal lump-sum wage increases for all. Combined with the drastic reduction in the array of job classifications—the latter a classic management tool to divide and rule—again within the metal industry the wage gap between the highest and the lowest job categories narrowed from 158.7 per cent (1968) to 129.7 per cent (1971) to 111.8 per cent (1975), and 71.3 per cent in 1977. The difference in wages paid to workers in the best-paid zone and the lowest-paid zone in the Italian state—along a sliding scale generally diminishing from north to south—amounting to 20 per cent before 1969, was reduced to 10 per cent in April 1969, further dropped to 5 per cent in January 1970, and was entirely eliminated by July 1972.[78]

Crucially, Italian labour conflicts went far beyond the pressure for material concessions. Rather than demanding monetary compensation for particular job assignments endangering the health and safety of the affected workforce, workplace delegates began to insist that the element of danger be removed from job assignments as much as possible. Such a move, however, demanded workforce involvement in the organization of labour at the point of production. And this is precisely what Italian workers moved towards from 1968 onwards. No one knew better than the workers involved how noxious chemicals, fumes, or high noise levels could become for the exposed workforce. They likewise were only too aware of the ill effects of monotonous labour, high intensity of labour, repetitive labour, awkward postures, or anxiety. In a series of semi-spontaneous actions, worker-controlled reduction of output became common practice in factories operating with piece-rate quotas and assembly lines. What would under normal circumstances never have got off the ground, given the context of rapidly spreading social conflict on all levels of Italian society, soon became reality in many flagship factories. An account of *autoriduzione* at the Pirelli works, for instance, notes that the factory still 'functioned with the regularity of a clock, but the tick-tock is more spaced out in time; it has a slowness that exasperates the bosses, who protest about the "irregularities" of this form of struggle. The workers, for their part, acquire consciousness of their power and learn to make the bosses dance to the rhythms of their music.'[79] The entire set of relations between workers, foremen, and managerial elite underwent tremendous changes. It was as if an entire country's workforce was finally able to breathe a collective sigh of relief.

If 1968 was the year of the CUB and 1969 the year of the *delegati*, Italy's Hot Autumn can be understood in part as a product of such semi-spontaneous and novel forms of workplace representation which were filling a gap left wide open by the lack of positive offensive actions on the part of traditional union hierarchies, the latter cautious to avoid unnecessary confrontations, a hesitancy that had arisen in part during the long years of cold war confrontations which had targeted Italy particularly hard. But, once again, Italian workers—and, crucially, even their unions—marched to a different drummer compared with many colleagues—and unions—to the west and to the north of the Alps. In the course of the intensifying social conflicts after 1968, all three trade union confederations, the Communist CGIL, the Catholic Italian Confederation of Free Trade Unions (CISL), and the social democratic Italian Federation of Labour (UIL), opened up to the innovative and militant spirit radiating upwards from the ranks. In the course of the Hot Autumn the traditional trade union confederations regained the initiative and began to eclipse the CUB.[80] But, despite protestations to the contrary emanating from the far left, at this stage of class struggle developments in the Italian state, such union recuperation of grass-roots initiatives did not translate into a moderation of conflicts. Indeed, the wave of overt challenges to the authorities of factory managements and even the state continued largely unabated for a half dozen years. First, strike-happiness continued relentlessly. The total number of strikes, which had never exceeded the 2,000 mark throughout the 1950s and which had averaged between 2,500 and 3,500 throughout the 1960s up to 1968, had jumped to 3,788 in 1969. But instead of diminishing after the concentrated explosions of the Hot Autumn, the trend continued upwards for a while: 4,162 (1970), 5,598 (1971), 4,765 (1972), 3,769 (1973), and 5,174 (1974). Data on strike participation are, if anything, even more indicative of continuing restlessness. The high water mark of 7.5 million strikers in 1969 owed much to the intensity of the last three months of that particular year. Subsequent strikes no longer occurred concentrated in a few weeks or months of any particular year; in short, there was no repeat of the particular intensity of the Hot Autumn. But here are the figures for strike participation in subsequent years: 3,722,000 (1970), 3,891,000 (1971), but then jumping to untold heights: 6,133,000 (1973), 7,824,000 (1974), and 10,717,000 in 1975! The number of hours lost due to labour conflicts parallels the developments reported above.[81] To be sure, the international economic conjuncture (oil price shock, etc.) contributed towards this explosion of unrest. But Italian strike statistics far surpass equivalent figures in other European states, once again highlighting the peculiarities of Italy.

Strike demands after the Hot Autumn of 1969 likewise retained their egalitarian thrust of the period 1968–9, resulting in an important victory in 1975 with the contractual stipulation of a vastly improved wage indexation to keep abreast of inflation. 'The Italian working class emerged as among the best protected in Western Europe against the inflation of the 1970s.' Crucially, unions began to concern themselves with issues which, elsewhere in Europe, tended to remain the exclusive terrain of politicians and parliaments. We may recall that the symbolic opening shot of the period of heightened working-class mobilization was the 7 March 1968 CGIL-led general strike for improvements in pension provisions. By February 1969, under continued pressures from the factory floor, major reforms were legislated which 'guaranteed 74% of his or her average annual wage in the five years prior to retirement' for anyone with forty years of paid employment, a level of pension provision most workers elsewhere in continental Europe could only dream of—and something which workers in the Anglo-Saxon world could not even imagine in their wildest dreams! Other trade union actions and contract negotiations concerned issues of housing policy, productive investments in Italy's impoverished south, and similar engagements in policy decisions on a national scale which resulted in further politicization of collective bargaining and, simultaneously, in the unionization of politics.[82]

Best of all—for promoters of working-class self-liberation—Italian trade unions for a time managed to integrate the radical impetus of the *biennio rosso* without compromising the decentralization of decision-making power which lay at the basis of the eruption of labour protest in 1969. The CUB for the most part disappeared in the wake of the Hot Autumn, and the *delegati*, freely elected by the entire workforce irrespective of trade union membership, were integrated into more permanent forms of representation, the factory councils (*consigli di fabbrica*). Yet, unlike similar bodies in most other European states, Italian factory councils were elected by the entirety of a given workforce, regardless of union affiliation, just as had been the case with the *delegati* earlier on. Rank-and-file workers thus retained an important measure of control and, though union federations regained significant influence from the Hot Autumn onwards, their recapturing of the initiative in labour conflicts after 1969 was in large part a reflection of the incontrovertible fact that their inner life had undergone tremendous qualitative changes. This process was most pronounced in the metalworking industry, where the three rival federations not only progressively merged their operations from 1972 onwards, but the ensuing unitary Metal Workers' Federation (FLM) then 'constituted the single most radical union in the country, wedded to egalitarianism, participatory democracy, militancy, and dreams of social revolution generated by direct action'.[83]

In sum, in Italy the process of collective and individual liberation, discussed at greater length in Chapter 5, went deeper, lasted longer and affected far more rank-and-file workers than anywhere else in Western Europe at that time. 'The rupture with traditional patterns of deference to hierarchical authority and the atmosphere of euphoria', characteristic of the spirit and the meaning of '1968', can be best studied in Italy between, roughly, 1968 and 1976. It was a period when the culture of permanent conflict and the ever-present atmosphere of strikes had become the rule and was no longer the exception.[84]

10. THE REVOLUTION OF THE CARNATIONS

Spanish workers after 1962 were instrumental in the destruction of a vicious dictatorship that had been established as a backlash to the popular conquests of the era of united and popular fronts in the mid-1930s. French workers during and after 1968 briefly imagined that it could be possible to finish the process of the destruction of the rule of privilege commenced in 1789. Italian workers, between 1969 and 1976, came closest to the spirit of 1917, with the authority of plant managers deeply shaken for a number of years. The final case study of this chapter combines various features of the national peculiarities of all of the above. Between 25 April 1974 and 25 November 1975, on the extreme south-western fringes of the European continent, Western Europe's longest-lived tyrannical regime not only crumbled overnight, but in the process an entire country went further than other European states in exuding the atmosphere of social revolutionary change. 'The Portuguese, who had been lagging behind [the rest of Europe] quite a bit, simultaneously lived through 1789, 1917, 1936 and May 1968.'[85]

The Portuguese Revolution began at 12.25 a.m on 25 April 1974, when young officers belonging to the Armed Forces Movement (MFA) launched a coordinated coup that swept away the crumbling authoritarian regime in power since 1926. Overnight, Portugal, for much of the twentieth century on the sidelines of

European history, obtained front-page news coverage across the continent, as the pent-up hopes and long-suppressed frustrations of the Portuguese population made themselves felt in open demonstrations, joyful celebrations of the arrival of democratic freedoms, and associated manifestations of their collective will to seize the moment. From the outset of the revolution in late April 1974, Portuguese workers played a prominent role. One of the largest workplaces in Portugal, the Lisnave shipyards in the capital city of Lisbon, employing 8,400 workers constructing or repairing ships, with an additional workforce of 4–5,000 in associated factories nearby, had already been the site of intermittent strike actions in pursuit of wage increases for several months prior to the unexpected coup of 25 April. On 25 and 26 April 1974 the entire Lisnave shipyard was shut down, and on 27 April approximately one thousand workers ransacked the head-quarters of the deeply compromised trade union organization set up by the authoritarian regime. While throngs of individuals massed the streets of Lisbon in an effort to dismantle the institutions of the repressive state, Lisnave workers gathered in the different sectors of this giant workplace in general assemblies, elect-ing delegates to represent the workforce, bypassing traditional regime-friendly unions, to construct the functional equivalent of the Spanish CCOO or the Italian CUB, called workers' commissions (CT) in Portugal. Indeed, it was as if Spanish labour struggles after 1962 or the Italian experience after 1968 was replicated— but within the time and space of very few days.[86]

In the first weeks after the coup, strikes were technically still illegal, but workers, smelling freedom, took matters into their own hands, and in Lisbon alone the month of May witnessed more than two hundred strikes. The new authorities, though worried about the implication of such newly found activism, were reluctant to intervene.[87] By the summer of 1974, the government became more proactive and the ongoing wave of labour disputes was increasingly met with repressive moves, including military intervention in production sites. A less-than-generous new strike law—sometimes dubbed the 'anti-strike law' in the relevant literature—passed in late August 1974 appeared to set the stage for a return to pro-employer 'normalcy'.[88] Yet, for a series of intercalated reasons which lie beyond the purview of this study, in subsequent months the Portuguese Revolution underwent a process of further radicalization, effectively laying to rest the best-made plans of a series of provisional governments that were attempting to govern unruly Portugal after 25 April 1974.

By the summer of 1974, it had also emerged that a sequence of events similar to that which had occurred at Lisnave in the immediate aftermath of the military coup was emulated in workplaces throughout the pockets of urban and industrialized Portugal. The practice of general assemblies of the entire workplace, the election of delegates, and the construction of CTs became a standard feature. Wage rises, but notably in combination with wage equalization measures, drastically reducing the wage gap between the lowest and the highest paid job categories, became central objectives of the newly formed CTs. Yet workers' commissions soon addressed concerns going far beyond normal practices of labour negotiations and disputes. After half a century of authoritarian dominance in state, society, and the point of production, workers felt it only natural that a series of purges of supporters of dictatorial rule in state and civil society under way since 25 April 1974 should be extended to workplace relations just as well. Worse yet—for the defenders of the prerogatives of property owners and their managerial elite—the demand for a purging of the most compromised managerial personnel became inextricably linked to the rapidly rising chorus of opinion asking for the removal of the most authoritarian line managers and foremen as well, regardless of their political involvement with figures belonging to the old regime. And, given the overall climate of sudden revolutionary changes, workers' demands were often heeded.[89]

It only stood to reason, then, that a spiral of radicalization began to take effect. 'New possibilities for action appeared almost daily, and initiatives often succeeded. Opportunities seized had a cumulative effect, for each new experiment or demand by one group of workers...became an example to workers elsewhere: either to be imitated directly, or to spur them on to even more audacious creativity.'[90] Soon, workers' commissions encroached even further on management prerogatives. In particular in those cases where property owners were suspected of considering disinvestment or capital flight, CTs began to keep records of the movement of capital and the shipment of goods.[91] In short, incipient forms of workers' control going beyond even the already exceptional circumstances in the Italian state after 1968 (*autoriduzione*) made inroads into another Western European state. Coming on the heels of the experience at LIP, which had served as an unifying magnet and inspiration for activists far beyond the eastern reaches of France, suddenly an entire country appeared to be in the throes of a collective endeavour to question the traditional alignment of political power and the authority over production sites.

Already in mid-June 1974, the first case of a factory takeover by its workforce with production and sales continuing, LIP-style, made headline news. The French-owned Sogantal textile factory, manufacturing jogging suits, had become contested terrain in the immediate aftermath of 25 April, when its workforce of forty-eight women demanded a wage increase. Even though the targeted increase would still have made wages hover just below the newly legislated national minimum wage, managers had refused to accede to the workers' demands. When the forty-eight women workers decided to press their claim with a slowdown of production, the owners announced on 12 June the closure of the plant. 'The workers refused to leave, continued production with the materials in stock and sold the suits to anyone who would buy.' In early August, a US-owned computer components' assembly plant, Applied Magnetics, employing 750 mostly women workers became the second Portuguese production site to experience a workplace occupation after a similar sequence of failed communication between workers and a management team opting for disinvestment and closure.[92]

The events at Sogantal and Applied Magnetics were widely advertised and soon found followers. By December 1974 more than a hundred workplaces in Portugal

were experiencing concrete applications of workers' control or operating under
outright self-management rules; by March 1975 this figure had risen to more than
two hundred concerns.[93] But the crest of the wave of movement towards forms of
self-management was reached in the summer of 1975, undoubtedly taking
advantage of heightened polarization and radicalization in society at large. 'By the
beginning of August 1975 it was estimated that some 380 factories had passed
into self-management.'[94] Looked at from a macro-economic point of view, the
socio-economic impact of *autogestion* within the contours of the overall Portuguese
economy remained rather marginal. 'Worker management has encompassed
fewer than 3 percent of all industrial firms and involved fewer than 6 percent of all
industrial workers.'[95] Yet where else in Europe—and indeed the world—could
workers' self-management be practised with impunity, and then in the context of
rising expectations in the middle of a social revolutionary process unseen in
Western Europe since the days of the Catalan Revolution in 1936?

The spirit of revolt soon began to affect non-industrial sectors of Portugal's
workforce. As late as the 1970s Portugal was still a country with a significant
workforce in agriculture. Whereas 39 per cent of Portuguese gained their
livelihood as members of the urban working class, no less than 33 per cent of
Portuguese earned their living from the land. Northern Portugal's landholding
patterns showed predominantly smallhold farmers owning their land, but vast
agricultural estates employing farm labourers with little or no land of their own
dominated most of central and southern Portugal.[96] It was in these southern
reaches of the country that the radical spirit of the Portuguese Revolution took
hold before too long. Agricultural unions were formed, and by the autumn of
1974 agricultural labourers forced employers in the Beja region to agree to a
contract which gave workers the right to establish hiring quotas overriding the
designs of regional proprietors. 'The unions' assertion of the right to impose
hiring quotas was unheard-of in Portugal, especially in a sector where unions had
not even existed six months before.' This important manifestation of agricultural
workers' control was soon extended to other regions.[97] In the winter of 1974–5,
the movement entered a further stage of development with outright land occupations replacing the ever-increasing encroachments by agricultural unions on
managerial rights. And, after the first cases of land occupations encountered little
effective opposition, the most concerted movement towards forms of workers'
self-management, far exceeding parallel processes in Portugal's urban industrial
base, began to get under way. 'More than 23 percent of Portugal's farmland
changed hands in less than twelve months, and every occupied hectare was farmed
and managed collectively.' The same process of the institutionalization of forms
of participatory democracy showcased elsewhere in Europe in this period of
heightened social movement activity became a ubiquitous feature of Portugal's
collective farms. General assemblies, egalitarian practices, the vanishing of many
forms of deference *vis-à-vis* all forms of hierarchy became standard features of
Portugal's collectivized agricultural establishments.[98]

No other European state experienced quite the same level of workers' experimentation with new forms of managerial control as did Portugal. No sector of the Portuguese economy experienced the revolution of everyday life to the same extent as the landless labourers on central and southern Portuguese landed estates, who believed that they had become the new shapers of their destiny by the autumn of 1975. The cycle of worker mobilization opened up in the valley of the Turón in Asturias in northern Spain thirteen years earlier had come full circle back onto the Iberian peninsula. But, whereas in the spring of 1962 Asturian miners had primarily engaged in defensive operations within the overall context of a powerful dictatorship which was to govern Spain for another fourteen long years, Portuguese agricultural labourers in the Alentejo operated within the context of a radicalizing regime, which seemed to express and facilitate—rather than repress—the desires of a long-oppressed urban and agricultural workforce.

NOTES

1. Sheelagh Ellwood, 'The Working Class under the Franco Régime', in Paul Preston (ed.), *Spain in Crisis: The Evolution and Decline of the Franco Régime* (Hassocks: Harvester, 1976), 171.
2. The most detailed narrative of the Asturian strike wave can be found in José Antonio Biescas and Manuel Tuñón de Lara, *España bajo la dictadura franquista (1931–1975)* (Barcelona: Labor, 1980), 340. The official rationale given for the dismissal of the seven miners at the Nicolasa mine is reported in Erich Rathfelder, Anna Stein, and Klaus Vogel, *'Alle oder keiner!': Comisiones Obreras—neue Arbeiterbewegung in Spanien* (Berlin: Rotbuch, 1976), 42.
3. A comprehensive survey of the function and activities of the *jurados de empresas* can be consulted in Jon Amsden, *Collective Bargaining and Class Conflict in Spain* (London: Weidenfeld & Nicolson, 1972), 105–28.
4. This was certainly the case during the 1970 wildcat strike at the Michelin works in Sint-Pieters-Leeuw, Belgium. I thank Rik Hemmerijckx for this intriguing piece of information, from a conversation with this author on 1 Feb. 2006.
5. Biescas and Tuñón de Lara, *España*, 340.
6. The higher end figure is reported in both Rathfelder *et al.*, *'Alle oder keiner'*, 43, and *Le Commissione operaie spagnole: Analisi e documenti di una originale e nuova esperienza di democrazia operaia* (Turin: Tommaso Musolini, 1969), 29. The spread of the strike movement beyond Asturias is best portrayed in Biescas and Tuñón de Lara, *España*, 340–2, who also report the lower end figure for strike participants on p. 342.
7. On the issues surrounding the personal intervention of José Solís, see Biescas and Tuñón de Lara, *España*, 342–3, and Ramón García Piñeiro and Francisco Erice Sebares, 'La reconstrucción de la nueva vanguardia obrera y las Comisiones Obreras (1958–1977)', in David Ruiz (ed.), *Historia de Comisiones Obreras (1958–1988)* (Madrid: Siglo XXI, 1994), 146–7.
8. Biescas and Tuñón de Lara, *España*, 343.
9. This process is best described in García Piñeiro and Erice Sebares, 'Nueva vanguardia', 148–62.

10. José Maravall, *Dictatorship and Political Dissent: Workers and Students in Franco's Spain* (London: Tavistock, 1978), 31.

11. Amsden, *Collective Bargaining*, 116.

12. None other than the most famous national spokesperson of the CCOO, Nicolás Sartorius, makes this claim in his *El resurgir del movimiento obrero* (Barcelona: Laia, 1976), 50. Most historians repeat Sartorius's claim.

13. Robert M. Fishman, *Working-Class Organisation and the Return to Democracy in Spain* (Ithaca, NY: Cornell University Press, 1990), 96. Thus, for instance, Joe Foweraker's bold assertion—'Contrary to the pervasive myth of La Camocha, the historical evidence suggests that the commissions first appeared in El Marco de Jerez'—should be taken with a grain of salt; see his *Making Democracy in Spain: Grass-roots Struggle in the South, 1955–1975* (Cambridge: Cambridge University Press, 1989), 99.

14. See Pedro Ibarra Güell and Chelo García Marroquín, 'De la primavera de 1956 a lehona 1978: Comisiones obreras de Euzkadi', in Ruiz (ed.), *Historia*, 116, and Fernando Claudín, 'El nuevo movimiento obrero español', in Lucio Magri, Rossana Rossanda, Fernando Claudin, and Anibal Quijano, *Movimiento obrero y acción política* (Mexico City: Era, 1975), 102. Fernando Claudín dates the Vizcaya province-wide CCOO to '1962–63'. Fernando Almendros Morcillo, Enrique Jiménez-Asenjo, Francisco Pérez Amorés, and Eduardo Rojo Torrecilla, *El sindicalismo de clase en España (1939–1977)* (Barcelona: Península, 1978), 62, claim 1963 as the year when the Vizcaya province CCOO, including the Greater Bilbao area, was founded.

15. Sebastian Balfour, *Dictatorship, Workers and the City: Labour in Greater Barcelona since 1939* (Oxford: Clarendon Press, 1989), 69–71.

16. Almendros Morcillo *et al.*, *Sindicalismo de clase*, 62, date this further qualitative and quantitative expansion of the network of CCOO to 1964; Marco Calamai, *La lotta di classe sotto il franchismo: Le Commissione Operaie* (Bari: De Donato, 1971), 41, mentions 1965 as the year of cross-provincial contacts on a regular scale.

17. Calamai, *Lotta di classe*, 43, gives Jan. 1966 as the date of this document; Almendros Morcillo *et al.*, *Sindicalismo de clase*, 45, report 31 Mar. 1966 as the date of publication.

18. Calamai, *Lotta di classe*, 52; Almendros Morcillo *et al.*, *Sindicalismo de clase*, 47.

19. Both José María Maravall, *El desarollo económico y la clase obrera* (Barcelona: Ariel, 1970), 103, and Ellwood, 'Working Class', 173–4, point to this important post-1962 move towards the expanding sectors of the Spanish economy as centres of labour conflict; all citations in this paragraph are taken from Ellwood, 'Working Class', 174.

20. Ellwood provides useful data on labour conflicts in Madrid in her 'Working Class', 174–5. Maravall, *Political Dissent*, provides some background to Madrid's rise to industrial fame and associated forms of labour militancy on pp. 57–9, citation on p. 58. Additional data on Madrid's top performance as centre of conflicts in 1966 and 1967 also readily emerges from information provided in Maravall, *Desarollo*, 144, 146, and 207.

21. On the particularly pronounced militancy and the political attitudes of bank workers in Madrid and elsewhere in Spain, see Maravall, *Political Dissent*, 61–2, and José Félix Tezanos, *Estructura de clases en la España actual* (Madrid: Cuadernos para el diálogo, 1975), 80–3. For unrest within the Spanish civil service, see Raymond Carr and Juan Pablo Fusi Aizpurna, *Spain: Dictatorship to Democracy* (London: Allen & Unwin, 1979), 84.

22. Maravall, *Political Dissent*, 54–5, is particularly good at highlighting the unusually politicized dimension of labour conflict in the Basque country.

23. Citations taken from Maravall, *Political Dissent*, 37–8 and 35–6.

24. See the relevant tables in Maravall, *Desarollo*, 106 and 124.

25. See Max Gallo, *Spain under Franco: A History* (London: George Allen & Unwin, 1973), 349, which includes the citation; but note also Calamai, *Lotta di classe*, 49, who concurs with Gallo's observation cited above.

26. On the National Day of Action of 27 Oct. 1967, see Calamai, *Lotta di classe*, 53–4; Gallo, *Spain*, 352, the latter again the source for the citation; and Balfour, *Dictatorship*, 94–5. The decline in strike activity for 1968 is reported by all available statistics; on this see, for instance, Biescas and Tuñón de Lara, *España*, 367–8, or Maravall, *Political Dissent*, 33.

27. For the weakened position of the CCOO which, however, did little to alter the dynamic of labour unrest, see Maravall, *Political Dissent*, 33–4, and Balfour, *Dictatorship*, 164. On the national state of emergency, which not only further politicized Spanish public opinion but alerted the international community to the worsening political climate in Franco's Spain, see Calamai, *Lotta di classe*, 60, and Gallo, *Spain*, 364–6.

28. Ellwood, 'Working Class', 179.

29. Almendros Morcillo *et al.*, *Sindicalismo de clase*, 52.

30. The 18 Oct. 1971 battle of the SEAT automotive plant is best described in Balfour, *Dictatorship*, 173–6, who notes that, symptomatically, 'the SEAT workers had little tradition of shop-floor organisation', see p. 173 of his informative text.

31. Ibid. 192.

32. For area general strikes 1972–4, see Almendros Morcillo *et al.*, *Sindicalismo de clase*, 54–5; for similar instances between 1973 and 1976, see Maravall, *Political Dissent*, 36–7 and 39, citation taken from pp. 36–7; Balfour, *Dictatorship*, 205–10, furnishes an in-depth description of the July 1974 area general strike in Baix Llobregat.

33. On the Assemblea de Catalunya, see Balfour, *Dictatorship*, 193–4, citations on p. 193.

34. Note that Pérez Díaz lists the number of *days*, not hours, lost to strikes! Franco's death in November 1975 thus was a catalyst in further heating up an already out-of-control situation. For the number of hours lost in Spain up to 1975, see Maravall, *Political Dissent*, 33; for the citation, see Víctor Pérez Díaz, *The Return of Civil Society: The Emergence of Democratic Spain* (Cambridge, Mass: Harvard University Press, 1993), 237. The figures for the comparative amount of wage earners in France and Spain are taken from Pérez Díaz, *Civil Society*, 326.

35. Raoul Vaneigem, *The Revolution of Everyday Life* (London: Rebel Press, 2003), 67–8.

36. Strike statistics for 1958–67 are taken from Werner Goldschmidt, 'Frankreich', in Detlev Albers, Werner Goldschmidt, and Paul Oehlke, *Klassenkämpfe in Westeuropa: Frankreich, Italien, Großbritannien* (Reinbek: Rowohlt, 1971), 42.

37. Information on the events in Caen in late Jan. and early Feb. 1968 is taken from Michael Seidman, *The Imaginary Revolution: Parisian Students and Workers in 1968* (New York: Berghahn, 2004), 163, and, above all, Gérard Lange, 'La Liaison étudiants–ouvriers à Caen', in René Mouriaux, Annick Percheron, Antoine Prost, and Danielle Tartakowshy (eds.), *1968: Exploration du mai français*, i. *Terrains* (Paris: L'Harmattan, 1992), 217–36, and Gérard Lange, 'L'Exemple caennais', in Geneviève Dreyfus-Armand and Laurent Gerverau (eds.), *Mai 68: Les Mouvements étudiants en France et dans le monde* (Nanterre: BDIC, 1988), 205–13.

38. On the political itinerary of the CFDT, the three central reference works are Frank Georgi, *L'Invention de la CFDT, 1957–1970: Syndicalisme, catholicisme et politique dans la France de l'expansion* (Paris: L'Atelier, 1995); Pierre Cours-Saliès, *La CFDT: Un passé porteur d'avenir. Pratiques syndicales et débats stratégiques depuis 1946* (Montreuil: La Brèche, 1988); and Hervé Hamon and Patrick Rotman, *La Deuxième Gauche: Histoire intellectuelle et politique de la CFDT* (Paris: Ramsay, 1982).

39. These are the words used by the *Le Monde* correspondent at that time, Jean Lacouture, a well-known historian and biographer of, amongst other figures, Charles De Gaulle, in a dispatch sent from Caen and published on 7 Feb. 1968, entitled 'De la grève à la jacquerie ouvrière', cited in Lange, 'Liaisons', 227.

40. Louis Vos, 'Rebelse generaties: Studentenprotest van de jaren zestig', in Louis Vos *et al.*, *De stoute jaren: Studentenprotest in de jaren zestig* (Tielt: Lannoo, 1988), 31.

41. The events of Nanterre have been retold many times. Some of the more insightful and comprehensive studies are Jean-Pierre Duteuil, *Nanterre 1965–66–67–68: Vers le Mouvement du 22 mars* (Paris: Acratie, 1988); Mouvement du 22 mars, *Ce n'est qu'un début, continuons le combat* (Paris: Maspero, 1968); Alain Touraine, 'Les Enragés de Nanterre', in *Le Mouvement de mai ou le communisme utopique* (Paris: Le Livre de Poche, 1998), 102–30; Adrien Dansette, *Mai 1968* (Paris: Plon, 1971), 56–86; Dreyfus-Armand and Gerverau (eds.), *Mai 68*, 100–35; and, last but not least, Ingrid Gilcher-Holtey, *'Die Phantasie an die Macht': Mai 68 in Frankreich* (Frankfurt: Suhrkamp, 1995), 115–38 and 154–63. The citation is taken from Patrick Seale and Maureen McConville, *French Revolution 1968* (Harmondsworth: Penguin, 1968), 30.

42. Accounts of events on the Left Bank of Paris between 3 and 11 May 1968 are legion. Good places to start are Daniel Singer, *Prelude to Revolution: France in May 1968* (Cambridge, Mass: South End Press, 2002), 115–42; Dansette, *Mai 1968*, 87–130; Seidman, *Imaginary Revolution*, 91–118; Seale and McConville, *French Revolution*, 71–89; Gilcher-Holtey, *Phantasie*, 177–209; and Hervé Hamon and Patrick Rotman, *Génération*, i. *Les Années de rêves* (Paris: Seuil, 1987), 447–88. For a map detailing the location of the most prominent barricades, located in an area flanked by the Boulevard Saint-Michel to the west, the Rue Mouffetard to the east, the Panthéon in the north, and the Hôpital du Val-de-Grace in the south, see René Viénet, *Enragés et situationnistes dans le mouvement des occupations* (Paris: Gallimard, 1968), 58. Starting on 6 May, the student uprising rapidly spread outside of Paris to encompass all French institutes of higher learning. Interestingly, there appears to be thus far no comprehensive study of the student movement of May 1968 outside of Paris, though there are plenty of individual case studies.

43. On the flurry of negotiations between 9 and 11 May, the most detailed source is Georgi, *La CFDT*, 495–7, with additional information in Gilcher-Holtey, *Phantasie*, 259–61, and Seidman, *Imaginary Revolution*, 164. Force Ouvrière was the most important union federation to belatedly join the worker-student united front.

44. On Pompidou's last-minute plea for a truce, see Singer, *Prelude*, 143–7, citations on p. 146; Gilcher-Holtey, *Phantasie*, 262–4; and Seale and McConville, *French Revolution*, 89–91.

45. On the organization of the demonstration in Paris, see Georgi, *CFDT*, 498–501; Gilcher-Holtey, *Phantasie*, 264–9; and Singer, *Prelude*, 147–51, citation on pp. 147–8. On demonstrations in provincial France, see Danielle Tartakowsky, 'Les Manifestations de mai–juin 68 en province', in Mouriaux *et al.* (eds.), *Terrains*, 148–50. On the strikes of 13 May in Paris, see Seidman, *Imaginary Revolution*, 164–6; curiously enough, little

substantive information appears to be available in comprehensive fashion on 13 May strike activity in provincial France.

46. Yannick Guin, *La Commune de Nantes* (Paris: Maspero, 1969), 58. A marvellous account by one of the workers in the affected factory can be consulted in François Le Madec, *L'Aubepine de mai: Chronique d'une usine occupée. Sud-Aviation Nantes 1968* (Nantes: Centre de Documentation du Mouvement et du Travail, 1988). The company director remained 'sequestered' on company property until 29 May.

47. For the events at Renault-Cléon, see the book collectively edited by activists at Cléon, *Notre arme c'est la grève* (Paris: Maspero, 1968).

48. For the spread of strikes throughout every administrative district of France see, amongst others, Gilcher-Holtey, *Phantasie*, 285–97; Seidman, *Imaginary Revolution*, 166–73; and Singer, *Prelude*, 152–85, citation on p. 157. For informed estimates on the total number of strikers, see Gérard Adam, 'Étude statistique des grèves de mai–juin 1968', *Revue française de science politique*, 20/1 (Feb. 1970), 105–19, who reports 6–7.5 million strikers on p. 118; but note also Jacques Kergoat, 'Sous la plage, la grève', in Antoine Artous (ed.), *Retours sur mai* (Paris: La Brèche, 1988), who suggests (p. 62) that between 6 and 8 million individuals participated in the work stoppage. For an evocative description of how the weeks-long general strike affected relatively insulated social milieux in remote corners of rural France, see the film by Louis Malle, *Milou en mai* (Orion Pictures, 1989).

49. Seidman, *Imaginary Revolution*, 167 and 169.

50. Sabine Erbès-Seguin, 'Militants et travailleurs: Organisation des relations dans la grève', in Pierre Dubois *et al.*, *Grèves revendicatives ou grèves politiques? Acteurs, pratiques, sens du mouvement de mai* (Paris: Anthropos, 1971), 262–4, citations on pp. 262 and 264. This collection of analyses of the May/June 1968 strike wave in France, a product of the fertile French tradition of industrial sociology quite popular at the time, remains the most informative and detailed assessment of various important aspects related to workers' participation in the social movement begun by students in early May.

51. Cited in Albert Detraz, 'Le Mouvement ouvrier, la CFDT, et l'idée d'autogestion', in Edmond Maire, Alfred Krumnow, and Albert Detraz, *La CFDT et l'autogestion* (Paris: Cerf, 1975), 77. Michael Seidman is, of course, aware of the CFDT's more 'democratic' image compared with the top-down functioning of the CGT, alluding to the 16 May document on p. 175, but in the vast bulk of his empirically rich volume, he never substantively distinguishes CFDT practice from CGT operations.

52. These are the final words of the concluding paragraph of Seidman, *Imaginary Revolution*, 282.

53. Erbès-Seguin, 'Militants', 307.

54. See, for instance, the case of middle-level managers in their forties, 'lugging their mattresses into their workplace, which had seen no form of agitation for twenty years, unable to explain what has happened to them once the seeming madness had drifted away', reported in Josette Blanchère *et al.*, *Les Événements de mai–juin 1968 vus à travers cent entreprises* (Paris: Centre National d'Information pour la Productivité des Entreprises, 1968), 18.

55. David Caute, *The Year of the Barricades: A Journey through 1968* (New York: Harper & Row, 1988), 236.

56. Blanchère *et al.*, *Cent entreprises*, 31.

57. Ibid. 26.

58. Pierre Dubois, 'Les Pratiques de mobilisation et d'opposition', in Dubois *et al.*, *Grèves politiques?*, 361, 368–9.

59. Tartakowsky, 'Manifestations', 148.

60. Olivier Kourchid and Cornelia Eckert, 'Les Mineurs des houillères en grève: L'Insertion dans un mouvement national', in Mouriaux *et al.* (eds.), *Terrains*, 99.

61. Cited in Georges Ribeill, 'SNCF: Une grève dans la tradition de la corporation du rail', in Mouriaux *et al.* (eds.), *Terrains*, 137.

62. For early CFDT-led discussions beginning in the mid-1960s, see Georgi, *CFDT*, 451–86; for the relevance of self-management as a theme for serious discussion in 24.5 per cent of 182 surveyed factories in the *nord*, with some workforces beginning to translate such desires into reality, see Dubois, 'Pratiques de mobilisation', 407–10. For an overall assessment of the role of *autogestion* in the French strike wave of 1968, see Frank Georgi, ' "Vivre demain dans nos luttes d'aujourd'hui": Le Syndicat, la grève et l'autogestion en France (1968–1988)', in Geneviève Dreyfus-Armand, Robert Frank, Marie-Françoise Lévy, and Michelle Zancarini-Fournel (eds.), *Les Années 68: Le Temps de la contestation* (Brussels: Complexe, 2000), 401–3; for one of the few exceptional cases of some form of *autogestion* occurring in 1968, see the case study by Danièle Kergoat, *Bulledor ou l'histoire d'une mobilisation ouvrière* (Paris: Seuil, 1973).

63. Pierre Dubois, 'New Forms of Industrial Conflict', in Colin Crouch and Alessandro Pizzorno (eds.), *The Resurgence of Class Conflict in Western Europe since 1968*, ii. *Comparative Analyses* (London: Macmillan, 1978), 2.

64. Serge Mallet, 'L'Après-mai 1968: Grèves pour le contrôle ouvrier', *Sociologie du Travail*, 12/3 (July–September 1970), 307–27.

65. Pierre Dubois, Claude Durand, and Sabine Erbès-Seguin, 'The Contradictions of French Trade Unionism', in Colin Crouch and Alessandro Pizzorno (eds.), *The Resurgence of Class Conflict in Western Europe since 1968*, i. *National Studies* (London: Macmillan, 1978), 61–5, citation on p. 64.

66. The information on the exemplary struggle at LIP is taken from Charles Piaget, *LIP* (Paris: Stock, 1973); Gaston Bordet, 'Les Lip: Rien ne se fait bien sans passion', in Claude Neuschwander and Gaston Bordet, *LIP, vingt ans après: 1973–1993: Propos sur le chômage* (Paris: Syros, 1993), 29–123; and Arno Münster, *Der Kampf bei LIP: Arbeiterselbstverwaltung in Frankreich* (Berlin: Rotbuch, 1974).

67. The positive impact of the Italian *movimento studentesco* on working-class communities has been highlighted, for instance, in Emilio Reyneri, 'Il "maggio strisciante": L'Inizio della mobilitazione operaia', in Alessandro Pizzorno, Emilio Reyneri, Marino Regini, and Ida Regalia, *Lotte operaie e sindacato: Il ciclo 1968–1972 in Italia* (Bologna: Il Mulino, 1978), 74–5; Marino Regini and Emilio Reyneri, *Lotte operaie e organizazzione del lavoro* (Padua: Marsilio, 1971), 88–91, who also draw attention to the link, made equally explicit in countless other studies, between the early prominence of young workers in Italian labour struggles of that era and their affinity for the values and the methods of the *movimento studentesco*; Bruno Trentin, *Autunno caldo: Il Secondo biennio rosso 1968–1969* (Rome: Riuniti, 1999), 63–7, 77–9, and 107–8, citation on p. 107. For one of many local studies reporting student–worker interaction, see Fabrizio Billi, 'Le lotte operaie e il sindacato a Bologna nel '67–'69', in Carmelo Adagio, Fabrizio Billi, Andrea Rapini, and Simona Urso, *Tra immaginazione*

e programmazione: Bologna di fronte al '68: materiali per una storia del '68 a Bologna (Milan: Punto Rosso, 1998), 71–4. On the overall context of student–worker interaction in Italy, see Marica Tolomelli, *'Repressiv getrennt' oder 'organisch verbündet': Studenten und Arbeiter 1968 in der Bundesrepublik Deutschland und Italien* (Opladen: Leske & Budrich, 2001), esp. pp. 202–31. On one of the many specific structures set up by students to influence factory struggles, see Liliana Lanzardo, *Cronaca della Commissione operaia del Movimento studentesco torinese: Dicembre 1967–maggio 1968* (Pistoia: Centro di documentazione, 1997).

68. A graph showing an almost continual increase in labour unrest in the Italian state from the mid-1950s up to 1976—with a clear temporary boost in 1969—is reproduced in Ida Regalia, Marino Regini, and Emilio Reyneri, 'Labour Conflicts and Industrial Relations in Italy', in Crouch and Pizzorno (eds.), *National Studies*, 105. Comparative strike statistics for five Western European states between 1958 and 1973 can be found in Dubois, 'Industrial Conflict', 2.

69. For one representative assessment of the meaning of the 7 Mar. 1968 general strike, see Robert Lumley, *States of Emergency: Cultures of Revolt from 1968 to 1978* (London: Verso, 1990), 169–70. For information on grass-roots pressure behind the CGIL decision to call the general strike, see Trentin, *Autunno caldo*, 79.

70. See Lumley, *Emergency*, 173–4; Guido Crainz, *Il paese mancato: Dal miracolo economico agli anni ottanta* (Rome: Donzelli, 2003), 328–9; and, in greatest detail, Giuseppe Bianchi *et al.*, 'Il conflitto alla Marzotto', in *Grande impresa e conflitto industriale* (Rome: Coincs, 1970), 113–38, who follow this conflict up to 1969.

71. On the events in Porto Marghera, Mestre, see above all Cesco Chinello, *Sindacato, PCI, movimenti negli anni sessanta: Porto Marghera, Venezia, 1955–1970* (Milan: Franco Angeli, 1996), ii. 616–40.

72. On Pirelli as the most visible centre of Italian labour unrest in autumn and winter 1968–9, see Lumley, *Emergency*, 181–96; Giuseppe Bianchi *et al.*, 'Il conflitto alla Pirelli', in *Grande Impresa*, 65–111; but above all Marianella Sclavi, 'Pirelli Bicocca di Milano ('68–'69)', in her *Lotta di classe e organizzazione operaia* (Milan: Gabriele Mazzotta, 1974), 33–179. Marianella Sclavi was a graduate of Trento's Sociology Department.

73. *Biennio rosso*, the two red years, is the term originally bestowed upon the period of radical activism in northern Italy in 1919–20. Given the turbulence of the student-dominated year of 1968, followed by the proletarian Hot Autumn 1969, the same term has frequently been applied to the latter period as well.

74. Italian strike statistics are taken from table 1 in Crainz, *Paese mancato*, 47. Evocative descriptions of events in Turin and Milan can be read in Lumley, *Emergency*, 207–16 (Turin) and 217–41 (Milan); citation on p. 167. On Turin in 1969, see also the two monographs by Diego Giachetti, *Il giorno più longo: La rivolta di Corso Traiano: Torino 3 luglio 1969* (Pisa: BFS, 1997), and Diego Giachetti and Marco Scavino, *La FIAT in mani agli operai: L'autunno caldo del 1969* (Pisa: BFS, 1999). For a richly detailed overall description of labour unrest in Italy between Mar. 1968 and Dec. 1969, see Crainz, *Paese mancato*, 326–62. A good chronological discussion of the strikes during the Hot Autumn of September through Dec.1969 is Detlev Albers, 'Italien', in Albers, *et al.* 152–61.

75. Lumley, *Emergency*, 167.

76. Anna Libera, *Italie: Les fruits amers du compromis historique* (Paris: La Brèche, 1978), 202.

77. The literature on *delegati* is extensive, but see Rainer Zoll, *Partizipation oder Delegation: Gewerkschaftliche Betriebspolitik in Italien und in der Bundesrepublik Deutschland* (Frankfurt: EVA, 1981), 90–115, and, above all, Roberto Aglieta, Giuseppe Bianchi, and Pietro Merli-Brandini, *I delegati operai: Ricerca su nuove forme di rappresentanza operaia* (Rome: Coines, 1970), for solid and informative surveys. An evocative photo of a general assembly of workers, in this case in the main courtyard at Turin's Mirafiori FIAT plant, is included in Joanne Barkan, *Visions of Emancipation: The Italian Workers' Movement since 1945* (New York: Praeger, 1984), 84.

78. On the victories of egalitarian wage demands, see, for instance, Regini and Reyneri, *Lotte operaie*, 73–84, and Marino Regini, *I dilemmi del sindacato: Conflitto e partecipazione negli anni settanta e ottanta* (Bologna: Il Mulino, 1981), 98–102. The concrete data mentioned in the text are taken from Libera, *Italie*, 205–6.

79. Again, the literature is replete with references to the ubiquity of such liberatory processes; see, for instance, Regini and Reyneri, *Lotte operaie*, 84–7; Regalia, 'Rappresentanza operaia e sindacato: Il mutamento di un sistema di relazioni industriali', in Pizzorno *et al.*, *Il ciclo 1968–1972*, 263–7; Regini, *I dilemmi*, 103–10; Dominique Grisoni and Hugues Portelli, *Les Luttes ouvrières en Italie (1960–1976)* (Paris: Aubier Montaigne, 1976), 118–22; and Lumley, *Emergency*, 185 and 189–91, citation taken from p. 189.

80. On trade union prominence during the Hot Autumn, see, for instance, Lumley, *Emergency*, 230, 243, and 247. Gino Bedani, *Politics and Ideology in the Italian Workers' Movement: Union Development and the Changing Role of the Catholic and Communist Subcultures in Postwar Italy* (Oxford: Berg, 1995), 161 and *passim*, is particularly good at pointing out the process of radicalization in Catholic working-class milieux and the CISL. On the Hot Autumn of 1969 as the beginning of the end of the flowering of the CUB, see the specific statements to this effect by Zoll, *Partizipation*, 96, and Giuseppe Bianchi, Franco Frigo, Pietro Merli Brandini, and Alberto Merolla, *I CUB: Comitati unitari di base* (Rome: Coines, 1971), 17.

81. Data taken from Marco Revelli, 'Movimenti sociali e spazio politico', in Francesco Barbagallo (ed.), *Storia dell'Italia repubblicana*, ii. *La trasformazione dell'Italia: Sviluppi e squilibri*, 2: *Istituzioni, movimenti, culture* (Turin: Einaudi, 1995), 452–3 Marco Revelli inexplicably omits data for 1972 from his narrative account.

82. Bedani, *Politics and Ideology*, *passim*, is, once again, particularly insightful on the interweaving of market and political strategies of Italian unions between 1968 and 1975. But see esp. Miriam Golden, *Labor Divided: Austerity and Working-Class Politics in Contemporary Italy* (Ithaca, NY: Cornell University Press, 1988), *passim*, with the citation on the impact of wage indexation taken from p. 65 of her work, whose first half, despite its misleading title and subtitle, is entirely devoted to a description and analysis of gains and conquests up to 1976 in Italy's all-important metalworking industries. The citation on the 1969 pension reform is taken from Paul Ginsborg, *A History of Contemporary Italy: Society and Politics 1943–1988* (London: Penguin, 1990), 328.

83. The most important study emphasizing the decentralization and democratization of Italian unions at that time remains Golden, *Labour Divided*, which focuses entirely on the activity and structures of the federation which had been most affected by the spirit of '1968', the FLM; citation taken from p. 21. Italian unions' adoption of the modus operandi of the *delegati* of the 1968–9 period into the newly created structures of the *consigli di fabbrica* is well-described by Zoll, *Partizipation*, 109–15. The same process

is also described, though with a decided emphasis on the negative consequences of union recuperation of labour conflict initiatives for rank-and-file participation, in Regini, *I dilemmi*, 69–74, and Marino Regini, 'Come e perchè cambiano la logica dell'organizazzione sindacale e i comportamenti della base', in Pizzorno *et al.*, *Il ciclo 1968–1972*, 125–31.

84. By far the most thoughtful reflection on the overall lessons and the impact of Italian labour movement culture between 1968 and 1976/8 can be read with great profit in Aris Accornero, *La parabola del sindacato: Ascesa e declina di una cultura* (Bologna: Il Mulino, 1992). But see also Regini, 'La logica', 151–75, citation taken from p. 151.

85. These are the words of Marcel Niedergang, writing in *Le Monde* on 26–7 May 1974, reporting on the events of the toppling of Portugal's almost fifty-year-old dictatorship; cited in Gérard Filoche, *Printemps portugais* (Paris: Actéon, 1984), 17.

86. On the proceedings at Portugal's premier industrial workplace, the Lisnave shipyard, see Filoche, *Printemps*, 44–7.

87. On the May 1974 strike wave, see John Hammond, *Building Popular Power: Workers' and Neighborhood Movements in the Portuguese Revolution* (New York: Monthly Review Press, 1988), 78.

88. Developments in summer 1974 are succinctly summarized in Filoche, *Printemps*, 224–5; for a detailed description of some viciously fought labour disputes in the summer of 1974, see Phil Mailer, *Portugal: The Impossible Revolution* (London: Solidarity, 1977), 107–16. On pp. 116–20, Mailer discusses what he terms 'the Anti-Strike Law and the resurgence of the Right'.

89. On the spreading functions of CTs, see Hammond, *Popular Power*, 77–81 and 98–105.

90. Hammond, *Popular Power*, 105.

91. Again, this process is best described in Hammond, *Popular Power*, 102–5.

92. Hammond, *Popular Power*, 82–3, citation on p. 82.

93. Data taken from Mailer, *Portugal*, 145.

94. Ibid. 247.

95. Nancy Bermeo, 'Worker Management in Industry: Reconciling Representative Government and Industrial Democracy in a Polarised Society', in Lawrence S. Graham and Douglas L. Wheeler (eds.), *In Search of Modern Portugal: The Revolution and its Consequences* (Madison: University of Wisconsin Press, 1983), 181–2.

96. For a statistical breakdown of Portuguese employment patterns, see Mailer, *Portugal*, 68.

97. Hammond, *Popular Power*, 115–16, citation on p. 116.

98. For a table detailing the spread of collectivization in the course of 1975 in three central and representative provinces, see Nancy Bermeo, *The Revolution within the Revolution: Workers' Control in Rural Portugal* (Princeton: Princeton University Press, 1986), 36, citation on p. 5. A more detailed discussion of the psychological impact of workers' self-management on Portugal's vast agricultural labour force will be reserved for Ch. 5.

4

Left, Left, Left: The Old, the New, and the Far Left

1. THE SUEZ CRISIS AND ITS AFTERMATH

'Tuesday, October 30, 1956. A date that will long be remembered.' Thus are the opening lines of the opening chapter in a book co-authored by a lifelong spokesperson for the British Labour Party's left-wing tendency, Michael Foot, and Mervyn Jones, who had dropped out of the British Communist Party in 1953 and soon became an early spokesperson for the British new left. 'In the Sinai desert, it was half past six in the evening; a warm day was ending in the sharpness that comes with twilight. It had been the first day of war. The Israeli Army had swept across the Egyptian border at dusk the night before.'[1] The authors continued: 'In Budapest it was half past five. The rebellion that had broken out exactly a week before seemed triumphant; Russian troops were moving out of the city and, many dared to hope, out of the country.'[2]

The Suez Crisis and the Hungarian Revolution, for several days running, competed for headline news around the world. No one following those turbulent events could have known or predicted that these seemingly unrelated incidents were to provide two catalysts for the most profound rearrangements of the European left since the heady days of 1917–20. For out of the international crises associated with the year 1956 arose a promising challenge to the traditional left. Both constituent parts of what became known as the old left, social democracy and communism, emerged badly tarnished from this sequence of events. In the aftermath of the twin crises of 1956, a new left arose. International communism had badly compromised itself by its support for the bloody Soviet suppression of the Hungarian Revolution in November 1956, but international social democracy had similarly exposed itself by its support for—or lack of critical distance to—the Suez Crisis, which soon was characterized as a naked defence of Western imperial powers.

Rather than trace the prehistory of the Suez Crisis here, it may suffice to highlight the decision of the Egyptian government on 26 July 1956 to nationalize the Suez Canal which had been operated by a private consortium of imperial origins up to that point. This Egyptian move, needless to say, did not please the Western powers, and the Suez Crisis quickly intensified in the second half of 1956. The first military moves against Egypt, however, were undertaken by the

Israeli proxy state. 'The attack began at the prearranged zero hour of 5 pm [on 29 October] with the dropping of 395 paratroopers at the Parker Memorial to the east of the Mitla pass, forty-five miles from the town of Suez and 156 miles from the Israeli border.'[3] The commander of these troops was none other than the young Ariel Sharon. But the imperial powers did not wait with their own contributions for very long. To return to Michael Foot and Mervyn Jones's narrative of the troubles of 30 October 1956: 'In London it was half past four. All day, as at every time of crisis, a small knot of anxious people had stood outside 10 Downing Street.... Those who drifted across to the Foreign Office observed the arrival of two ambassadors obeying an urgent summons—the Egyptian at 4:15, the Israeli at 4:25', and five minutes later the British Foreign Minister 'Sir Anthony Eden spoke amid an attentive silence' to the assembled members of parliament in Westminster just down the street. After a few preliminaries, he announced that the great powers with the greatest stake in the fate of the freshly expropriated Suez Company, Great Britain and France, had urged Egypt and Israel to cease fighting. 'And, to safeguard free passage and separate the belligerents, Egypt had been asked to agree "that Anglo-French forces should move temporarily—I repeat, temporarily—into key positions at Port Said, Ismailia, and Suez".'[4]

Unsurprisingly, Egypt refused to acquiesce in this unequal deal. With customary imperialist arrogance, in the early evening of 31 October 1956 French and British bombs began to rain on Egyptian targets. It was no consolation for the Egyptians that the very first sorties flown by British teams missed their original targets, not once but twice. British bombers had been ordered to wipe out the airfield of Cairo West, where Soviet-manufactured fighter planes were located. Literally at the last moment, following up on an urgent message from the British Embassy in Cairo, Eden, quickly glancing at a map, realized 'that the American community, some thirteen hundred strong, was being evacuated by the road which bordered on that airfield'. Fearing possible repercussions for Britain's 'special relationship' with its former rebel colony, Eden ordered the bombers to switch targets. The British Foreign Minister did not know that the map he relied on was not only outdated but wrong. In reality, the road ran at a safe distance from any airborne attack on Cairo West. Meanwhile pilots and navigators, some operating at 'only ten minutes' warning of the change,... had to work out new flight plans in the air'. Ill-preparedness took its toll. 'For all the British familiarity with Cairo, the briefing material available for this last-minute work was poor; no attention was called to the close proximity of Cairo International Airport to Almaza', a military airport. Predictably, after dropping Cairo West as a target because of faulty maps, the new target, Almaza, was missed as well. 'In the end, going for Almaza, they hit Cairo International', a civilian airport.[5] After several days of bombing raids on Egyptian targets, the British and French airborne expeditionary teams were whistled back by American action. US pressure did not arise from humanitarian concerns, but what parenthetically saved Egyptian lives was perceived in Paris and London as a bitter and humiliating diplomatic defeat. Coming less than ten years after Britain's handing over of Greece to the Americans and less than three years after the French retreat at Dien Bien Phu, it reinforced perceptions of French and British imperial decline. Why did this affect the lifeworld of the European left?

The impact of Suez on the inner life of Europe's left was most self-evident in the case of France, as from January 1955 until May 1957 France's Fourth Republic was headed by the Socialist Guy Mollet. In short, it was a socialist who was responsible for the joint attack on Egypt, and Guy Mollet and his 'comrades' were by no means passive victims of the vagaries of international diplomacy. Identifying socialist policies with the interests of the Suez Company, the French Section of the Socialist International (SFIO), as the French Socialist Party was officially called, had few doubts which side of the Suez Crisis they were on. 'When the Anglo-French invasion of Egypt occurred, it was defended by the Socialists as a logical extension of their previous arguments against the nationalisation of the Suez Canal.'[6] The SFIO's support for imperialist military intervention, of course, was only a logical consequence of its principled support for French colonialism elsewhere, most importantly in Algeria, about which more below. The Suez Crisis nonetheless helped crystallize inner-party opposition which, a few years later, developed into a fully fledged split and the birth of the French new left.

In Britain, Labour Party attitudes towards Suez differed, undoubtedly in part because of the happy circumstance that British Labour was then in opposition to Tory government control. Not only in parliament but elsewhere in the public sphere, Labour and others raised embarrassing questions, and public meetings, telegrams, and petitions exerted pressure on Tory policy-makers to pursue a policy of 'Law Not War'.[7] Even so, Labour opposition was kept within safe limits. While desiring to exploit this opportunity to showcase a distinctive Labour policy alternative to the ruling Tory consensus, Labour was fearful that it might lose control over an antiwar movement that proved to be popular. Labour called for pressure on Tory figureheads to be exercised 'through normal constitutional parliamentary methods' and, faced with calls for strike actions against British bombings, enacted measures to ensure that activists would 'refrain from taking industrial action as a means of influencing national policy in the present crisis'.[8] A keen analyst of Labour Party policies and procedures, Ralph Miliband then added: 'British military operations did in fact come to an end within the next few days. No one, however, has so far seriously claimed that the Labour Party's opposition had much to do with this outcome.' Furthermore, Miliband continued: 'Labour's campaign came to an end as abruptly as the Government's military operations, and Labour pressure upon the government soon subsided altogether.'[9] The lessons of the Suez Crisis and the opposition movement in Britain became one of two key factors explaining the subsequent emergence of a British new left.[10]

The other crucial determinant undermining the continued hegemony of the old left was intimately related to the fate of the other headline event of 30 October

1956. The Anglo-French military intervention of Egypt was halted at midnight on Tuesday, 6 November 1956. The brief flowering of the anti-Stalinist Hungarian Revolution came to an end even earlier. On 4 November 1956, Soviet armies intervened in Hungarian affairs for the second time in less than a fortnight. And, this time around, they were there to stay. Similar to the case of the military intervention of Czechoslovakia twelve years later, various forms of grass-roots self-organization continued to spread in the initial period of Soviet occupation, but the dice had been cast. The most prominent attempt to date to construct a democratic socialist society within the sphere of influence of Soviet power had been decisively and brutally crushed.[11] It was a turn of events which was bound to affect the world of international communism.

What made the impact on communist parties around the world so obvious and direct was not solely the naked brutality of Soviet terror. But this barbaric display of feigned 'proletarian internationalism', Moscow-style, happened to materialize less than nine months after another landmark event in the annals of world communism. When, on 14 February 1956, in front of 1,436 delegates hailing from fifty-five communist parties around the world, Nikita Khrushchev delivered the opening address to the Twentieth Congress of the Soviet Communist Party, his listeners were intensely aware that they were present at an extraordinary event in world communist history, for the death of Stalin less than three years earlier had begun to effect certain positive changes in the Soviet Union and its satellite states. 'Nonetheless, none of them could have possibly imagined the way the congress would conclude.' For, at a session closed to all foreign delegates held at midnight on 24–5 February 1956, Khrushchev delivered a stinging indictment of the personality cult of Joseph Stalin and the 'excesses' associated with his iron-fisted rule over Soviet society and international communism.[12] News of the Secret Report soon filtered into communist party circles around the world, where it provoked consternation, incredulity, but also a flurry of creative thoughts and hopes. Thus the suppression of the Hungarian Revolt towards the end of that fateful year appeared to a growing minority of party activists and intellectuals as living confirmation of the need to move beyond the increasingly compromised world of communist party politics. If the Suez Crisis, particularly for Britain and France, stirred socialist activists to take an increasingly hostile attitude to official party policies, the Hungarian Revolt served as catalyst for similar manifestations of an increasingly critical distance from official communist politics around the world. For, even the communist politician supposedly at the origin of the post-1968 polycentrist drift within European communism, the Italian Communist Party's (PCI) Palmiro Togliatti, defended the Soviet invasion of Hungary which he deemed 'necessary to prevent counter-revolution', a position continuously upheld by the flagship Eurocommunist party until January 1979.[13] The new left, fuelled by the events of 1956, thus benefited from political crises affecting both strands of the old left: social democracy and communism.

2. A SOCIAL DEMOCRATIC FOREIGN POLICY?

Suez and Hungary were, of course, only the tip of the iceberg. Neither of these two landmark events determining the subsequent evolution of the left diverged to any significant extent from pre-existing patterns of social democratic or communist politics. To take a closer look at social democratic policy, post-Second World War developments were remarkable only for the near-total absence of any qualitatively distinct social democratic foreign policy. A key authority on post-1945 socialism, Donald Sassoon, put it like this: 'There was never a "socialist foreign policy" or, at least, no one knew where to find it or how to make it.'[14] And this renunciation of an independent stance in foreign policy not only had consequences for the concrete crises punctuating the international arena of world politics in the boom years of the post-war decades; it also served to alienate precisely those countless individuals who were taking sides with regard to international politics, and who did not opt for the side of Western policy-makers.

No single foreign policy issue served to heat up debates in the second half of the 1960s as much as the Vietnam War. Yet the policy shapers of social democratic parties were most notable for their abstention in this debate. Confirmation of the self-incriminating passivity of leading social democrats is found in Henry Kissinger's comments in his memoirs *The White House Years*. His relevant observations pertain to all European leaders of the 'left' or 'right', though the final sentence underscores the culpability of leading social democrats:

Strangely, Vietnam played a minor role in the visits of European leaders. European public opinion, at least as represented by the media, opposed the war. But European leaders registered no objection. During the entire period of the war I recall no criticism by a European leader in even the most private conversation.... Brandt and Wilson [social democratic luminaries in West Germany and the United Kingdom] volunteered no comment and made sympathetic noises when Nixon outlined our Vietnam strategy.[15]

The increasingly politicized generation of young activists coming of age in the 1960s and described in preceding chapters no longer considered social democracy as a vehicle for foreign policy change.

And this accommodation to the international status quo long preceded America's involvement in South-east Asia and the growing international opposition to it after 1965. For the political generation of the late 1950s and early 1960s French policies in Algeria played an equally critical role, though opposition movements were far smaller in scale and, for practical purposes, limited to the Gallic state. It has been noted that the Suez Crisis broke with a Socialist Prime Minister as French head of state. For critics of France's Algerian course, '1956 was a recurring watershed' as well.[16] Having campaigned on a platform widely regarded as a commitment to a peaceful solution to the Algerian crisis, the victorious coalition government headed by Guy Mollet jettisoned its cautious veneer and embarked on a vicious and brutal terror campaign against Algerian independence fighters, the military intervention serving as a rehearsal in all but name for US tactics applied to the Vietcong ten years later. 'In order to secure the country against rebel terrorism and to enact immediate reforms in the face of expected Algerian European opposition, a law granting the government special powers was submitted to and passed by the National Assembly on March 12, 1956.'[17] Special powers in a colonial war meant kidnappings and the liberal recourse to torture. 'The usual reaction of the Socialists, in the beginning, was either to deny or to ignore reports of torture.' 'Another practice...was the attempt to suppress those critics who protested against the use of torture.'[18] It is small wonder, then, that French socialism in the form of the SFIO entered the turbulent decade of the 1960s as a mere shadow of its former self.

3. SOCIAL DEMOCRACY'S DOMESTIC AGENDA

For the predominantly young activists of the generation of '1968' social democratic foreign policy in the 1950s and 1960s was the source of consternation and condemnation and rarely a fount of inspiration. This alignment with the imperial status quo, eliciting, as we have seen, surprise and approval by brutal power brokers à la Henry Kissinger, had enormous consequences for the outlook of socialism with regard to the domestic agenda as well. In a brilliant passage of his modern classic, *One Hundred Years of Socialism*, Donald Sassoon highlights the pioneering role of ostensibly socialist foreign policy conceptions for the evolving policy debates within the lifeworld of European socialism in other areas as well. Sassoon notes that the social democrats'

adoption of a non-socialist and fundamentally bipartisan concept of international political and economic relations provided the model for their ideological renewal. They accommodated their internal programme to the exigencies of a world economy.... To be real 'innovators,' it was necessary to adapt in domestic policy as well. Thus, it is in the 1950s and not in the 1980s or the 1990s that the revision of the socialist tradition effectively began.[19]

The classic case of post-war success at the ballot box of an organization belonging to the Socialist International was the July 1945 Labour Party victory which propelled Clement Attlee into 10 Downing Street for six important post-war years. Prior to the election, the eminent political scientist and Labour politician Harold Laski had called the forthcoming national vote 'a fight between private enterprise now expressed as monopoly capitalism, and socialism that realises that the new age is born and that only through the establishment of a Socialist Commonwealth can we realise the purposes for which we have been fighting this war'.[20] A quick look at British post-war realities may serve to place this pronouncement in a proper perspective. Apart from the introduction of the National Health Service, itself a policy entirely compatible with the continued prosperity of a market economy, a number of nationalization measures served to imbue post-war Labour with a radical hue. Looked at more closely, this aura of radical change quickly began to dissipate. One of the most cogent analysts of Labour Party policy mutations, Ralph Miliband, had this to say in his pathbreaking study first published in 1961: 'From the beginning, the nationalisation proposals of the Government were designed to achieve the sole purpose of improving the efficiency of a capitalist economy, not as marking the beginning of its wholesale transformation', the latter a pious wish reserved for party conferences and Sunday speeches. 'In fact, one consequence of the Government's compensation policies was to release vast financial resources for profitable investment in the "private sector"; another was to saddle the nationalised industries with a burden of debt which materially contributed to difficulties that were later ascribed to the immanent character of public ownership.'[21]

Nonetheless, for all its faults, the limited nationalizations carried out in the immediate post-war era could have conceivably been employed to permit experiments in grass-roots participation in the running of economic and political affairs to take hold and serve as inspiration for subsequent, deeper structural reforms. Nothing could have been further from the minds of Labour politicians in the Attlee cabinets. Heeding the examples of Tory-inspired wartime economic oversight bodies, 'in close consultation with the industrial interests concerned', the Labour government 'relied at least as much as its predecessors upon the advice of private industry and finance and gave their representatives a major share in the operation of controls: if there was no workers' participation in those years, there was at least employers' participation'.[22]

From 1948 onwards even such limited nationalizations as had occurred up to that year were no longer seriously on the agenda—with the partial exception of iron and steel, where Labour had made grand promises from which it could not easily retreat. 'From then onwards, the Government was mainly concerned to preach "austerity" to its supporters, who might have responded with greater enthusiasm had austerity been less obviously reserved for wage earners.'[23] A pattern had now been established which was only interrupted by the long period of Tory control of British politics between 1951 and 1964. When Harold Wilson entered Downing Street as the first Labour prime minister since Attlee's departure in 1951, in terms of foreign and domestic policy agendas there was a near-seamless continuity from the Attlee era, minus the reform euphoria of 1945–8. Sure enough, Wilson, like all politicians, continuously stressed 'the need for change, renewal, modernisation and reform in every area of British life, most of all in economic life'. But, in effect, this was not to be confounded with a radical critique of moribund British capitalism. Instead, Huddersfield's most famous son energetically advocated the need to construct 'a renovated capitalism, freed from its aristocratic and gentlemanly accretions, dynamic, professional, entrepreneurial, numerate and efficient'.[24] There were other continuities as well. Austerity politics was merely rebranded 'incomes policy', resulting in 'people earning £1,000 a month (or more) telling people earning £1,000 a year (or less) that they must stop being greedy'.[25] In short, under Wilson as under Attlee, British Labour displayed an 'unconsciously reverential and touching faith in the capabilities of the capitalist system'.[26] 'The main problem with Labour was not that it did not have policies for transforming the capitalist economy into a socialist one, but that it did not know how to run the capitalist economy.'[27] Another thoughtful critic of the European left put it like this, commenting on European social democracy in general and not just British Labour in particular: 'Socialist strategists took prosperity's permanence as an appealing substitute for abolishing capitalism, for which in any case they had no plan. The rhetoric of revolution, as a challenge to state power, was long gone. But any extraparliamentary politics, via local government, workplace democracy, or direct action, however vestigial, now too disappeared.'[28]

4. YOUTH REVOLT AND THE OLD LEFT

Yet the rot of social democratic policy conceptions—seen from the vantage point of social movement activists described in earlier chapters—went even deeper than its 'mere' accommodation to the foreign and domestic status quo. For, had many young rebels chosen to join the Labour fold, they would have found themselves almost on another planet, even within its youth organization, the Young Socialists (YS). 'Like its forerunners, the YS had neither representation on the NEC [National Executive Committee], at Party conference, at Transport House, nor the right to produce its own publications.'[29] And in the mother party itself, even Anthony Crosland himself considered it 'a depressing fact, for a party of change, that the average Labour candidate in 1959 was several years older than his Conservative counterpart'.[30] Official Labour Party culture regarded Teddy boys and rock'n'roll in a way similar to that in which anthropologists study remote Amazonian cultures, though most likely with far less respect. In Coventry, for instance, then still a thriving industrial town, Teddy boy culture arrived 'in 1954, and caught on so wildly that by 1957 the promoters responsible for bringing Bill Hayley to Britain felt it appropriate to open the star's tour at the city's 2000-seat Gaumont theatre'.[31] Nonetheless, the city fathers of Coventry, a city then long governed by unrestrained Labour Party control, in 1959 'refused to intervene over a management ban on Teddy Boys and Girls' at a prominent city centre café.[32] British Labour was no more closed minded than the average European social democrat. In West Germany, the Young Socialists performed their function as a loyal conveyor belt for mother party electioneering tasks without noticeable complaints until the mid-1960s. The German Young Socialists, when left to their own devices, organized beauty contests, and brainstorming sessions for electoral campaigns of its mother party came up with slogans such as 'Listen to your Wife—Vote SPD'.[33]

Official communist culture was no less traditionalist. In 1956, the Communist Party of Great Britain's (CPGB) *Daily Worker* referred to rock'n'roll as a 'depraved offshoot' of authentic popular music.[34] Other modernist musical trends did not necessarily fall on more receptive ears. 'The CPGB formally regarded [jazz] as "decadent"—in its vernacular a euphemism for American.' Eric Hobsbawm, preferring to publish his classic study of jazz—his 1959 *The Jazz Scene*—under a pseudonym, Francis Newton, in part to avoid friction with his Communist Party comrades, in turn had little appreciation for rock'n'roll. Hobsbawm, reflecting on the meaning of the Elvis fad, wrote in the *New Statesman*, 'why the fashion has grown up is anybody's guess'.[35] But the most telling indictment of the disjuncture between communist culture and youth culture emerges from a closer look at the practices and moral judgements proffered by the supposedly least Stalinist and most open-minded of Western Europe's communist parties, the largest communist party west of the Iron Curtain, the Italian Communist Party (PCI).

The Italian Communist Youth Federation (FGCI) suffered from the same problem as its social democratic counterparts elsewhere in Europe. 'Youth leaders, who in any case were often men in their late twenties or early thirties, found it difficult to latch onto new trends in society because they felt obliged to play to the gallery, to take the adult party and its leadership, in other words, as their point of reference.'[36] The PCI's culture tsars were almost exclusively concerned to exercise a distinct influence over important sections of Italian intellectuals in the area of high culture. Most forms of mass culture, particularly when associated with new media, were rejected outright, an attitude of disdain which came all the more natural when American influence could be detected at will. Throughout the 1950s, PCI notables railed against the pernicious influence of TV culture, sometimes going as far as refusing to sanction the installation of TVs in party branch offices and associated social clubs. In a 1958 article in the FGCI's journal, *Nuova Generazione*, the caption underneath photos of Elvis Presley decried the 'hysteria and paroxysm' triggered by the Memphis idol, and the Beat Generation poets suffered no better fate at the hands of Communist culture tsars. The Beat phenomenon was described as 'a mind-boggling mixture of mysticism, escapism, jazz and marihuana, the latest and most exasperated example of that banality and fear of facing up to reality, that "infantile" complex that is sapping the great objective possibilities of the new generation in the United States.'[37]

And such 'curious' observations did not improve in style or content in the course of the 1960s. When, in 1965, the Piper Club in Rome opened its doors, the functional equivalent to Liverpool's Cavern Club or Hamburg's Star-Club, Communist publications railed against the propagation of 'false models taken from the world of show business', and the PCI's national daily, *L'Unità*, ventured onto the terrain of comparative analysis: 'In England the style of the Beatles represents a youth protest against conformism, puritan boredom, the proper comportment of their parents, middle-class comforts. Here in Italy young people, if they wish to protest, have other ways, other possibilities, other means to find release.'[38] Small wonder that Italian youth began to turn away from the FGCI as an outlet of their political and cultural urges. In a national culture still heavily influenced by the teachings of Catholic moral apostles firmly ensconced in Rome, the puritan Stalinism of PCI high culture did not provide a viable alternative. As a letter to the editor of one of the new youth magazines appearing in Italian kiosks at that time, *Big*, underscored, faced with the concrete concerns of young people trying to carve out a niche for themselves, the old left's concentration on 'the so-called structural reforms' of economy and high politics simply 'makes us laugh'.[39]

Predictably, the PCI, which had exercised a certain type of cultural hegemony over radical intellectuals up to the late 1950s, eventually began to suffer the consequences of the party's lack of adaptation to changing times and mores. A keen and sympathetic analyst of the PCI's plight in matters of cultural politics, Stephen Gundle, suggests the following important paradigm shift: 'Undoubtedly, one of the most significant developments of the early 1960s was the emergence of a broad, heterogenous area of left-wing cultural and intellectual activity outside and beyond the reach of the PCI.'[40] Sure enough, the PCI in the 1960s was confident enough to begin a process of gradual opening up to the concerns, morals, and ideas of a new generation, whose socialization had not been shaped by the exigencies and sacrifices of war, Nazi occupation, resistance, and post-war reconstruction. The letters column in the party magazine, *Vie Nuove*, in particular became a central site for the frank exchange of opinions with few holds barred. Nonetheless, in a decade when radical ferment grew by leaps and bounds, such partial openings to new realities turned out to be too little too late.

Crucially, such Communist reluctance to accommodate new mass cultures and youth concerns was closely linked to an intimately related political conservatism. Thus, the totally unexpected desperate militancy of young *teppisti* in the streets of Genoa and Turin in 1960 and 1962 (see Chapter 1) not only caught PCI commentators unawares but led to a chorus of condemnations and insinuations in the Communist press. To take the case of the *rivolta di Piazza Statuto* in 1962 in Turin, comprehensively documented by Dario Lanzardo: the PCI's *L'Unità* headlined an extensive nine-column article on the street battles in purposefully provocative terms: 'The Operation "Piazza Statuto": We Reveal the Background to the Provocation.' The subheading then gave away the PCI's game: '1,500 lire and a packet of cigarettes: Who paid?' Clearly, in the eyes of PCI politicians, such acts of militance could only be the direct result of wilful manipulation by sinister forces. The Milanese PCI daily paper, *Stasera*, then dotted all the remaining 'i's. Its headline confidently proclaimed: 'The fascists in the city square.' And *Stasera* did not refer to the police. For PCI journalists, the 'fascists' and 'provocateurs' were the *teppisti*! Not all headlines and articles in the PCI press had recourse to equally grotesque distortions. Nonetheless, the PCI approach can be judged from the joint appearance of two separate articles in the party's flagship national journal, *Rinascità*, on 14 July. On the one hand, there was a reasoned article by Togliatti himself, expressing certain sympathies for the combatants of the Piazza Statuto, who had exhibited, Togliatti wrote, 'a sense of collective solidarity that can find expression in the most diverse and improvised forms'. Elsewhere in the same issue, under the heading 'Seven Days of Union Struggles', an anonymous author referred to the Turin event as 'provocations by fascist Teddy boys (*teppisti fascisti*), evidently inspired by rightwing business interests', hardly a reasoned judgement or supported by any cumbersome facts.[41] A demonstration of PCI openness towards competing currents of thought? Very unlikely, given the centrality of this affair and the tight hierarchical control over PCI publications. However, such polemical denunciations most definitely would not have attracted youthful rebels sympathizing with the *teppisti* revolt.

One of the standard rituals of post-war Italian civil society has been (and remains to the present day) anniversary celebrations of the official day of liberation from Nazi occupation and the Republic of Salò, 25 April 1945. By the early 1960s a growing chorus of voices began to express disagreement with the official culture of patriotic celebrations of an event which had in part been the product of a bitter civil war but which was now presented as an occasion for festive pleas for national unity and reconciliation. An editorial in one of the journals belonging to the emerging new left, *Quaderni Piacentini*, called for a reappraisal: 'No, no, no. We do not wish those killed in the resistance to be "honoured" via monuments "to the fallen of all wars", inaugurated by bishops, prefects, judges, military commanders, commissars, policemen, and police chiefs. It is better to remain silent.'[42] The PCI and its dense network of satellite organizations, including its association of resistance fighters, were of course deeply implicated with these patriotic and nostalgic affairs.

The twenty-year anniversary in 1965 witnessed a first public manifestation of dissent. The final march and rally to celebrate the event occurred on 9 May 1965 in Milan, assembling 80,000 former partisans but likewise 'a restless crowd of about a thousand youth who ill-supported the celebratory rites and the atmosphere of unanimity and fraternization erasing all differences between political parties and social classes', occuring precisely at the moment when the Vietnam War began to dominate international news, a war fully supported by Italy's Christian Democratic political elite. Keynote speakers addressing the crowd were confronted with chants, such as 'Yankees Go Home', 'Johnson Murderer', and 'Free Vietnam'. And when the official demonstration was over and the crowd began to disperse, the dissident youthful protestors marched to the American consulate instead.[43] Less than two weeks later, on 22 May 1965, a public rally in Milan organized by the PCI and addressed by key party spokespersons led to similar verbal altercations. This time, the PCI decided to restrain the dissident crowd. Party marshals and police physically assaulted the dissenters, followed by a denunciation in the party's *L'Unità* two days later.[44] In May 1967, during an antiwar march in Turin, marshals organized by the PCI once again carried out a vicious attack on left-wing dissidents who were planning to diverge from the official route in order to demonstrate in front of the American consulate. In the second half of the 1960s, such clashes soon became the norm.[45] It is not difficult to imagine what impact the repeated incidents 'of finding oneself on city streets as the object of the same blows and the same insults meted out by PCI marshals and police' had on the consciousness and the political choices of a young generation in open revolt.[46]

When the Italian student movement developed and prospered in an unprecedented radical spiral after 1966, PCI responses were only more measured by degree. It usually did not come to any blows, but the PCI and its youth wing, the FGCI, lagged behind the rapid radicalization of an entire generation of young intellectuals.[47] It did not help the fading star of the PCI as vehicle for social change that, in response to the Battle of Valle Giulia in Rome on 1 March 1968, the symbolic high point of the Italian student movement (see Chapter 2), one of the most well-known party intellectuals, the film director and novelist Pier Paolo Pasolini, composed a poem that must be considered one of the most embarrassing faux pas in the long history of bitter infighting within the European left. In his composition, paternalistically entitled 'The PCI to Young People', Pasolini identified the rebel student militants with the Italian upper classes, while expressly declaring his sympathies for the club-swinging policemen which he, by contrast, identified as representatives of impoverished working-class migrants hailing from Italy's south. This overt tastelessness was compounded by Pasolini's decision to publish his poem in Italy's premier mass-market-oriented weekly magazine, *L'Espresso*.[48]

It is no surprise, then, that the PCI lost its attraction for young activists coming of age in the 1960s, a generation plentiful in numbers throughout the Western world but arguably most numerous precisely in Italy. There is no better way to dramatize the losing touch with the realities of actually existing social movements of the largest and supposedly the most innovatory Communist party in the entire Western world than a quick glance at FGCI membership figures. At a time when young Italians radicalized in massive numbers and in particular in 1968, at the very moment when the entire system of higher education in Italy had ground to a halt under the onslaught of a student cohort no longer willing to tolerate a conservative and hierarchical mandarinate of omnipotent professors ill-supported by an antiquated infrastructure, precisely at this promising conjuncture for radical politics, the FGCI experienced an astounding contraction of its membership. There exists no better indictment of the irrelevance of PCI politics for radical activism than the documentation of FGCI membership decline in the years of greatest youth revolt: 1961 (240,000), 1962 (180,000), 1963 (175,000), 1966 (154,485), 1967 (135,012), 1968 (125,438), 1969 (68,648), 1970 (66,451).[49]

5. *IL CASO MANIFESTO*

As if this disastrous implosion of the Communist youth organization was not enough, a similar process, though ultimately of less dramatic impact on membership figures, affected the mother party itself. Throughout the post-war decades there had never been any doubt amongst PCI strategists that the Leninist revolutionary strategy for political power no longer conformed to the realities of the modern world. A socialist society remained the ultimate and desirable goal, but the road map leading in this direction no longer contained instructions for sudden, radical breaks and associated cataclysmic events but, instead, a series of intercalated structural reforms which, in due time, would bring about the same result but without running the risks associated with the outbreak of revolution and possible negative reactions to such events. Disagreements arose, however, over the precise articulation of such gradual reforms, as the strategic orientation towards structural reforms permitted a variety of alliance strategies to be formulated and practised.

This is not the place to discuss the finer points of Communist debates on the roadway to meaningful social change in the post-war decades. May it suffice to note that, by the late 1950s, a distinct political current arose within the PCI, crystallized around Pietro Ingrao, which increasingly questioned what they considered a self-defeating path of increasing moderation on the part of the PCI leadership. This Ingrao left did not wish to return to Leninist models, but nonetheless expressed their fear that, in jettisoning the Leninist model, official PCI policies were losing sight of their ultimate goal. The Ingrao left stressed the continued need for frontal attacks on bourgeois power, if by non-revolutionary means, and they warned the PCI leadership that the latter's search for ever more numerous allies was effectively beginning to relegate anticapitalism to the sidelines of PCI politics. The Ingrao left also advocated decentralization measures within the lifeworld of the PCI itself, to empower grass-roots activists at the party's base, the latter regarded as the crucial agents for inner-party and societal change.[50]

Though suffering a stinging inner-party defeat in 1966, a left current within the PCI survived, and it lay at the origins of an important crisis which erupted in the open in the course of 1969. The remnants of the Ingrao left proved to be far less hostile to the various social movements polarizing Italian society after 1966 than the official PCI hierarchy. Indeed, Rossana Rossanda, the spokesperson for PCI cultural affairs and a supporter of this dissident tendency, wrote the rather sympathetic portrayal of the *movimento studentesco, l'anno degli studenti*, repeatedly cited in Chapter 2. The Warsaw Pact invasion of Czechoslovakia in August 1968 had led to public condemnations of this repressive move by the PCI leadership, but the left-wing dissidents were not content with such a limited critique and pushed for a radical reassessment of PCI attitudes towards the communist east, something the party hierarchy refused to entertain at that time. The year 1969, of course, was also the central year of the Italian working-class revolt. Between June and September 1969, the left opposition within the PCI published four issues of a journal, *Il Manifesto*, which led to open attacks by the PCI in return for this breach of party protocol. The differences of opinion could no longer be reconciled, and in November 1969 the brains trust behind *Il Manifesto*, Aldo Natoli, Luigi Pintor, and Rossana Rossanda, were expelled, leading to subsequent successive waves of further expulsions across the entire Italian state.

Thus, precisely during the Hot Autumn 1969, at the moment when 'the most extensive and radical wave of social conflicts which Republican Italy had ever seen was under way', the PCI responded by closing itself off, expelling those party members who came closest to expressing activist agendas at the centre of public attention in the *biennio rosso* of 1968–9.[51]

6. INTELLECTUALS AND THE NEW LEFT

Out of the contradictions of Europe's social democracy and international communism arose a political current which assumed the mantle of a new left. The similarity of this new label across most national frontiers—*Neue Linke, Nieuw Links, Nouvelle Gauche, Nuova Sinistra, Izquierda Nuova*—in some respects helped to paper over important qualitative and quantitative differences between the various manifestations of this increasingly prominent international political trend. But, for the purposes of this study, the similarities and parallels are more decisive for an analysis of the impact of '1968' on the left than the corresponding disjunctures and discontinuities. First, however, it is incumbent to define the parameters of what has generally become known as the new left.

In an important recent survey of the political ferment associated with '1968' Ingrid Gilcher-Holtey reserves pride of place in her definition and description of the new left to a select grouping of intellectual currents, personified in such leading social thinkers as C. Wright Mills, Herbert Marcuse, E. P. Thompson, Raymond Williams, Edgar Morin, and Cornelius Castoriadis, a list that should rightfully be extended to include the Italians Lelio Basso and Raniero Panzieri.[52] And it is beyond doubt that individual social theorists and the larger circles of intellectuals with which the former were usually associated, often producing high quality journals of international repute, were instrumental in helping a new generation of social movement activists to break from the habits and traditions of the old left and to form a new identity and political orientation. In virtually every single country in Western Europe, including Great Britain and the United States, top quality journals and magazines played a crucial role in the preparation of the terrain. Usually arising from various dissident forces within the respective social democratic and communist parties, in Catholic Europe frequently energized by a healthy admixture of left Catholic activists and intellectuals, the emerging transnational new left was inseparable from the publication and associated discussion projects arising in the course of the 1950s and 1960s. Catalysed by the twin crises of the year 1956, the British new left, for instance, was an exemplary case in point. John Saville and E. P. Thompson's *Reasoner* (1956) and *New Reasoner* (1957–9), combined with the *Universities and Left Review* (1957–9), edited by Stuart Hall, Charles Taylor, Raphael Samuel, and others, to form the aptly named *New Left Review* in January 1960.[53] In France, the equivalent pride of place must be ascribed to *Arguments* (1956–62), *L'Internationale Situationniste*

(1958–69), and *Socialisme ou Barbarie* (1949–66), although the emergence of the latter journal highlights the pre-existence of proto-new left currents long before the crisis point of 1956 gave rise to a proliferation of such tendencies and corresponding publications on a far larger scale.[54] In the United States, *Liberation* (1956–77) and *Monthly Review* (1949–present) performed a similar role. In Italy, corresponding to its particularly vibrant culture of social movement activism, the menu of available options in the world of innovative journals included *Ragionamenti* (1955–7), *Passato e Presente* (1958–60), *Quaderni Rossi* (1961–5), *Lettere dei Quaderni Rossi* (1963–8), *Classe Operaia* (1964–7), *Quaderni Piacentini* (1962–85), and many others.[55]

A quick glance at the editorial boards of this kaleidoscope of dissident left-wing journals, usually located at some distance from established political organizations of the old left, is a who's who of post-war left-wing intellectuals outside of the organizational influence of the mainstream old left, though in the initial period overlapping party memberships continued to exist. In Chapter 1, attention was briefly drawn to the microcosm of Bernese intellectuals and artists who provided the nutrient medium for the steady growth and development of a Bernese—and, by extension, Swiss—new left in the course of the 1960s. Parallel processes, if normally on a much larger scale, characterized the creative intermixture of political and cultural fermentation in other countries, eventually giving rise to a powerful national, European and North American new left.[56] Crucially, leading social theorists, just like their counterparts in the closely related artistic realm, joined forces in the huge enterprise to restructure and reshape the European left. Lelio Basso, born in 1903, had first made a major impact on Italian left-wing political culture between 1943 and 1945, at the high point of antifascist resistance activism, when he became a central figure in several attempts to break through the virtual monopoly of social democracy and communism by organizing alternative outlets for Italy's vibrant Marxist underground left. Subsequently carving out a niche for himself and like-minded unorthodox individuals within the left wing of Italian social democracy, Basso remained a card-carrying member of the Italian Socialist Party (PSI) until 1964. From 1958 until his death in 1978, he became the editor and guiding spirit of one of the more memorable products within the kaleidoscope of dissident left journals, *Problemi del socialismo* (1958–91).[57] Raniero Panzieri, born in 1921, like Basso a long-time member of the PSI, during his term as editor of the PSI's theoretical journal, *Mondo Operaio*, from March 1957 until December 1958, effectively transformed this into a dissident left-wing journal which debated and prefigured many of the themes and issues central to the emerging new left. As the guiding spirit of *Quaderni Rossi* until his premature death in October 1964, Panzieri blazed a trail of new directions for critical inquiry and thus helped shape the flagship intellectual circles and corresponding debates of the Italian new left.[58]

It would take too long to provide similar, if rough, biographical notations for other intellectual figureheads of the emerging new left. May it suffice to note that the two quintessentially French thinkers mentioned above, Edgar Morin and Cornelius Castoriadis, originated from two mutually exclusive political milieux dating back to the inter-war period of European history: Moscow-oriented communism (Morin, one of the editors of *Arguments*), and Trotskyism (the Greek-born Castoriadis, one of the editors of *Socialisme ou Barbarie*). And the personal-political background of the five names of British new left journal editors listed above is equally varied, in addition to the fact that two of them were transplants from other geographic regions of the world—Charles Taylor, of Canadian descent, and Stuart Hall, a native of the Caribbean.

7. MARCUSE AND MILLS

Yet the two internationally most influential intellectuals and social theorists had their home base neither in Italy, France, Britain, or anywhere else in Western Europe. C. Wright Mills and Herbert Marcuse were the principal intellectual fixtures of the North American new left. And it is undoubtedly due to the pioneering role of North American social movements in spawning the international student revolt that Mills and Marcuse were catapulted to front-rank position amongst the large number of intellectual, academic and activist protagonists intimately associated with the new left. Until his untimely death in 1962, C. Wright Mills was in all likelihood far more integrated within—and representative of—the intellectual currents composing the nascent, fledgling North American new left than the German-born Herbert Marcuse, who was then researching and writing his dystopian vision of the contemporary age, *One-Dimensional Man*, which ends with a quotation from Walter Benjamin: 'It is only for the sake of those without hope that hope is given to us.'[59] Mills, an untiring traveller, roaming the US West on his BMW motorcycle, Kerouac-style, was also a frequent visitor to Europe, where he helped construct a dense network of new left co-thinkers. In the summer of 1957, for instance, together with Ralph Miliband, Mills visited Poland for extended intellectual exchanges with Leszek Kolakowski and other Polish dissidents, the latter then searching for similar answers to the questions posed by Western exponents of the developing new left. It is highly symptomatic that two important personalities in the West German and US student new left, Michael Vester and Tom Hayden, in 1964 both finished major academic studies on C. Wright Mills, the latter clearly a role model for young, nonconformist rebels in search of heroes. The single most important North American document announcing the birth of an activist new left, *The Port Huron Statement*, was to a significant extent inspired by the thoughts and writings of C. Wright Mills.[60]

The death of C. Wright Mills at the age of 45 left the field wide open for the ascendancy of Herbert Marcuse as the transnational lodestar of the 1960s new left. Born and raised in Germany, Herbert Marcuse had already graduated from high school and had been drafted into the German Imperial Army by the time C. Wright Mills was born in Waco, Texas. Marcuse had already made a name for himself as a promising philosopher when he was forced to emigrate, first to Switzerland and then to the United States, where he arrived on 4 July 1934. By the time Marcuse published *One-Dimensional Man* thirty years later, he had become one of the world's leading nonconformist Marxist intellectuals. And *One-Dimensional Man*, despite its generally rather pessimistic air, captured the mood of the young generation of rebels at the centre of the spirit of '1968'.[61] For, like other prescient and imaginative pioneers of innovative theories and practices, such as the Situationists or the Provos, Marcuse's 1964 opus adopted Antonio Gramsci's dictum: 'Pessimism of the intellect, optimism of the will'. Finding subversive agents of revolutionary change in 'the substratum of the outcasts and outsiders, the exploited and persecuted of other races and other colors, the unemployed and the unemployable', Marcuse invested all his hopes in these 'marginal' strata. 'The fact that they start refusing to play the game may be the fact which marks the beginning of the end of a period' of hegemony by what Marcuse liked to call the 'totalitarian tendencies of the one-dimensional society' he was attempting to dissect. Still, Marcuse immediately added after his invocation of 'the Great Refusal' by his favoured outcasts and dropouts from advanced industrial society: 'Nothing indicates that it will be a good end.'[62] But by the time Marcuse's closing passages in *One-Dimensional Man* appeared in print, the deep freeze of the 'American Century' had begun to thaw. 'During precisely the five years in which Marcuse had been writing about "the closing of the political universe" characteristic of one-dimensional society, an unprecedented confluence of political forces was maturing that would enable him to move the analysis to a higher stage.' Students were soon added to Marcuse's list of promethean forces that could perhaps redeem the world. 'Within five years [of publication], Marcuse's "Studies in the Ideology of Advanced Industrial Society" had sold over 100,000 copies in the United States, and had been translated into sixteen languages.'[63]

From 1967 to 1969 Marcuse, for the first time ever, exchanged academic conferences for raucous public meetings in overcrowded and smoke-filled auditoria, addressing student activists in New York, London, Berlin, Amsterdam, Paris, Oslo, Rome, and other cities where new left radicalism suddenly politicized hundreds, then thousands, and finally hundreds of thousands in search of a non-alienated way of life.[64] Even in France, where Marcuse's fame never quite reached the same cult status as in most other Western European states, Marcuse was a revered public figure for the student left. The ageing British poet Stephen Spender recalls a telling incident during his tour of hot spots of revolutionary agitation in the calendar year of 1968 when, present at one of the many open-ended public discussion fora in the constantly overcrowded nerve centre of the Parisian youth revolt, the occupied Odéon Theatre, Spender, who had not been invited to speak, at the spur of the moment decided to ask the chairperson whether he could address the crowd:

There was only one disapprobating yell (which was silenced by the young chairman with a severe, 'We even listened to Jean-Louis Barrault [the artistic director of the Odéon National Theater of France, disinvested of his powers in the course of the month-long occupation]; why not him?'), and I started to speak my poor French to what seemed an electric silence. To my amazement they listened and then started asking questions.... I struggled to answer these questions and then, at the first opportunity, left the theater and walked to a bar. I was followed there by three students. One of them came up to me very shyly and said: 'Monsieur... Monsieur... Is it true that you are Monsieur Marcuse?'[65]

8. THE MEDITERRANEAN NEW LEFT

Intellectuals, social theorists, the world of journals and magazines, and the practice of discussion and debate were vital elements in the mix of factors underlying the genesis of a new left. Gilcher-Holtey repeatedly stresses the centrality of such theoretical elaborations in her concise survey of social movements occurring in '1968'. For a successful mobilization of such movements, their 'cognitive constitution' is decisive, the author suggests. A thorough intellectual comprehension of means and goals is seen as a prerequisite for any given social movement's success in the conquest of everyday life and the pursuit of ongoing social conflicts. Accordingly, Gilcher-Holtey's brief history of the determinants of new left identity begins with an exploration of leading dissident intellectuals, seen as primary forces behind the emergence of the new left, before going on to depict a subsequent generation of new left activists, who applied the lessons drawn from their intellectual pathfinders and who then proceeded to constitute the first numerically important manifestations of the spirit of new left ideology in actual practice. Symptomatically, Gilcher-Holtey exclusively refers to student movements—above all the West German and American SDS—as the incorporation of this activist spirit within the emerging new left.[66] Such a view of the paramount importance of intellectual labour in the constitution of the new left is relatively widespread, though it should be noted that such convictions tend to be most prominent with academics in countries in which new left activism took a distinct and particular route (about which below).[67]

What this particular approach leaves out is an additional, at least equally central determinant in the shaping of a new left: political organizations, often with significant membership figures, that had arisen to the left of the old left and which survived and prospered concurrently with the ivory tower efforts of prominent intellectuals. Indeed, in those countries where new left forms of activism had most impact on society, such a favourable evolution was the concrete result of the creative interplay of forces between new left political organizations, dissident intellectuals often integrated within or highly sympathetic to such new left parties, and a wider periphery of supporters hailing from all walks of life, with students a pivotal but by no means exclusive mass base. The new left political parties relevant in this particular context can be best outlined and described by a cursory survey of three particular experiences: the Socialist Party of Proletarian Unity (PSIUP) in Italy; the Unified Socialist Party (PSU) in France; and the Popular Liberation Front (FLP) in Francoist Spain. All three organizations were mass-based political parties with a significant presence within actually existing social movements—and a noticeable presence in the sphere of parliamentary politics in those nation-states permitting open discussion and debates. Given their importance within the spectrum of the left in these three crucial states at the centre of the experience of '1968', it is an extraordinary fact that the few existing monographs claiming to present a transnational view of the fledgling new left neglect to include such eminently influential organizations in their survey of the life and times of the activist 1960s.[68]

Chronologically, the first of the three flagship organizations to the left of communism and social democracy to be considered here was the Spanish Popular Liberation Front (FLP), officially constituted in 1958, but with its roots traceable to the 1956 emergence of two student groupings in Barcelona and Madrid, both groupings significantly adopting the name of University New Left.[69] The title 'Popular Liberation Front' was a conscious admixture of the names of two model organizations which stood godfather to the FLP: the Algerian National Liberation Front (FLN) and the French Left Catholic Popular Liberation Movement (MLP).[70] By the time of its constitution in the anti-Franco underground, its support base already extended far beyond its original nuclei in Barcelona and Madrid. And the FLP soon agitated in all corners of the Spanish state. From early on, it strove to extend its influence beyond the university milieu, and at the time of the 1962 Asturian general strike (see Chapter 3), the FLP played a prominent role in the popularization and extension of the strike wave.[71] By 1968, its Catalan federation was the dominant organization within the all-important workers' commissions operating within the province of Barcelona,[72] at the same time as it continued to agitate the Catalan university milieu. No study of Spanish student and worker protest in the second half of the 1960s can afford to ignore the central contributions of the Spanish FLP and its affiliated Catalan and Basque federations.[73]

Symptomatically—and clearly demonstrating its affinity to new left politics elsewhere in the Western world—the FLP always operated as a broad umbrella group of dissident left-wing tendencies, open to all sorts of currents and counter-currents within the anti-Stalinist radical left. From the beginning including a prominent number of left Catholic activists, its political syncretism and openness towards any promising radical ideas were a constant hallmark of FLP political culture—and, indeed, the worldwide new left.

In contradistinction to the monolithic nature of other parties, [the FLP] opted for the free interpretation of the greatest variety of authors, the latter frequently of obviously heterodox provenance. Activists could therefore simultaneously read Rosa Luxemburg, Lenin, Mao, Trotsky, Marx, André Gorz, Teilhard de Chardin, or Mounier; profiting from a pluralism connecting the various traditions from which FLP members could draw, such as Marxism, Christian humanism, or libertarian thought.[74]

Or, in the words of another observer, 'within its sphere of influence coexisted a thousand and one differing theoretical approaches', such as 'Castro-Guevarists, Trotskyists of old or new extraction, spontaneists, anarcho-Marxists; . . . a hundred different doctrinal flowers blossomed and intermingled within its ranks, but without a gardener who could put order into such chaos'.[75] The heterodox FLP served as training ground for several generations of Spanish social movement activists, most notably labour leaders such as Nicolás Sartorius, but also a string of intellectuals such as the novelist Manuel Vázquez Montalbán, the sociologist Manuel Castells, or the political scientist José María Maravall. The FLP's closest international allies were the Italian PSIUP and the French PSU.

Founded on 3 May 1960, the PSU provided a home to the entire kaleidoscope of dissident communist, left socialist, and left Catholic currents that had made French political culture *sui generis* even in the cold war deep freeze in the 1950s. In May 1954, in Paris, a two-day conference, called 'Study Days of the New Left', gave rise to the first political organization anywhere in the world employing the signature label of 'new left,' in this case the Nouvelle Gauche. The Nouvelle Gauche never managed to become more than one amongst many such tendencies to the left of the old left, and it was the founding of the PSU which finally crystallized the forces of the dissident left.[76] Total PSU membership throughout the 1960s fluctuated between 10,000 and 15,000, no small feat in a country generally hostile towards party affiliation.[77] The PSU never managed to cross the 4 per cent threshold in national elections, but in 1967 it obtained four seats in parliament.[78] In 1967, on the eve of the May revolt, the PSU had 26 members of departmental parliaments, 421 municipal councillors, and 96 mayors throughout France, the latter including two medium-sized regional centres (Brive-la-Gaillarde and Saint Brieuc) as well as the city of Grenoble.[79] In January 1967, the PSU's student organization, the Unified Socialist Students (ESU), had obtained control over the National Union of French Students (UNEF), a leading voice of dissident activism ever since its campaign against French policies in Algeria—and a major force in May 1968.[80] In 1968 the PSU 'leaders were as surprised as everyone else when the students' demonstrations spread and the strike wave began. The PSU did, however, react in a unique way. It was the only left-wing party that supported both the students and the workers.' 'In the next six months at least six thousand new members flocked to the party, more than compensating for its losses of the year before. These new members, with their revolutionary aspirations, kept the party moving to the left',[81] transforming the PSU in the aftermath of the May events into the political expression par excellence of the spirit of *autogestion*. It is more than symbolic that the spokesperson of the 1973 Besançon LIP revolt, Charles Piaget, was a long-time member of the PSU.

An equally multifaceted, pluralist, open-minded, and open-ended organization at the centre of the 1960s worldwide new left was the Italian PSIUP. Officially constituted in January 1964 in reaction to the Italian Socialist Party's entry into a coalition government with Italy's Christian Democracy, the bulk of its forces were disaffected members of the PSI. The PSI, of course, had always included a strong dissident left-wing tendency within its ranks. In 1959, for instance, the traditional 'Socialist Left' within the PSI garnered 33 per cent of the vote at the PSI's annual conference. Another left tendency, Lelio Basso's 'Alternative', obtained an additional 8 per cent of the vote.[82] Not all supporters of the PSI left went along with the organizational split in 1964, but the PSIUP counted 150,000 members nonetheless.[83] Twenty-five members of parliament, eight senators, and many union leaders helped constitute the PSIUP, and indeed the proportion of PSI leaders going along with the split was higher than the disaffection from the PSI's ranks. 'There always continued to exist two souls at the heart of the PSIUP with frequent communication problems between each other: one which strove to regain the territory lost by the decline of the PSI, and another one which, once again, aimed for the construction of a completely new organization', an inner division which 'was aggravated by the decentralized nature of the party, differing from local party to local party, from one sector of industry to another, devoid of a strong identity and common reference points'.[84] Yet this very same ambivalence also served as a point of attraction for radical activists of varying persuasions. Leading activists of the *movimento studentesco*, such as Luigi Bobbio, Mauro Rostagno, or Marco Boato, were members of the PSIUP. And, time and again, working-class members of the PSIUP performed crucial roles in the unleashing of the proletarian revolt in countless factories in the *biennio rosso* of 1968–9.[85] Despite apparent divisions and prevarications, the PSIUP stood far closer to the spirit of the Italian *sessantotto* than any of its old left rivals. The May 1968 national elections rewarded the PSIUP with an unexpected total of 4.5 per cent of the popular vote.[86]

To write a history of the new left without giving prominent attention to the PSIUP, PSU, and FLP is like composing a study of Eurocommunism (about which below) in the 1970s without a reference to the French, Spanish, or Italian Communist parties. Rather than viewing the European and North American new left as a product of intellectual combustion, combined with the fresh energies of a restless new generation of students, in reality the new left included a much vaster sociological heritage and organizational spectrum of forces. The interpretation of the new left as a unique combination of intellectual ferment and university unrest is, of course, not entirely inappropriate for the 'northern' tier of European states, including the United States, although even here student activism was at least as crucial to new departures in intellectual explorations as were academic stimulants for student unrest. But when including the all-important 'southern' tier of European states, where the spirit of '1968' affected workers as much as students, the limits of such a partial 'northern' vision become readily apparent to anyone who cares to see. In the 'southern' European states, the ideology and practice of the new left had a much deeper impact on society at large than the far more exclusively student-oriented variants further north. In 'northern' European states, including the United States, the limited social reach of new left thinking allowed student organizations to gain pride of place. But, when compared with the French, Italian, and Spanish examples where radical student movements were also second to none, the centrality of the West German and American SDS turns out to have been an expression of new left weakness and not of strength. Naturally, given the context of relative societal isolation, the radicalized student organizations gained prominent media attention and were able to rock the boat of consensual high politics as usual. In the southern tier of European states, however, the stakes were distributed in a rather different fashion. Given the strength of oppositional new left sentiments amongst far wider social strata in the south, here the political expression of new left sentiment found its quasi-natural outlet in solidly implanted political parties of the new left—but political parties of a special kind: open to a large variety of views, decentralized, non-dogmatic, and attractive to a new generation of rebels who, further north and across the Atlantic, only found solace in the isolated pockets of a student new left.

9. CHARACTERISTICS OF THE NEW LEFT

How, then, can one summarize the intellectual character and the organizational nature of the new left? Given its pluralist nature—itself a classic hallmark of the new left—any summary will necessarily be partial, incomplete, and fraught with inherent dangers of misrepresenting the manifold national specificities and peculiarities. Nonetheless, the following generalizations may serve as useful signposts for an understanding of the 1960s new left. It is instructive to use the old left view of political and social action as a point of comparison.

The old left was, by definition, intimately associated with its political parties, in addition to its trade union wings in those countries where the structures of trade unions permitted such party-political appendices. Moreover, for practical purposes, significant political changes were, for the old left, by the 1960s almost entirely associated with parliamentary manœuvres and establishment politics as usual, at least in those countries where parliamentary politics was the name of the game. For the new left, including in countries with well-respected new left political parties, such as France, Italy, and underground Spain, organizations as such and the realm of customary politics played a decidedly less central role. Stress was placed on the decentralization of decision making, the empowerment of grass-roots activists—in short, the politicization of everyday life. Often, stress was placed on the anticipation of a non-alienated future in counter-institutions, such as cooperative ventures of any kind, community projects, or communal living arrangements. Direct action or civil disobedience took precedence over party building. Small groups were to enable the immediacy of membership interaction with each other to persist. Personal interaction was stressed, in part to avoid bureaucratization. At the same time, broad mass mobilizations, social movements, regardless of their social class composition, were seen as the key agents for meaningful social change. The old left habitually regarded workers, more often than not specifically blue-collar workers, as the central force pushing society in the direction of progressive change. Social democracy in the 1960s, of course, was increasingly moving to replace workers with a diffuse definition of an amorphous 'people' as their coveted target audience and recruiting ground, but even here old habits died hard. By contrast, the new left, though rarely entirely neglecting workers as an instrument for social change, actively searched for other agents as well. They found them, just as Marcuse suggested, clustered in a variety of social groupings, such as intellectuals, students, Third World peasants, disadvantaged ethnic minorities, and youth in general.

By the 1960s both elements of the old left, communism and social democracy, had long discarded revolution as a mechanism and a goal. While, to varying degrees, still paying lip service to the necessity for radical changes in society and economy, in concrete moments of societal crises nothing seemed to be further from their actual practice of politics. Communism's ongoing identification with the non-capitalist East still imbued its Western organizations with a certain system-transforming aura, but the brutal crushing of democratic socialist aspirations in Hungary (and Poland) in 1956, combined with the increasing moderation of actual practice in the capitalist West, placed Western Communist parties either in the counter-revolutionary or reform-oriented rather than the revolutionary camp. Not all new left activists were firmly committed social revolutionaries. Indeed, the new left usually combined individuals and political currents devoted to structural reforms together with self-proclaimed and unabashed supporters of a revolutionary approach in one multifaceted and free-flowing institutional and organizational framework. The difference from the old left, however, not only lay in the greater affinity for revolutionary tactics and changes—however ill-defined—on the part of many new left activists. Above all else, when faced with the outburst of revolutionary energies and opportunities, new left supporters were generally found in the vanguard—and not in the rearguard—of actually existing radical processes and social movements.

For the old left, traditionally, material conditions and economic preconditions and prospects were central for their self-understanding of the mechanisms behind political and social changes. Inasmuch as old left parties still paid homage to 'socialism' as their ultimate political goal, they generally imagined such desirable changes in almost exclusively economistic terms. Where the old left stressed economics, the new left stressed culture. The desirable society of the future should not just be characterized by a revolution in property relations: it would also have to be a cultural revolution or it would be no revolution at all. A post-capitalist society should not just bring economic and institutional changes, but it would have to be accompanied by a whole new way of living and interacting. The focus for new left activists was thus no longer exclusively exploitation but included in equal measure the consequences of alienation. Not just capitalism but authority structures in general were to be opposed. Replacing capitalism with another exploitative and alienating social system would not usher in the end of authoritarian rule. The new left was centrally concerned with the promotion of anti-hierarchical, anti-institutional, and anti-bureaucratic means and goals. Self-determination and self-management in all walks of life was their ultimate aim.

Whereas the old left—inasmuch as sections of it still proclaimed the ultimate 'inevitability' of 'socialism'—generally argued that economic and social contextual conditions eventually would bring about this inescapable future utopian state, the new left stressed the crucial role of individual and collective will in order to bring about radical change. Consequently, new left activists by and large showcased a high degree of individual commitment and personal engagement. Their firm belief that without active resistance change would rarely come about instilled the tell-tale voluntarism of the European and North American new left. One consequence of the new left refusal to regard progressive changes as inevitable was their keen attention to international politics. For, if individual human beings, singly and combined, were ultimately responsible for revolutionary change, then any example of successful radical activism elsewhere in the world could potentially serve as role model at home. From the very beginning, the new left proved to be internationalist to the core. Its journals were full of analyses of foreign politics. If the brutal crushing of the Hungarian Revolution was a notable negative model behind the rise of the new left, the Cuban Revolution provided a positive alternative for many. And the European and North American student movements, largely non-existent up to the mid-1960s, found positive inspiration in the early upsurge of student struggles in Turkey, South Korea, and, above all, Japan.

In the end, however, one could summarize the growing separation between old left and new left in the following terms. What best explains the growing alienation of 1960s activists from the politics and the organizations of the old left was the ever-growing distance between old left politics and politicians from the great variety of social movements making headline news in the course of the 1960s. This is not the time and place to enter the debate on the supposed or real differences between 'old' and 'new' social movements. It may suffice to suggest that social activism in the first one hundred years following *The Communist Manifesto* was rarely as exclusively identified with pure 'working-class' concerns as the relevant literature purports to portray. What makes old left behaviour between 1848 and 1948 differ from its outlook between 1948 and 1968 is 'merely' that, roughly speaking, up to 1948 social democrat and communist parties were generally oriented towards—and identified with—critical engagement with all sorts of social movement activities, be it working-class strikes, suffrage movements, abortion rights campaigns, or antifascist resistance movements. Clearly, the degree of concrete old left involvement and the nature of their support to such actually existing social movements was—and remains—subject to debate. But there was little question that, despite contradictions and a thousand and one hesitations even in the golden age of the old left, their fundamental identification with social movement activism crucially contributed to their political identity and popularity.

The post-Second World War decades, by contrast, turned out to be the period when old left parties began to sever their umbilical cord to actually existing social movements. Social democracy and communism—two political currents born in the heat of struggle out of vibrant and highly contested social struggles—increasingly came to be identified as passive bystanders, if not outright opponents, of the most dynamic social movements taking place in the decades of the post-war boom. In the genesis of the new left, 1956 became the crucial watershed year for three reasons: Hungary, Algeria, and Suez. Old left identification with the repressive actions of colonial and imperial acts provided the catalyst for the paradigm shift analysed in preceding pages of this chapter. The abandonment of the last vestiges of old left independent thinking in the area of 'foreign policy' found its domestic counterpart when the rise of social struggles in the 1960s forced old left parties to take up position on either side of the literal and proverbial barricades. With few exceptions, old left machine politics abandoned the new generation of activists. With the old left abandoning the classic terrain of the left, the old was thus bound to be replaced by an activist new left.

10. THE LIMITS OF NEW LEFT ORGANIZATIONAL PRACTICE

The honeymoon of new left politics lasted until 1968. The variety of often cataclysmic social movements occurring in the course of that year—first the Italian *movimento studentesco* and then, above all else, the French May—served simultaneously as the summit and supersession of seemingly limitless new left activism and its concomitant spirit of boundless optimism. The French May in particular proved to be the beginning of the end of new left hegemony within the activist left. For, many participant-observers began to argue, how could such a tremendous social movement, uniting broad social strata in a joint campaign to paralyse a modern industrial state in a three-week-long general strike, quietly end with a mere wage increase and then the reinforcement of the Gaullist state? May 1968 and especially the 'morning after' with the massive Gaullist counterdemonstration on the Champs-Elysées on 30 May suddenly forced countless activists—within but likewise outside of France—to reconsider and to question the value and utility of new left organizational practices. The perceived failure of what many interpreted as a classic revolutionary situation triggered a deep and long-lasting process of rethinking on the part of the activist-oriented new left, which had itself recently emerged from what many regarded as the shambles of the old left. May 1968 became the moment of conception of a far left.

Criticism of—and discontent with—new left politics, of course, preceded 1968. Furthermore, given the carefully cultivated pluralism of new left operational methods, any general observations at this point will, once again, necessarily be partial and incomplete. Taking the case of southern Europe's new left parties—the PSIUP, PSU, and FLP—first, their consciously decentralized nature was no longer regarded as an asset but as a liability. Organizations that permitted a limitless variety of local experiences, with party branches differing from town to town not only with regard to their ideological outlook but in matters of organizational practices as well, were no longer regarded as a point of attraction but as an obstacle on the pathway to radical social change. If only activists had been better organized and capable of goal-oriented action, or so many began to think, the disastrous outcome of May 1968 could have been avoided. In the case of Italy, it did not help matters that the PSIUP leadership, at the time of the Soviet invasion of Czechoslovakia in the middle of the eventful year of 1968, proved to be far less willing to criticize Soviet great power politics than its main old left rival, the PCI. Small wonder then, that when the PSIUP, originally the numerically largest of the new left parties in the southern tier of European states, dissolved in 1972 its membership had dwindled from its original 1964 high water mark of 150,000 to no more than 20,000.[87] The PSIUP was simultaneously the most promising and the weakest link within the rainbow spectrum of organizations belonging to the new left.

In the northern tier of European states, including the United States, where new left student organizations provided the key organizational outlets and focal point for new left thinking, the problem was different only by degree. The open-ended, decentralized nature of new left student politics was, if anything, even more accentuated than in southern Europe, where the formal party status provided less irregular structures, although this was obviously not the case in underground Spain. The process behind the ultimate self-dissolution of the American and West German SDS are two parallel cases in point. One of the criticisms of old left politics by the new left had been the condemnation of old left rock-solid commitment to representative democracy—simultaneously as the optimal means and the desirable goal. Many of the shortcomings of old left policies and practices had likewise been explained as the logical consequence of the unmitigated belief of old left politicians in the virtues of traditional party organization. Robert Michels, the ruthless critic of the iron law of oligarchies afflicting political parties, quickly became an authority for the early new left, which was then trying to find a way out of what it perceived as the morass of parliamentary politics. Indeed, in the early years of the American SDS, next to C. Wright Mills, Robert Michels was the most frequently cited authority, 'and his description of the inevitable bureaucratisation in traditional organisations provided the chief framework for analysis of both the domestic trade union movement and the Old Left Communist Party'—by the early 1960s there was no more functional social democracy in the US, if it had ever existed.[88]

Convinced of the counterproductive nature of representative democracy, and equally certain of the real and imagined promises of 'participatory' democracy, SDS in America rarely operated in accordance with parliamentary procedures or *Robert's Rules of Order*. 'From 1962 until 1966, a small and unified elite virtually ran SDS. But this national leadership, which everyone recognised, however reluctantly, was not reflected in SDS's official structure, was rarely elected to office, and was never ratified through any formal democratic process.'[89] And after 1966 matters got even worse. The story of SDS's self-dissolution in 1969, driven to paralysis by bitterly contested faction fights, is fairly well-known.[90] But what is often forgotten is that 'factionalism was forced upon all opponents by the nature of the initial elite's control'.[91] Top positions and leadership bodies were progressively abolished, and control was nominally handed down to grass-roots activists at SDS's base. Yet, in reality, this merely increased the actual control over SDS policy and procedures by the 'much more experienced and politically sophisticated' top cadre. 'Thus, leadership was transformed into manipulation; in addition, it is always harder to hold informal leadership accountable for mistakes than it is to hold formal leadership accountable—especially if the prevailing ethos requires a denial that any leadership exists at all.'[92] Where elections to high offices survived as a regular feature of SDS organizational life, the principle of rotation of office ensured that power here too was increasingly removed from the SDS ranks. For, what was seen as 'a necessary antidote to bureaucracy' in actual practice meant that top organizational posts went to relatively inexperienced newcomers and that the more seasoned activists now, here too, operated behind the scenes. 'The successive SDS leaders and activists who dismantled that structure [of formal representative democracy nominally operational within early SDS] did so out of a belief that it was responsible for the absence of full democratic participation in SDS,... but in so doing these SDS leaders and activists intensified the very problems they had set out to remedy.'[93] It was almost as if SDS leaders were driven to prove Michels's iron law of oligarchy—Mark II.[94]

Virtually identical processes were responsible for the concurrent implosion of the German SDS. Increasingly the playing field of local movement leaders competing for national attention, the standard history of SDS concludes: 'At the last regular delegate conference of SDS before its self-dissolution, held in Frankfurt from 12 to 16 September 1968, it became apparent that the organization was unable to dismantle the local power elites; instead of democratization it promoted decentralization—but decentralization of a special kind: each local elite would obtain its own proper duchy (*Fürstenreich*) as its sphere of influence.'[95] On 21 March 1970, almost as an afterthought, a haphazard and unrepresentative gathering in Frankfurt officially proclaimed the death of SDS. No one appeared to oppose this move. The informal burial of SDS was—in the minds of new left strategists—to clear the way for ill-defined grass-roots organs of 'participatory' or 'direct' democracy to lead the way into a non-alienated and libertarian red dawn.[96] As it happened, things evolved in rather different directions.

11. MAOISM AND TROTSKYISM

As if choreographed behind the scenes but in reality quite independently from each other, in virtually every single country that had experienced the presence of a fledgling new left, in 1968–9 moves got under way to construct an entirely different political project that was designed to avoid the pitfalls of both the old left and the new. If the new left had lived in splendid isolation from the historical debates at the centre of old left concerns—the latter singlemindedly focused on the experiences of fascism and world war; the former proving to be innocent children of the post-war boom, happily unconcerned with what had come before—the far left certainly paid close attention to the politics of the 1930s, but above all they rediscovered an even earlier event. Aiming to avoid a repetition of the French post-May 1968 defeat, the far left's eyes were suddenly opened to the perceived lessons of the Bolshevik Revolution. Here, or so it seemed, the organizational antidote to new left passivity and disorganization was beckoning for anyone who cared to see. Growing disillusioned with the tyranny of new left structurelessness while retaining new left disdain for the policies and practices of the old left as it existed in the 1960s, the far left latched onto the lessons of 1917 as the answer to the problems radical activists were encountering more than half a century later. A tightly—certainly by comparison with new left structures—organized political party would be capable of leading the wished-for assault on the foundation of the economic and political order. If decentralized social movements had been able to rock—though not to capsize—the boat of advanced industrial society, how much more effective would centralized action turn out to be?[97]

A flurry of party-building activity set in, just as a year or two earlier grass-roots decentralization had been rigidly enforced. In Barcelona, Paris, Turin, San Francisco, and Berlin, new left organizations were abandoned almost overnight for newly founded revolutionary parties or—where a measure of moderation still held sway—circles of like-minded 'revolutionaries' who set themselves the task of constructing such parties as soon as the necessary critical mass of activists had been assembled. Given that the old left remained wholly discredited and the new left was on the verge of collapse, the emergence of multiple and competing new revolutionary parties, even and especially within the borders of one state, was only logical. For, given a perceived vacuum of revolutionary politics, a tabula rasa of sorts, why not permit a variety of revolutionary parties to test their mettle? Would not the marketplace of revolutionary politics soon inevitably sift the chaff from the wheat? Nonetheless, from the very beginning, the suddenly multiplying 'revolutionary parties' tended to fall into a rather limited number of categories. Two variants proved to be most promising. One, the Trotskyist variant, was, strictly speaking, not a product of '1968'. But, tracing its traditions and carefully cultivated organizational continuities back into the inter-war period, in most countries targeted by this study the turbulences associated with '1968' for the first time propelled Trotskyist organizations into the limelight of national and international politics. The second strand of far left politics can be subsumed under the Maoist label. Inspired by a limited and selective understanding of China's Cultural Revolution, encouraged by Chairman Mao's public break with the Soviet Union, significant portions of an entire generation of politicized activists of the '1968' generation sought salvation in the Red East.[98]

With hindsight and following a series of harrowing experiences, it has become common practice for former far left activists, academic analysts, and other interested observers to proclaim the post-1968 era of far left politics an unmitigated disaster and a regression, which put a prolonged but brutal end to the period of bright-eyed innocence usually ascribed to the relevant milieux of the preceding new left. And there certainly is no shortage of detailed and painful accounts highlighting the negative consequences of prolonged personal engagement with the frequently frenetic pace of activism demanded by many key organizations of the far left. Whether it be the extent of personal self-sacrifice demanded of individual far left party members or the growing frustration with the absence of meaningful internal party democracy; be it the transference of the cult of personalities, pioneered by Joseph Stalin, enthusiastically adapted by the Chinese Communist Party, and then copied by the miniature Maoist 'revolutionary parties' populating the political map of Europe and North America, or the exactions of iron party discipline imposed on far left activists from Naples to New York; there is no disputing that the post-1968 era of far left hegemony within the activist left resulted in at least as many broken promises and empty hopes as new left structurelessness was responsible for in the years leading up to 1968.[99]

But, just as it would be ahistorical and counterproductive to condemn the new left and everything it stood for because of its failures, contradictions, and unachieved goals, it would be equally self-limiting and ineffective to paint all of the experiences and variegated contributions by the plethora of far left parties with the same shade of grey.[100] For one thing, not all far left organizations were alike, leaving aside their cursory categorization as belonging to either the Trotskyist or Maoist fold. To be sure, Maoist organizations, on balance, showed a far greater willingness to ride roughshod over the principles and practices of inner-party democracy than did Trotskyist groups, but there are plenty of important exceptions. The 'soft' Maoist French Gauche Prolétarienne or the Italian Lotta Continua, for all their structural faults and shortcomings, were fundamentally anti-hierarchical political parties and, if anything, they thus incorporated some of the corresponding faults of the new left organizations they sought to replace. It is true, of course, that top-down hierarchical authority structures were most pronounced in those Maoist organizations most closely pretending to please the Great Helmsman in the Far East. But Trotskyist organizations, too, though generally derisive of the supposed model character of China's Cultural Revolution or Mao himself, were rarely shining examples of practices where members controlled their leadership and not the reverse. Still, most organizations affiliated to the largest of the Trotskyist umbrella groups, the Unified Secretariat of the Fourth International in Brussels, were, on balance, far more democratic than the average Maoist group. Some, such as the Austrian Revolutionary Marxist Group (GRM), or the early French Revolutionary Communist Youth (JCR) or the early British International Marxist Group (IMG) were downright pluralist or 'chaotically libertarian'.[101]

12. THE GENESIS OF THE FAR LEFT

What is often completely forgotten in the discussion of far left politics in its heyday between, say, 1969 and 1976 is the fact that, despite apparent differences from the immediately preceding new left, the far left emerged from the contradictions of the experiences of the new left. Although far left organizations frequently took on all the trappings of hierarchical organizations, with choreographed performances not only on the theatrical stage, sometimes complete with mini-personality cults, virtually none of them embraced such celebrations of uniformity in their earliest stages. And it could not have been any different as most of the leading figures in what became the far left came politically of age in the preceding new left. Thus, in the formative years of the far left, its organizations and its inner political life showed remarkable flexibility and a penchant for pluralism and debate. The British IMG, for instance, did not adapt a strict Leninist line until 1970. Earlier on, the 'style of IMG...was suggestive of Marcuse rather than Lenin'.[102] The early JCR was 'more Guevarist than Trotskyist', and their Swiss co-thinkers organized in the Revolutionary Marxist League (LMR) were openly pluralist until 1971.[103] The wide array of competing far left organizations in Francoist Spain, admirably covered by Consuelo Laíz, confirms the near-universality of an identical process elsewhere, and for Maoist as much as for Trotskyist groups. After a period of intellectual casting about and institutional consolidation in underground Spain, 'the organizations abandon[ed] their initial ideological eclecticism', adopted the Leninist party-building model, and began to insulate themselves from outside influence, a process promoted but by no means necessitated by repressive measures of the Francoist state.[104]

The ideological pluralism of the early far left was paralleled by an equally contingent process of individual membership choice. 'Many individuals quickly passed through contradictory and seemingly mutually exclusive political experiences in rapid succession; spontaneists became Maoists and Marxist-Leninists, whereas others followed an opposite trajectory from orthodox Leninism to highly energised anti-party activism.'[105] This process of serial commitment to apparently irreconcilable organizational alternatives was reinforced—and reflected—by high turnover. The early years of the Ligue Communiste, the successor organization to the JCR, saw an annual membership turnover of 33 per cent![106] Another legacy of new left practice was the persistence of regional and even local differentiation within the far left. The decentralization within new left organizational structures resulted, as we have seen, in the creation of regional power bases headed by more or less charismatic leaders. When the paradigm shift from new left structureless-ness to far left centralism began to occur, local and regional peculiarities did not vanish overnight. If local SDS chapters or PSIUP party branches had already developed a certain style of politics and a specific 'personality', such informal tendencies towards particularization became, if anything, more pronounced when informal rule by new left regional barons was replaced by centralized authority over local activists by the same dominant individuals, now sanctioned by the precepts of centralized party building characteristic of the far left. For all its debilitating faults, Gerd Koenen's pioneering study of the German far left is most persuasive in his reconstruction of the way in which regional new left fiefdoms smoothly converted into ever so many proletarian combat parties in specific locations and with—at least initially—limited national reach: 'But each group, once constituted, formed a specific milieu or micro-community, engendered particularistic styles and traditions, and attracted individuals with distinct individual and social characteristics.'[107] In Italy, identical geographical differenti-ations determined the regional peculiarities of both the new and the far left.[108] Other countries' experience replicated this trend.

13. THE FAR LEFT AS INSPIRATION

But what about the perception of fully developed far left organizations on the part of its growing army of members and sympathizers? Was there much that was positive about the far left once most of its organizations had adopted some version of the Leninist model? Given the prominence of the redemptive literature alluded to above, was far left activism solely a self-destructive generational flop? For Italian far left activists, Diego Giachetti avers,

to engage in politics was by no means an alienating activity, an onerous obligation, experienced as a painful loss of precious time that had to be subtracted from one's regular social and emotional life. These activists submerged themselves in political work, investing all sorts of energies, participating in concrete and daily actions, experiencing a certain joy of living and concrete measures of personal growth resulting from such choices.[109]

Or, in the words of the former Trotskyist, Gérard Filoche, later on a leading campaigner in the French Socialist Party's left: 'All those young people evolved, read, studied, campaigned, travelled, were engaged in exceptional activities; and the sum total of their efforts was spellbinding. We do not need to be told the opposite today when the pundits complain about the depoliticization of youth.'[110]

The frequent get-togethers at party branch headquarters, the typing of leaflets, the distribution of newspapers at school or factory gates was experienced as a great communal effort and uplifting of spirits. The proliferation of associated cultural venues and products served as simultaneously stimulating and entertaining digressions. After leafleting the giant FIAT Mirafiori works for most of the day, to listen to a concert by Paolo Pietrangeli or to experience a live performance of Franca Rame and Dario Fo was an experience no one was likely to forget anytime soon. A dense network of far left publishing houses—often pluralist in orientation even and especially when the individual far left parties tightened their organizational rules—and bookstores, newspapers and magazines, served to update and refine one's political horizons. Cooperative ventures, such as food co-ops, restaurants, or repair shops were widely available as communal living had become the norm. A long-time member of the extensive far left squatter community in Frankfurt, Germany, a woman rather reluctant to romanticize her environment in her incisive memoirs, remembers:

The sole thing which was expected was 'solidarity,' i.e. the willingness to help out and a generalised altruism—to an extent which is today difficult even to imagine. . . . Solidarity meant to help comrades and soulmates alike—with a move, when painting an apartment or room, when looking for a job, with term papers, or in emotional crisis situations.[111]

Even the production and distribution of written documents, whether stencilled leaflets, posters, pamphlets, newspapers, or books—a proliferation of printed matter later on often ridiculed by detractors—must be understood as a key element 'in a process of democratization of debate', which Michel de Certeau aptly phrased as 'the capture of speech' or 'the capture of the word'.[112] In short, far left activism was first of all experienced as a fulfilling, pleasurable, and meaningful way of life.

And far left politics, in virtually all national settings and all ideological permutations, affected far larger circles of activists and sympathizers than new left politics was able to affect even in the best of days. Precise figures of total membership are notoriously elusive, but the best guesstimates of far left membership at the point of maximum expansion in the Spanish state, for instance, claim 50,000 card-carrying activists.[113] In Italy, the equivalent figure for total numbers of far left activists approaches the 100,000 mark.[114] Attentive readers may, of course, recall that in 1964 the new left PSIUP claimed 150,000 members. But new left activism in general, though generally decidedly more pronounced than equivalent engagement within the old left, rarely approached the level of near-full-time commitment demanded of most far left members. Thus, the far left was unquestionably disproportionately more visible in the public sphere even in those few regions or countries where new left membership had equalled it in numbers. Consequently, the years of the greatest far left presence are usually remembered as 'the red years', much more so than the preceding era of new left hegemony on the radical left.[115]

Already in 1969, according to a well-respected national opinion survey, 30 per cent of West German secondary and university students expressed sympathies for Marxist or communist ideologies, a choice which, given German politics, rarely indicated a spiritual home in the vicinity of either traditional West German social democracy or Moscow-oriented communism but a distinct proximity to either the new or the far left camps. This figure, Gerd Koenen correctly reports, was likely to have grown even higher by the early 1970s.[116] At the high point of Maoist influence in the relatively conservative United States, the independent Maoist weekly, *Guardian*, sold more than 20,000 copies of each issue; the intellectual house journal of academic 'soft' Maoism at that time, *Monthly Review*, peaked at over 11,000 copies per issue.[117] If the 1960s was the classic decade of the new left, the years from 1969 to 1976 were the period of hegemony of the even more radical and activist-oriented far left. Precisely in the years following the events of 1968, the Western European and North American 'radical left', the latter expression a label of convenience subsuming both the new and the far left, reached the peak of its influence in terms of membership, geographical spread, and societal depth.

Still, in terms of numbers, even the flourishing far left of the 1970s did not even come close to the mass support which the organizations belonging to the old left continued to enjoy. With regard to their impact on social movements, however, the forces of the far left benefited from—and, indeed, further strengthened—the winds that had propelled the sails of the 1960s new left. The ongoing disinvestment by old left social democracy and communism from the compromising baggage of its formerly radical social critique left the field wide open for the post-1968 far left to shape the activist discourse of the 1970s. Nonetheless, precisely during these turbulent 1970s the old left experienced one last bout of left-wing opposition and dissent from within its own ranks. Just as had happened during the last generalized wave of societal critique in the 1930s, there were signs that social democracy would once again turn to the left.[118]

14. A SOCIAL DEMOCRATIC TURN TOWARDS THE LEFT?

France had experienced the almost total disappearance of social democracy even as an electoral force in the run-up to 1968. The shock effect of 1968 reinstilled vitality into a seemingly moribund organization. A veritable 'new' Parti Socialiste (PS) arose from the ashes of 1968. In June 1971, the Épinay Congress of the PS combined the energies of a variety of competing social democratic tendencies, and the new organization managed to adopt some of the most dynamic concepts emerging from 1968: the decentralization of decision-making powers, an enlargement of the vision of 'socialism' to encompass non-economistic means and goals and, last but not least, *autogestion*. As the French far left began its process of rigidification, PS politics gained in attraction. One-time guerrilla fighter Régis Debray was only one amongst many former critics of the social democratic tradition who jumped on the bandwagon of renovated PS politics. Increasing numbers of PSU spokespersons and rank-and-file members abandoned the fledgling new left, with PSU figurehead Michel Rocard switching allegiance in

1974. Soon entering an electoral pact with left bourgeois parties and the French Communist Party, the second half of the 1970s saw a groundswell of hopes for this Union of the Left. Correspondingly, PS membership figures rapidly grew from 90,000 (1971) to 150,000 in 1975.[119]

But even in countries less unequivocally affected by the moment of opportunity and crisis exemplified by 1968, the social democratic old left felt the rumblings of a left challenge within its own ranks.[120] In West Germany, as early as 1969, the social democratic youth organization, the Young Socialists (Jusos) were caught up in the whirlwind of activity affecting university campuses across the land. From an organization providing a steady stream of eager recruits for the SPD party apparatus, the Jusos evolved into a debating ground where 'the most common references in discussions were the names of [the Belgian Trotskyist Ernest] Mandel, [the French new left sociologist André] Gorz, [the Italian PSIUP's leading intellectual Lelio] Basso and [the new left philosopher par excellence Herbert] Marcuse'. By December 1969 the 'revolutionary reformist' currents obtained a majority of votes at the Munich congress of their organization. For the succeeding half a dozen years, they determined the political atmosphere within the German social democratic youth organization, and their rebellious spirit made inroads into the SPD itself, though interest in the ideologies and practices of the new and far left were, in a peculiar twist of the German mind, eventually eclipsed by admiration of the Communist East. Forty-five out of 240 SPD members of parliament elected in 1972 sympathized with the Young Socialist critique. At the Hanover SPD congress in 1973, 11 out of 36 national executive committee members belonged to the camp of the social democratic radical left.[121]

Of all European social democratic parties, perhaps the British Labour Party saw the most deep and long-lasting combined efforts of an assortment of radical currents and traditions to force an old left organization to remember its more radical past. In the United Kingdom, efforts to reform British Labour from within did not get seriously under way until the early 1970s, but then an unexpected if often conflict-ual 'alliance' made its presence felt. The traditional Labour left aimed to push for greater inner-party democracy, together with Trotskyist forces operating from within the Labour Party and aiming to turn the latter's practices upside down. Both currents took advantage of a fresh influx of new members seeking to alter British society and politics. Their tenacious fight almost led to a victory of sorts. At the 1981 Labour Party Conference, the figurehead of the insurgent left, Tony Benn, lost the campaign for deputy leadership by the narrowest of all margins. Benn obtained 49.574 per cent of all votes against Denis Healey's 50.426 per cent majority.[122]

15. THE PROMISE OF EUROCOMMUNISM?

Yet the spark of innovation within the old left did not only target its social democratic component. Within the world of communism, too, important changes were forthcoming contemporaneous with the revolts of 1968. The Soviet invasion of Czechoslovakia, putting a brutal end to 'socialism with a human face', jolted large portions of Western European communist parties into a rebellion of their own. If the bloody suppression of the 1956 Hungarian Revolt had still obtained unanimous support from communist parties around the world, twelve years later such total submission to the dictates of their Kremlin leadership had become increasingly impossible to maintain. A number of the most important Western European communist parties openly condemned the snuffing out of the Prague Spring. This act of insubordination became the declaration of independence for the more dynamic portions of the communist movement around the world. Above all the Italian, the Spanish, and the French Communist Parties became increasingly identified with the 'Eurocommunist' promotion of discussion and dissent *within* the communist movement, although other communist parties, notably the British and the Belgian parties, were affected even more deeply by this spirit of revolt.[123] Yet, in a curious difference from reverberations of '1968' within the social democratic universe, efforts to reform or revolutionize traditional policy conceptions and modes of operation within the communist component of the old left frequently evolved in a moderate direction rather than to the left.

The belated discovery of the values of democracy and openly conducted inner-party debates was greeted by a large portion of a broadly sympathetic interested public with a collective sigh of relief. Finally, or so it seemed, one no longer had to compromise one's personal beliefs when organizationally linking up with the communist tradition. One of the major obstacles to a broader acceptance of communism as a potentially major player in the Western world seemed to disintegrate, leaving wide open the possibilities of a reinforcement of social movement activity now reinvigorated by constructive communist critique. Yet it soon became all too apparent that radical hopes invested in Eurocommunism were to be bitterly disappointed. For, in practice, the abandonment of sectarian traditionalism on the part of Eurocommunist parties led to accommodation with—and not to challenges to—the late capitalist status quo. To take the case of the most famous and influential party of the Eurocommunist camp: the PCI. As we saw in earlier portions of this chapter, its first organizational decision after declaring its opposition to the Moscow invasion of Prague's reforming efforts was the expulsion of the PCI's left opposition, which had crystallized around *Il Manifesto*. Intransigence towards left-wing critics was more than matched by openness to and accommodation of forces standing considerably further to the right. In a series of moves the PCI sought to overcome the cold war divide, which had rendered Italian politics seemingly immovable since the late 1940s, by offering a historic compromise with reform-minded elements amongst Italy's ruling Christian Democrats. But, if such a policy reorientation was designed to break open encrusted stalemates on the domestic policy front, it also encouraged and promoted a further moderation of PCI politics. In the mid-1970s, for instance, important cultural and political battles broke out in Italy around the issues of abortion and divorce. In these major parliamentary and, above all, extraparliamentary social conflicts the embarrassed Communist Party stood on the sidelines.

A referendum on the liberalization of divorce laws was held in May 1974. 'After a campaign in which the Socialists and the extra-parliamentary Left, particularly *Lotta Continua*, were much more vigorous in defense of secular values than the Communists, the PCI was startled to find that divorce was approved by no less than 59.1 per cent of the electorate.'[124] Yet, fearful of alienating its coveted Christian Democratic potential allies, the PCI learnt few lessons for the subsequent abortion fight, where a 1981 referendum found a staggering 68 per cent of Italians in favour of drastic liberalization. Instead, the party which was proud to be regarded 'as a force both for the preservation of order and for change'[125] continued on its rightward drift.

When the PCI's *primus inter pares* Enrico Berlinguer openly embraced austerity politics as a weapon to promote progressive social change, he went one step too far. At a PCI-sponsored conference in January 1977, which assembled leading representatives of Italy's influential progressive intellectual community, the non-conformist Norberto Bobbio, for instance, lectured the PCI's leader: 'Dear Berlinguer; with sacrifices alone one will not transform society. On the whole, austerity is a recommendation by the employing classes. The austerity of the poor is a part of [poor people's] everyday life.'[126] And 1977 became a watershed year for PCI politics in more ways than one. For, in the course of that year, a series of unpredicted political and cultural rebellions broke out in urban centres throughout Italy, with a new youthful generation of rebels at the helm. Confronting PCI-led municipal administrations in the many population centres then under communist local control, the Movement of '77 challenged authorities of both the political (old) left and the right. 'For the first time a social movement developed that regarded the PCI not as an ally but as an enemy. In marked contrast to the evenhanded attitude shown in 1968, the party sharply criticised the student movement [of 1977] as a source of disruption and destabilisation.'[127] And PCI functionaries contributed wholeheartedly to the ensuing indiscriminate repressive campaign. It marked the end of an era. 'The PCI had become the party of law and order, the bulwark of democratic legality, the shield of the constitution.'[128]

Efforts to change the outlook of social democracy ended on a similar note. Young Socialists in West Germany could not sustain their dynamic after 1973, and the reform euphoria which had greeted Willy Brandt's election to German chancellor in 1969—a victory in part responsible for the subsequent influx of rebellious new energies into the SPD, despite the fact that Brandt was no friend of such youthful enthusiasms—ended in McCarthyite witchhunts triggered by Brandt's 1972 explicit call for *Berufsverbote*, a policy aiming to remove social movement activists and radical critics from public employment in the cold war state. The French PS's embrace of *autogestion* fell out of fashion soon after the presidential victory of François Mitterrand in 1981.[129] The same year, as we have seen, also proved to be the summit and supersession for the campaigning forces within the British Labour Party's insurgent left. The latter never again came even close to repeating Tony Benn's near-successful challenge to unseat the forces of tradition. With hostile challenges from the left safely removed, Europe's social democracy continued its secular drift towards the centre and the centre-right. 'Socialists had run out of ideas. In the 1960s they had abandoned the aim of abolishing capitalism; in the 1970s and 1980s they proclaimed that they were the ideal managers of it.'[130] The erstwhile Moscow-oriented communists were not far behind.

NOTES

1. Michael Foot and Mervyn Jones, *Guilty Men, 1957: Suez and Cyprus* (New York: Rinehart & Co., 1957), 13.
2. Ibid. 14.
3. Keith Kyle, *Suez* (London: Weidenfeld & Nicolson, 1992), 349.
4. Foot and Jones, *Guilty Men*, 15–16.
5. Kyle, *Suez*, 383.
6. Harvey G. Simmons, *French Socialists in Search of a Role: 1956–1967* (Ithaca, NY: Cornell University Press, 1970), 36.
7. For the controlled outpouring of oppositional sentiments, see Foot and Jones, *Guilty Men*, 236–43.
8. Citation from the 1957 Labour Party Annual Conference Report, reported in Ralph Miliband, *Parliamentary Socialism: A Study in the Politics of Labour* (London: Merlin, 1973), 338.
9. Ibid.
10. On the explicit link between Suez and the genesis of a British new left, see Michael Kenny, *The First New Left: British Intellectuals After Stalin* (London: Lawrence & Wishart, 1995), 19.
11. Still today the superior study of the Hungarian Revolution of 1956 remains Bill Lomax, *Hungary 1956* (London: Allison & Busby, 1976); but see, amongst others, also Chris Harman's substantive chapter on the Hungarian revolt in his *Bureaucracy and Revolution in Eastern Europe* (London: Pluto, 1974), 124–87.
12. The citation is taken from Marcello Flores, *1956* (Bologna: Il Mulino, 1996), 33. This volume is the single most important transnational study of the events of 1956 east and west of the Iron Curtain. For a concise account of the impact of '1956' on Eastern European societies, see Geoffrey Swain and Nigel Swain, *Eastern Europe since 1945* (New York: St Martin's Press, 1993), 77–100. Khrushchev's 'Secret Report to the 20th Party Congress of the CPSU' is most accessible in English translation in Tariq Ali (ed.), *The Stalinist Legacy: Its Impact on Twentieth-Century World Politics* (Harmondsworth: Penguin, 1984), 221–72.
13. See Keith Middlemas, *Power and the Party: Changing Faces of Communism in Western Europe* (London: André Deutsch, 1980), 99, a passage which includes the Togliatti quote.
14. Donald Sassoon, *One Hundred Years of Socialism: The West European Left in the Twentieth Century* (New York: New Press, 1996), 167.
15. Henry Kissinger, *The White House Years* (London: Weidenfeld & Nicolson, 1979), 424.
16. Here, again, the crucial reference work is the chapter on 'The Socialists and Algeria', in Simmons, *French Socialists*, 19–52. A brief synopsis can be found in Martin Evans,

The Memory of Resistance: French Opposition to the Algerian War (1954–1962) (Oxford: Berg, 1997), 137–9, where the citation can be found on p. 137.

17. Simmons, *French Socialists*, 28. Simmons did not neglect to add: 'The PCF [French Communist Party] voted unanimously for the law.'

18. Both citations can be found ibid. 45. The young Jean-Marie Le Pen was, of course, one of the torturers officially covered by Socialist tolerance of such 'interrogation techniques'.

19. Sassoon, *One Hundred Years*, 239–240.

20. Laski's grandiloquent pronouncement is cited in Miliband, *Parliamentary Socialism*, 284.

21. Ibid. 288.

22. Ibid. 290.

23. Ibid. 305.

24. Ibid. 354–5.

25. Ibid. 364. The fundamental continuities of Labour Party advocacy of austerity politics from 1945 onwards are convincingly portrayed in much greater detail in Leo Panitch, *Social Democracy and Industrial Militancy: The Labour Party, the Trade Unions and Incomes Policy, 1945–1974* (Cambridge: Cambridge University Press, 1976).

26 Sassoon, *One Hundred Years*, 156.

27. Ibid. 155.

28. Geoff Eley, *Forging Democracy: The History of the Left in Europe, 1850–2000* (New York: Oxford University Press, 2002), 317.

29. Lawrence Black, *The Political Culture of the Left in Affluent Britain, 1951–64: Old Labour, New Britain* (Basingstoke: Macmillan, 2003), 70.

30. Ibid. 65.

31. Nick Tiratsoo, *Reconstruction, Affluence and Labour Politics: Coventry 1945–60* (London: Routledge, 1990), 96.

32. Ibid. 116.

33. Peter Lösche and Franz Walter, *Die SPD: Klassenpartei—Volkspartei—Quotenpartei* (Darmstadt: Wissenschaftliche Buchgesellschaft, 1992), 269.

34. Cited in Black, *Culture of the Left*, 77.

35. Both citations can be found ibid. 78; the second one is a quote from a 1956 Hobsbawm article. On the precautionary use of a pseudonym by Hobsbawm, see personal communication by Lawrence Black to author, 16 Mar. 2005.

36. Stephen Gundle, *Between Hollywood and Moscow: The Italian Communists and the Challenge of Mass Culture, 1943–1991* (Durham, NC: Duke University Press, 2000), 114.

37. Both quotes, ibid. 111.

38. The Mar. 1965 denunciation of the Piper Club is taken from *Noi Donne* and reported in Gundle, *Between Hollywood*, 111; the June 1965 recommendation of a specifically Italian road to youth rebellion is taken from Diego Giachetti, *Anni sessanta comincia la danza: Giovani, capelloni, studenti ed estremisti negli anni della contestazione* (Pisa: BFS, 2002), 97.

39. Letter, dated Aug. 1965, reported ibid. 60.

40. Gundle, *Between Hollywood*, 115. This widening gap between the PCI and left wing youth and intellectuals is at the centre of Nello Ajello's 2-vol. study of PCI policies and their interactions with Italian intellectuals. His first volume, *Intellettuali e PCI*

1944/1958 (Bari: Laterza, 1979), covers the golden age of PCI hegemony. The title of his subsequent volume gives away the process of increasing alienation: *Il lungo addio* (The Long Good-Bye): *Intellettuali e PCI dal 1958 al 1991* (Bari: Laterza, 1997).

41. The PCI response to the *rivolta di Piazza Statuto* is documented in Dario Lanzardo, *La rivolta di Piazza Statuto: Torino, Luglio 1962* (Milan: Feltrinelli, 1979), 47–56, citations on pp. 49, 51, and 56.

42. Editorial entitled '25 Aprile 1945–25 Aprile 1962', in *Quaderni Piacentini* 1 bis (April 1965), reprinted in Goffredo Fofi and Vittorio Giacopini (eds.), *Prima e dopo il '68: Antologia dei 'Quaderni Piacentini'* (Rome: Edizioni minimum fax, 1998), 11.

43. Giachetti, *Anni sessanta*, 36.

44. Ibid. 157, and Guido Crainz, *Il paese mancato: Dal miracolo economico agli anni ottanta* (Rome: Donzelli, 2003), 174–5, for this episode.

45. See Giachetti, *Anni sessanta*, 157–62, and Crainz, *Paese mancato*, 175, for a representative listing of such altercations; for the Turin occasion see p. 157 in Giachetti's informative study.

46. Giachetti, *Anni sessanta*, 161.

47. See Walter Franz, *Jugendprotest in Italien: Die lange revolutionäre Welle 1968–1977* (Frankfurt: Haag & Herchen, 1993), 50–4; Crainz, *Paese mancato*, 302–5; and Franco Ottaviano, *La rivoluzione nel labirinto: Sinistra e sinistrismo dal 1956 alla fine degli anni ottanta* (Soveria Mannelli: Rubbettino, 1993), 257–7, for concise and virtually identical assessments of the relationship between the *movimento studentesco* and the PCI. The most detailed commentary on this conflictual coexistence remains, however, Romano Luperini, *Il PCI e il movimento studentesco* (Milan: Jaca, 1969).

48. The tragedy of Italian Communist youth politics is best recounted in Ajello, *Lungo addio*, 72–7.

49. The figures are reported in Giachetti, *Anni sessanta*, 163.

50. The overall parameters of post-war PCI strategies up to the late 1950s are best set out in Livio Maitan, *Teoria e politica comunista del dopoguerra* (Milan: Schwarz, 1959); an update for the 1960s, taking into account PCI interactions with other forces on the Italian working-class left, was published by the same author as *Il movimento operaio in una fase critica* (Rome: Samonà e Savelli, 1966). But see also Grant Amyot, *The Italian Communist Left: The Crisis of the Popular Front Strategy* (London: Croom Helm, 1981), which is particularly illuminating on the stances of the Ingrao left.

51. For the Il Manifesto affair, see Crainz, *Paese mancato*, 310–12, citation on p. 312; Ajello, *Lungo addio*, 94–9; Amyot, *Italian Communist Party*, 170–97; but above all Sergio Dalmasso, *Il caso 'Manifesto' e il PCI degli anni '60* (Turin: Cric, 1989), 99–135.

52. Ingrid Gilcher-Holtey, *Die 68er Bewegung: Deutschland, Westeuropa, USA* (Munich: Beck, 2001), 11–17.

53. The two key studies of the history of the British new left and its associated journals are Kenny, *First New Left*, and Lin Chun, *The British New Left* (Edinburgh: Edinburgh University Press, 1993).

54. The most insightful description of this French intellectual milieu finding public recognition and acceptance via the aforementioned journals remains Ingrid Gilcher-Holtey, *'Die Phantasie an die Macht': Mai 68 in Frankreich* (Frankfurt: Suhrkamp, 1995), 47–81. The movement around the journal *Socialisme ou Barbarie* has found its chronicler in Philippe Gottraux, *'Socialisme ou Barbarie': Un engagement politique et*

intellectuel dans la France de l'après-guerre (Lausanne: Payot, 1997). The literature on the Situationist International is plentiful but of uneven quality. There exists as of yet no convincing study of its political impact on the French new left. Reference to a plethora of publications on this small but highly influential grouping can be culled from my notes in Ch 1. *Arguments* remains curiously understudied, but see Gil Delannoi, '*Arguments*, 1956–1962: ou la parenthèse de l'ouverture', *Revue française de science politique*, 34 (1984), 127–45.

55. For a thorough assessment and bibliographic registration of the world of Italian new left journals produced in the 1960s, see Attilio Mangano and Antonio Schina, *Le culture del sessantotto: Gli anni sessanta, le riviste, il movimento* (Pistoia: Centro di Documentazione di Pistoia, 1998). A special issue of the journal *Classe* devoted to dissident new left journals up to 1969—*Gli anni delle riviste (1955–1969)*, constituting the entirety of *Classe*, 17 (1980)—provides another excellent starting point for the comprehension of this phenomenon.

56. Two national case studies of paradigmatic value for similar processes elsewhere are the imaginative observations on the mutual interaction between the worlds of literature and activist politics in West Germany and Italy, Klaus Briegleb, *1968: Literatur in der antiautoritären Bewegung* (Frankfurt: Suhrkamp, 1993), and Giuseppe Muraca, *Utopisti ed eretici nella letteratura italiana contemporanea* (Soveria Mannelli: Rubbettino, 2000).

57. Interestingly, Lelio Basso has yet to find his biographer. For some preliminary notes, however, see Sergio Dalmasso, *Lelio Basso nella storia del socialismo italiano* (Milan: Punto Rosso, 1995).

58. On Raniero Panzieri, see, for instance, the biographical materials included with the selection of essays Panzieri wrote in the last half dozen years of his creative life, Raniero Panzieri, *Spontaneità e organizazzione: Gli anni dei 'Quaderni rossi', 1959–1964* (Pisa: BFS, 1994); the two chapters devoted to Panzieri in Attilio Mangano, *L'altra linea: Fortini, Bosio, Montaldi, Panzieri e la nuova sinistra* (Catanzaro: Pulano, 1992), 75–121; above all, Salvatore D'Albergo *et al.*, *Ripensando Panzieri trent'anni dopo* (Pisa: BFS, 1995), and now Paolo Ferrero (ed.), *Raniero Panzieri: Un uomo di frontiera* (Milan: Punto rosso, 2005).

59. Herbert Marcuse, *One-Dimensional Man: Studies in the Ideology of Advanced Industrial Societies* (Boston: Beacon, 1964), 257.

60. The sole published biography of C. Wright Mills which pays central attention to his role as mentor of the new left is Andreas Hess, *Die politische Soziologie C. Wright Mills: Ein Beitrag zur politischen Ideengeschichte* (Opladen: Leske & Budrich, 1995). The joint trip to Poland by Mills and Miliband is alluded to in Michael Newman, *Ralph Miliband and the Politics of the New Left* (London: Merlin, 2002), 66–7. On the German student activist Michael Vester finishing his *Diplomarbeit* on C. Wright Mills two years after a lengthy stay in the US, where he participated in the Port Huron Conference of June 1962, see Michael Schmidtke, *Der Aufbruch der jungen Intelligenz: Die 68er Jahre in der Bundesrepublik und den USA* (Frankfurt: Campus, 2003), 49 n. 73. On Tom Hayden's 1964 graduate thesis on Mills, see James Miller, *Democracy is in the Streets: From Port Huron to the Siege of Chicago* (Cambridge, Mass.: Harvard University Press, 1994), 261–2; Miller's book conveniently reprints *The Port Huron Statement* in a documentary appendix on pp. 329–77. More generally on C. Wright Mills's influence on Tom Hayden, see Tom Hayden, *Reunion: A Memoir* (New York: Random, 1988), 76–82 and *passim*. Tom Hayden, of course, was a central

leader of the radical US student organization Students for a Democratic Society, which, by a fluke of linguistic contingency, became known by the identical acronym as its German counterpart: SDS. On Mills's radiance amongst wider American SDS circles, see Miller, *Democracy*, 78–91.

61. The two superior studies of the life and œuvre of Herbert Marcuse remain Barry Katz, *Herbert Marcuse: Art of Liberation* (London: Verso, 1982), and, above all, Jean-Michel Palmier, *Marcuse et la nouvelle gauche* (Paris: Belford, 1973).

62. The citations are all from the closing paragraphs of Marcuse, *One-Dimensional Man*, 256–7.

63. Citations taken from Katz, *Marcuse*, 176 and 168.

64. On the extraordinary reception of Marcuse in Italy, see Francesca Sidotti, 'Emancipazione e politiche culturali negli anni sessanta: Marcuse in Italia', *Rassegna Italiana di Sociologia*, 15 (1974), 241–90. Perhaps the high point of Marcuse's activist engagement with new left student leaders was reached in the course of a four-day symposium in his native Berlin shortly after the police murder of Benno Ohnesorg, a curious onlooker at an SDS-sponsored demonstration against the state visit to Berlin of the dictatorial Persian Shah, an incident ushering in the hot phase of student protests in West Berlin. The transcript of Marcuse's lectures and his discussions with leading student activists are now conveniently published as Herbert Marcuse, *Das Ende der Utopie: Vorträge und Diskussionen in Berlin 1967* (Frankfurt: Neue Kritik, 1980).

65. This episode is told in Stephen Spender, *The Year of the Young Rebels* (London: Weidenfeld & Nicolson, 1969), 52–3, with citations taken from p. 53. The words spoken by the chairperson and the students in the bar are rendered in the original French in Stephen Spender's text.

66. Note, above all, the chapter on 'Alte Linke—Neue Linke: Die kognitive Konstitution der Bewegung', in Gilcher-Holtey, *68er Bewegung*, 11–24, citation on p. 11.

67. Examples of such single-minded focus on intellectuals preparing the terrain for subsequent social action are Kevin Mattson, *Intellectuals in Action: The Origins of the New Left and Radical Liberalism, 1945–1970* (University Park, Penn.: Pennsylvania State University Press, 2002), an excellent study of four US intellectuals, two journals, and the corresponding milieux; and an earlier investigation of fifteen 'dissident intellectuals and the breathing spaces that they carved out of the postwar American landscape' by Andrew Jamison, with the tell-tale title *Seeds of the Sixties* (Berkeley Calif.; University of California Press, 1994), citation on p. 1.

68. George Katsiaficas, *The Imagination of the New Left: A Global Analysis of 1968* (Boston: South End Press, 1987) was perhaps the very first English-language effort to chart the rise and fall of the new left from a comparative point of view. One searches in vain for even a single reference to any of the three organizations mentioned above. Though clearly ascribing secondary importance to this party-political dimension of pre-1968 new left practice, Ingrid Gilcher-Holtey, in her 1995 study of the French May, still devoted a few pages to the PSU (*Phantasie an die Macht*, 96–104). Her subsequent comparative analysis includes not even a hint at the mere existence of such political parties.

69. Julio Antonio García Alcalá, *Historia del Felipe (FLP, FOC y ESBA): De Julio Cerón a la Liga Comunista Revolucionaria* (Madrid: Centro de Estudios Políticos y Constitucionales, 2001), 39.

70. Ibid. 45.

71. On Felipe activity in the strike wave of 1962, ibid. 115–23.

72. Bernhard Pöter, *Von der Ohnmacht zur Gegenmacht: Die Arbeiterkommissionen der Provinz Barcelona unter dem Franquismus* (Saarbrücken: Verlag für Entwicklungspolitik, 1996), 52.

73. Here the relevant two central chapters in García Alcalá, *Historia del Felipe*, 215–50, are the most detailed available sketches of FLP activity in these two most prominent sectors of anti-Franco oppositional activism in Spain: the university student and the working-class milieux.

74. Ibid. 21–2.

75. Ernesto Portuondo, 'Forja de rebeldes: Una aproximación a los orígenes de las vanguardias militantes del radicalismo de izquierdas en la segunda mitad de los sesenta: el movimiento estudiantil (1964–1970)', in José Manuel Roca (ed.), *El proyecto radical: auge y decline de la izquierda revolucionaria en España (1964–1992)* (Madrid: Los Libros de la Catarata, 1994), 111.

76. The most detailed reconstruction of the genesis and evolution of the PSU remains Jean-François Kesler, *De la gauche dissidente au nouveau Parti socialiste: Les Minorités qui ont rénové le P.S.* (Toulouse: Privat, 1990); for the experiment of the original *Nouvelle Gauche*, see pp. 210–14.

77. Ibid. 405.

78. Charles Hauss, *The New Left in France: The Unified Socialist Party* (Westport, Conn.: Greenwood, 1978), 31.

79. Kesler, *Gauche dissidente*, 410.

80. Alain Monchablon, *Histoire de l'UNEF de 1956 à 1968* (Paris: PUF, 1983), 182.

81. Citations taken from Hauss, *New Left*, 35 and 36.

82. Massimo Teodori, *Storia delle nuove sinistre in Europa (1956–1976)* (Bologna: Il Mulino, 1976), 154.

83. Ibid. 155.

84. Sergio Dalmasso, 'L'arcipelago delle sinistre: Partiti, gruppi, riviste', in Carmelo Adagio, Rocco Cerrato, and Simona Urso (eds.), *Il lungo decennio: L'Italia prima del 68* (Verona: Cierre, 1999), 279–80. This somewhat 'schizophrenic nature of the PSIUP' is also alluded to by Steve Wright, *Storming Heaven: Class Composition and Struggle in Italian Autonomist Marxism* (London: Pluto, 2002), 92.

85. On the ambivalent track record of the PSIUP amongst Italy's politicized students, see Marco Boato, 'PSIUP: L'alibi dell'autonomia e la pratica della burocrazia', in his *Il '68 è morto: Viva il '68!* (Verona: Bertani, 1979), 240–55. On PSIUP factory activism, note the exemplary case of PSIUP member Francesco Morino, who on 11 Apr. 1969 organized the very first open meeting within the vast Mirafiori FIAT works in Turin to take place since the mid-1950s, when he jumped on a table in the canteen and addressed a crowd of 1,500 co-workers. On this opening shot of the Hot Autumn in Italy's largest assembly plant, see Marco Revelli, *Lavorare in FIAT: Da Valletta ed Agnelli a Romiti. Operai sindacati robot* (Milan: Garzanti, 1989), 41–2.

86. For additional comments on 'a party which is today unjustly forgotten', see Diego Giachetti, *Oltre il sessantotto: Prima, durante e dopo il movimento* (Pisa: BFS, 1998), 35. On the election returns in 1964 and 1968, see Teodori, *Nuove sinistre*, 155.

87. On PSIUP's official sanctioning of Warsaw Pact intervention in Aug. 1968, see Daniele Protti, *Cronache di 'nuova sinistra': Dal PSIUP a Democrazia Proletaria* (Milan: Gammalibri, 1979), 14. PSIUP membership in 1972 is calculated on the basis of information reported in Giachetti, *Oltre il sessantotto*, 134.

88. Robert Michels's classic 1910 study *Zur Geschichte des Parteiwesens in der modernen Demokratie* has usually been published in English as *Political Parties*. The quotation is taken from Richard Rothstein, 'Representative Democracy in SDS', *Liberation* (Feb. 1972), 11, a stimulating critique of SDS practices by a leading long-time SDS activist.

89. Norman Fruchter, 'SDS: In and Out of Context', *Liberation* (Feb. 1972), 28.

90. Note, above all, the classic—and thus far unsurpassed—study by Kirkpatrick Sale, *SDS* (New York: Random, 1973).

91. Fruchter, 'SDS', 31.

92. Rothstein, 'Representative Democracy', 16.

93. Ibid. 12.

94. Another eloquent discussion of the consequences of consciously chosen informality in social movements emerged out of the trials and tribulations of the US women's movement at roughly the same time. See Jo Freeman, 'The Tyranny of Structurelessness', first published in various versions between 1971 and 1973, but now most readily available at http://www.jofreeman.com/joreen/tyranny.htm (1 May 2004). Note, for instance, Freeman's following observation: 'If the movement continues deliberately to not select who shall exercise power, it does not thereby abolish power. All it does is abdicate the right to demand that those who do exercise power and influence be responsible for it.'

95. Tilman Fichter and Siegward Lönnendonker, *Kleine Geschichte des SDS* (Berlin: Rotbuch, 1977), 142.

96. This passage is based in part on pertinent insights contained in Tilman Fichter and Siegward Lönnendonker, 'Von der "Neuen Linken" zur Krise des Linksradikalismus', in Georgia Tornow *et al.*, *Die Linke im Rechtsstaat*, ii. *Bedingungen sozialistischer Politik 1965 bis heute* (Berlin: Rotbuch, 1979), 111–12.

97. The centrality of the French 1968 experience—even, and especially, outside of France itself—as the trigger in this process of rediscovery of Leninist organization principles is best documented in the Italian and Spanish cases: see, for instance, the relevant comments in Giachetti, *Oltre il Sessantotto*, 73–4, and Manuel Garí, 'El "Felipe": Una historia por escribir', in Roca (ed.), *Proyecto radical*, 131. Note, for instance, the symptomatic observations by a Spanish new left activist reflecting on the 1969 dissolution of the FLP: 'The FLP died from the complications of May 1968'; cited in García Alcalá, *Historia del Felipe*, 261.

98. There exists no satisfactory transnational survey of Trotskyism and Maoism after 1968, although a handful of informative specific case studies within the limits of one state are beginning to be published; see, for instance, on the Maoist variant, Michael Steffen, *Geschichten vom Trüffelschwein: Politik und Organisation des Kommunistischen Bundes 1971 bis 1991* (Berlin: Assoziation A, 2002), or Kees Slager, *Het geheim van Oss* (Amsterdam: Atlas, 2001).

99. Out of the denunciatory literature on the ravages of far left hyper-politics on the personal lives of far left rank-and-file activists, two edited volumes are particularly perceptive and representative. A series of reports on the peculiarly self-contained worlds of West German Maoisms can be consulted in *Wir warn die stärkste der Partein...: Erfahrungsberichte aus der Welt der K-Gruppen* (Berlin: Rotbuch, 1977). The oftentimes destructive interaction between far left activism and the fledgling second-wave women's movement is at the heart of Marie-Claire Boons *et al.*, *C'est terrible, quand on y pense* (Paris: Galilée, 1983).

100. For an early, insightful critique of the tendency to view new left activism up to 1968 as a golden age of youthful enthusiasms, compared with the supposed subsequent descent into increasingly counterproductive militant tactics and confrontations, see Wini Breines, 'Whose New Left?', *Journal of American History*, 75 (1988), 529–45. Her cogent observations on US radical politics can easily be extended to cover European conditions as well.

101. The most balanced assessment of Gauche Prolétarienne remains A. Belden Fields, *Trotskyism and Maoism: Theory and Practice in France and the United States* (New York: Praeger, 1988), 99–130. Lotta Continua is probably the best researched far left grouping of those years. See, above all, Luigi Bobbio, *Storia di Lotta Continua* (Milan: Feltrinelli, 1988); Aldo Cazzullo, *I ragazzi che volevano fare la rivoluzione: 1968–1978. Storia di Lotta continua* (Milan: Mondadori, 1998); and Corrado Sannucci, *Lotta Continua: Gli uomini dopo* (Arezzo: Limina, 1999). For the IMG, see John Callaghan, 'The New Left and the Politics of the International Marxist Group', in his *British Trotskyism: Theory and Practice* (Oxford: Blackwell, 1984), 122–62. An evocative description of the three key strands of French Trotskyism in 1968, including the JCR, is provided by Gérard Filoche, *Ces années-là, quand Lionel . . .* (Paris: Ramsay, 2001). The ascription of 'chaotically libertarian organizational structures' is taken from Wilhelm Svoboda, 'Die Gruppe Revolutionäre Marxisten (GRM)', in his *Sandkastenspiele: Eine Geschichte linker Radikalität in den 70er Jahren* (Vienna: Promedia, 1998), 172.

102. Callaghan, 'International Marxist Group,' 133.

103. See Fields, *Trotskyism and Maoism*, 50, for the characterization of the JCR in 1967 and 1968. On the Swiss LMR, see Benoît Challand, *La Ligue Marxiste Révolutionnaire en Suisse romande (1969–1980)* (Fribourg: Université de Fribourg, 2000), 70–1.

104. Consuelo Laíz, *La lucha final: Los partidos de la izquierda radical durante la transición española* (Madrid: Los Libros de la Catarata, 1995), 95; for a table listing the chronologically parallel stages of the various consecutive permutations of the Spanish far left, see p. 36 of her work. For the Italian case of the mutation of initially often pluralist far left groupings into generally much more homogeneous 'mature' political parties, see Giachetti, *Oltre il Sessantotto*, 80–1.

105. Giachetti, *Oltre il Sessantotto*, 81.

106. Filoche, *Quand Lionel*, p. 194.

107. Gerd Koenen, *Das rote Jahrzehnt: Unsere kleine deutsche Kulturrevolution 1967–1977* (Cologne: Kiepenheuer & Witsch, 2001), 261.

108. For the *movimento studentesco* phase, the most straightforward depiction of such mechanisms and circumstances is Attilio Mangano, 'La geografia del movimento del '68 in Italia', in Pier Paolo Poggio (ed.), *Il Sessantotto: L'evento e la storia* (Brescia: Fondazione 'Luigi Micheletti', 1988–9), 231–56.

109. Giachetti, *Oltre il Sessantotto*, 89.

110. Filoche, *Quand Lionel*, 160.

111. Ulrike Heider, *Keine Ruhe nach dem Sturm* (Hamburg: Rogner & Bernhard, 2001), 120–1.

112. On de Certeau's discussion of *la prise de parole*, see the following chapter. The citation is, once again, from Giachetti, *Oltre il Sessantotto*, 89.

113. José M. Roca, 'Una aproximación sociologica, politica e ideologica a la izquierda comunista revolucionaria en España', in Roca (ed.), *Proyecto radical*, 35.

114. Giachetti, *Oltre il Sessantotto*, 87. For the most comprehensive available analysis and description of the chief organizations and currents of the multiform Italian far left, see Franco Ottaviano, *La rivoluzione nel labirinto: Sinistra e sinistrismo dal 1956 agli anni ottanta*, ii. *I partiti del sinistrismo (1969–1976)* (Soveria Mannelli: Rubbettino, 1993).

115. Note e.g. Louis Vos's characteristic employment of such terminology when describing the student milieu in the Flemish city of Leuven *after* 1968. In Ch 2, we have seen that Leuven in the years 1966–8 experienced wholly unprecedented instances of student radicalism. But radicalization became far deeper and more widespread when the most visible altercations in early 1968 were over. In 1978, the former student activist and subsequent historian of student activism, Louis Vos, described the years 1969–73 as the experience of 'the Red Leuven', the subtitle of the author's relevant section in his 'Terugblik op roerige jaren: De Leuvense studentenbeweging sinds de jaren sestig', *Onze Alma Mater*, 32/4 (1978), 235. Fifteen years later, the same author utilized identical terminology but extended the period of 'the Red Leuven' all the way to 1979—see Louis Vos, 'Van Vlaamse Leeuw tot rode vaan… en verder: De naoorlogse Leuvense studentenbeweging', *Onze Alma Mater*, 47 (Aug. 1993), 249. I thank Patricia Quaghebeur for getting copies of these articles.

116. Koenen, *Rote Jahrzehnt*, 184–5.

117. Max Elbaum, *Revolution in the Air: Sixties Radicals Turn to Lenin, Mao and Che* (London: Verso, 2002), 203. As Michael Kazin underscored in his critical comments on an earlier manuscript version of this book, a number of local 'underground' publications generally associated with the free-flowing US new left benefited from much higher press runs. And, indeed, the United States, the pioneer and beacon of social movement practices in the 1960s, may very well be the most important exceptional case of a country where an earlier new left was stronger than the subsequent far left.

118. On the all-but-forgotten phenomenon of the significant radicalization of major portions of European social democracy during the early to mid 1930s, see Gerd-Rainer Horn, *European Socialists Respond to Fascism: Ideology, Activism and Contingency in the 1930s* (New York: Oxford University Press, 1996), and Gilles Vergnon, *Les Gauches européennes après la victoire nazie: Entre planisme et unité d'action, 1933–1934* (Paris: L'Harmattan, 1997).

119. The atmosphere of optimism and renewal within France's old left is captured well in Bernard E. Brown, *Socialism of a Different Kind: Reshaping the Left in France* (Westport, Conn.: Greenwood, 1982). An English-language study of one of the key currents pushing for renewal within France's social democratic tradition is David Hanley, *Keeping Left? Ceres and the French Socialist Party* (Manchester: Manchester University Press, 1986). The most comprehensive survey of the variety of new left currents which joined up their efforts to revitalize the PS is Kesler, *Gauche dissidente*. Massimo Teodori was one of the first observers to draw attention to this revitalization of social democracy as a transnational trend in the 1970s. His comments on the French dimension can be found on pp. 467–95 of his *Nuove sinistre*. I have culled PS membership statistics from pp. 484 and 486 of his work. An important French-language document of that era is Jean-François Bizot, *Au parti des socialistes: Plongée libre dans les courants d'un grand parti* (Paris: Bernard Grasset, 1975), as is Michel Charzat and Ghislaine Toutain, *Le C.E.R.E.S: Un combat pour le socialisme* (Paris: Calmann-Lévy, 1975).

120. Paul Lucardie, for instance, underscores the left wing challenge arising within Dutch social democracy precisely at this time. See his unpublished 1980 dissertation, where, amongst other highlights, the author attempts to understand the phenomenon of radicalization within social democracy as a transnational phenomenon. Lucardie's comments on the left wing currents operating within Dutch, French, and German social democracy can be found in Anthonie Paul Marius Lucardie, 'The New Left in the Netherlands (1960–1977): A Critical Study of New Political Ideas and Groups on the Left in the Netherlands with Comparative References to France and Germany', Ph.D. dissertation, Queen's University, Kingston, Ontario, pp. 140–68, 280–313, and 359–85.

121. Some bibliographic references may serve to provide a useful starting point for the reconstruction of this radical impulse within West German social democracy. Siegfried Heimann, Gitta Martens, and Peter Müller, 'Die Linke in der SPD', *Prokla*, 7/3 (1977), 58–107, is a broadly sympathetic portrayal of this current within the Jusos and the *Arbeitsgemeinschaft für Arbeitnehmerfragen* (AfA) within the mother party itself. Dietmar Süß, 'Die Enkel auf den Barrikaden: Jungsozialisten in der SPD in den Siebzigerjahren', *Archiv für Sozialgeschichte*, 44 (2004), 67–104, is an insightful recent reassessment of the rise and decline of radical energies within the Young Socialists. For a book-length study of this phenomenon, see the comparative study by Thomas A. Koelble, *The Left Unravelled: Social Democracy and the New Left Challenge in Britain and West Germany* (Durham, NC: Duke University Press, 1991), but now above all Martin Oberpriller, *Jungsozialisten zwischen Anpassung und Opposition: 100 Jahre Arbeiterjugendbewegung* (Bonn: Dietz, 2004), 169–301. Note also Ferdinand Müller-Rommel, *Innerparteiliche Gruppierungen in der SPD* (Opladen: Westdeutscher Verlag, 1982), 69–95 and 132–61. For some interesting, if consistently disparaging, comments on the left-wing opposition within the Jusos and the SPD, see Lösche and Walter, *Die SPD*, 256–85 and 336–78. The concrete data in my text are, once again, taken from Teodori, *Nuove Sinistre*, 505.

122. For the left challenge to Labour Party traditionalist complacency, see, amongst others, John Gyford, *The Politics of Local Socialism* (London: Allen & Unwin, 1985), and Patrick Seyd, *The Rise and Fall of the Labour Left* (Basingstoke: Macmillan, 1987). The superior study, however, is now Leo Panitch and Colin Leys, *The End of Parliamentary Socialism: From New Left to New Labour* (London: Verso, 2001).

123. On Eurocommunism, see, amongst many, Carl Boggs and David Plotke (eds.), *The Politics of Eurocommunism: Socialism in Transition* (Basingstoke: Macmillan, 1980), and Keith Middlemas, *Power and the Party: Changing Faces of Communism in Western Europe* (London: André Deutsch, 1980). A classic document of the Eurocommunist tradition is Santiago Carrillo, *Eurocommunism and the State* (Westport, Conn.: Lawrence Hill, 1978). Within the English-speaking world, the following book-length interview popularized the emerging trend: *The Italian Road to Socialism: An Interview by Eric Hobsbawm with Giorgio Napolitano of the Italian Communist Party* (Westport, Conn.: Lawrence Hill, 1977). A comprehensive critique of Eurocommunism from the point of view of the Trotskyist far left is Ernest Mandel, *From Stalinism to Eurocommunism: The Bitter Fruits of 'Socialism in One Country'* (London: NLB, 1978). On the impact of Eurocommunism in Belgium, see now, above all else, Nicolas Naif, *L'Eurocommunisme en Belgique: Crises et débats autour d'une voie belge au socialisme* (Brussels: Éditions CARCOB, 2004); for Britain, see

Keith Laybourn, *Marxism in Britain: Dissent, Decline and Reemergence 1945–c. 2000* (London: Routledge, 2006), 106–47 and *passim*.

124. Tobias Abse, 'Judging the PCI', *New Left Review*, 153 (Sept.–Oct. 1985), 24.

125. Gundle, *Between Hollywood*, 139.

126. Cited in Ajello, *Lungo addio*, 123.

127. Gundle, *Between Hollywood*, 161. On the 1977 youth revolt, see amongst others, Marco Grispigni, *Il Settantasette: Un manuale per capire, un saggio per riflettere* (Milan: Il saggiatore, 1997); Claudio Salaris, *Il movimento del settantasette: Linguaggi e scritture dell'ala creativa* (Bertiolo: AAA Edizioni, 1997); but above all Sergio Bianchi and Lanfranco Caminiti (eds.), *Settantasette: La rivoluzione che viene* (Rome: DeriveApprodi, 2004). By the 1970s, the PCI had obtained important gains in local elections in many key cities, large and small, of northern and central Italy. Today the most comprehensive study of the promise of PCI local government control in the era of Eurocommunism remains Max Jäggi, Roger Müller, and Sil Schmid, *Red Bologna* (London: Writers and Readers Publishing Cooperative, 1977).

128. Sassoon, *One Hundred Years*, 585.

129. Note, for instance, the instructive observation by Frank Georgi: 'Paradoxically, the 1981 capture of governmental control by the Union of the Left served as an excuse for the weakening of autonomous action by civil society, the decline of trade union activism, and the fading of the ideal of self-management'; see Frank Georgi, ' "Vivre demain dans nos luttes d'aujourd'hui": le syndicat, la grève et l'autogestion en France (1968–1988)', in Geneviève Dreyfus-Armand, Robert Frank, Marie-Françoise Lévy, and Michelle Zancarini-Fournel (eds.), *Les Années 68: Le Temps de la contestation* (Brussels: Complexe, 2000), 400. The classic autopsy of the Union of the Left's governmental record remains Daniel Singer, *Is Socialism Doomed? The Meaning of Mitterand* (New York: Oxford University Press, 1988).

130. Sassoon, *One Hundred Years*, 649.

1. Existentialist Coffeehouse Scene, Café De Welkom, Brussels, 1963. The Café De Welkom was located in the city center's Rue des Bouchers, nowadays crammed with tourist-trap restaurants offering indoor and al fresco dining. Note the 'existentialist' hairstyles of the young couple sitting across from Derroll Adams and observing his fingerpicking.

2. Derroll Adams, Café De Welkom, Brussels, 1963. Derroll Adams came to Brussels at the occasion of the 1958 Brussels World Exhibition. Belgium then remained his home until his death in February 2000. The Oregon-born folk musician retained many links to English-language folk and pop musicians, influencing in particular the Scottish Donovan.

3. May 1st Demonstration, Kapelle-op-den-Bos. This undated photograph exemplifies the grim deter-mination of Flemish union members and their families, showcasing that at this particular point in time union membership and the traditional First of May demonstrations were still solidly embedded commu-nity concerns. Kapelle-op-den-Bos is located roughly halfway between Brussels and Antwerp. The Zeekanaal, a major artificial waterway, visible on the right, cuts through this industrial town.

4. Brussels Tramway Workers, May Day Demonstration, Brussels, early 1970s. The Brussels Tramway Workers and their leader Arthur Vercruyce had been one of the strongholds of far left influ-ence in Brussels trade union circles in earlier years. The pictured banner had been given as a present to the 'Brussels Revolutionary Tramwaymen' by Moscow trade unionists in the 1920s. By the 1970s it had become a venerated relic of the heroic period symbolising international solidarity.

5. Socialist Party Parade, Saint-Gilles/Sint-Gillis. Well into the 1970s, Belgian Socialist Party parades were blissfully unaffected by the spirit of second-wave feminism.

6. Provocative Poses by Brussels Provos, 1966. This photo showcases the ludic aspirations of Provo activism. Several of the pictured characters-in-disguise represent figures from Belgian history and culture. The slogan displayed, of particular relevance in a country proud of its monarchical tradition, has yet another and more sinister meaning. On 11 August 1950, several Belgian Communist Party deputies, at the occasion of the pledge of allegiance by the new Belgian King Baudoin in parliament, stood up and shouted: 'Vive la République.' One of the hecklers was the Communist Party chairman, Julien Lahaut. One week later, Julien Lahaut was shot dead in front of his home in Seraing near Liège.

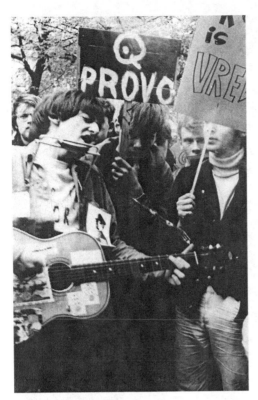

7. Anti-Vietnam War Protest, organised by Brussels Provos. Note the relatively 'smart' dress style of the pictured protesters in 1966.

8. Anti-Vietnam War and Anti-NATO Protest, organised by the far left, Brussels. The distinctly more unkempt dress style and overall comportment—compared to the previous picture taken a few years earlier—is not entirely due to the rainy weather in this picture taken in the early 1970s. It was a sign of changing moods and changing times.

9. Anti-Vietnam War Protest, Brussels, early-to-mid-1970s. Note the ubiquity of motorcycle helmets, the protective headgear of choice by far left activists in the early-to-mid-1970s.

10. Frans Pans never abandoned the ludic touch. This photo shows his brother, Werner Pans, posing as a far left demonstrator wielding a particularly dangerous weapon. Frans Pans entitled this picture: 'Ice Cream Project.'

11. Masked police confront demonstrators, Brussels.

12. Police take aim at protestors, Brussels.

13. Police water cannon in action, Brussels.

14. The aftermath of confrontation, Brussels.

15. Anti-Militarism Protest at the occasion of Belgian Christian Democratic Defense Minister Paul van den Boeynants' plans for a reorganisation of the Belgian armed forces. Note the visible presence of the Flemish Young Socialists, the social democratic youth group, amongst the demonstrators in Saint-Gilles/Sint-Gillis in 1972–3.

16. Anti-Franco Protest, Brussels. The Spanish dictatorship remained a central target for the European left until the dictator's natural death in November 1975. Up to that moment, many Spanish demonstrators, even and especially when demonstrating abroad, attempted to protect their identity out of fear of reprisals to themselves or to their families living in this Iberian stronghold of the 'free world.'

17. Anti-Abortion Protest, passing in front of the Feminist Bookstore La Rabouilleuse in the Ixelles/
Elsene district of Brussels. Note the sceptical pregnant onlooker in front of the store.

18. Workers' Protest Rally, Charleroi, Hainaut. The Hainaut, a region dominated by heavy industry,
had been a focal point of radical protest for many decades. By the 1970s, the ravages of deindustriali-
sation were beginning to take a particularly heavy toll.

19. Picket Line, Glaverbel, Gilly (Charleroi), Hainaut. The wildcat strikes at the Glaverbel glassmaking plant in Gilly (Charleroi) in the Hainaut took on a particular prominence amongst the wave of unofficial labor struggles in Belgium between 1970 and 1975.

20. Picket Line, 'The End of Paternalism.' Women workers were just as actively involved in the labor struggles of this era. Quite often feminist demands made deep inroads into the labor movements of the 1970s and beyond.

21. Il Manifesto Contingent, LIP Solidarity Demonstration, Besançon, France, 1973. The highpoint of international solidarity actions in Western Europe in this period was undoubtedly the string of mobilisations in support of the self-managed watch factory LIP in Eastern France. Numerous delegations from other European states made the trek to Besançon, including the Italian far left organisation named after its daily newspaper Il Manifesto.

22. French Trotskyist Contingent, LIP Solidarity Demonstration, Besançon, France, 1973. Rouge was and remains the newspaper of the Ligue Communiste Révolutionnaire. The Trotskyist forces were one of several tendencies in the European far left to focus on LIP solidarity work at that time.

23. LIP Solidarity Demonstration, Besançon, France, 1973. The pictured activist became a type of 'poster boy' for the European far left. This image was utilised on multiple occasions and for various purposes unrelated to the LIP events.

24. LIP Solidarity Demonstration, Besançon, France, 1973. The watch factory being located on the outskirts of Besançon, demonstrators had to walk some distance to reach their destination. A few years later, similar pictures were commonplace in the course of the first major 'new' social movement erupting in the second half of the 1970s: the anti-nuclear power plant movement.

25. 'The Strike is Over,' Glaverbel, Gilly, 1973. Frans Pans purposefully left this picture slightly blurry. The serene expression on the striker's face provided a fitting complement to the ending of a major strike. Frans Pans adapted this photo for other purposes in subsequent years, including various versions serving as advertising posters for the social democratic Belgian Socialist Party, which proved to be a particular source of satisfaction for Frans Pans, as the pictured striker was a card-carrying member of the Belgian Trotskyists.

5

Participatory Democracy: The Meaning of '1968'

1. MEASURING FAILURE AND SUCCESS

The preceding pages were designed to concentrate on process rather than outcome, for social movements generally leave their mark on the societies they aim to affect regardless of the measure of success in obtaining their goals. It is in the struggle to change their world that activists leave their imprint on their environment, and the learning curve of activists, sympathizers, and onlookers alike is dependent on any number of factors, only one of which is the relative degree of success in reaching stated objectives. Indeed, quick and easy achievements of ambitions and hopes may very well contribute to the rapid demise of a fledgling campaign before it can begin to affect substantial numbers of people. To some extent, then, it is the failure to achieve success which often produces a snowball effect. Unable to satisfy limited objectives, social movement activists become progressively embittered, and their change of tactics often leads in the direction of greater radicalism and the involvement of ever-larger numbers of individuals. On the other hand, victories, particularly when achieved after prolonged bouts of struggle, can also embolden activists to reach for ever-more distant and seemingly utopian goals. Which way the particular dynamic of any given social movement will evolve is usually difficult to predict. The contingency factor in the reality of everyday life is one of the underlying elements which makes it often exceedingly difficult to predict the trajectory of actually existing, much less embryonic social movements.

Uncertainty is greatest when there are multiple overlapping and parallel movements operating within a location or a nation-state. And, by extension, the unpredictability is most pronounced when movements coincide not just within the borders of one state but when they occur roughly simultaneously across national frontiers. In the case of '1968' they occurred not just in more than one state, but they transcended oceanic frontiers.[1] It was this peculiarly volatile conjuncture which shaped '1968' into a transnational moment of opportunity and crisis with few parallels in modern history.

Success, of course, can be measured in various ways. The process of personal growth, the ability to speak up for oneself, to stand one's ground, may count for many at least as much as the achievement of particular and measurable goals. Berkeley's Free Speech Movement, as we have seen, after a protracted struggle lasting several months, did in fact manage to retain the student organizations' right to set up tables in various locations on campus traditionally reserved for such student campaigns. But in the process of achieving this tangible and important victory, countless individuals underwent a learning process which changed their habits and outlook for at least a dozen subsequent years. In addition, the example of the Berkeley student revolt became an inspiration for students elsewhere in the sprawling system of university campuses, large and small, from San Diego, California, to Portland, Maine. What's more, as we have seen, the example of Berkeley was eagerly studied across the Atlantic. And Trento students in the Catholic Institute of Sociology on the western edge of the Dolomites were not the only ones fascinated by the ways and means in which a small but determined and fearless group of individuals could affect their immediate environment—and the larger world around them. Who is to say, then, that the reacquisition of the right of Berkeley students to set up tables where they wished counted for more than their inspirational impact on Berkeley and the wider world?

Nonetheless, a history of '1968' without attention paid to concrete and tangible changes is like a history of the Bolshevik Revolution without attention to the ensuing Soviet state. And this historical analogy was chosen for a good reason. For just as most of the processes and many of the goals of the October Revolution were soon forgotten or transformed, the experience and goals of 1968 had often little in common with the actual and measurable changes that were readily visible and apparent when the movements giving shape to 1968 subsided sometime in the second half of the 1970s. Just like parents sometimes wonder about their offspring entering their teenage years, activists of 1968 were often disappointed when taking stock of movement goals and actual accomplishments ten, twenty, or more years later.

2. CULTURAL REVOLUTION AND MATERIAL GAINS

It has become a standard feature of the serious historical literature on 1968 to proclaim a cultural revolution as the most noticeable product of the period under review. Arthur Marwick's modern classic, *The Sixties*, has done more than anything else to fashion a consensus on this contentious issue: 'There was no economic revolution, no political revolution, no advent of the proletariat to power, no classless society, no destruction of mainstream culture, no obliteration of language.'[2] Instead, 'another kind of revolution did happen', Marwick convincingly argues, 'a "revolution," or "transformation" in material conditions, lifestyles, family relationships and personal freedoms for the vast majority of ordinary people'; in short, 'a "cultural revolution" '.[3] And the 800 densely packed pages of his remarkable tome are an eloquent and empirically rich verification and demonstration of the validity of such a view. When judged from some distance in time and place, thirty-odd years in Marwick's case, indeed the evidence is incontrovertible that the most important and long-lasting concrete changes effected by the turmoil of 1968 can be located in the socio-psychological domain.

This author grew up in the cold war-determined post-war West German state, and it is in this front-line state that the cultural revolution postulated by Marwick and others can best be exemplified by means of two longitudinal poll results. A set of identical questions was asked in 1954, 1965, and 1976. They pertained to the 'qualities education should encourage in children'. To focus solely on two particular results: the percentage of adults who stressed the stereotypically Germanic values of 'obedience and subordination' dropped preciously little between 1954 (28%) and 1965 (25%), but then experienced a precipitous decline in 1976 (10%). Conversely, the percentage of West German adults favouring 'independence and free will' rose from 28 per cent (1954) to 37 per cent (1965) to 51 per cent (1976). Changing social mores and, in particular, gender relations can best be showcased in another set of poll results. The question asked of West German respondents was: 'When a young man and a young woman live together, without being married, do you think that this is going too far or do you think it doesn't matter?' The years of comparison are 1967 and 1973. In 1967 43 per cent of unmarried men and 65 per cent of unmarried women thought such cohabitation transgressed social norms; 48 per cent of men and 24 per cent of women thought it did not matter. Only six years later a dramatic sea-change had occurred. By 1973 only 5 per cent of men and 2 per cent of women registered continued objections. Correspondingly, the figure of unmarried men and women who claimed not to care had risen to 84 per cent (men) and 92 per cent (women).[4] There is thus no contest that in the all-important realm of interpersonal relationships and societal norms the period of 'the sixties'—and in particular its hottest activist phase in the second half of the 1960s and the first half of the 1970s—left behind a positive legacy and helped fashion advanced industrial societies into less cramped and restrictive places in which to live. In the words of Arthur Marwick, the 'long sixties' was a time when 'people gained power to make decisions for themselves. Life became more varied and enjoyable.'[5] Few denizens of the contemporary age would want to dismiss such tangible gains.

But there is more to the balance sheet of '1968' than these medium- to long-term mentality changes at the heart of the cultural revolution of the 1960s. As Marwick's reference to the 'transformation of material conditions' suggests, in the course of 1968 itself, or in its immediate aftermath, a series of concrete and tangible improvements were effected as well. For the student movement at the heart of Chapter 2, such improvements are less material than institutional, though the abandonment of tuition for undergraduate university education in a number of European states or the increased provision for stipends were about as tangible and real as university reforms at the time could possibly get. Yet many of the efforts to improve university life were geared towards a thoroughgoing and radical reform of the way in which universities were governed.

It would take too long to detail the variety of reform plans for the entirety of states covered in this study. The case of West Germany may stand for many others. Unlike the United States, for instance, where the administration of such institutions was already then firmly in the hands of an autonomous university bureaucracy which regarded universities much like any other businesses, in West Germany the professoriate remained firmly in control. But the downside to the German model was the retention of almost exclusive control of academic life by the rather exclusive club of full professors. The much larger fleet of younger assistant or associate professors—lecturers or readers in the British world—was on principle excluded from meaningful decision-making positions at the top of the university hierarchies. Students, let alone support staff, were obviously kept completely out of the loop. To turn the tide against institutional autocracy, the West German SDS, as early as 1961, had entered on a campaign to drastically reshape this authoritarian system. Full professors, less senior faculty, and notably students were to obtain a third of all seats in the important committees retaining effective power over universities. By the late 1960s and early 1970s, several comparatively 'progressive' states—education is a matter for state, not federal control in West Germany—enacted legislation approximating such radical demands. Yet in 1973 the German Supreme Court declared significant portions of the necessary legislation sanctioning such laws unconstitutional. Some bits and pieces of such far-going reforms were nonetheless translated into concrete measures by some universities, depending on local power constellations and party-political arrangements. Plans for grand revisions, however, went nowhere. In the end, the climate of instruction may very well have changed for the better; yet the overall hierarchical division remained essentially intact.[6]

For Europe's industrial and white-collar workers material improvements were concrete, tangible, and important. First, in matters of real wages the years of contestation resulted in noticeable purchasing power improvements. Following two decades of post-war boom, European workers had become accustomed to experiencing a series of wage increases rather than stagnation or income regression. But the greater militancy embarked upon—depending on the country involved—between 1968 and 1970 and then continuing for several more years, paid off as well. Two sets of relevant data may underscore the material advantages of the experience exemplified in Chapter 3.

A British team of authors compared real wage increases in four countries, dividing up their data into a set of earlier years of lower militancy and then a number of immediately following years with heightened labour action. Here is what they report. In Great Britain, average annual real wage increases of 2.4 per cent in the more quiescent years 1967–9 were followed by purchasing power improvements of 3.9 per cent in 1970–1. In France, the years 1965–7 saw average annual increases of 2.9 per cent; in the period 1968–9 French workers on average pocketed an additional 5.4 per cent per year. For Italy, the respective data contrast 4.3 per cent (1966–8) with 7.3 per cent (1969–70); in Germany 3.3 per cent

(1966–8) compared with 9.2 per cent in 1969–70.[7] The French sociologist Pierre Dubois computes somewhat different figures, but the overall trend is identical: Years of militancy help bolster workers' income. Pierre Dubois divides his data into three time slots rather than two. Between an earlier and a later period roughly corresponding to the other data set, Dubois inserts a single central year in which often, but not always, industrial militancy was at its peak. Once again trailing behind comparable countries, the United Kingdom reported real wage rises of 2.3 per cent (1965–9), 6.2 per cent (1970), and 4.1 per cent (1971–3). French workers pocketed average annual wage increases of 3.2 per cent (1965–7), 8 per cent (1968), and 5.5 per cent (1969–73). West German workers benefited from the following improvements in purchasing power: 2.8 per cent (1966–8), 7.5 per cent (1969—the year of major wildcat strikes) and 5.7 per cent (1970–3). Belgium's relevant figures are 3.3 per cent (1967–9), 7.1 per cent (1970), and 8.4 per cent (1971–3); and, last but not least, Italian workers could point to real wage rises of 1.7 per cent (1965–8), 7.2 per cent (1969), and 12.8 per cent per year (!) in 1970–3.[8] Europe's workforce, however, benefited from '1968' not only in terms of substantial wage improvements. 'The only significant reduction of working time since World War II was due to the militancy of the working class itself in the late 1960s.'[9] If nothing else, then, the dependent wage force in Europe—less so in the United States—proved to be a huge beneficiary of the various social movements unleashed in the course of the 1960s. Concrete, tangible, material improvements, then, also constituted an important short-to-medium-term consequence of 1968.

But there is yet another dimension which must be listed as an achievement of this era, in addition to medium-to-long-term paradigm shifts in modes of inter-personal and institutional behaviour and short-to-medium-term material advances. Perhaps the most important rearrangements occurred on yet another, rather elusive, constantly shifting, and ultimately vanishing terrain: the concrete experience of a qualitatively different way of life, the exposure to non-hierarchical modes of social interaction, the lived environment of solidarity, the heated atmosphere of open debate, the concrete strivings for a common and mutually beneficial system-transcending goal. Without these factors, it is unlikely that the 'cultural revolution' referred to above would have been brought about, and such influences should thus be included in any balance sheet of the revolutions of 1968. But, more importantly, they pointed in an entirely different direction from the way the 'cultural revolution' was eventually perceived.

3. PARTICIPATORY DEMOCRACY

Careful readers of the preceding pages may be somewhat puzzled by the return of elements of 'participatory' or 'direct' democracy to centre stage. Having spent some time in Chapter 4, section 10, depicting the deterioration of, for instance, the American Students for a Democratic Society (SDS) from an association of like-minded and egalitarian idealists into a cluster of warring factions galvanized around locally influential charismatic leaders, it may appear to add insult to injury to suddenly revalidate a moment in the history of social movement activism apparently laid to rest with much eloquence and analytic precision by Richard Rothstein, Norm Fruchter, Jo Freeman, and many others. Yet, just as some of the less enticing features of the post-1968 far left should not unduly colour the overall appreciation of that particular phenomenon which arose in part as a response to the disintegration of the new left, the new left in turn should not be solely judged by its ultimate phase of decomposition. Also, many of the features of 'direct democracy' were not exclusively the property of the burgeoning new left. As we shall see, the far left was responsible for at least as many experiences of participatory democracy as its new left antecendent.

The practice of direct or participatory democracy is, of course, as ancient as social movements themselves. Within the mobilization cycle culminating in 1968, one of the earliest manifestations of 'grass-roots democracy' occurred in the daily practices of the Student Nonviolent Coordinating Committee (SNCC) in the American Deep South. All important decisions by this young band of idealistic volunteers were reached in endless discussions where everyone was invited to speak, where everyone was listened to, and where everyone was considered as important as anyone else. Organized into small groups dispersed throughout Mississippi, the white northern volunteers arriving for Freedom Summer 1964 were immediately taken by the spirit of the 'beloved community' governing personal interactions and group decisions, reached after often harrowing debates by SNCC members and volunteers alike. Northern volunteers were originally earmarked to be housed in separate, dispersed, single-family dwellings, hosted by supportive members of the local black community, but such well-made plans collapsed under the weight of the fear of local sympathizers, dreading acts of terrorist revenge by the local white establishment. Consequently, volunteers usually had no other choice than to take up residence in so-called Freedom Houses, rental units shared by small groups of SNCC staff and northern whites. Such unintended and intense daily contact with like-minded 'strangers' strongly reinforced the inevitable intermixture of the personal and the political on the level of individual experiences. Doug McAdam, in his modern classic, *Freedom Summer*, points to the institution of Freedom Houses in Mississippi Freedom Summer as the contingent circumstance triggering subsequent political 'communes' further north.[10] Such 'political communes', of course, became a hallmark of both the new left and the far left in Europe as well as America in subsequent years.[11]

SNCC ran many projects, and the 1964 Mississippi Freedom Summer was only the most media-savvy and therefore visible one. For the most part, SNCC concentrated its efforts on what has often been termed 'community organizing', the tireless endeavours to have members of the black community in locations throughout the Deep South take matters into their own hands. After centuries of enforced subordination such self-organization on the part of the American black poor did by no means come naturally or easily. Inspired by didactic techniques popularized by the Highlander Folk School, itself an institutional product of an earlier period of intense social movement activity in the 1930s, SNCC community organizers sought to build 'indigenous leadership', and their methods were 'deliberately educational. The point was to give people the tools to articulate their grievances and goals and to organize to realize them. The process of decision-making was as important as its endpoint. Just providing the time that people unschooled in political strategizing needed to think through unfamiliar issues was important.'12 In a supportive environment, inhibitions and obstacles could tendentially be overcome. 'People learned how to stand up and speak', the guiding spirit behind SNCC organizing tactics in America's Deep South, Bob Moses, remembers today. 'The meeting itself, or the meetings, became the tools.' 'Folks were feeling themselves out, learning how to use words to articulate what they wanted and needed. In these meetings, they were taking the first steps toward gaining control over their lives, by making demands on themselves.'13 Freedom Summer, argues Doug McAdam, spawned 'many of the specific cultural elements that were later associated with the counterculture' and the new left. 'Among these were communal living, a more liberated sexuality, interracial relationships, and a distinctive style of speech and dress.'14 Participatory democracy, later popularized by SDS, was the most important product of the experimental laboratory of SNCC communities built up throughout the American Deep South. Seen 'as a commitment to surmount the usual barrier of status, a commitment on the part of participants to treat each other as equals, not by dividing power up equally, but by fostering each person's self-development',15 participatory democracy was enthusiastically carried north by Freedom Summer volunteers, and it quickly developed into a constituent part of the standard operating procedure of SDS.

For the blossoming and rapidly expanding student movement in America's north, participatory democracy seemed tailor-made: 'Groups characterised by direct democracy and dialogue seemed to form naturally in action situations during the sixties. Spontaneous assemblies arose and were incorporated into the emergent new left culture and experience.' Berkeley's Free Speech Movement was merely the first amongst many social movements turning campuses into a debating ground. 'A deep desire for democratic participation surfaced in new left political practice, mandating its inclusion in the history of radical and democratic insurgency.'16 Student politics in 1960s America was characterized by countless demonstrations alternating with mass meetings where seemingly everything was up for debate. Describing one such giant open forum where 3,000 participants in the October 1967 Stop-The-Draft Week in Oakland, California, deliberated their next tactical moves, Wini Breines pinpoints the unusual quality of such events: 'That three thousand people engaged in a discussion and debate appears not to have distressed or inconvenienced them. It seemed, in fact, the natural and necessary way to decide how to proceed or to share analyses, and created enormous exhilaration.

Time and again during the decade, huge meetings formed in the midst of political action to debate and discuss politics.' 'For people who were rarely given an opportunity to express their political views and effect an outcome—and students were afforded it more than most people—such collective democratic forms were thrilling and confirming.'[17]

Similar manifestations of grass-roots democracy occurred near-spontaneously on radicalized campuses around the world. In francophone Belgium, similar 'mass meetings' (as they tended to be called in the US) were termed *assemblées libres*, in Germany *Vollversammlungen*, in France *assemblées générales*, in Italy, most frequently, just *assemblee*. Everywhere, or so it seemed, activists were gathering in unprecedented numbers for an intense experience of seemingly never-ending debates. Before long, however, it became clear that such huge mass gatherings only permitted the least inhibited to step to the microphone and to enter the fray. Thus, smaller subcommittees soon began to proliferate, usually formed to address specific issues or to carry out certain tasks, but in the process becoming the forum par excellence for less outspoken activists to develop initiatives and influence the flow of events. A veritable panoply of independent, interlocking, and mutually supportive initiatives flourished in the heyday of student activism. Eric Hobsbawm, when describing the joyful atmosphere of earlier popular revolts in his *Primitive Rebels*, accurately captured such exuberant moods: 'Liberty, equality, above all fraternity may become real for the moment in those stages of the great social revolutions which revolutionaries who live through them describe in the terms reserved for romantic love.'[18]

Repeated mention was made earlier on of student occupations of university buildings, starting with the occupation of Sproul Hall on the Berkeley campus in October 1964. Building, faculty, and campus occupations soon multiplied and became a preferred activist tactic by students elsewhere. Chapter 2 highlights a certain number of such transgressions in Italy and elsewhere. Often, such periods of student occupation of university property furnished the circumstances and facilities for a maximum extension of experiments with radical grass-roots democracy. For the duration of the general strike, for instance, the old central building of the venerated Sorbonne with its many tracts and copious meeting spaces served as organizational nodal points for the proliferation of subcommittees designed to give structure and purpose to the Parisian student May.[19]

But possibly the most central challenge to the smooth functioning and continuation of university business as usual were not the physical occupations of university buildings and property. Instead, the most subversive undertakings by student activists from Berkeley to Berlin were various parallel efforts to construct blueprints for alternative modes of university education. Not content to physically challenge traditionalists on university campuses, radical student activists began to develop alternative curricula for a non-alienated future society. And, in due time, these utopian plans began to take on concrete shape. In a number of locations, efforts to translate such strivings into concrete reality were crowned by limited and temporary success. Curiously, there exists to date not a single serious study which has attempted to describe and analyse such longings within the confines of a given state, let alone on a comparative or transnational scale.

4. FREE SCHOOLS AND UNIVERSITIES

The notion and the practice of alternative education models is nearly as old as schooling itself. But, when analysing the mobilization cycle of the 1960s and early 1970s, the earliest traces of such strivings are, once again, located to the west of the Atlantic and, more specifically, in the Deep South. One of the concrete projects associated with Mississippi Freedom Summer 1964 was the provision of 'freedom schools' for local black children, alternative forms of education for a population group that, left to the tender loving care of the state school system, remained steeped in state-mandated ignorance. As of 1960, 42 per cent of all white residents in Mississippi had finished at least twelve years of schooling, whereas 'only 7 percent of the black population had managed to do so. . . . Nor did state officials do anything to discourage this pattern.' State expenditure for black pupils barely surpassed 25 per cent of the—by no means generous—level reserved for white pupils. 'In rural areas, especially in the Cotton Belt, the figures were often many times more skewed than the state average. North Pike County, for instance, spent $30.89 for each of its white students and a bare $0.76 per black student.'[20]

Small wonder that, when northern volunteers began to set up alternative schools, they soon discovered the true dimensions of race relations in the American South. 'The county superintendent of schools ordered that neither foreign languages nor civics shall be taught in any Negro schools, nor shall American history from 1860 to 1875 be taught', wrote one northern student cum teacher of freedom schools. 'My students are from 13 to 17 years old, and not one of them had heard about the Supreme Court decision of 1954' mandating desegregation of schools, reported another.[21] 'Freedom Schools sprang up like wildflowers all over Mississippi, until 2000 [children] were attending over thirty schools.' 'The object of the Freedom School was not to cram a prescribed amount of factual material into young minds, but to give them that first look into new worlds which would, some day if not immediately, lead them to books and people and ideas not found in the everyday lives of Mississippi Negroes.'[22] 'The freedom school teachers eliminated traditional classroom rules and developed innovative teaching techniques designed to encourage the free expression of ideas.' 'The free-dom schools, which survived the summer [of 1964], represented one of the first attempts by SNCC to replace existing institutions with alternative ones.'[23] 'They didn't always succeed, but even their failures were warmed by the affection that sprang up everywhere between teachers and students—both aware that they talked with one another inside a common cradle of concern.'[24] The immeasurable

impact of such alternative education projects can be gauged by yet another letter
sent home by a northern volunteer:

We were sitting on the steps at dusk, watching the landscape and the sun folding into the
flat country, with the backboard of the basketball net that is now netless sticking up into
the sunset at a crazy angle. Cotton harvesters went by—and the sheriff—and then a
6-year-old Negro girl with a stick and a dog, kicking up as much dust as she could with her
bare feet. As she went by, we could hear her humming to herself 'We shall overcome. . . .'[25]

Such alternative school projects soon cropped up outside of the Deep South.
Targeting a whole range of ethnically diverse communities, including white
middle-class children, their label changed from Freedom Schools to Free Schools.
By 1971, 350 alternative 'free' schools in thirty-nine states employed 4,500 teachers
and volunteers.[26] But the link with the emerging university student movements in
the US and elsewhere was made most explicit when the creative spark of alternative teaching methods and curricula transferred from primary and secondary
education to the domain of higher education itself. Here, once again, Berkeley led
the fray. Michael Rossmann, one of the spokespersons of the Free Speech
Movement, later reminisced about the origins of what became known as the Free
University of Berkeley. Describing the second occupation of Sproul Hall,
Rossmann remembered:

It is true that we barricaded the offices. But we also showed movies on the walls, danced in
the corridors, held a religious service, smoked weed and played music in the stairwells,
made love on the roof, ate from our cafeteria in the vestibule, sought aid at the pre-meds'
infirmary, published leaflets in corners, *organised a new educational institution in the
basement*, and met to govern ourselves in the halls and the johns. In those eighteen hours in
liberated territory, at the core of an institution in crisis, waiting for the teargas and murders
that came only later, we acted out a precise miniature image of the scope in which
we would engage our freedom—an image of a whole society, newly recreated, many-
dimensioned and united in cooperation and purpose.[27]

When the Free Speech Movement emerged victorious, activists rented facilities
on nearby Telegraph Avenue where, in 1965, the first twenty courses of the Free
University of Berkeley (FUB) were offered. By 1966 the number rose to thirty,
and by 1969 the FUB had 119 courses on offer. The curriculum concentrated on
topics and themes unavailable in the regular university fare, such as 'State and
Society: The Dialectics of Alienation', 'Social Thought since the De-Stalinisation
Congress of 1956', 'Community Organising', or 'Revolutionary Thought and
Action'.[28] The idea caught on like wildfire elsewhere in the United States. In 1965
alone, more than fifty free universities or experimental colleges were founded
across the entire country. By 1970, their numbers ranged between 300 and 500.[29]
Michael Schmidtke calculates that more than 100,000 students were enrolled at
one point or another in one of the free universities organized across the United
States.[30] Already by 1966, however, their idea had spread eastwards across the
Atlantic.

The first such rumblings occurred in Trento, one of the cradles of the Italian *movimento studentesco* where the entire student body was trained to keep their eyes on the American prize. As we saw in Chapter 2, during the October–November 1966 occupation of the Sociology Faculty, the sole faculty at Trento at that time, a series of guest lecturers and performance artists had been invited by the student insurgents, and the experience of the Berkeley Free Speech fight served as inspiration for Trento activists. In late 1966, Trento student radicals published a detailed alternative sociology curriculum, explicitly designed to clash with the regular progress of study administered by the academic authorities.[31] Starting with the autumn 1966 occupation of Trento University, Trento student leaders, with Renato Curcio in editorial control, began to work on a text in which they aimed to generalize and popularize a framework for the construction of an alternative university. As already mentioned in Chapter 2, the 'Manifesto for a Negative University' was completed in the spring of 1967, first published in June 1967 and then received wide distribution with its publication in *Lavoro Politico* in November 1967, just in time for the hot phase of the *movimento studentesco* throughout the Italian state.[32]

In 1967 free universities spread to England, the Netherlands, and Germany. Easter break saw the first effort at a free university in Great Britain, when activists in the midst of 'the trouble at the LSE [London School of Economics]' set up a 'free university that was in some curious way to maintain the protest during the [Easter] vacation', though, in the words of the erstwhile student radical Colin Crouch, it was 'doomed to a half-hearted existence and an early demise'.[33] In September 1967, the first Dutch 'critical university' was set up at the University of Amsterdam, followed by the Critical University of Nijmegen set up in November.[34] Already in the summer of 1967 West Berlin activists around Rudi Dutschke had begun to make plans for such a 'critical university' to take shape in Berlin. The founding conference of the 'critical university' in the main assembly hall of the Free University of Berlin took place on 1 November 1967. In the winter semester 1967/8, thirty-three alternative courses were on offer. Similar 'critical universities' saw the light of day in the course of 1967–8 in Hamburg, Frankfurt, Heidelberg, Kiel, Mainz, Münster, Freiburg, Tübingen, Erlangen, and Bochum.[35]

By 1968, in England, the idea had spread out from the LSE to Cambridge University, the University of Essex, but above all to the art colleges, the traditional testing ground for all sorts of nonconformist ideas in the generally rather paternalistically regulated sphere of British higher education.[36] In France, the May explosion placed such free universities on the agenda as well. Usually given the label Summer Universities, as they were set up for the summer months of 1968 to keep alive the flame of university revolt after the Gaullist rollback of June, they were set up in Paris, Strasbourg, Montpellier, Grenoble, and probably elsewhere, though the dearth of serious discussions of such alternative educational experiments in the relevant literature suggests that the Strasbourg experience may have been not the exception but the rule. The chronicler of the Strasbourg student revolt, Pierre Feuerstein, recalls: 'Much verbiage, banalities, various contributions characterised by disarming naïveté.'[37] Perhaps the most noteworthy contribution of the French student movement of 1968 to the construction of alternative educational experiments was a series of detailed blueprints for such counter-universities emerging from the strikes and occupations of May–June 1968.[38]

'Critical,' 'free', or 'summer' universities were a mixed success. Even the mother of them all, the Free University of Berkeley, though prospering for more than a half dozen years, eventually began to lose its emancipatory drive. 'By the late 1960s, the Free University was a joke; it was primarily a good place to meet someone to get laid.'[39] And perhaps it was indeed impossible to construct long-lasting islands of non-alienated learning and interaction within an ocean representing hierarchically organized traditional advanced industrial society or, to employ a different terminology, late capitalist postmodernity. Perhaps the same forces which eventually perverted the emancipatory ideals of the new left and, a few years later, the far left could not but emerge victorious, given the failure to change society at large. Perhaps Gramsci's pessimism of the intellect was more prescient than his optimism of the will. Yet no serious discussion of university revolt, including alternative educational concepts and experiences, should over-look two important, though all but forgotten, experiments in this field.

5. AN EXPERIMENTAL LABORATORY IN THE BOIS DE VINCENNES

Michael Schmidtke, in his important study of the West German and American new left, points to several important instances of free universities in the United States being created not exclusively by radical student demand. Here the Experimental College at San Francisco State University stood godfather to a series of explorations of free universities called into existence through joint efforts by students, faculty, and university administrations alike. But such tripartite experimentation was not limited to the unique political environment of the Bay Area. At the Catholic University of Notre Dame and universities in New Mexico and Utah, students, faculty, and administrators likewise joined forces to create alternative educational curricula to supplement regular course offerings. In two private colleges in Iowa, Schmidtke reports, similar initiatives were instigated not by radical students or faculty but by university administrators deeply affected by the spirit of the times.[40]

Yet the two most spectacular attempts to fashion an alternative university to become part and parcel of an overall effort to promote the progressive cause took place in Europe—more precisely, in Italy and France. By ministerial decree, on 7 December 1968, a pilot project was launched just east of the Paris city limits proper, in a compound within the urban forest called the Bois de Vincennes, on a piece of land belonging to the city of Paris, though surrounded by Vincennes.

What became known as the University of Paris VIII–Vincennes started out as an 'experimental laboratory', where new forms of interdisciplinary learning and didactic methods could be tried out. Designed as a temporary teaching and learning facility for 7,500 students, the experiment commenced with a small number of departments in January 1969. By the academic year 1970–1, the number of students had swelled to 9,500, though only less than half of the prefabricated buildings planned for the 'laboratory experiment' had been constructed by then. Overcrowding and less-than-optimal infrastructure provision made this experience a rather trying one—but few students and even fewer faculty opted for Vincennes out of desire for comfort or a traditional learning environment.

The experimental laboratory, which obtained university status in December 1970, immediately became a point of attraction for large numbers of dissident faculty members contesting the forces of tradition at older universities across France. From the beginning, Paris VIII attracted innovatory spirits who had long dreamt of creating a university of their own. In effect, Paris VIII–Vincennes became the proving ground for various and sometimes conflicting ideas behind earlier movements for 'free,' 'critical', or 'summer' universities set up to oppose and subvert higher education methods and principles. Consequently, Paris VIII became, to all intents and purposes, the place where a 'critical university' could be built from scratch. Only, in this particular instance, the primary push for such a radical solution came from the arriving faculty members—and such a counter-institution was not designed as a modest underground effort but it was explicitly fashioned to represent the institution as a whole.

University students on the urban campus in the Bois de Vincennes played a decidedly secondary role in the construction of this state-sponsored 'free university', though this was largely the result of the phenomenally high degree of activism by the faculty involved, and not because Vincennes students were an usually quiet lot. Indeed, faculty initiatives consistently encouraged and promoted student involvement and decision making. But the high concentration of activist faculty continuously outdistanced student campaigns. It may serve to highlight the unusual relationship of forces on the campus at Vincennes to contrast its faculty politics with faculty debates on other French campuses. The usual line-up of forces with regard to French university faculty internal debates saw a powerful centre-right arrayed against a rather solid phalanx of the political left. At Vincennes, the former was virtually absent. Faculty politics was no less bitterly contested, however: only, at Vincennes, the two hostile camps were roughly evenly divided between supporters of old left politics and activists gravitating towards the far left.

As a result, the courses on offer at Vincennes differed drastically from regular French university menus of modules on offer, thus approximating the reality within the Bois de Vincennes to some of the wilder dreams of strategists of 'critical' universities elsewhere. But departments functioned along entirely different principles and management theories as well. Various forms of self-management formulas, usually involving students and staff alongside faculty members, were continuously debated, practised, altered, and contested. A roughly 100-page series of documents drawn up after several years of experimentation by a large array of departments, showcase the ongoing efforts to develop and refine the workings of this state-sponsored 'critical university'.[41] But the innovatory nature of this laboratory encompassed more than 'just' course content and management models. By contrast to regular French university fare, small group teaching was not the exception but the rule. Again in contradistinction to normal French higher education curricula, students could choose their modules from a large menu of options. Not the least significant of initiatives was the abolition of intake selection. To be able to attend Vincennes, standard high school diplomas (baccalaureates) were expressly removed as the most important admissions criteria. The student body was rather different as a result, and much of the teaching took place in the late afternoon and early evenings. Traditional exams were frowned upon and often quietly subverted. University education at Vincennes thus turned out to be non-traditional in more ways than one. It only stood to reason, then, that Vincennes became a haven for various generations of student activists as well. Michel Debeauvais reports:

Serge Mallet [the industrial sociologist teaching at Vincennes's Department of Political Science] once said that at Vincennes small administrative posts were distributed to former barricade fighters [of May 1968] in the same manner in which *bars-tabacs* [a combination of tobacconist shop and small standing-room-only pub] were distributed to war widows after World War One. He called these minor jobs at Vincennes *les bars-tabacs de la Sorbonne*.[42]

6. THE ALBERONI PROJECT

The Université de Paris VIII–Vincennes was a product of fermentation on the faculty front. An even more portentous experiment occurred in Trento, Italy, where, as we have seen in Chapter 2, the Higher Institute of Social Sciences—the Trento Institute did not obtain official university status until 1972—had been a laboratory experiment all of its own ever since 1966, when sociology students decided to apply critical sociological inquiry to determine activist practice on location. In late 1968, a further stage in its turbulent history began with the arrival of Francesco Alberoni as the new president of the Higher Institute. Formerly at the Catholic University of the Holy Cross in Milan, itself a hotbed of student unrest, Alberoni brought along a team of like-minded researchers and teachers, including Giorgio Galli and Gian Enrico Rusconi. Fundamentally sympathetic to the fresh wind of student politics which was then beginning to shake up trad-itional university politics and Italian society as a whole, Alberoni soon established a cordial and working relationship with Trento student leaders, the latter notably including individuals performing crucial roles in Italian far left politics in the subsequent decade.

Trento thus became the showcase example of a system-transcending cooperation between radical faculty and administrators on the one hand and vanguard student militants on the other. Unlike Vincennes, where faculty politics always outshone student activism, Trento University, though only half a dozen years old by that time, had already produced a battle-hardened *movimento studentesco*, whose activist potential was second to none. When some of the most brilliant minds employed by Italy's university system combined their efforts and ideals with a fresh generation of student radicals, it unsurprisingly produced a time bomb. Spurred into action by the ceaseless enthusiasm of Trento students—amongst them Marco Boato, Mauro Rostagno, and Renato Curcio—and ably encouraged by University President Alberoni, whose series of 'Working Documents' provided a running commentary and incitement to further progress by the university community for the duration of this experience, the entire curriculum and course content was restructured to conform to the desires of students and teachers alike to construct a better world. And how could it be any different when none other than the university president himself wrote in Working Document No. 6:

Our mode of operation...constitutes a threat to all those who want to sit back and go to sleep, to those who dream of a secure salary of an irresponsible bureaucrat, to those who wish for a university to be organised like an elementary school, to those who do not want to be creative scholars but who are, instead, predisposed to become or to try to be reasonably well-informed regurgitators of information....[43]

A 'research laboratory' saw the light of day which coordinated a series of working groups that gave empirical sociology in Italy an entirely new meaning. With faculty members heading up the various campaigns, students set out to investigate a variety of social issues and institutions, including prisons, psychiatric hospitals, elementary schools, teachers, 'capitalist development and consequences of large-scale industries', 'peasants in the Trento region', or the local newspaper press.[44] Given the collusion of radical reformers in institutional seats of power in Trento with locally entrenched student revolutionaries, no one expected such applied sociological methods to produce ringing defences of the status quo. Just as was happening in the Bois de Vincennes, an entire higher education establishment had transformed itself into a 'critical university'. An alternative curriculum had replaced traditional teaching and course content, only, whereas in Vincennes the initiative was always firmly lodged in the hands of faculty, in Trento the active sponsorship encompassed the entire university community.

A number of consequences derived from this unique circumstance. The *movimento studentesco antiautoritario trentino* (MSA) retained a crucial measure of autonomy, though initially firmly wedded to the idea and practice of the critical university of Trento operating as a full-scale, officially sanctioned higher education institute, unlike the 'critical' or 'free' universities elsewhere, which were at best running as small-scale alternative challenges alongside official business as usual. In due time, however, precisely this unique synergy amongst top-level administrators, faculty, and students was bound to create certain frictions. The most detailed reflections on this experience from the student activist side, Renato Curcio and Mauro Rostagno's *Fuori dai denti*, written in the heat of the moment in December 1968, repeatedly reflect the worries amongst student radicals that their revolutionary intentions could eventually become compromised by what could be regarded as a form of cooptation from above. Nonetheless, for the moment, the alliance held firm. An organizational diagram of the MSA graphically underscored how the Alberoni project and MSA efforts clearly overlapped. From the diagram it remains unclear where the empirical research efforts of the officially sanctioned critical university ended and where the MSA terrain of activity began.[45] In all probability, for much of the first year of this experiment, the boundaries must have remained fluid.

In the most detailed step-by-step reconstruction of the various stages of the critical university of Trento, Marco Boato, curiously without ever mentioning the role of Francesco Alberoni and his team, points out how, by April 1969, students organized in the various working groups no longer regarded the university as the primary reference point for their activist sociological efforts. With the 'discovery' of the working class as the hoped-for agent of social change, Trento students now focused all their energies 'outside the university proper within the social practices on the level of the factory, the neighborhood and the country-at-large. The town of Trento was now subdivided into "intervention zones" within which the working groups pursuing their theoretical and practical efforts were to combine their factory agitation with relevant activities in the neighborhoods and secondary schools',[46] the latter, the reader may recall from Chapter 2, not only providing future generations of university student activists but constituting hotbeds of radicalism in and of themselves. Despite the support by Alberoni and his team for the concentration on extra-university investigatory practices, the critical university of Trento was beginning to reach a crisis point.[47]

To overcome the splendid isolation of ivory tower concerns had been a central platform point for Alberoni when arriving in Trento. In many ways, he succeeded in transforming this dream into reality. But the spiral of increasing radicalization of Italian politics soon took its toll. Student radicals began to sever their ties with the Alberoni project. And even formerly respected Trento student leaders suffered the consequences for their continued belief in the validity of the unique opportunity offered by the critical university of Trento. Mauro Rostagno recalls: 'They attacked me and told me that the Critical University was aristocratic, anti-working class, a golden ghetto, and so forth. I abandoned Trento, haunted by the terror of being considered a traitor of the working class.'[48] By February 1970 Francesco Alberoni had vacated his post as university president. The Alberoni project had come to an end.

Did the revolutionary instincts of Trento students lead to the failure of institutional innovation? Or was the critical university of Trento yet another instance of institutional failure to revolutionize society? In one of his last

'Working Documents', Francesco Alberoni took stock and noted that the significance of the critical university as it had developed in the course of 1969 was, after all, that it had provided an opportunity 'to administer revolutionary power in an exemplary fashion, in a way that produced a working utopia', and Alberoni continued: 'The experience of management and self-management has been, both within and outside of the university proper, a real and fundamental practical experience.'[49] But what of the growing divorce between supporters of the Alberoni project and the radical faction dominating the MSA? Already in early 1969 Alberoni, as always, did not mince words. He had soon recognized the authoritarian streak in his closest collaborators within the Trento MSA. The *movimento studentesco*, Alberoni wrote,

in Trento is intimidating. It remains stuck within that old shitty logic (*vecchia logica di merda*); it is unable to shake it off its back. It has seen shit happening to others (*Ha visto la merda adosso agli altri*); it has recognized other people's way of thinking in repressive, vengeful, and oppressive ways; but, in the course of the fight itself, it has been unable to leave behind its own traditional baggage. Accordingly, it has gained 'power', but it is losing support (*In questo modo ha il 'potere' ma perde gli uomini*).'[50]

Or, in the words of a former sociology student at Trento, Marianella Sclavi, 'the only way of doing politics we had at our disposal after '68, on the outside and among ourselves, was an authoritarian way'.[51] Was this legacy of authoritarian traditions an inevitable millstone around the neck of antiauthoritarian student insurgents?

7. PARTICIPATORY DEMOCRACY AT THE POINT OF PRODUCTION

Working-class mobilization between 1962 and 1976 took on forms quite similar to processes occurring within the university milieu. The democratization of factory and office relations, including the inner workings of trade unions which often had experienced an arteriosclerosis of their own, proceeded apace and was closely related in all but name to participatory democracy found in university student milieux. Most visibly present during labour conflicts, the working-class dimension of 1968 showcased a similarly bewildering array of imaginative institutional innovations to that illustrated for the world of student politics. General assemblies of the combined workforce on the factory or office floor became standard features of working-class self-mobilization in the heyday of labour insurgency. When the realization quickly set in that huge general assemblies merely allowed the most assertive individuals to address the crowd, as was the case in the university milieu, other smaller bodies, commissions and subcommissions, were created, usually designed to resolve specific problems but in the process providing the necessary free space and a less intimidating atmosphere to allow less outspoken blue- or white-collar workers to speak up for themselves and for each other.

If strike committees and subcommittees provided precisely such a nurturing environment fostering self-expression by the ranks, in several countries central to the 'proletarian May' more permanent forms of organization operating along precepts of 'participatory democracy' arose at least for some time. In Italy, in 1968–9, such rank-and-file institutions transcending union demarcation were called unitary base committees, in France and francophone Belgium strike committees, in Flanders workers' committees, and in Spain and Portugal workers' commissions. In each case, such innovative forms of working-class self-organization were nothing other than 'participatory' or 'direct' democracy applied to the working-class milieu. Bypassing or simply ignoring traditional social divisions between wage or craft categories, union membership, or other markers of internal division, the workforce of a given plant, office complex, or mine pit simply gathered in a 'general assembly' to discuss their concerns, deliberated on strategies to pursue and then, if necessary, took action. What distinguished the French experience of strike committees, where a similar unitary dynamic was at work, from the Belgian, Italian, and Spanish organizational models was that, in France, they generally disappeared when the specific labour conflict which had spawned such committees was resolved. In Portugal, Belgium, Italy, and Spain they survived the settlement of specific conflicts and evolved into more long-lasting features of the period under review. In Portugal, however, their lifespan was determined by the rise and fall of the Portuguese Revolution. In Belgium they generally disappeared in the second half of the 1970s, coterminous with the decline of labour unrest in the country at large.[52] In Spain, undoubtedly fuelled by the extraordinary circumstances of illegality or semi-legality, the workers' commissions (CCOO) retained their democratic impulse by and large from the early to mid 1960s until the mid-1970s when, benefiting from legal protection with the demise of Franco and the transition to democracy, the CCOO quickly evolved into 'just' another ordinary, hierarchically structured trade union, which it remains until the present day.

Italy, in many ways, provides a special case. The unitary base committees (CUB), already discussed in Chapter 3, began to vanish from the scene precisely when the intensity of labour conflicts reached its peak. The Hot Autumn of 1969 saw the return of traditional trade union structures to centre stage. But, unlike in France, where traditional union federations—with the partial exception of the erstwhile Catholic CFDT—reclaimed control over their 'natural' constituency with full hierarchical lines of communication, in Italy all three major trade union confederations underwent significant changes with regard to their modes of internal functioning. The CUB disappeared because 'regular' trade unions increasingly absorbed the CUB's methods and, for at least a half dozen years, Italian labour relations witnessed a revitalized trade union militancy, in which formerly rival union federations increasingly cooperated and created structures of rank-and-file democracy which gave blue-collar workers maximum control over their working lives.

Even in 1968–9, the CUB never came to dominate labour relations in all of Italy or even 'just' northern Italy. Yet their democratic impulse soon spawned a truly nationwide wave of new institutional departures within the previously rather fractured Italian labour movement. The Hot Autumn witnessed the generalization of grass-roots *delegati*, representatives of a given unit of production within the factory or office complex. But, in contrast to, for instance, British shop stewards, the *delegati* did not have to be members of a particular union or, for that matter, any union at all. Structurally, the Italian *delegati* thus came closest to the German *Betriebsräte* who, likewise, could be members of any union or none at all. The crucial difference lies in the vastly different political cultures of Italy and West Germany in these years. German *Betriebsräte* were a legacy of the 1918–19 German Revolution, but half a century later elections to the *Betriebsräte* in West Germany usually tended to be rather staid affairs. The same could not be said for their Italian equivalents. Springing up in the midst of a huge national wave of social movement activity paralysing universities and factories alike, the average Italian delegate was rather different in nature and mentality from the average German *Betriebsrat*. Two graphic descriptions of the origins of the *delegati* in the giant FIAT Mirafiori works may serve to demonstrate the highly irregular background to this (for Italy) new phenomenon: 'We jumped up on the tables of the canteen and organized assemblies and the first strikes. In the course of these strikes we then discovered the organizational medium, the *delegati*. The elections were immediate, and the most combative colleagues were chosen.' 'The delegates arose spontaneously, out of the groups of workers on strike who put forth demands, especially the assembly line workers. Whoever displayed the greatest amount of rage and whoever was most experienced politically became the spokesperson for the production unit.'[53]

Born out of struggle, the Italian worker delegates incorporated in a quasi-natural fashion the organizational parameters of 'participatory democracy'. As a rule directly elected from the factory floor, this close connection to their constituency remained in force by virtue of an additional feature. Factory delegates could be recalled at any time by majority decision of their electors.[54] This crucial mechanism not only ensured that delegates would stay in close touch with the factory floor, but the fact that delegates were thus most often the most militant and articulate members of a given workforce served to heat up further the already highly volatile climate surrounding labour relations in Italy after 1968. A product of unusual militancy, the innovation of such permanently accountable delegate structures consolidated the first gains and stimulated workers to set ever higher goals.

In Chapter 3, I described the situation on some factory floors, where workers—rather than management—controlled the speed of production. Workers who, for generations, had regarded factories as necessary but infernal production sites gradually began to derive a certain amount of satisfaction from their activity on the company floor. When the tables began to be turned against management,

Italian workers, for the first time since the wave of factory occupations after the First World War, began to feel a certain pride in their 'choice' of profession. This process of individual and collective liberation experienced by countless blue- (and white-)collar workers after 1968, has been given superb literary form in the epic novel on the FIAT Mirafiori workforce by Nanni Balestrini, *Vogliamo tutto*, a novel chronicling the migration of a southern Italian migrant to the north and the corresponding rise in his self-assertiveness when labour struggles at FIAT swept away many of the obstacles and inhibitions keeping the FIAT workforce silent and unfree. The experience of a rapid increase in control by workers over their working and their private lives was likewise converted into artistic form by one of the songwriters par excellence of the Italian *sessantotto*, Alfredo Bandelli. In his classic 'La Ballata della FIAT' Bandelli gave voice to long-standing resentments against management and remote union structures alike, then summarizing the profound shift within the relationship of forces at the giant Mirafiori works in the course of 1969:

> Mister boss [Signor padrone], this time around things have turned out badly for you:
> From now on you need to turn to no one but us if you want to negotiate.
> And this time around you won't be able to buy us off with a five lire increase:
> If you offer us ten, we will demand a hundred,
> If you offer us a hundred, we will want a thousand.

Italian workplace relations underwent a similar radicalizing dynamic to that which propelled Italian students from idealistic and reform-minded supporters of innovation to radical revolutionaries in the space of two short years.[55]

When comparing French and Italian labour relations after 1968, it is at first sight puzzling to note that, whereas the French May 1968 saw countless workplace occupations and in the course of the first half of the 1970s several experiments of workers' control, Italy experienced virtually none of those forms of labour conflict supposedly denoting maximum combativity. But upon closer observation, what initially may appear as French strength and Italian weakness turns out to be exactly the reverse. Italy, too, experienced instances of factory occupations in these years, but they were few and far between and generally located in towns that were not at the centre of the working-class revolt. Rather than an indicator of militancy and self-assuredness, factory occupations could very well be seen as instances of desperation and weakness rather than strength.[56] In the frontline battle zones of the Italian north, in Turin, Milan, or Porto Marghera, there was no need for factory occupations. Workers were often in control of their work environment without having to engage in such needlessly risk-laden open confrontations. Why go to the extent of occupying the factory floor in an open show of force when workers could obtain their goals by less intimidating but at least equally persuasive measures? The absence of major instances of site occupations or forms of self-management should therefore be read as proof positive of the energy and power of factory activists—and not the reverse!

But, to return to the interaction between grass-roots rebellion and union structures in the Italian state, the largely spontaneous birth of the movement of *delegati* not only turned management–labour relations upside down; it also profoundly altered the mode of operation of trade unions themselves. In France, only the formerly Catholic CFDT absorbed the spirit of 1968 and emerged drastically changed as a result. The other two important national union feder-ations, the General Labour Confederation (CGT) and Workers' Power (FO), in most respects continued as before. In Italy, however, the spirit of direct democ-racy, as expressed in the rise of the CUB (1968) and then the *delegati* (1969), changed all three Italian trade union confederations in roughly equal measure. Certainly within the crucial metalworking industry, all three federations adopted rank-and-file militancy and modes of operation. The advantages of union adaptation to the incursions of participatory democracy into Italian labour relations were immediately visible to all. Given their powerful organizational presence across the entire state, union backing to 'delegate democracy' would serve to strengthen and consolidate these novel institutions of direct democracy. Correspondingly, the democratic impulse from below stimulated union flexibility and adaptation to new organizational models. Thus a virtuous cycle of fruitful cooperation between grass-roots movements and union structures characterized the Italian labour movement after 1969.[57] It was this unique confluence of activist and institutional energies which ultimately made Italian factories (and not only Italy's factories) into virtual 'free zones' of experimentation with all sorts of elements of participatory democracy which, further north in Europe and in North America, appeared to be the exclusive property of the student movement and the new and far left.

General assemblies, working groups, subcommittees, and commissions flour-ished after 1969. But there was more. Given a stamp of approval by the three union federations, the delegate structures underwent further refinement and, above all, strengthening. Factory councils (*consigli di fabbrica*, CdFs) were created—most prominently so in Italy's flagship metalworking industry—which were in practice assemblies of the various delegates elected on the factory floor. And by combining the already not inconsiderable powers of delegates into such company-wide bodies, the explosive power of delegates was further enhanced. Having sufficiently imbibed the grass-roots message of that era, the Metalworking Federations in particular remained generally rather careful not to patronize or exert undue control over these increasingly numerous and powerful factory councils. 'In 1972 there were close to 1,000 factory councils in Italy, with just under 10,100 delegates, according to confederal sources. By 1977 there were over 32,000 councils and more than 200,000 delegates elected.'[58] Most importantly, decision-making power with regard to contract negotiations, grievance procedures, and other vital interests of rank-and-file workers was consciously decentralized by the union federations so that individual factory councils were in maximal control. 'CdFs not only bargain, but bargain continually; there are no formal restrictions on their right to strike or the scope of issues they may consider. Articulated bargaining in Italy thus both raises the wage floor set in industrywide contracts and improves plant-specific working conditions.'[59] But, above all else, such gains of participatory democracy on the company floor made individual workers feel that they were finally in control of their destiny.

What, then, of the role of *autogestion* or workers' self-management? Narratives of the French proletarian May in particular tend to give pride of place not only to the factory occupations occuring in May and June 1968 but to the experiments with workers' control over production or workers' self-management. And in Chapter 3 emphasis was placed on the inspirational role of the LIP struggle, capturing the imagination of an entire post-1968 generation of activists and radiating far beyond the borders of the French state. Mention was made, too, of 'the children of LIP', several instances of strikes followed by wildcat production under workers' control à la LIP. In the summer and autumn of 1973, for instance, female workers at a textile plant in western France decided to respond to management intransigence by resuming production of shirts on their own. A local member of a radical farmers' union provided the necessary space on his property, the necessary machinery was collected, and for two months shirts were produced and sold under the self-management label PIL (*Populaires Inventés Localement*).[60] From late January until early March 1974, poultry workers in a small town in Brittany, with the active assistance of radical farmers and support committees in fifteen Breton towns, responded to a management ultimatum by organizing the purchase, processing, and sale of chicken on their own.[61] And, a bit further to the north, in neighbouring Belgium, a number of instances of workers' self-management made waves throughout the 1970s as well.[62]

But in virtually all such instances, recourse to such radical measures was decided upon out of a defensive mode, not as part of a system-transforming radical offensive strategy. As was the case with LIP itself, workers' self-management was usually opted for only when the alternative was certain closure of the production site. In Chapter 3, I drew attention to the case of Portugal in 1974–5 as the country with by far the most extensive experience of workers' control in industry. But even there the motivations for such drastic measures were generally of a desperate, defensive rearguard nature. Only in Portugal's rural sector were collectivization measures, the functional equivalent to workers' control or workers' self-management in industry, part of an offensive campaign. But, then, rural agriculture in semi-peripheral Portugal could hardly be proclaimed a model for the generally more developed industrial West. To proclaim measures of *autogestion* as yardsticks for working-class mobilization and collective liberation from the oppressive rule of capital may therefore entirely miss the point in the radical upsurge after 1968. The most exemplary and long-lasting legacy of the workings of participatory democracy in working-class milieux should rather be located in the variety of practices described above for the hotbed of social movement activism after 1968: Italian factory floors.

8. PARTICIPATORY DEMOCRACY AND THE LEFT

To briefly compare new left with far left contributions to the innovation of participatory democracy, it is symptomatic that—in Italy at the very least but also in Belgium and elsewhere—the high point of direct democracy at the point of production occurred long after the new left had faded to give rise to a powerful and multiform far left.[63] The Italian far left was responsible for many of the manifestations of grass-roots or direct democracy long after the rising star of the new left PSIUP and the *movimento studentesco* had faded to make room for Potere Operaio, Lotta Continua, Avanguardia Operaia, and other formations on the burgeoning far left. The CUB, the first organizational product of radical ferment in Italian factories, for instance, were strongest precisely where radicalized students and workers sought and found mutual trust and cooperation, most often under the auspices of Avanguardia Operaia in and around Milan, the latter's stronghold. Participatory democracy was therefore by no means the exclusive property of the northern European and American student new left. The social relevance of direct democracy was at least as strong in southern Europe and under the creative leadership of individuals generally sympathetic to the far left. Indeed, inasmuch as working-class milieux in Italy and elsewhere encompassed far wider sectors of society than the university milieux most centrally affected further to the north, the true social impact and potential of participatory democracy can best be gauged and studied in the southern European working-class milieux rather than the campus-oriented communities in northern Europe and the United States.

As to the role of the old left, the picture is somewhat uneven and contradictory. In France, the Communist Party (PCF) had little time for the ideas and practices of participatory democracy. In Italy, the PCI was less averse to such initiatives, though it rarely led the pack, instead sanctioning and then popularizing certain gains when far left-inspired actions had proved to be beneficial to the larger cause. Social democracy in Italy was then eclipsed by the powerful PCI. In France, the newly rebranded Parti Socialiste (PS), as we have seen in Chapter 4, was keen to jump on the bandwagon of *autogestionnaire* ideas and practices, absorbing and thereby neutralizing the self-management party par excellence, the new left Parti Socialiste Unifié (PSU). Both PS and PCI, however, jettisoned the ideological baggage and most practical gains of participatory democracy when the time seemed right to make peace with late capitalist postmodernity in the wake of an increasingly unfavourable political and economic conjuncture after 1976.

9. NEIGHBOURHOOD ASSOCIATIONS IN IBERIA

In earlier historical instances of central challenges to the dominant social order, grass-roots or participatory democracy had not stopped at the university or factory gates. In the most famous instance of transnational political upheavals in Europe, the wave of radicalism and revolution between 1917 and 1920, direct democracy developed to the point of creating representative bodies assembling factory, neighbourhood, and other 'councils' in an entire town, region, and even an entire state.[64] In the late 1960s and early 1970s, clearly, such radical steps were never taken. Even in Italy, such efforts to link up individual organs of direct democracy into 'zonal councils' never went beyond the drawing board.[65] But in this particular domain, it seems, the Iberian peninsula, in the peculiarly tense atmosphere experienced just before and after the transition to democracy, went furthest in the direction of coordinating such organs of 'popular power', yet another expression for participatory democracy, most common in the Portuguese- or Spanish-speaking world. Curiously, such efforts were most visible in working-class residential areas rather than production sites.

Neighbourhood associations in Francoist Spain had been given legal status as a pacifying measure in 1964. They soon became an outlet for underground activists to mobilize concerned members of communities, and they provided a legal cover for social movement activists under conditions of dictatorial rule. In Bilbao, for instance, the neighbourhood associations grew in importance after a series of setbacks to the underground labour movement encouraged activists to turn their attention to these officially sanctioned bodies in the second half of the 1960s.[66] By the early to mid 1970s, these neighbourhood groups increasingly took on a life of the own, wholly divorced from the original function of such institutions as state-supported channels for the controlled diversion of popular discontent. 'There were many causes for dissatisfaction on the working-class estates' where such associations flourished—'lack of proper sewerage, street lighting, or paving; poor-quality housing; inadequate health, educational, or recreational facilities; cuts in social services; flooding; and schemes of urban renewal that smashed through old neighbourhoods'. Soon 'demands for amnesty and democracy' were mixed in with location-specific grievances. 'The actions were particularly defiant in the new working-class districts, where residents staged rent strikes, blocked main roads, occupied churches, organised delegations to seek support among influential people, and campaigned against the local structures of power.'[67]

Neighbourhood associations cropped up throughout urban Spain, from Las Palmas on the Canary Islands to La Coruña in Galicia, north-western Spain. Perhaps the strongest movement along such lines existed in Greater Barcelona where, on the eve of Franco's death, 120 such groupings functioned with an average membership of between 50 and 200 supporters in each individual organization. Coordinating bodies were created to give greater meaning and power to such attempts to improve the quality of life while subverting the Francoist state. As early as 1972, the Barcelona neighbourhood associations formed a federation. By 1976 a similar federation was set up in Madrid, though of the 138 associations in the capital city only 28 had managed to obtain legal status by that time.[68] They experienced an even greater influx of supporters after

Franco's death in late 1975, but by the late 1970s their importance diminished as other forms of legal protest gained in popularity instead.[69]

Residents' commissions was the term for identical organizations springing up throughout neighbouring Portugal in the wake of the overthrow of its dictatorship in April 1974. Unlike Spain, however, the overall political context at the time of their growth and development was far more conducive to radical demands and, accordingly, Portuguese residents' associations not only created an even denser network of such bodies most firmly implanted in poor working-class neighbourhoods, but openly engaged in housing squats and set firm limits on the manœuvring room for landlords and municipalities. Just like in neighbouring Spain, Portuguese residents' commissions became part and parcel of the experience of participatory democracy for countless citizens. 'The commissions adopted the model of direct democracy to which the neighborhood movement aspired. Constituents had the right to recall elected commission members at any time. Voting in general assemblies was by a show of hands.' 'Unlike workers' commissions [see Chapter 3], neighbourhood commissions attempted to go beyond the issues of economic necessity to questions of culture. By building parks, establishing day care centres, taking children to museums or the beach, founding musical and theater groups, and similar activities, they worked to improve the quality of their members' and their neighbourhoods' lives.' 'Activists believed that the commissions, close to their constituency and open to everyone, embodied direct democracy and foreshadowed a new society in which all would share in making the decisions by which they were governed.'[70] As was the case in neighbouring Spain, residents' commissions soon federated into city-wide coordinating committees, and Portuguese urban centres in the eighteen months of the Portuguese Revolution began to experience the changes emanating from these rank-and-file organs of 'popular power'.[71]

Residents' commisions, of course, faced many obstacles even during the 'brief summer' of popular mobilization in the Portuguese state. Phil Mailer presents a brief listing of such difficulties, including meddling by political organizations, often by groups of the Maoist far left, and corresponding passivity of 'unorganized' residents.[72] But, on the whole, such residents' commissions came closer to actually representing their nominal constituency than any other organs of 'popular power', including the workers' commissions which became far more easily the plaything of the grandstanding Maoist far left. Encouraged by the most radical factions in Portugal's Armed Forces Movement, in the course of 1975 a number of popular assemblies were set up, most frequently in the Greater Lisbon area, which combined delegates from residents' commissions and workers' commissions, attempting to replace traditional forms of local government. Yet here the problems besetting such commissions were multiplied by the controlling instincts of the Communist Party and the far left, and only a few such organs of dual power prospered and survived.[73] The counterrevolution after 25 November 1975 ensured that all such assemblies and commissions would eventually wither and die.

10. THE COMMUNE OF NANTES

Outside of Iberia, such organs of city-wide popular power appeared nowhere—with one curious exception. In the middle of the upheavals of the weeks-long general strike in May–June 1968, the town of Nantes in western France was for a period of eighteen days in effect ruled by a strike committee composed of delegates from all local trade union federations. Nantes, of course, was also the location where the very first factory occupation of the French springtime upheaval took place on 13 May (see Chapter 3). A closer look at local politics and leading social movement activists explains why Nantes became a battleground *sui generis* and once again underscores the relevance of the far left. The dominant figure in union politics at Sud-Aviation, the factory which triggered the nationwide strike wave and the parallel moves towards workplace occupations throughout France, was Yvon Rocton, a young Trotskyist militant. Student politics at the University of Nantes was dominated by a curious and combative alliance of Trotskyists, anarchists, and Situationists. The leading figure with the greatest authority in Nantes union circles as a whole was an anarcho-syndicalist by the name of Alexandre Hébert.

The creation of a central, city-wide strike committee was already an anomaly and happened virtually nowhere else in France. But what upped the ante even more was the adoption by this coordinating body for Greater Nantes of Alexandre Hébert's proposition to become proactive and in effect take control of the city government. City hall was thus taken over by the insurgent strikers, and for the duration of the conflict the mayor of Nantes 'could not take a single decision without the approval of the municipal strike committee, and indeed the mayor of Nantes had to obtain prior agreement to go about his regular business'.[74] The most pressing business was the distribution of increasingly scarce provisions, and it became the task of the strike committee, not the regular authorities, to issue rationing coupons for petrol and the like. 'In the city, emptied of the daily traffic composed of countless private automobiles, one could not but notice the vehicles belonging to the various trade unions criss-crossing the main arteries, not always paying heed to traffic regulations. These vehicles, filled with activists wearing red armbands, recalled in an astounding manner the revolutionary period of the immediate post-liberation era.'[75]

The Commune of Nantes remained a fascinating but exceptional case of popular power in municipal control. Portuguese organs of direct democracy were plentiful and full of energy but subject to the vagaries of high politics as usual. Italian workers may have controlled the line speed and caused ulcers for managers experiencing a distinct sense of loss of control, but the country as such remained firmly in the hands of conservative Christian Democracy. What precisely did all these instances of participatory democracy mean for the individuals concerned? How did modes of behaviour and social interaction change for the hundreds of thousands, even millions of rank-and-file individuals at the heart of such campaigns? How did all this affect their perception and the reality of everyday life?

11. INDIVIDUAL AND COLLECTIVE LIBERATION

The most profound changes of any economic sector in any European country at that time occurred in rural Portugal, where collectivization measures and cooperatives fundamentally altered the relationship of forces between formally subordinate workers and the former elites. It is therefore not unexpected that attitudinal changes would be noted here on an unprecedentedly large scale. Nonetheless, precisely rural Portugal was also an area of the modern world where the forces of tradition held great sway and where traditional notions of deference to authority were not just habits but reflected ingrained norms. Here is what the most thorough student of revolutionary rural Portugal reports when the old power structures had been safely removed:

Egalitarian norms were not confined to formal statutes and pay schemes. They were also embodied in a whole range of symbolic behavior. The professional titles that are so prominent in daily communication throughout Portugal were totally absent within cooperatives and collectives. Instead of being called 'doctor' or 'engineer,' as is the rule in other parts of Portugal, the trusted outsider with post-secondary education was called 'friend' or, under some circumstances, 'comrade.' Within the cooperative, men used nicknames, family names, or first names, but never the formal *Senhor*.

Though some older 'women were the occasional exception to the rule'. 'Though worker-members often deferred to the judgement of elected leaders in a formal setting, there was no fear-based deference between individuals. There was, instead, a camaraderie and solidarity that contrasted markedly with the organisation of work in the past.'[76]

The experience of individual and collective liberation at the heart of the spirit of 1968 could be felt in countless other locations by activists experiencing the possibility of a different world. Interviewed years later, for instance, a woman worker who had lived the brief experience of the self-managed PIL textile plant in Cérizay reminisced: 'We experienced an extraordinary moment. The girls wanted everything.'[77] Almost identical wording, of course, became the unifying slogan of the rebellious workforce at the FIAT Mirafiori plant repeatedly referred to earlier in this study: *Vogliamo tutto!* (We Want Everything!). And, indeed, in the process of fighting for initially often relatively limited goals, new worlds of possibilities opened up in more ways than one. Few accounts of the beehives of activity which strike committees, subcommittees, and commissions soon became neglect to mention the countless incidents when previously shy and quiet individuals suddenly began to talk.

One of the most evocative reconstructions of this process is the left Catholic historian and anthropologist Michel de Certeau's series of essays 'The Capture of Speech'. Several trips to Latin America, where he experienced first-hand the attraction of liberation theology which instilled self-confidence and an activist spirit into vast numbers of disenfranchised urban poor, had prepared de Certeau to be attuned to the symbolic markers of freedom filling the air. Here are some excerpts from his remarkable text, whose second chapter opens up with the observation: 'Last May speech was taken the way, in 1789, the Bastille was taken.' He then goes on to recreate the atmosphere of individual and collective liberation as experienced in the Parisian May:

Something happened to us. Something began to stir in us. Emerging from who knows where, suddenly filling the streets and the factories, circulating among us, becoming ours but no longer being the muffled noise of our solitude, voices that had never been heard began to change us. At least that was what we felt. From this something unheard of was produced: we began to speak. It seemed as if it were for the first time. From everywhere emerged the treasures, either aslumber or tacit, of forever unspoken experiences. At the same time that previously self-assured discourses faded away and the 'authorities' were reduced to silence, frozen existences melted and suddenly awoke into a prolific morning.[78]

This process was by no means unique to France. Wini Breines, in her compelling defence of the American new left, reports how outside observers witnessing student protest meetings were often 'surprised that student speeches were short and sentences clear and simple in contrast to the usual "convoluted" expressions that the faculty find characteristic of students. And most astonishing, many students who hardly ever spoke in the classroom spoke to large numbers of demonstrators often urging them to a particular tactic or strategy.'[79] Virtually identical reports recall the atmosphere elsewhere. Gianni Statera describes the Italian case:

What occurred in the Italian universities during the academic year 1967–68 [the first year of generalized university revolt] was an extraordinary experience for thousands of young people, most of whom were just discovering politics, ideal commitment, collective excitement: in a tumultuous environment, everybody could and even was obliged to take the floor to say whatever he had in mind, the audience being composed of 'comrades' who made up 'general assemblies,' fluid bodies which operated in the name of direct democracy without any delegation of power. These assemblies were designed to be occasions for debate and free individual expression, providing students with the opportunity 'to find themselves,' to change their minds, to exert their own repressed drives by the means of verbal violence.[80]

12. THE BIRTH OF SECOND-WAVE FEMINISM

It was precisely out of this atmosphere of antiauthoritarian challenges to the hierarchical structures of the status quo that second-wave feminism emerged to confront male domination of public space in general and social movements in particular. Much has been written about the persistence of male chauvinism within the left. And it is clearly symptomatic of this particular facet of gender relations that not a single internationally known spokesperson or 'leader' of the 1968 student left was a woman. By contrast, pictorial evidence is overwhelming that activists in faculties and streets were to an equal extent represented by both sexes. Nonetheless, it would be wholly ahistorical and misleading to present the feminist movement of the 1970s and subsequent decades primarily as a reaction to 1968. Second-wave feminism was simultaneously a product and a response to 1968. For, without the opening of windows onto the wider world, without the partial dismantling of traditional power structures, without a widespread questioning of authority, it would have been far more difficult for feminist ideologies and practices to take root in Western European and North American societies.

No better proof of the intricate and intimate relationship between the upsurge of social movements in the period of '1968' and the genesis of a women's liberation movement exists than the parallel—if somewhat delayed in the case of the latter—growth of challenges to traditional authorities and the feminist critique. It is, for instance, one of the empirical observations repeatedly highlighted throughout this book that social movements in the United States, the civil rights movement above all else, provided a critical mass and impetus which inspired subsequent radical challenges to traditional conceptions of social order in North America and Western Europe alike. In an astounding confirmation of the thesis of the crucial link between generalized questioning of authority—first exercised in the campaign for civil rights—and the specific concerns of women, the US women's movement can be traced precisely to the ebullient atmosphere of innovations and challenges characteristic of SNCC.

Second-wave feminism in the United States as an organized response to male hegemony was born in hesitant but unmistakable fashion out of women's experience of discrimination within the civil rights movement. Just like the subsequent student movement in the United States, the civil rights movement was almost exclusively represented by male voices. 'Nevertheless, in comparison to the division of roles in most of American society, the civil rights movement was strikingly egalitarian.'[81] No civil rights group was more egalitarian than SNCC. Still, even SNCC remained best known to the outside world through its male spokespersons, such as Robert Moses, James Forman, or Stokely Carmichael. But its high degree of relative openness provided the fertile breeding ground for proto-feminist ideas. The historic first document of American second-wave feminism was written as an anonymous position paper by Mary King and Casey Hayden for an SNCC gathering in November 1964.[82] And the distribution patterns of second-wave feminist ideas in North America, Western Europe, and elsewhere further strengthens the argument that social movement engagement and critique was crucial in instilling in a new generation of activist women the power to carry out the feminist 'capture of speech'. The spark of condemnation of male chauvinist habits in the United States first jumped from women in the civil rights community to women in the new left—often aided by individual women's personal and political itineraries from the civil rights movement into the new left.[83] Gaining important allies amongst women members in the US new left, the feminist critique then transferred to European soil via the transnational communication circuits of the student new left. Accounts of the early history of Western European feminism in the late 1960s convincingly recall the model character of the US women's liberation movement for their European sisters.[84] And in Western Europe too, with an astonishing regularity, women within the student movement and the flourishing new and far left became the early spokespersons of the feminist critique.[85] In short, the capture of speech, a hallmark of social movement activism throughout the ages, in the concrete context of the mid to late 1960s, gave rise to a whole sequence of condemnations of authorities, with portentous consequences for many decades to come.

13. CAGED BIRDS BREAK FREE

Such socio-psychological processes are, indeed, in no way an invention of 1968. They occur throughout history at such extraordinary moments of opportunity and crisis as are presented by revolutions and revolts. Hannah Arendt, for instance, describes a similar atmosphere in revolutionary Paris after 1789: 'An enormous appetite for debate, for instruction, for mutual enlightenment and exchange of opinion, even if all these were to remain without immediate consequence on those in power, developed in the sections and societies; and when, by fiat from above, the people in the sections were made only to listen to party speeches and to obey, they simply ceased to show up.'[86] The events of 1968 were merely the most recent of such collective anticipations of a different way of organizing social life and interpersonal communications across the boundaries of social class and station.

But if the process de Certeau coined as 'the capture of speech' was already astounding when witnessing the shedding of inhibitions by mostly middle-class students, its impact and meaning was amplified in the case of blue-collar workers. The final series of citations is thus reserved for the experience of workers at the FIAT Mirafiori works which, in Italy but not only in Italy, became the crucial symbol for the humiliations of the past and the promise of redemption. Referring to a favourite tactic of Italian workers in the course of 1969, the organization of demonstrations on the factory floor (*cortei*), moving from one production area of the vast site to another, often to the sound of makeshift drums, designed to rouse hesitant workers and to encourage them to join the swelling crowd of protestors, one FIAT line worker recalled: 'The first *cortei* were an incredible thing. You have to imagine the fear of the workers to leave their workstation. After fifteen, twenty years under Valletta, with that boss with that medal who had always terrorized us, we saw those ten, fifteen workers, shouting along the corridors, and we were fearful to leave the line.' Another FIAT worker, Rino Brunetti, remembers that

When you felt the *corteo* come closer, 'boom, boom, boom', even the walls were shaking. But not like they did from the noise of the machines. This must be an earthquake, for heaven's sake. What's happening? Then the *corteo* arrived. And already about one kilometre ahead of the *corteo* some people began to scatter. The little bosses ran away. And in a moment I see Luciano Parlanti, Roby, Antonio il Prete, Zappalà [leading FIAT activists] walk in . . . . When we saw this, I swear to you, we here in the Mechanics department, we began to weep. We began to understand . . . , perhaps our time has come. Perhaps we can redeem ourselves, right now. We have done well to come north. I swear to you, you know how it is when you want to speak and you can't . . . . We embraced each other, and this truly meant everything to us. It could mean 'we have won', 'we have finally pulled ourselves out of the muck', 'we have redeemed our honour, our pride'. You thought about your father, the miserable life he had led, you thought about all those older people who had been here.

Rino Brunetti then recalled how life had been experienced up to now:

Our atrophied brains reminded me of those birds one keeps in cages which, when we go to set them free, to let them escape, no longer know how to fly. I was overcome by sadness. I told myself: 'For God's sake! We do not know how to use our brains any more because something is blocking them.' Then, suddenly, in '69, they began to function again. We broke the cage, and we began to fly again.[87]

To assert that the social movements of 1968 were only a passing, youthful fancy, a momentary diversion, or at best an ill-fated radical upsurge which merely sped up inevitable cultural changes is tantamount to missing the forest for all the trees. For how did one of the Situationist graffiti on the walls of Paris proudly proclaim?

> When the Finger Points At the Moon
> The Idiot Looks At the Finger
>
> (Chinese Proverb)[88]

NOTES

1. For a graphic representation of 1968 as a high point in international social movement activism, see table 1 in Andre Gunder Frank and Marta Fuentes, 'Civil Democracy: Social Movements in Recent World History', in Samir Amin, Giovanni Arrighi, André Gunder Frank, and Immanuel Wallerstein, *Transforming the Revolution: Social Movements and the World System* (New York: Monthly Review Press, 1990), 146.
2. Arthur Marwick, *The Sixties: Cultural Revolution in Britain, France, Italy, and the United States, c.1958–c.1974* (Oxford: Oxford University Press, 1998), 805.
3. Ibid. 14–15.
4. The data—and the quotations—can be found in Werner Hülsberg, *The German Greens: A Social and Political Profile* (London: Verso, 1988), 73.
5. Marwick, *The Sixties*, 802–3.

6. An entertaining account of German university reform plans and realities can be found in Uwe Wesel, *Die verspielte Revolution: 1968 und die Folgen* (Munich: Blessing, 2002), 169–76 and 232–8.

7. Philip Armstrong, Andrew Glyn, and John Harrison, *Capitalism since 1945* (Oxford: Basil Blackwell, 1991), 193.

8. Pierre Dubois, 'New Forms of Industrial Conflict', in Colin Crouch and Alessandro Pizzorno (eds.), *The Resurgence of Class Conflict in Western Europe since 1968*, ii. *Comparative Analyses* (London: Macmillan, 1978), 16.

9. These are the words of the most authoritative and thorough study of actual working hours laboured by workers in the modern world, Pietro Basso, *Modern Times, Ancient Hours: Working Lives in the Twenty-First Century* (London: Verso, 2003), 30.

10. Doug McAdam, *Freedom Summer* (New York: Oxford University Press, 1988), 140–2.

11. See the stimulating and informed case study of the role of communal lifestyles within West Germany's far left, Detlev Siegfried, '"Einstürzende Neubauten": Wohngemeinschaften, Jugendzentren und private Präferenzen kommunistischer "Kader" als Formen jugendlicher Subkultur', *Archiv für Sozialgeschichte*, 44 (2004), 39–66. For similar 'beloved communities' in the expansive sphere of influence of the Italian far left organization Lotta Continua, see Aldo Cazzullo, *I ragazzi che volevano fare la rivoluzione: 1968–1978. Storia di Lotta continua* (Milan: Mondadori, 1998), 163–8, a subsection entitled 'Vivere insieme' (Living Together).

12. Francesca Polletta, *Freedom is an Endless Meeting: Democracy in American Social Movements* (Chicago: University of Chicago Press, 2002), citations on pp. 63 and 64.

13. This text by Bob Moses, published in 2001, is cited in the important recent study by Polletta, *Endless Meeting*, 69–70.

14. McAdam, *Freedom Summer*, 139–40.

15. Polletta, *Endless Meeting*, 128.

16. Both citations are taken from the marvellous volume by Wini Breines, *Community and Organisation in the New Left 1962–1968: The Great Refusal* (New Brunswick, NJ: Rutgers University Press, 1989), 46.

17. Breines, *Community and Organisation*, 36 and 36–7.

18. Eric J. Hobsbawm, *Primitive Rebels: Studies in Archaic Forms of Social Movement in the 19th and 20th Centuries* (Manchester: Manchester University Press, 1959), 61. Accounts of mass meetings, the plethora of subcommittees, action committees, and other forms of student self-organization are legion. Perhaps the most well-documented instance is the Paris student rebellion in May–June 1968. Jean-Claude Perrot, Michelle Perrot, Madeleine Rebérioux, and Jean Maitron (eds.), *La Sorbonne par elle-même* (Paris: Éditions Ouvrières, 1968), special issue of *Le Mouvement Social*, 64 (July–Sept. 1968), was one of the very first in a flood of publications highlighting student self-organization. Note, for instance, on p. 267 of this volume the map of neighbourhood-oriented action committees set up by university students in central Paris. Bernard Brillant, *Les Clercs de 68* (Paris: PUF, 2003), 205–56, provides a detailed look at radical student ferment beyond the Sorbonne proper, including notably the Grandes Écoles. The classic collection of documents hailing from the French student May remains Alain Schnapp and Pierre Vidal-Naquet (eds.), *The French Student Uprising November 1967–June 1968: An Analytical Record* (Boston: Beacon,

1971). Originally published in 1969, its materials, though Paris-centred, do include a sprinkling of reports emanating from the equally activist campuses in other parts of France.

19. Note, for instance, the floor plan of the Old Sorbonne and the corresponding diagram of room locations for the profusion of subcommittees, then unofficially in full control of public life in and near the Sorbonne, reproduced in Perrot *et al.* (eds.), *Sorbonne par elle-même*, 106–7.

20. McAdam, *Freedom Summer*, 25 and 25–6. Note that these figures refer to state allocations per pupil per year!

21. Both citations can be found in Elizabeth Sunderland (ed.), *Letters from Mississippi* (New York: McGraw-Hill, 1965), 93. Mention of the lack of lessons on American history in the fifteen years between 1860 and 1875 refers to the period of the Civil War and Reconstruction in US history.

22. Howard Zinn, *SNCC: The New Abolitionists* (Cambridge, Mass.: South End Press, 2002), 247 and 248.

23. Clayborne Carson, *In Struggle: SNCC and the Black Awakening of the 1960s* (Cambridge, Mass: Harvard University Press, 1995), 120 and 121.

24. Zinn, *SNCC*, 248. For a relatively recent academic article on Freedom Schools, see Daniel Perlstein, 'Teaching Freedom: SNCC and the Creation of the Mississippi Freedom Schools', *History of Education Quarterly*, 30 (1990), 297–324.

25. Sutherland (ed.), *Letters from Mississippi*, 117, ellipses in the original.

26. A stimulating brief survey of such US Free Schools is provided in the excellent comparative study by Michael Schmidtke, *Der Aufbruch der jungen Intelligenz: Die 68er Jahre in der Bundesrepublik und den USA* (Frankfurt: Campus, 2003), 117–20, with the information on the 1971 statistics on p. 119. For a lively presentation of some primary sources, see Mitchell Goodman (ed.), *The Movement toward a New America: The Beginning of a Long Revolution* (Philadelphia: Pilgrim Press, 1970), 266–306.

27. Cited in English by Schmidtke, *Aufbruch*, 229; emphasis added.

28. Ibid. 229–30.

29. Ibid. 225; Kirkpatrick Sale, *SDS* (New York: Random, 1973), 264–9, provides another brief survey of this phenomenon. Again, a stimulating illustrated collection of some relevant primary sources is contained in the section on 'Colleges, Jails and Other Institutions of Higher Education', in Howard (ed.), *New America*, 307–46.

30. Schmidtke, *Aufbruch*, 234.

31. The relevant document, 'Sul piano di studi per il corso di lavoro in sociologia dell'Istituto di Trento', is reprinted in Movimento studentesco (ed.), *Documenti della rivolta universitaria* (Bari: Laterza, 1968), 15–22. For a discussion of the context out of which this first Italian countercurriculum arose, see Ch. 2.

32. The most comprehensive discussion of the Manifesto can be found in Jan Kurz, *Die Universität auf der Piazza: Entstehung und Zerfall der Studentenbewegung in Italien 1966–1968* (Cologne: SH-Verlag, 2001), 109–16. The first published version was printed on 30 June 1967 by the Centro di Informazione in Verona—I thank Marica Tolomelli for providing me with a copy of this rare document. The subsequently revised edn., 'Trento—università negativa', can be consulted in *Lavoro Politico*, 2 (1967), 20–2. I thank Valentina Marchegiani for sending me a copy of yet another version, a typescript by Renato Curcio which differs from both published accounts, in all likelihood a very early draft. It notably includes a list of relevant bibliographic

inspirations, including the Italian translation of Hal Draper's first-hand account of the 1964 Berkeley revolt, referred to in Ch 2.

33. Colin Crouch, *The Student Revolt* (London: Bodley Head, 1970), 59.

34. Mark Derez, Ingrid Depraetere, and Wivina van der Steen, 'Kroniek van het studentenprotest', in Louis Vos, Mark Derez, Ingrid Depraetere, and Wivina van der Steer, *De stoute jaren: Studentenprotest in de jaren zestig* (Tielt: Lannoo, 1988), 114–15, and Paul Goossens, *Leuven '68 of het geloof in de hemel* (Zellik: Roularta, 1993), 82.

35. Schmidtke, *Aufbruch*, 234–40; Gerhard Bauß, *Die Studentenbewegung der sechziger Jahre: Handbuch* (Cologne: Pahl-Rugenstein, 1983), 253–70. The May 1968 attempt to construct a Political University in Frankfurt is the best-documented West German case; see Detlev Claussen and Regine Dermitzel (eds.), *Universität und Widerstand: Versuch einer Politischen Universität in Frankfurt* (Frankfurt: Europäische Verlagsanstalt, 1968).

36. Crouch, *Student Revolt*, 101 (Cambridge), 104 (Essex), and 111 (art colleges). On British art colleges as breeding grounds for innovative practices and nonconformist thought, see Simon Frith and Howard Horne, *Art into Pop* (London: Methuen, 1987), *passim*. For the most famous instance of unrest affecting a British university campus, see the volume edited anonymously by the students and staff of the Hornsey College of Art, *The Hornsey Affair* (Harmondsworth: Penguin, 1969).

37. On the Summer University of Strasbourg, see Pierre Feuerstein, *Printemps de révolte à Strasbourg: Mai–juin 1968* (Strasbourg: Saisons d'Alsace, 1968), 59–62, citation on p. 60. Alain Touraine lists Summer Universities in Grenoble and Montpellier at the very end of his chronology of events in his *Le Mouvement de mai ou le communisme utopique* (Paris: Livre de poche, 1998), 313. Bernard Brillant concentrates solely on summer universities in Strasbourg and Paris; see his discussion of these alternative institutions in his *Clercs de 68*, 420–4. Interestingly, Arno Münster, in his *Paris brennt: Die Mai-Revolution 1968* (Frankfurt: Heinrich Heine Verlag, 1968), devotes an entire chapter to what he termed the *Kritische Universität Sorbonne* on pp. 121–7.

38. Here the best sources are Schnapp and Vidal-Naquet (eds.), *French Student Uprising*, *passim*; Perrot *et al.* (eds.), *Sorbonne par elle-même*, *passim*; but above all the anthology of texts presented by the Centre de Regroupement des Informations Universitaires (ed.), *Quelle université? Quelle société?* (Paris: Seuil, 1968).

39. W. J. Rorabaugh, *Berkeley at War: The 1960s* (New York: Oxford University Press, 1989), 46.

40. Schmidtke's evocative discussion of US Free Universities can be found on pp. 225–34 of his *Aufbruch*.

41. The aforegoing and following discussion is largely based on the remarkable series of documents, comprising protocols of faculty discussions of the Vincennes experiment, individual interviews of both student and faculty protagonists, and many other materials, in Michel Debeauvais (ed.), *L'Université ouverte: Les Dossiers de Vincennes* (Grenoble: Presses Universitaires de Grenoble, 1976). The various 'mission statements' of university departments, referred to in my text above, can be consulted on pp. 77–162 ('Innovations pédagogiques et auto-gestion dans les Départements') of this suggestive volume.

42. Ibid. 237.

43. Cited in Diego Leoni, 'Testimonianza semiseria sul '68 a Trento', in Aldo Agosti, Luisa Passerini, and Nicola Tranfaglia (eds.), *La cultura e i luoghi del '68* (Milan: Franco Angeli, 1991), 183.

44. A listing of the core curriculum for the academic year 1968–9 is reproduced in Vincenzo Calì, 'Università e Ricerca tra movimenti e istituzioni: Il caso trentino,' in Giuliana Gemelli, Girolamo Ramunni, and Vito Gallotta (eds.), *Isole senza arcipelago: Imprenditori scientifici, reti e istituzioni tra Otto e Novecento* (Bari: Palomar, 2003), 171 n. 51.

45. The diagram is reproduced in Renato Curcio and Mauro Rostagno, *Fuori dai denti* (Milan: Gammalibri, 1980), 95.

46. Marco Boato, 'Il movimento studentesco trentino: Origine storica, esperienze di lotta, prospettive politiche', in his *Il '68 è morto: Viva il '68!* (Verona: Bertani, 1979), 338–9.

47. The growing rift between Alberoni and increasingly radical student activists can be gleaned, for instance, in the memoirs of Giorgio Galli, who taught at Trento in the first half of 1967; see Giorgio Galli, *Passato prossimo: Persone e incontri 1949–1999* (Milan: Kaos edizioni, 2000), 136–54.

48. Cited in Leoni, 'Testimonianza', 185.

49. Cited ibid. 184.

50. Cited ibid. 188.

51. Cited in Luisa Passerini, *Autobiography of a Generation: Italy, 1968* (Hanover, NH: Wesleyan University Press, 1996), 127.

52. For Belgian strike or workers' committees, see Rik Hemmerijckx, 'Arbeiterprotest und "1968" in Belgien', in Bernd Gehrke and Gerd-Rainer Horn (eds.), *Die Arbeiter und '1968': Ein europäischer Vergleich* (Hamburg: VSA, forthcoming), and Jaak Brepoels, *Wat zoudt gij zonder 't werkvolk zijn: Anderthalve eeuw arbeidersstrijd in België*, ii. *1967–1980* (Leuven: Kritak, 1981), 51–110.

53. Citations taken from Rainer Zoll, *Partizipation oder Delegation: Gewerkschaftliche Betriebspolitik in Italien und in der Bundesrepublik Deutschland* (Frankfurt: EVA, 1981), 91.

54. See, for instance, Roberto Aglieta, Giuseppe Bianchi, and Pietro Merli Brandini, *I delegati operai: Ricerca su nuove forme di rappresentanza operaia* (Rome: Coines, 1970), 103.

55. Nanni Balestrini, *Vogliamo tutto: Romanzo*, was originally published in 1971 by Feltrinelli. It has most recently been reissued in Oct. 2004 by DeriveApprodi in Rome. It has been translated into many languages but, symptomatically, not into English. 'La ballata della FIAT' can be found on the CD: Alfredo Bandelli, *Fabbrica galera piazza* (Modena: Dischi del Sole, [1974]).

56. For one such factory occupation at Pancaldi in Bologna, see Fabrizio Billi, 'Le lotte operaie e il sindacato a Bologna nel '67–'69', in Carmelo Adagio, Fabrizio Billi, Andrea Rapini, and Simona Urso (eds.), *Tra immaginazione e programmazione: Bologna di fronte al '68. Materiali per una storia del '68 a Bologna* (Milan: Punto rosso, 1998), 75. For the case of two sequential factory occupations at the Parma Salamini plant, see Diego Melegari, 'I lavoratori della Salamini in lotta: Nuove pratiche contestative e organizzazioni tradizionali in un conflitto operaio', in Margherita Becchetti et al., *Parma dentro la rivolta: Tradizione e radicalità nelle lotte sociali e politiche di una città dell'Emilia "rossa". 1968/1969* (Milan: Punto rosso, 2000), 142–3. Both the Bologna and the Parma occupations ended with a working-class defeat.

57. I have adapted the term 'virtuous cycle' from Vittorio Rieser, who coined this term in a related—though somewhat different—context in his presentation at a conference on 'Workers and 1968: A European Comparison', in Hattingen, Germany, 11–13 Feb. 2005, forthcoming in Gehrke and Horn (eds.), *Arbeiter und '1968'.*

58. Miriam Golden, *Labor Divided: Austerity and Working-Class Politics in Contemporary Italy* (Ithaca, NY: Cornell University Press, 1988), 105.

59. Ibid. 110. Another excellent source on the role of *delegati* and the *consigli di fabbrica* is Guido Romagnoli, *Consigli di fabbrica e democrazia sindacale* (Milan: Mazzotta, 1976). Romagnoli takes a slightly more critical attitude with regard to the democratic impulse of factory councils.

60. Xavier Vigna, 'Le mot de la lutte? L'autogestion et les ouvrières de PIL à Cérizay en 1973', in Frank Georgi (ed.), *Autogestion: La Dernière Utopie?* (Paris: Publications de la Sorbonne, 2003), 381–93.

61. Vincent Porhel,'L'Ambiguïté de la référence autogestionnaire: L'Exemple d'un conflit breton (Pédernec, 4 décembre 1973–1 mars 1974)', in Georgi (ed.), *Autogestion*, 395–412.

62. Patrick Pasture, 'Histoire et représentation d'une utopie: l'idée autogestionnaire en Belgique', in Georgi (ed.), *Autogestion*, 143–56.

63. The often crucial role of the Belgian far left in the post-1970 upsurge of working-class mobilization in Belgium is highlighted by Rik Hemmerijckx in his 'Arbeiterprotest'. For a recent case study showcasing the 'virtuous cycle' (Vittorio Rieser) of direct democracy, union involvement, and activist engagement by Italy's powerful far left, see Claudia Finetti, 'Autonomia operaia: L'Alfa Romeo di Arese (1970–1973)', *Novecento*, 1 (July–Dec. 1999), 71–98.

64. Instructive introductions to the experience of councils in the period between 1917 and 1920 are, for what became the Soviet Union, Oskar Anweiler, *The Soviets: The Russian Workers, Peasants and Soldiers Councils, 1905–1921* (New York: Pantheon, 1974); for Germany and Austria, F. L. Carsten, *Revolution in Central Europe, 1918–1919* (London: Maurice Temple Smith, 1972); and, for Italy, Gwyn A. Williams, *Proletarian Order: Antonio Gramsci, Factory Councils and the Origins of Italian Communism, 1911–1921* (London: Pluto, 1975).

65. Robert Lumley, *States of Emergency: Cultures of Revolt in Italy from 1968 to 1978* (London: Verso, 1990), pp. x–xi. Some efforts at coordination of Belgian strike and workers' committees are mentioned in Hemmerijckx, 'Arbeiterprotest', and Brepoels, *Werkvolk 1967–1980*, 86–9.

66. Jordi Borja, *Qué son las Asociaciones de Vecinos?* (Buenos Aires: La Gaya Ciencia, 1976), 69.

67. Sebastian Balfour, *Dictatorship, Workers, and the City: Labour in Greater Barcelona since 1939* (Oxford: Clarendon Press, 1989), 195 and 196.

68. Borja, *Asociaciones de Vecinos*, 52–76, furnishes a survey for the entire Spanish state, from which the concrete figures in the text have been taken.

69. Some additional information on the overall socio-economic and political context behind the rise of the urban protest movements linked with the fostering of associational life are furnished by Jordi Borja, *Movimientos sociales urbanos* (Buenos Aires: SIAP, 1975), 95–122. A local study which also suggests some causes for the Associations' ultimate demise is Joan Camós and Clara C. Parramón, 'The Associational Movement and Popular Mobilisation in L'Hospitalet: From the Anti-Francoist

Struggle to Democracy, 1960–80', in Angel Smith (ed.), *Red Barcelona: Social Protest and Labour Mobilisation in the Twentieth Century* (London: Routledge, 2002), 206–22.

70. John L. Hammond, *Building Popular Power: Workers' and Neighborhood Movements in the Portuguese Revolution* (New York: Monthly Review Press, 1988), 132, 200, and 199.

71. The most detailed study of these commissions exists for the town of Setubal, 'an industrial city some twenty-five miles south of Lisbon, which witnessed the most widespread and coordinated urban struggles and organisations of any city during the Portuguese revolution'; see Charles Downs, *Revolution at the Grassroots: Community Organisation in the Portuguese Revolution* (Albany, NY: State University of New York Press, 1989), citation on p. 13. The most concise overall survey of such urban social movement in Portugal as a whole is Charles Downs, 'Residents' Commissions and Urban Struggle in Revolutionary Portugal', in Lawrence S. Graham and Douglas L. Wheeler (eds.), *In Search of Modern Portugal: The Revolution and its Consequences* (Madison: University of Wisconsin Press, 1983), 151–79.

72. Phil Mailer, *Portugal: The Impossible Revolution?* (London: Solidarity, 1977), 260–2.

73. Mailer, *Portugal*, 285–7, and Hammond, *Popular Power*, 200–3, are the best sources on these overarching, grass-roots, council-like structures.

74. Adrien Dansette, *Mai 1968* (Paris: Plon, 1971), 263.

75. Yannick Guin, *La Commune de Nantes* (Paris: Maspero, 1969), 99.

76. Nancy Gina Bermeo, *The Revolution within the Revolution: Workers' Control in Rural Portugal* (Princeton: Princeton University Press, 1986), 113 and 121.

77. Vigna, 'Ouvrières de PIL', 390.

78. Michel de Certeau, 'The Capture of Speech (May 1968)', in his *The Capture of Speech and Other Political Writings* (Minneapolis: University of Minnesota Press, 1997), 11–12; trans. slightly amended, with the correct full title of the essay rendered from the original French-language text. For similar descriptions emerging from the French context, see also the section entitled 'Liberated Speech' in Jean-Pierre Le Goff, *Mai 68, l'héritage impossible* (Paris: La Découverte, 2002), 69–84.

79. Breines, *Community and Organisation*, 37.

80. Gianni Statera, *Death of a Utopia: The Development and Decline of Student Movements in Europe* (New York: Oxford University Press, 1975), 174.

81. Sara Evans, *Personal Politics: The Roots of Women's Liberation in the Civil Rights Movement and the New Left* (New York: Vintage, 1980), 41.

82. The most detailed reconstruction of the genesis of the Nov. 1964 position paper and its Nov. 1965 sequel, 'A Kind of Memo from Casey Hayden and Mary King to a Number of Other Women in the Peace and Freedom Movement', can be consulted in the memoirs of Mary King, *Freedom Song: A Personal Story of the 1960s Civil Rights Movement* (New York: William Morris, 1987), 437–74; the two documents are reproduced on pp. 567–74 and in Evans, *Personal Politics*, 233–8. Sara Evans's *Personal Politics* remains the most detailed and convincing study of the civil rights origins of American second-wave feminism, although McAdam, *Freedom Summer*, 178–85, makes some additional important points.

83. Casey Hayden, for instance, was then married to Tom Hayden, a key national figure in SDS.

84. Sheila Rowbotham, for instance, in her vivid portrayal of her own conversion to feminist ideals underscores the vital role of American feminists in challenging British

(and European) traditions: 'Unlike the approach usually taken on the left then, in which new relations in the family were to follow a "revolution," [US feminists] were intent on making changes in the here and now. Along with their anti-authoritarianism and belief in participatory democracy, the North American women brought into the British Women's Liberation movement a belief in prefiguring a desired future in the way you organised. They also possessed an openness to new realities and perceptions and a respect for knowledge rooted in experience'; see Sheila Rowbotham, *Promise of a Dream: Remembering the Sixties* (London: Allen Lane, 2000), 222. For the equally crucial American stimulus to French and West German second-wave feminism, see Kristina Schulz, *Der lange Atem der Provokation: Die Frauenbewegung in der Bundesrepublik und in Frankreich 1968–1976* (Frankfurt: Campus, 2002), 45–52.

85. Here, again, some relevant observations in the remarkable autobiography of Sheila Rowbotham may stand for many others in Britain and elsewhere: 'I could conveniently forget that I was in a left group because the International Socialist group was so completely dismissive of Women's Liberation that it did not have a "line" on us. Paradoxically, while the leadership simply felt that we should not exist, individual women IS members or the girlfriends and wives of IS members were the ones who actually played a key role in starting the early Women's Liberation groups in many cities'; see Rowbotham, *Promise of a Dream*, 235–6. For West Germany, the same general picture emerges from the individual biographies contained in Ute Kätzel (ed.), *Die 68erinnen: Porträt einer rebellischen Frauengeneration* (Berlin: Rowohlt, 2002).

86. Hannah Arendt, *On Revolution* (London: Penguin, 1990), 246.

87. All citations taken from Marco Revelli, *Lavorare in FIAT: Da Valletta ad Agnelli a Romiti. Operai sindacati robot* (Milan: Garzanti, 1989), 49, 48, and 50. I thank Andrea Mammone for assisting in the translation of this passage.

88. Daubed on the wall of the Paris Conservatoire de Musique, May 1968; see Tom Nairn and Angelo Quattrocchi, 'Foreword', in *The Beginning of the End: France, May 1968* (London: Verso, 1998), p. x.

Conclusion: A Moment of Crisis and Opportunity

1. A TALE OF TWO EUROPES

So '1968' was a period of roughly ten years (*c.*1966–*c.*1976) in which various material and socio-psychological changes suddenly and forcefully made headline news. After an intellectually vibrant preparatory period (*c.*1956–*c.*1966), a whole series of states experienced a range of momentous events which made it seem possible that a new society could be constructed, a society where individuals and communities could finally be in control of their own destiny. No longer did it seem preordained that traditional economic, political, and cultural elites would continue to set the narrow parameters within which millions of individuals had to run on the treadmill of their alienated lives. The horizon of a different way of organizing social life shone most brightly, I argue, in those parts of Europe where the challenges to the status quo affected a broad cross-section of society, most notably when the spirit of 1968 began to affect dependent wage workers on the factory and office floors of the late industrial First World. For a number of conflicting reasons, this tendency was most pronounced in Mediterranean Europe. To the north of Romance-language Europe, the process of questioning traditional authorities and received wisdoms for the most part affected young people—and in particular youth enrolled on various rungs of the educational ladder. While the relative isolation of radical experiments in university and secondary school environments in what I term the 'northern European' tier of states (including the United States) contributed to a particularly acute sense of 'lived rebellion', in effect the social depth of radical transformations was by and large far more pronounced in southern Europe than elsewhere. Why was this so?

Spain and Portugal experienced the tensions associated with the transition from brutal dictatorial control to parliamentary democracy precisely in these years. In Spain this process was spread out over a period of more than a dozen years; in Portugal change arrived far more abruptly than in neighbouring Spain. It makes sense that the greater turbulence associated with the Portuguese Revolution compared with the Spanish *transición* was closely related to the suddenness with which the Lusitanian dictatorship crumbled after fifty years of seemingly total control. But why, then, did the challenges to the status quo go deeper in Italy than anywhere else? Italy had left behind its dictatorial phase several generations earlier. And what about France? The concentrated period of society-wide revolt of May–June 1968 left Charles De Gaulle teetering on the edge—if only for a few fascinating weeks. Yet France had been a pillar of Western European post-war democracies since the summer of 1944.

Is there, perhaps, an underlying pattern determining the distinctly differing trajectories of 'Mediterranean' compared with 'northern' European states? It is a commonplace of the comparative literature on industrial relations that northern European labour movements (excluding the special case of the United Kingdom) by and large operate on a far less conflictual basis than their comrades to the south. Consensus politics is common in the north; strike propensity is far higher in the south. Also, readers may recall a similar discrepancy with regard to the social composition of the new left. In northern Europe, I argue, the new left remained mostly a student-based and thus a middle-class affair, whereas in southern Europe the new left included students in central positions but also other social strata in significant ways to shape the Mediterranean new left into a multilayered phenomenon clearly distinct from the northern European trajectory of the new left. Why this apparent discrepancy between 'northern' and 'Mediterranean' Europe? If one could confirm such patterns over significant periods of time, then perhaps one could move one step closer to furnishing answers to explain such obvious differences between sets of countries. If it were possible to isolate underlying reasons for the posited phenomenon of the 'two Europes', perhaps one could then develop a more fine-tuned analysis which could begin to make sense of why, for instance, Italian patterns differed from French ones or why the Swedish model differed from the Dutch. In other words, not only differences between 'north' and 'south' but individual country differences could perhaps be satisfactorily explained.

Most countries indeed follow given transnational patterns for an undetermined number of decades without deviating excessively from the chosen model's predetermined norm. This is, of course, not exactly surprising. For one thing, any pre-existing political culture shapes the contours of national politics and social movement practices, a process which partially explains the presence of long-term continuities. But at various, seemingly 'random', moments some countries suddenly jettison traditional arrangements. Over time, certainly in the decades that I have intensely studied in my own historical work, that is, the 1930s to the 1970s, some countries which tended to fall squarely into one particular framework for a lengthy period suddenly 'switched sides', so to speak, and developed rather different long-term patterns. When looked at more closely, the important moment in the determination of a given country's political paradigm turns out to be the *moment of transition* when that country experiences a major change in orientation. It appears, thus, that the study of such crisis moments, when one set of social regulations makes way for a completely different set of rules, may be the route to pursue in order to uncover possible mechanisms undergirding the adoption of a new model.[1] If there are any structural explanations for the adoption of a given way of organizing social and political life, then a close look at these moments of transition may very well discover them. What explains the urge to 'jump ship'?

One example for such a trajectory is Germany. Until the 1930s, German patterns of political behaviour and political culture tended to be rather conflictual and were far closer in spirit and substance to what I term the Mediterranean model than to the northern European model, as I describe it above. By contrast, in all decades of the post-Second World War period Germany appears to have wholly abandoned most vestiges of its conflictual past and fits much better into the northern European way of 'doing business'. Here of course an easy answer would be to point to the caesura of fascism, which is often said to have engendered such a major paradigm shift. Maybe so. But some other countries, too, have experienced similar major paradigm shifts *without* having undergone the experience of fascism. Sweden, for instance, until the 1920s had a rather conflictual political culture and class struggle traditions dominating labour–management relations. But, then, in the course of the 1930s a major sea-change began to occur which has made Sweden a model of consensus politics with low incidents of labour–management conflicts in the form of serious strikes. Here, of course, the usual answer is to point to innovative moves on the part of Swedish social democracy, whose Keynesian welfare state ideas and practices (notions of a *people's home*) managed to become hegemonic without open struggle and thus turn the tide for Sweden to become a haven for labour peace coupled with high quality welfare state policies.

The case of the Netherlands may be instructive as well. Today for the most part known and admired (by some) for its progressive, cosmopolitan outlook on life, the Netherlands throughout the inter-war period was neither a haven of labour peace nor a model for consensus politics. Quite the contrary! But in the post-Second World War era, the Netherlands, for practical purposes, joined the 'camp' of countries that followed what I call the northern European route. Why? Here opinions differ, but once again social democracy was at the heart of the changes, as it was Dutch social democracy which pioneered (earlier than any other continental social democracies) the move away from the politics and the language of *class* to a politics and language emphasizing an amorphous and cross-class *people* at the centre of their concerns. Unlike Sweden, the Netherlands of course experienced a major bout of fascist occupation policies. But so did many other countries in Europe, most of which did *not* switch 'camps' in the post-war European constellation of political forces. So why did Holland do it, and others not? Were Dutch and Swedish social democrats better 'communicators'? Perhaps so, but this does not exactly provide a 'scientific' answer to the question as to why some countries choose distinctly different trajectories compared to others. And, of course, in West Germany the post-war recovery took place under Christian Democratic—not social democratic!—hegemony.

In short, I find few structural factors which may cast light on the processes behind 'strategic switches'. Ultimately, I suggest, the answer to such queries can only be found in conjunctural factors. I am by no means suggesting that there are no overarching patterns and that each individual country's history is always unique. Alas, after close to twenty years of transnational studies involving continental Western European states between the 1930s and the 1970s, I have become increasingly sceptical that structural explanations for underlying trends—desirable as such solutions may very well appear to be—can be found. To be sure, to return to the subject matter of this study, there are plenty of transnational parallels between Western European (and even North American) states included in this study. For all the obvious differences between 'northern' and 'Mediterranean' European states, there are plenty of commonalities that serve to unify the two decades from *c.*1956 to *c.*1976 as a distinct period in its own right. The rise of a new and, eventually, a far left, the ubiquity of student revolts, the preparatory groundwork laid by countercultural rebels; these and many other features constitute ever so many elements which were remarkably similar across the entirety of countries covered. But, indeed, one cannot and should not ignore the fact that other fundamental traits which I highlight in this study were particular to one set of countries—and largely absent from the other—even if they 'merely' form a subset of factors which do not alter the overall coherence of 1956–76 as a period in its own right including both Europes, north and south.

I cannot offer a satisfactory overall explanation why things heated up more decisively south-west of a line drawn from Antwerp to Porto Marghera, rather than at points to the north-east of this imaginary boundary, which is in any case porous, fluid, and uneven. What I do have on offer, however, is a narrative—and an analysis—of what happened and how it happened. In very many crucial ways, the twenty-year period at the centre of my study, despite the apparent division into 'north' and 'south', forms a distinct period with certain crucial overarching parallels between a great variety of states. And it cannot be stressed enough—indeed it is a central argument of this book—that the individual actors and collective social movements which engendered '1968' opened up possibilities that fundamentally questioned the social, political, economic, and cultural status quo. Yes, Arthur Marwick and others are absolutely correct that, ultimately, the most tangible achievement of 1968 was the socio-cultural paradigm shift which qualitatively loosened the moral and material strictures determining interpersonal relationships up to the mid-1960s in virtually every single one of the afflicted states. Yes, Western Europe and North America by and large became far less inhospitable places to live and work in as a result of these by no means insignificant socio-psychological transformations engendered by the process of 1968. But what is the larger meaning of the various processes described in the aforegoing pages, which potentially (and, for some time, *actually*) pointed in a far more radical direction of social change? What of the legacy of the experiences of what I lumped together into the catch-all category of 'participatory democracy' in the preceding chapter? Did such societal experiments vanish without leaving a trace?

2. THE LEGACY OF 1968

On the one hand, of course, it is undeniable that most of the concrete gains described in preceding pages were eventually rescinded. Wage increases on the scale experienced in the hot phase of 1968 were never to be repeated and, worse yet, for some time now the pendulum has swung the opposite way. Contrary to widespread sociological mythmaking, the average duration of the work week has begun to lengthen rather than shorten again, and the starting point of this regression has been traced back precisely to the second half of the 1970s, that is, exactly to the moment when the two-decade long process of '1968' had come to an end.[2] Workers' control over workplace conditions, including line speeds, a phenomenon which let Italian workers (but not only Italian workers) playfully predict the imminent arrival of paradise on earth,[3] began to disintegrate and ultimately vanish—even in Italy—in the course of the post-1976 decades.[4] Student input into the running of university affairs, despite some well-intentioned reforms here or there, has made few meaningful qualitative steps forward, although the climate of interaction may well have become less overtly paternalistic. Virtually none of even these cosmetic changes affecting higher education, however, have trickled down to the level of secondary schools, whose repressive regulations closely resemble authoritarian factory or office regimes, presumably the more effectively to socialize the next generations of waged and salaried workers.

What about the legacy of the all-important socio-psychological changes brought about by the 'capture of speech' described in earlier pages? Clearly, mental transformations cannot be as easily and quickly reversed as percentage wage increases or reductions in line speed. Nonetheless, here too, there is incontrovertible evidence that many of the gains of 1968 vanished in the course of the last quarter of the twentieth century. With the creeping reversal of the material improvements brought about by 1968, over time, inevitably, mental attitudes began to readjust as well. The previously caged birds, briefly soaring to untold heights, eventually were recaptured again, placed back into a slightly more spacious and less discomforting cage perhaps, but nonetheless put under lock and key.

On the other hand, of course, on the level of mentalities the reverseal was rarely complete. Important holdovers and pockets of resistance survived in often unexpected locations. The generation of the 1960s student new left soon matured to become the next generation of the managerial and academic elite. It is this generational turnover, so to speak, which, to a significant extent, made possible the easing of interpersonal relationships—within families, within companies, within faculties—cogently highlighted by Marwick and other proponents of the cultural revolution of the 1960s. And within academia, to take but one such locus of change, as (post)graduate students began to take up posts as entry-level lecturers, for some time into the 1980s and beyond the quality of education and the topic of modules taught began to reflect the interests these entry-level lecturers or assistant professors had evinced a few years earlier as students. In a certain sense, the 'critical' or 'free' universities, those fragile pockets of alternative education schemes described in Chapter 5, made way for partially reshaped curricula in universities at large.

Within the world of industrial and office labour, too, the sea-change in mentalities experienced in the course of 1968 did not vanish overnight. Little serious work appears to have been carried out on tracing continuities between radical labour activists responsible for the injection of the spirit of 1968 into the world of labour and the survival of combative tendencies within certain industries, certain production sites, or certain unions throughout the 1980s, into the 1990s, and even, on occasion, all the way up to the present day.[5] But circumstantial evidence permits a tentative hypothesis to be made that, here too, lines of continuities can be easily detected between the conscious construction of militant networks of social movement activists in certain locations—often first seeing the light of day precisely in the early to mid-1970s—and activist traditions characterizing certain industries or factories or office complexes in subsequent decades and even today.[6] Along similar lines, though on a larger societal terrain, it surely is no coincidence that the country with the most well-developed social movement practice in Western Europe today is the very same country which was in the forefront of 1968: Italy!

But here the limits of such a legacy must be highlighted as well. The refusal to comply with the forces of top-down globalization may be most widespread in Italy, but the viciousness of the Italian state's response is also second to none. The European Social Forum in Florence in 2002 may have been the high point of recent social movement culture in Europe as a whole, but the brutal police-state repression in Genoa in 2001 was also without parallel up to now. Italy may have a dense network of *centri sociali*, autonomous youth centres that keep the flames of rebellion alive; and the Italian spontaneous response to the Allied invasion of Iraq in March 2003 may have been the most impressive such show of force in the Western world, as this author was able to witness first-hand in Rome the day after Baghdad was chosen for Anglo-American target practice, when even the Central State Archive shut its doors in protest against this naked display of imperial might, with widespread strikes followed in the evening by huge demonstrations winding their way through Italy's capital city. Yet at the same time the Italian head of state (at least at the time of writing) remains Silvio Berlusconi, the media magnate cum politician par excellence.[7] It may remain a source of pleasure and satisfaction for a foreigner to be able to step off a train or plane anywhere in Italy and to be able to pick up at any kiosk across the land not just one but two quality daily newspapers published in the orbit of the radical left, *Il Manifesto* and *Liberazione*, but such surviving strongholds of the spirit of 1968 pale in comparison to the creeping *Gleichschaltung* of Italian television.

The survival of militant traditions of social movement culture in Italy, then, has ultimately had preciously little impact on high politics in Italy today. Similar observations can be made for the actual impact of radical academics of the generation of 1968 on the academic environment as such. First of all, such conquests, wherever they occurred in the 1970s and early 1980s, were only partial conquests. Increasingly so, even if administrative interlocutors remained effectively neutral, which was certainly not everywhere the case, radical academics, if they managed to stay 'true' to their initial calling, found themselves confronted by an increasingly conservative student body. Over time, many academics, advancing along the career ladder, began, for various reasons, to moderate their views. This process was enhanced when the next wave of academics began to obtain teaching posts. Young academics, who had been (post)graduates in the 1960s or 1970s, had all the reason in the world to be affected by the spirit of 1968. Those who became (post)graduates in the late 1970s, the 1980s, or later, had little exposure to the social movement culture which had socialized their 'elder' colleagues.[8]

Last but not least, the survival of activist traditions on the shopfloor level became increasingly tenuous as well. The same societal pressures which affected the outlook of society at large, the same pressures towards conformity, the return to passivity, and the search for solace in private and/or family life took its toll amongst office and shopfloor militants as well. Here, too, the work of tracing the deradicalization of personal/political itineraries has barely begun. But there are indications that the process of moderation and the concomitant marginalization of surviving pockets of militancy took multiple forms. One such route towards accommodation that calls out for further investigation was the pathway of integration of leading activists into the overall institutional hierarchies of trade unions or old left political parties.[9] Participant observers familiar with a given national political culture can easily rattle off a long list of names of leading grass-roots militants in '1968' who subsequently became integrated into trade union official-dom, parliamentary factions of the old left, or who found comfortable niches in the world of the media. And, once again, it would be one-sided to focus solely on the negative consequences of such career moves. After all, it is this process which accounts to some extent, no doubt, for the actual experience of relaxation of certain psycho-social tensions and the greater ease of interpersonal communication often vaunted as the primary product of 1968.

More crucially, not all activists of the new and far left followed identical itineraries. And, indeed, there is reason to believe that many grass-roots activists of the erstwhile new and far left in actual fact have held on to key components of their personal/political belief systems, acquired during the high point of their activist phase, for significant periods of the rest of their lives. The evidence is sketchy, and I cannot lay claim to comprehensive study of this phenomenon, but it seems likely that for every Joschka Fischer or Lionel Jospin there are dozens, hundreds, and thousands of former far left activists who, to be sure, usually no longer agitate within the ranks of the organized far left, but who frequently engage in social movement activism nonetheless and who, in a vague but determined sort of way, remain ready to engage in battles for a different way of organizing social life, should the opportunity occur. The wave of so-called 'new' social movements in the last quarter of the twentieth century would be impossible to imagine without the active engagement of former new and far left activists, who could very often be seen in the new social movements' frontline ranks.[10]

Still, for all the hidden potential that may be at large, the overall balance sheet is rather bleak—at least for advocates of system-transforming radical changes. Was

1968, then, a flash in the pan devoid of larger consequences? Is it not true that, in the end, to paraphrase a passage I wrote some time ago, the rules of the game may have changed in the aftermath of 1968, but the game remained the same?[11] Was 1968 a momentary diversion on the road towards the modernization of class society? Was 1968 a brief error message in the transition phase from modernity to postmodernity?

3. THE GREAT REHEARSAL?

In the late 1970s, at the high point of the radicalization of 1968 in Great Britain, when, with customary British delay, the high tide of the waves engendered by 1968 elsewhere finally caused a ripple along Albion's shores, one of the most interesting debates within late twentieth-century Marxism occurred, a vibrant and committed polemic, which has been all but forgotten today. Initiated by the pugnacious English historian E. P. Thompson, it initially took the form of a more than 200 page polemical essay by Thompson against the French structuralist Marxist Louis Althusser, 'The Poverty of Theory or an Orrery of Errors'. First published in 1978, Thompson also railed against what he had come to regard as the British import agency of French structuralist Marxism, the *New Left Review*, a magazine which Thompson had helped to found but which had soon been 'taken over' by a younger generation of British new left writers. Two years later, one of the key shapers of the reconfiguration of the editorial board of *New Left Review* in 1961–2, Perry Anderson, perhaps the most important Marxist theoretician to emerge from Britain in the second half of the twentieth century, published a cogent, measured but nonetheless straightforward response to Thompson, Anderson's book-length *Arguments within English Marxism*.[12]

Coming at the tail end of the resurgence of activist interest in Marxist theory and associated strategy debates, the brilliant exchange of opinion elicited preciously few rejoinders and virtually no substantive further elaborations by later commentators. It did not help matters that, in 1980, the year of Perry Anderson's thoughtful attempt at synthesis between what he regarded as the two extremes exemplified by Thompson and, respectively, Althusser, the latter embarked on his final journey into the world of mental illness from which he never returned, while the former began to devote most of his energies to the campaign for nuclear disarmament, after the NATO 'double track' decision, spearheaded by West Germany's social democratic chancellor, Helmut Schmidt, had cleared the way for the latest generation of nuclear missiles to cloud the future of the planet. What was the point of this triangular succession of reflections on the Marxist theory of history? And why mention it in the context of my discussion of the meaning of 1968?

Suffice it to say that Althusser, Thompson, and Anderson, each in their own way, dissected the age-old problem of the interaction between—and the relative relevance of—human agency and the constraints imposed by objective and material circumstances. In the eyes of E. P. Thompson, Althusser subscribed to a view of societal change which gave minimal role to individual human beings and human agency as such. Anderson in turn partially defended Althusser from some of the more outlandish claims by Thompson but, more importantly, Anderson then went on to criticize some of what Anderson regarded as Thompson's voluntarist exaggerations. Just as Althusser may have been off the mark when stressing the tight embrace of humanity by the material forces of production and exchange, Thompson's invocation of human agency and free will was felt to be on occasion losing sight of the fact that not everything is possible at all points in time. Where is the link to the problematic of 1968?

It has become a standard misinterpretation of Marxism—by both wilful detractors and simplistic adherents alike—to suggest that Marxism mandates a determinist vision of history. In this partial view, Marxism is equated with an approach to history which supposedly decrees that history is a lawful progression from one stage of socio-economic development to the next, in lockstep with the growth of productive forces. After slavery, feudalism; after feudalism, capitalism; after capitalism, socialism; and then the cycle would magically end. This is obviously not the time and place to engage with such overarching theories of societal development. May it suffice to point to another central element of Marxist theory, which was mentioned above: the role of human agency. It will, of course, never be very difficult to find within most major Marxists' writings exaggerations or distortions which, on various occasions, stress one or the other element in this conceptual pair: human agency and material constraints, base and superstructure, or determinism and free will. But, on balance, most of the writings of those authors most likely to be regarded as authorities in this field, certainly Marx and Engels themselves, place emphasis on both elements necessary to achieve what they viewed as societal progress. In that sense the debate entered into by Althusser, Thompson, and Anderson a quarter of a century ago constituted merely a recapitulation—but also an updating—of a century-old debate. It would be a most interesting task to reconstruct the degree to which the particular distortions clung to by Althusser on the determinist end and Thompson on the voluntarist side—as well as the place of Perry Anderson himself—may have been inadvertent reflections of the impasse of 1968, which, by the end of the 1970s, was most definitely beginning to make itself felt.

For our purposes, however, the recollection of this debate is meant, above all else, to draw attention to the conjunctural topicality of this high-calibre and high-powered, if ultimately unresolved and, since then, strangely neglected theoretical debate. The events of 1968 had put a sudden end to earlier establishment notions of an 'end of ideologies'.[13] The possibility (and not only the necessity) to change society had suddenly been placed at centre stage for an entire generation of activists. The failure of 1968 to change the world placed a question mark over this project once again. Were the missed opportunities merely due to inadequate preparation by individuals and organizations? Was insufficient human agency at fault? Is it proper to speak of 'missed opportunities' at all? Or were the objective constraints and limits imposed by the structures and the strictures of actually existing late capitalism indeed too strong to overcome? What were the lessons of 1968? In the late 1970s, such questions were still considered relevant, relevant enough to produce the aforementioned sequence of exchanges by leading Marxist historians and theorists of that era. In subsequent decades, once again, the clock was turned back to the cold war climate of the 1950s and 1960s, when all thought of radical social transformations had been deemed safely left behind. Notions and debates with regard to 'The End of Ideology' were updated and reinforced as invocations of 'The End of History' and not just ideology.[14] Is there, then, finally, no future for the ideas, practices, and ideologies which came to the fore—for the last time, perhaps?—in 1968?

Social revolutions—or, for that matter, peaceful transformations of social systems as well—are never guaranteed to succeed. This much may stand uncontested. As the brilliant aphorisms by one of Europe's leading historians of the twentieth century, Jürgen Kuczynski, written shortly after the collapse of 'actually existing' communist regimes in 1989, remind us, even the presumed standard succession of social systems, slavery–feudalism–capitalism, widely accepted as near-universal on European soil, may not have been as inevitable as often regarded in historical hindsight. Kuczynski's comments on the rise, decline, and subsequent return of 'new' social systems in the most recent two thousand years of European history warrant far more detailed considerations than his stimulating essay thus far appears to have provoked. Frustratingly, Kuczynski does not elaborate the various reasons why certain systemic transformations may have undergone a series of false starts before eventually succeeding.[15] It stands to reason, however, that even in the best of all possible circumstances, human agency was necessary to bring about the desired (or the dreaded) social changes—and sometimes it was lacking. So much more so when objective circumstances are less than optimal for the successful conclusion of a revolutionary project. And, as social revolutions go, the passage from actually existing capitalism to a simultaneously more humane and rational future society, be it called democratic socialism, libertarian communism, or whatever, is generally recognized as a particularly tough nut to crack. For, unlike earlier transitions in the Western world, where new forms of production and corresponding human interactions prospered and grew long before the victory (whether peaceful or violent) of the new social system was assured, where, to use 'old-fashioned' terminology to exemplify the argument, bourgeois financiers could become wealthy and influential personalities even in the age when aristocracy still ruled the roost, the hoped-for transition from (late) capitalism to libertarian, self-management-oriented socialism can count on no such independent pockets of anticipatory economic and political power preceding the desirable systemic switch. Quite to the contrary! Even when, in the middle of a revolutionary phase, certain early experiments with grass-roots 'popular power' or 'participatory democracy' emerge, they rarely coexist for very long with traditional forms of capitalist domination—be it in the realm of politics, culture, or the economy. Witness the fate of the short-lived and more often than not embryonic experiments sketched in Chapter 5!

On the other hand, it is equally self-evident that, on irregular occasions and at unpredictable moments, dissatisfaction with the (capitalist) status quo and a desire to move to a less destructive and irrational mode of production make themselves felt in no uncertain terms. It used to be that such moments of societal opportunity and crisis tended to erupt at historical conjunctures when societies were experiencing a generalized state of collapse, most frequently brought about by the ravages of war, foreign occupation, or a combination of the two. The first brief flicker of an anti-capitalist societal revolt, the 1871 Paris Commune, certainly fits this bill exceedingly well. Not only had French troops been defeated in battle, but Prussian troops stood on the outskirts of Paris when the Commune rose. The wave of revolutions of 1917–20 powerfully reconfirmed this nexus of wars engendering revolts. Last but not least, the nadir of popular acceptance of capitalism as a semi-tolerable social system in 'the West' was reached at the moment of liberation from Nazi occupation in 1944–5, another crisis moment engendered by occupation and war.[16]

But, then, there have been other moments in recent history when capitalism was challenged from within—without a military conflagration precipitating such a grave societal crisis. The radical turn by important sections of the European (old) left between May 1934 and May 1935 was one such moment, although here one can argue that the threat of fascism was the virtual equivalent of an actual war.[17] Yet how to explain the explosion of 1968? Neither internal mortal enemies (fascism) nor external threats (war) may account for the ferocity and vitality of this transnational revolt. To be sure, one need not underscore that self-management-oriented libertarian socialism was nowhere victorious. But, then, as we now know, nor was it in 1944–5, in 1934–5, in 1917–20, or in 1871. Can one therefore conclude that the dream of a non-alienating society is bound to remain . . . a dream?

This remains to be seen. What is certain, however, is that 1968 was only the latest instalment in a long series of unpredicted and unpredictable popular insurrections which have, time and time again and in a great variety of historical contexts, attacked privilege, autocracy, and hierarchy in the name of justice, equality, and self-determination. Giovanni Arrighi, Terence K. Hopkins, and Immanuel Wallerstein have pointed out that there was at least one other wave of radical revolts which was equally unpredicted, and one might add that the 1848 wave of continent-wide revolt was likewise unrelated to any foreign or domestic catastrophes: 'There have only been two *world* revolutions. One took place in 1848. The second took place in 1968. Both were historical failures. Both transformed the world.'[18] Even if one does not fully share the optimism exuded by the world systems theorists, one cannot help but recognize that, indeed, no one had predicted either one of these transnational revolts. Therefore, the sentiment that it can never happen again is somewhat bemusing to anyone with a historical memory.

NOTES

1. The study of transnational crisis moments or, better, moments of crisis and opportunity has been at the heart of my various projects as a historian. For an anthology of different approaches to the phenomenon of transnational choice points, with an emphasis on social movement practices at such crucial conjunctures, see Gerd-Rainer Horn and Padraic Kenney (eds.), *Transnational Moments of Change: Europe 1945, 1968, 1989* (Lanham, Md.: Rowman & Littlefield, 2004).

2. Pietro Basso, *Modern Times, Ancient Hours: Working Lives in the Twenty-First Century* (London: Verso, 2003), 57.

3. For an artistic rendering of this sentiment, see the film by Elio Petri, *La classe operaia va in paradiso* (Italy, 1971).

4. Note here, symptomatically, the decline in just about every index of labour movement activism for Italian labour after the high point of the early 1970s reported in table 16.3, 'Industrial Disputes 1952–95', in Ida Regalia and Marino Regini, 'Italy: The Dual Character of Industrial Relations', in Anthony Ferner and Richard Hyman (eds.), *Changing Industrial Relations in Europe* (Oxford: Blackwell, 1998), 485. Here are, for instance, the numbers of strike days per year per 100,000 employed Italian workers: 1952–8: 44,527; 1959–67: 93,167; 1968–73: 148,506; 1974–9: 110,545; 1980–4: 59,481; 1985–9: 17,856; 1990–4: 11,420.

5. Labour activism in the 1970s fed on many fertile sources, most of them emerging from within the working class itself. But one such stimulus derived from the decision by thousands upon thousands of far left activist students to give up their university career and to enter factories in order to agitate for revolutionary change where it seemed to them to matter the most. Most such moves occurred in the first half of the 1970s. Symptomatically for the unhealthy state of the historical literature today, studies of this transnational phenomenon are sorely lacking. For an evocative description of this process in Belgium, however, see Imelda Haesendonck, *De Fabriek* (Antwerp: EPO, 1999). The relevant literature is most developed for the French case; see Marnix Dressen, *De l'amphi à l'établi: Les Étudiants maoïstes à l'usine (1967–1989)* (Paris: Belin, 1999); Virginie Linhart, *Volontaires pour l'usine: Vies d'établis 1967–1977* (Paris: Seuil, 1994); Marnix Dressen, *Les Établis, la chaîne et le syndicat: Évolution des pratiques, mythes et croyances d'une population d'établis maoïstes 1968–1982. Monographie d'une usine Lyonnaise* (Paris: L'Harmattan, 2000); and, the prototype of them all, Robert Linhart, *L'Établi* (Paris: Minuit, 1978).

6. For the case of (West) Germany, these hypotheses have been validated in several conversations with Heiner Dribbusch, researcher for the West German Trade Union Federation's Wirtschafts- und Sozialwissenschaftliches Institut, 12 Feb. 2005 and 1 Feb. 2006.

7. For a stimulating essay on Berlusconi, note Paul Ginsborg, *Silvio Berlusconi: Television, Power and Patrimony* (London: Verso, 2004).

8. I have traced the generational lines of (dis)continuities for the field of American labour studies in Gerd-Rainer Horn, 'Labor History in Nordamerika: Eine Zustandsbeschreibung', *Internationale wissenschaftliche Kommunikation zur Geschichte der deutschen Arbeiterbewegung*, 35 (Sept. 1999), 362–73, esp. pp. 365–6.

9. For some suggestive comments in this regard, see Rik Hemmerijckx, 'Arbeiterprotest und "1968" in Belgien', in Bernd Gehrke and Gerd-Rainer Horn (eds.), *Die Arbeiter und '1968': Ein europäischer Vergleich* (Hamburg: VSA, forthcoming).

10. Note the relevant pages on the mid- to long-range trajectory of Freedom Summer activists in Doug McAdam, *Freedom Summer* (New York: Oxford University Press, 1988), 199–232. For all the various prevarications included in the editorial comments, the case studies by Heinz Bude, *Das Altern einer Generation: Die Jahrgänge 1938–1948* (Frankfurt: Suhrkamp, 1995), suggest similar lines of continuities for West Germany to those noted by McAdam for the activists involved in Mississippi Freedom Summer. The continuities of life choices between 1968 and later decades for erstwhile activists in West Germany's student left emerge even more clearly in Ute Kätzel, *Die 68erinnen: Porträt einer rebellischen Frauengeneration* (Berlin: Rowohlt, 2002). For France, note, amongst others, the relevant observations in Elisabeth Salvaresi, *Mai en heritage* (Paris: Syros, 1988), and, more recently, Jean Birnbaum, *Leur jeunesse et la nôtre: L'Espérance révolutionnaire au fil des générations* (Paris: Stock, 2005).

11. See Gerd-Rainer Horn, 'The Changing Nature of the European Working Class: The Rise and Fall of the "New Working Class" (France, Italy, Spain, Czechoslovakia)', in Carole Fink, Philipp Gassert, and Detlef Junker (eds.), *1968: The World Transformed* (Cambridge: Cambridge University Press, 1998), 371.

12. For the debate, see E. P. Thompson, 'The Poverty of Theory or An Orrery of Errors', in E. P. Thompson, *The Poverty of Theory and Other Essays* (New York: Monthly Review Press, 1978), 1–210, and Perry Anderson, *Arguments within English Marxism* (London: New Left Books, 1980).

13. Daniel Bell, *The End of Ideologies: On the Exhaustion of Political Ideas in the Fifties* (Glencoe, Ill.: Free Press, 1960).

14. Francis Fukuyama, *The End of History and the Last Man* (Harmondsworth: Penguin, 1992).

15. Jürgen Kuczynski, *Asche für Phönix: Aufstieg, Untergang und Wiederkehr neuer Gesellschaftsordnungen* (Cologne: PapyRossa, 1992). But see also Georg Fülberth, *Sieben Anstrengungen den vorläufigen Endsieg des Kapitalismus zu begreifen* (Hamburg: Konkret, 1991), esp. his fifth chapter, 'Gegengesellschaften', pp. 91–145.

16. I hope to return to this little-understood and much-obscured 'moment of liberation' in a future monograph.

17. See Gerd-Rainer Horn, *European Socialists Respond to Fascism: Ideology, Activism and Contingency in the 1930s* (New York: Oxford University Press, 1996), and Gilles Vergnon, *Les Gauches européennes après la victoire nazie: Entre planisme et unité d'action, 1933–1934* (Paris: L'Harmattan, 1997), for this little-known moment of opportunity and crisis, which has been largely forgotten, soon eclipsed by the more heroic but also far more moderate period of popular fronts—and the corresponding and successive waves of celebratory literature on popular fronts.

18. Giovanni Arrighi, Terence K. Hopkins, and Immanuel Wallerstein, *Antisystemic Movements* (London: Verso, 1989), 97; emphasis in the original.

Bibliographic Essay

Few monographs cover '1968' from a transnational perspective. Those books covering 'just' one particular theme covered in this study, even if in a variety of countries, will be listed under the respective subheadings. The modern classic on 1968 is Arthur Marwick, *The Sixties: Cultural Revolution in Britain, France, Italy and the United States, c.1958–c.1974* (Oxford: Oxford University Press, 1998). Despite his emphasis on the 'cultural revolution' as the key legacy of 1968, the author amasses a wealth of evidence on a wide range of topics. Another flagship volume focusing on the transnational dimension of 1968 is Peppino Ortoleva, *I movimenti del '68 in Europa e in America* (Rome: Riuniti, 1998). A further important Italian publication written from a transnational perspective is Marcello Flores and Alberto De Bernardi, *Il Sessantotto* (Bologna: Il Mulino, 2003). Both publications focus on the calendar year of 1968 and therefore, understandably, on the phenomenon of youth and student revolt. Two edited volumes likewise focus on the international context: Ingrid Gilcher-Holtey (ed.), *1968: Vom Ereignis zum Gegenstand der Geschichtswissenschaft* (Göttingen: Vandenhoeck & Ruprecht, 1998), and Carole Fink, Philipp Gassert, and Detlef Junker (eds.), *1968: The World Transformed* (Cambridge: Cambridge University Press, 1998). At least one other work, though mostly geared towards French events, should be mentioned in this introduction. Kristin Ross, *May '68 and its Afterlives* (Chicago: University of Chicago Press, 2002), is the first serious academic study which attempts to interpret the various waves of interpretations of '1968'. Her pioneering effort for the French context will hopefully inspire others to do the same for other countries. Last but not least, two books by the well-known Pakistani-born activist at the heart of the British '1968', Tariq Ali, provide additional insights. His *1968 and After: Inside the Revolution* (London: Blond & Briggs, 1978) is a partisan survey of the post-1968 decade from the perspective of the far left. But note also his intelligently illustrated running commentary on the keynote events of the calendar year of 1968, co-edited with Susan Watkins, *1968: Marching in the Streets* (New York: Free Press, 1998).

NONCONFORMITY AND YOUTH REVOLT

The two most insightful works on the history of the key artistic influence on Situationism, *COBRA*, are Jean-Clarence Lambert, *COBRA* (London: Sotheby, 1983), and Willemijn Stokvis, *Cobra: 3 Dimensions* (London: Lund Humphries, 1999). On Situationism itself, the choices are wider. Stimulating overviews with an eye on the political dimension of the Situationist critique are Roberto Ohrt, *Phantom Avantgarde: Eine Geschichte der Situationistischen Internationale und der modernen Kunst* (Hamburg: Nautilus, 1990), which covers the period up to the early 1960s, and Laurent Chollet, *L'Insurrection Situationniste* (Paris: Dagorno, 2000), covering a wider spectrum up to the present day; both volumes are superbly illustrated. The most stimulating English-language overview remains Sadie Plant, *The Most Radical Gesture: The Situationist International in a Postmodern Age* (London: Routledge, 1992). There are plenty of anthologies of Situationist texts; the two most interesting English-language collections are Ken Knabb (ed.),

Situationist International Anthology (Berkeley, Calif.: Bureau of Public Secrets, 1981), and Dark Star (ed.), *Beneath the Paving Stones: Situationists and the Beach: May 1968* (Edinburgh: AK Press, 2001). No study of Situationist theory and practice would be complete without a close look at two classic monographs: Guy Debord, *The Society of the Spectacle* (New York: Zone Books, 1995), and Raoul Vaneigem, *The Revolution of Everyday Life* (London: Rebel Press, 2003). Two monographs on Situationism in May 1968 in Paris are René Viénet, *Enragés and Situationists in the Occupation Movement, France, May '68* (London: Rebel Press, 1992), and Pascal Dumontier, *Les Situationnistes et Mai 68: Théorie et pratique de la révolution (1966–1972)* (Paris: Ivrea, 1995); though indispensable, both monographs emerge from within the Situationist tradition and should be read with some degree of caution.

On the Beat poets and the San Francisco Renaissance, see, above all, Steven Watson, *The Birth of the Beat Generation: Visionaries, Rebels, and Hipsters, 1944–1960* (New York: Pantheon, 1995), and Dennis McNally, *Desolate Angel: Jack Kerouac, the Beat Generation, and America* (New York: McGraw-Hill, 1979). On the North American counterculture as such, note the stimulating comments in Theodore Roszak, *The Making of a Counter Culture: Reflections on the Technocratic Society and its Youthful Opposition* (London: Faber & Faber, 1971). On literature and the spirit of '1968' see, for particularly outstanding examples of analyses of particular national literary cultures, Morris Dickstein, *Gates of Eden: American Culture in the Sixties* (Cambridge, Mass.: Harvard University Press, 1997); Klaus Briegleb, *1968: Literatur in der antiautoritären Bewegung* (Frankfurt: Suhrkamp, 1993); and Giuseppe Muraca, *Utopisti ed eretici nella letteratura italiana contemporanea* (Soveria Mannelli: Rubbettino, 2000). For a wonderful microstudy of the literary 'underground' in the Swiss capital city of Bern, see Fredi Lerch, *Begerts letzte Lektion: Ein subkultureller Aufbruch* (Zurich: Rotpunkt, 1996), and Fredi Lerch, *Muellers Weg ins Paradies: Nonkonformismus im Bern der sechziger Jahre* (Zurich: Rotpunkt, 2001). For the contributions to '1968' in the realm of theatre plays and productions, see, amongst others, John Tytell, *The Living Theatre: Art, Exile and Outrage* (London: Methuen Drama, 1995), on the prototype of radical theatre troupes; for Europe's best-known radical playwright and actor, Dario Fo, see Tony Mitchell, *Dario Fo: The People's Court Jester* (London: Methuen Drama, 1999), and Tom Behan, *Dario Fo: Revolutionary Theatre* (London: Pluto, 2000).

On the working-class youth rebellions of the mid to late 1950s, note, for France, the recently reissued 1962 monograph by Émile Copfermann, *La Génération des blousons noirs: Problèmes de la jeunesse française* (Paris: La Découverte, 2003), and, for Germany, Thomas Grotum, *Die Halbstarken: Zur Geschichte einer Jugendkultur der 50er Jahre* (Frankfurt: Campus, 1994), as well as Uta Poiger, *Jazz, Rock and Rebels: Cold War Politics and American Culture in a Divided Germany* (Berkeley, Calif.: University of California Press, 2000), the latter admirably covering both sexes and both Germanies. Many of the studies by the Birmingham Centre for Contemporary Cultural Studies touch on the Teddy boy phenomenon in Britain, though no monograph on this topic appears to have been published by one of the Centre's creative associates. On the Italian variant, the *teppisti*, and their involvement in political protest movements of a peculiar kind, note above all the relevant sections in Dario Lanzardo, *La rivolta di Piazza Statuto* (Milan: Feltrinelli, 1979), and the articles by Paola Ghione and Giovanni De Luna in Paola Ghione and Marco Grispigni (eds.), *Giovani prima della rivolta* (Rome: Manifestolibri, 1998), the latter volume an excellent collection of writings on various aspects of the Italian youth revolts throughout the 1960s.

Incredibly enough, no satisfactory study of the socio-political dimension of British rock music has been published to date. For the possibilities opened up by a multidisciplinary approach to a key phenomenon of the 1960s, see the stimulating recent monograph by Diego Giachetti on the (sub)cultural prehistory of the Italian youth revolt, including notably the impact of new musical styles, *Anni sessanta comincia la danza: Giovani, capelloni, studenti ed estremisti negli anni della contestazione* (Pisa: BFS, 2002). Likewise covering far more than 'just' music, the article contribution by the Swiss researcher Jakob Tanner, ' "The Times They are A-Changin": Zur subkulturellen Dynamik der 68er Bewegungen', in Gilcher-Holtey (ed.), *1968*, showcases the possibilities of a creative interdisciplinary route towards a comprehension of the meaning of '1968'. For the British context, thus far the most suggestive volumes focus on the British underground in general. Note, above all, the monograph by Jonathon Green, *All Dressed up: The Sixties and the Counterculture* (London: Pimlico, 1998), and the collection of interviews edited by the same author, *Days in the Life: Voices from the English Underground 1961–71* (London: Pimlico, 1998). An insightful contemporary record of great value remains the vivid essay by Jeff Nuttall, *Bomb Culture* (London: Paladin, 1970). As any glance at Giachetti's volume listed above will tell, young Italians in the mid to late 1960s, though listening to the same tunes as their generational cohort elsewhere in Europe and North America, were marching to a different drummer. The remarkable mixture of subcultural hippy rebellion and political revolt can be best gauged in the extensive reprint of the short-lived Milanese journal *Mondo Beat*, Gianni De Martino and Marco Grispigni (eds.), *I Capelloni: Mondo Beat, 1966–1967. Storia, immagini, documenti* (Rome: Castelvecchi, 1997).

The unique blend of provocative Dutch nonconforming practices, which made Amsterdam into a pilgrimage site for many youthful rebels in Europe and North America for a long period even and especially after the Provo movement had literally buried itself, has found a number of intelligent chroniclers. The most comprehensive survey of the Provos is now Niek Pas, *Imaazje! De verbeelding van Provo 1965–1967* (Amsterdam: Wereldbibliotheek, 2003). The first book-length attempt to place the Provo movement in perspective was Yves Frémion, *Provo, la tornade blanche* (Brussels: Cahiers JEB, 1982). But note also the observations by a key actor at the centre of the Provo revolt, Roel van Duijn, *De geschiedenis van de provotarische beweging 1965–1967* (Amsterdam: Meulenhoff, 1985). The superior book-length study of the various waves of Dutch urban social movements spawned by the provocative methods of the Amsterdam Provos, including Provo itself, remains Virginie Mamadouh, *De stad in eigen hand: Provo's kabouters en krakers als stedelijke sociale beweging* (Amsterdam: Sua, 1992).

STUDENTS

The literature on students in the years under consideration is endless. The following suggestions are meant to highlight certain texts which were of particular use in the construction of case studies. In two final paragraphs, additional volumes covering the student movement in other countries will be listed to open up further avenues for investigation and critique. Four volumes should, however, be mentioned up front, for they attempt to cover the topic from a comparative perspective. First of all, a standard reference work partially consisting of interviews of student activists in a variety of states is Ronald Fraser (ed.), *1968: A Student Generation in Revolt* (New York: Pantheon, 1988). Gianni Statera, *Death of a Utopia: The Development and Decline of Student Movements in Europe*

(New York: Oxford University Press, 1975), is an early product of the fertile Italian academic and activist tradition. Two more focused monographs are Ingo Juchler, *Die Studentenbewegung in den Vereinigten Staaten und der Bundesrepublik Deutschland der sechziger Jahre: Eine Untersuchung hinsichtlich ihrer Beeinflußung durch Befreiungsbewegungen und -theorien aus der Dritten Welt* (Berlin: Duncker & Humblot, 1996), and Michael Kimmel, *Die Studentenbewegungen der 60er Jahre: BRD, Frankreich, USA: Ein Vergleich* (Vienna: Wiener Universitätsverlag, 1998).

For SNCC, the classic books remain the 1964 volume by Howard Zinn, *SNCC* (Cambridge, Mass.: South End Press, 2002), and the 1981 monograph by Clayborne Carson, *In Struggle: SNCC and the Black Awakening of the 1960s* (Cambridge, Mass.: Harvard University Press, 1995), although the relevant chapters in Taylor Branch, *Parting the Waters: Martin Luther King and the Civil Rights Movement 1954–1963* (London: Macmillan, 1990), add further depth and colour. Mississippi Freedom Summer 1964 is best analysed in Doug McAdam, *Freedom Summer* (New York: Oxford University Press, 1988), but anyone interested in the phenomenon of Freedom Summer and its impact on the northern white volunteers should include the 1965 collection of letters collected by Elizabeth Sutherland Martínez (ed.), reissued as *Letters from Mississippi: Personal Reports from Civil Rights Volunteers of the 1965 Freedom Summer* (Brookline, Mass.: Zephyr Press, 2002). A remarkable autobiography of an early leader of SNCC, who played a major role in subsequent black nationalist revolts, is the recently reissued 1972 volume by James Forman, *The Making of Black Revolutionaries* (Seattle, Wash.: University of Washington Press, 1997).

On the Berkeley Free Speech Movement, the classic study remains the on-the-spot account by Hal Draper, *Berkeley: The New Student Revolt* (New York: Grove Press, 1965). The most comprehensive and detailed history is Max Heirich, *The Spiral of Conflict: Berkeley 1964* (New York: Columbia University Press, 1971). A recent memoir by the then-leader of the campus Young Democrats, who later on became a prominent early feminist campaigner, is Jo Freeman, *At Berkeley in the Sixties: The Education of an Activist, 1961–1965* (Bloomington: Indiana University Press, 2004). Note, also the voluminous anthology recently published by Robert Cohen and Reginal E. Zelnik (eds.), *The Free Speech Movement: Reflections on Berkeley in the 1960s* (Berkeley Calif.: University of California Press, 2002). The US student movement, of course, had barely begun by the time the Berkeley rebels won their victories. In lieu of an endless list of titles, three case studies of American university towns in the 1960s may suffice to indicate the breadth of materials. W. J. Rorabaugh, *Berkeley at War: The 1960s* (New York: Oxford University Press, 1989), a study focusing on processes and conflicts in the second half of the decade; the brilliant monograph on the radical decade in Austin, Texas, Douglas C. Rossinow, *The Politics of Authenticity: Liberalism, Christianity, and the New Left in America* (New York: Columbia University Press, 1998); and, last but not least, the documentary film on the 1960s in Madison, Wisconsin, by Glenn Silber and Barry Alexander Brown, *The War at Home* (USA, 1979). The classic study of the all-important US radical student organization, Students for a Democratic Society (SDS), remains Kirkpatrick Sale, *SDS* (New York: Random, 1973).

Historiography on many topics of Belgian history suffers from the restricted market for its products. Many book-length studies, which would easily find publishers in other states, remain solely accessible as unpublished dissertations with often heavily restricted access. For the Belgian student movement, however, the situation appears to be even worse. There are very few published or unpublished studies, despite the importance of this phenomenon. On the peculiarities of the Belgian student revolt, which began in Leuven, the best place to start is Christian Laporte, *L'Affaire de Louvain:1960–1968* (Paris: De Boeck Université, 1999). For an overview with a helpful chronology, including major dates and conflicts outside the Belgian state, note Louis Vos, Mark Derez, Ingrid Depraetere, and Wivina van der Steen, *De stoute jaren: studentenprotest in de jaren zestig* (Tielt: Lannoo, 1988). The indispensable inside story of the Leuven protest is Paul Goossens, *Leuven '68 of het geloof in de hemel* (Zellik: Roularta, 1993). Two other protagonists coming of age in the Leuven student milieu wrote a more general volume on the Belgian 1968 from a hard-line Maoist perspective, Ludo Martens and Kris Merckx, *Dat was 1968* (Berchem: EPO, 1978). For the events of 1968 at the Free University of Brussels and the capital city as a whole, note the stimulating volume by Serge Govaert, *Mai '68: C'était au temps où Bruxelles contestait* (Brussels: Politique et Histoire, 1990). The history of the Belgian student revolt remains to be written, but for some preliminary remarks on the Belgian '1968' as a whole, see Gerd-Rainer Horn, 'The Belgian Contribution to Global 1968', *Revue Belge d'Histoire contemporaine/Belgisch Tijdschrift voor Nieuwste Geschiedenis*, 35 (2005), 597–635.

The rich publishing tradition in Italy has resulted in plentiful materials for the historical reconstruction of the most persistently radical student movement of these years in all of Europe. It is nonetheless curious that the most convincing overall study of the Italian student movement was recently written by a non-Italian: Jan Kurz, *Die Universität auf der Piazza: Entstehung und Zerfall der Studentenbewegung in Italien 1966–1968* (Cologne: SH-Verlag, 2001). Two informative contemporaneous surveys are Rossana Rossanda, *L'anno degli studenti* (Bari: De Donato, 1968), and Carlo Oliva and Aloisio Rendi, *Il movimento studentesco e le sue lotte* (Milan: Feltrinelli, 1969). Indispensable document collections remain the anonymously edited volumes, Movimento studentesco (ed.), *Documenti della rivolta universitaria* (Bari: Laterza, 1968), and *Università: l'ipotesi rivoluzionaria: documenti delle lotte studentesche: Trento, Torino, Napoli, Pisa, Milano, Roma* (Padua: Marsilio, 1968). The local idiosyncrasies of the Italian student revolt, of course, are partially responsible for the lack of overall syntheses. For important studies of local milieux, see various contributions in Aldo Agosti, Luisa Passerini, and Nicola Tranfaglia (eds.), *La cultura e i luoghi del '68* (Milan: Franco Angeli, 1991), and Pier Paolo Poggio (ed.), *Il Sessantotto: L'evento e la storia* (Brescia: Fondazione 'Luigi Micheletti', 1988–9). An excellent 'atmospheric' account of the Italian student revolt remains the translated text by Luisa Passerini, *Autobiography of a Generation: Italy, 1968* (Hanover, NH: Wesleyan University Press, 1996).

For the student movement in Spain, a key opposition stratum in the anti-Franco underground, see José Álvarez Cobelas, *Envenenados de cuerpo y alma: La oposición universitaria al franquismo en Madrid (1939–1970)* (Madrid: Siglo XXI, 2004), and Josep M. Colomer i Calsina, *Els estudiants de Barcelona sota el franquisme* (Barcelona: Curial, 1978). The student movement in Great Britain was, in comparison to most continental experiences, a rather subdued affair; the essential monograph remains Colin Crouch, *The Student Revolt* (London: Bodley Head, 1970). For two specific incidents of student activism in the British Isles, note Harry Kidd, *The Trouble at L.S.E.* (London: Oxford University Press, 1969), and the collectively and anonymously edited volume on the most famous university occupation in England, *The Hornsey Affair* (Harmondsworth: Penguin, 1969). For the French case, the ideal way to approach this topic is by means of intensive study of the vast collections of documentary materials emanating from the events of May. One of the best of these anthologies has been translated into English: Alain Schnapp and Pierre Vidal-Naquet (eds.), *The French Student Uprising November 1967–June 1968: An Analytical Record* (Boston: Beacon, 1971). Other indispensable sources are the recently reissued 1968 volume by the Mouvement du 22 mars, *Ce n'est qu'un début, continuons le combat* (Paris: La Découverte, 2004); Jean-Claude Perrot, Michelle Perrot, Madeleine Rebérioux, and Jean Maitron (eds.), *La Sorbonne par elle-même* (Paris: Éditions Ouvrières, 1968); Centre de Regroupement des Informations Universitaires (ed.), *Quelle université? Quelle société?* (Paris: Seuil, 1968); and Michel Debeauvais (ed.), *L'Université ouverte: Les Dossiers de Vincennes* (Grenoble: Presses Universitaires de Grenoble, 1976).

For some additional countries not directly covered in my text, here are some further suggestions for introductory reading. The standard work on the Dutch student revolt is Hugo Kijne, *Geschiedenis van de Nederlandse studentenbeweging 1963–1973* (Amsterdam: Sua, 1978). For West Germany the equivalent publication is Gerhard Bauß, *Die Studentenbewegung der sechziger Jahre in der Bundesrepublik und Westberlin* (Cologne: Pahl-Rugenstein, 1983). But note now, for the all-important Socialist German Student Association (SDS), Siegward Lönnendonker, Bernd Rabehl, and Jochen Staadt, *Die antiautoritäre Revolte: Der Sozialistische Deutsche Studentenbund nach der Trennung von der SPD*, i. *1960–1967* (Wiesbaden: Westdeutscher Verlag, 2002). A rare gem not only from a literary perspective is the autobiographical account of the student movement in Mexico by Paco Ignacio Taibo, *'68* (New York: Seven Stories Press, 2003).

WORKERS

There are preciously few comparative or transnational studies of this phenomenon, and none of them are single-author monographs. Classic reference works remain the two volumes by Colin Crouch and Alessandro Pizzorno (eds.), *The Resurgence of Class Conflict in Western Europe since 1968* (London: Macmillan, 1978). But note also the texts by Lucio Magri, Rossana Rossanda, Fernando Claudin, and Anibal Quijano, *Movimiento obrero y acción política* (Mexico City: Era, 1975). With regard to the historiography of specific countries, Spain is the logical starting point, as it was in Spain that the working-class underground first developed the characteristic features of 'participatory democracy', given organizational expression in the workers' commissions. Here the superior study is David Ruiz (ed.), *Historia de Comisiones Obreras (1958–1988)* (Madrid: Siglo XXI, 1994). An early comprehensive text was authored by an Italian trade unionist, Marco Calamai, *La lotta di classe sotto il franchismo: Le Commissioni Operaie* (Bari: De Donato, 1971). The most useful English-language study remains Sebastian Balfour, *Dictatorship, Workers and the City: Labour in Greater Barcelona since 1939* (Oxford: Clarendon Press, 1989).

The French May 1968 events may, for starters, be best accessed via the recently reissued 1970 first-hand account by Daniel Singer, *Prelude to Revolution: France in May, 1968* (Cambridge, Mass.: South End Press, 2002). Another observant on-the-spot report is Patrick Seale and Maureen McConville, *French Revolution 1968* (Harmondsworth: Penguin, 1968). The superior French-language contemporaneous account remains Adrien Dansette, *Mai 1968* (Paris: Plon, 1971). A well-known team of investigative journalists and historians produced an important two-volume study, Hervé Hamon and Patrick Rotman, *Génération* (Paris: Seuil, 1987/8). A recent comprehensive academic study of the May events is Jean-Pierre Le Goff, *Mai 68, l'héritage impossible* (Paris: La Découverte, 2002). An excellent German-language overview and analysis remains Ingrid Gilcher-Holtey,

'Die Phantasie an die Macht': Mai 68 in Frankreich (Frankfurt: Suhrkamp, 1995). An empirically rich recent publication is Michael Seidman, *The Imaginary Revolution: Parisian Students and Workers in 1968* (New York: Berghahn, 2004). Two edited collections should be mentioned in this context. The two-volume set of articles edited by René Mouriaux, Annick Percheron, Antoine Prost, and Danielle Tartakowsky (eds.), *1968: Explorations du mai français* (Paris: L'Harmattan, 1992), will remain a quintessential reference work for some time; likewise Geneviève Dreyfus-Armand, Robert Frank, Marie-Françoise Lévy, and Michelle Zancarini-Fournel (eds.), *Les années 68: Le Temps de la contestation* (Brussels: Complexe, 2000), is a treasure trove for detailed investigations into particular aspects of that era in France. All titles listed in this paragraph cover the working-class dimension as part of a larger study of May 1968 as a whole.

There are surprisingly few book-length monographs on just the working-class dimension of '1968' in France. A good place to start is the semi-autobiographical account of the very first factory occupation in all of France, François Le Madec, *L'aubepine de mai: Chronique d'une usine occupée. Sud-Aviation Nantes 1968* (Nantes: Centre de Documentation du Mouvement et du Travail, 1988). Likewise the account of the LIP self-management experience by the spokesperson for the LIP workforce should be a must, Charles Piaget, *LIP* (Paris: Stock, 1973). Yannick Guin, *La Commune de Nantes* (Paris: Maspero, 1969) is another classic text that should not be overlooked. The standard expert sociological investigation of the French strike movements of 1968 is Pierre Dubois et al., *Grèves revendicatives ou grèves politiques? Acteurs, pratiques, sens du mouvement de mai* (Paris: Anthropos, 1971). Perhaps the best way to access French workers' contributions to the spirit of 1968 is via three excellent studies of the most flexible and open-minded union confederation in the French state, the CFDT. Here note, in chronological order of publication, Hervé Hamon and Patrick Rotman, *La Deuxième Gauche: Histoire intellectuelle et politique de la CFDT* (Paris: Ramsay, 1982); Pierre Cours-Saliès, *La CFDT: Un passé porteur d'avenir. Pratiques syndicales et débats stratégiques depuis 1946* (Montreuil: La Brèche, 1988); and, last but not least, Frank Georgi, *L'Invention de la CFDT, 1957–1970: Syndicalisme, catholicisme et politique dans la France de l'expansion* (Paris: L'Atelier, 1995). But note also the various contributions to Frank Georgi (ed.), *Autogestion: La Dernière Utopie?* (Paris: Publications de la Sorbonne, 2003).

There exist important English-language studies which pay careful attention to the working-class dimension of the all-important Italian example of social unrest. Robert Lumley, *States of Emergency: Cultures of Revolt from 1968 to 1978* (London: Verso, 1990), remains one of the very best monographs on the entire spectrum of Italian social struggles in these years. Gino Bedani, *Politics and Ideology in the Italian Workers' Movement: Union Development and the Changing Role of the Catholic and Communist Subcultures in Postwar Italy* (Oxford: Berg, 1995), covers more than the post-1968 period, but is excellent on the latter years as well. Last but not least, Miriam Golden, *Labor Divided: Austerity and Working-Class Politics in Contemporary Italy* (Ithaca, NY: Cornell University Press, 1988), despite its misleading title, reconstructs the cultural revolution within the metalworking unions in exemplary fashion. The classic sociological survey of this period of working-class activism in Italy is Alessandro Pizzorno, Emilio Reyneri, Marino Regini, and Ida Regalia, *Lotte operaie e sindacato: Il ciclo 1968–1972 in Italia* (Bologna: Il Mulino, 1978). Stimulating contemporaneous accounts of key aspects of Italian labour relations in the *biennio rosso* are Giuseppe Bianchi et al., *Grande impresa e conflitto industriale: Ricerca su quattro casi di conflitto sindacale. Fiat–Pirelli–Marzotto–Italcantieri* (Rome: Coines, 1970); Roberto

Aglieta, Giuseppe Bianchi, and Pietro Merli Brandini (eds.), *I delegati operai: Ricerca su nuove forme di rappresentanza operaia* (Rome: Coines, 1970); and Giuseppe Bianchi, Franco Frigo, Pietro Merli Brandini, and Alberto Merolla (eds.), *I CUB: Comitati unitari di base. Ricerca su nuove esperienze di lotta operaia: Pirelli–Borletti–Fatme* (Roma: Coines, 1971). Two important case studies of central hot spots of labour unrest are Diego Giachetti and Marco Scavino, *La FIAT in mani agli operai: L'autunno caldo del 1969* (Pisa: BFS, 1997), and the second volume of Cesco Chinello, *Sindacato, PCI, movimenti negli anni sessanta: Porto Marghera, Venezia, 1955–1970* (Milan: Franco Angeli, 1996). But note also Attilio Mangano, *1969: L'anno della rivolta. Uno studio sull'immaginario sociale* (Milan: M&B, 1999), a reflective and insightful essay on the central year of working-class revolt. The book-length interview of a key CGIL trade union leader, Bruno Trentin, *Autunno caldo: Il secondo biennio rosso 1968–1969* (Rome: Riuniti, 1999), and the masterful assessment by Aris Accornero, *La parabola del sindacato: Ascesa e declina di una cultura* (Bologna: Il Mulino, 1992), are likewise mandatory reading for anyone wishing to understand the peculiarities of Italian labour relations in these years.

Portuguese worker unrest is inseparable from the events of the Portuguese Revolution in 1974–5, a symbiosis which is reflected in the secondary literature. The superior study remains Gérard Filoche, *Printemps portugais* (Paris: Actéon, 1984). The two most convincing English-language studies are Phil Mailer, *Portugal: The Impossible Revolution?* (London: Solidarity, 1977), and John Hammond, *Building Popular Power: Workers' and Neighborhood Movements in the Portuguese Revolution* (New York: Monthly Review Press, 1988). A marvellous study of the rural collectivization efforts in central and southern Portugal is Nancy Bermeo, *The Revolution within the Revolution. Workers' Control in Rural Portugal* (Princeton: Princeton University Press, 1986). The closely related case of community organization on the grass-roots level is well-described for the case of Setubal in Charles Downs, *Revolution at the Grassroots: Community Organisation in the Portuguese Revolution* (Albany, NY: State University of New York Press, 1989).

Mention should be made of at least one classic title on the key North American dimension of worker revolts in '1968'. First published in 1975, Dan Georgakas and Marvin Surkin, *Detroit: I do Mind Dying: A Study in Urban Revolution* (Cambridge, Mass.: South End Press, 1998), should be required reading for anyone who wishes to engage with America in the 1960s. Heather Ann Thompson, *Whose Detroit? Politics, Labor, and Race in a Modern American City* (Ithaca, NY: Cornell University Press, 2004) brings this story up to date. The year of greatest unrest for labour relations in Great Britain was 1972; a solid introduction is provided by Ralph Darlington and Dave Lyddon, *Glorious Summer: Class Struggle in Britain, 1972* (London: Bookmarks, 2001). On Belgium, an empirically rich study is Jaak Brepoels, *Wat zoudt gij zonder 't werkvolk zijn: anderthalve eeuw arbeidersstrijd in België*, ii. *1967–1980* (Leuven: Kritak, 1981).

THE LEFT

There are countless volumes on the political itinerary of the old left. The superior overall approach to the material is Donald Sassoon, *One Hundred Years of Socialism: The West European Left in the Twentieth Century* (New York: New Press, 1996), a book which, despite its title, focuses primarily on the post-Second World War decades; note also the relevant chapters in Geoff Eley, *Forging Democracy: The History of the Left in Europe, 1850–2000* (New York: Oxford University Press, 2002). For social democracy in particular, the most convincing study of the key policy mutation in this era is now Gerassimos Moschonas, *In the Name of Social Democracy: The Great Transformation, 1945 to the Present* (London: Verso, 2002). Rather than listing individual volumes for all of the countries investigated in my text, the British Labour Party's experience may stand for that of many of its sister parties on the continent. The classic autopsy of British Labour is Ralph Miliband, *Parliamentary Socialism: A Study in the Politics of Labour* (London: Merlin, 1973), a wonderful read despite its dry title, first published in 1961. The trade union dimension of Labour Party identity is ably dissected by Leo Panitch, *Social Democracy and Industrial Militancy: The Labour Party, the Trade Unions and Incomes Policy, 1945–1974* (Cambridge: Cambridge University Press, 1976). The cultural inertia of the Labour Party is well depicted by Lawrence Black, *The Political Culture of the Left in Affluent Britain, 1951–1964: Old Labour, New Britain* (Basingstoke: Macmillan, 2003). Finally, Leo Panitch and Colin Leys, *The End of Parliamentary Socialism: From New Left to New Labour* (London: Verso, 2001), cover the final years in which the Labour Party still had meaningful ties to what remains of the British left.

The most comprehensive study of post-war Western European communism remains Keith Middlemas, *Power and the Party: Changing Faces of Communism in Western Europe* (London: André Deutsch, 1980). Due to the centrality of Italian communism in the post-war era, the rich variety of contributions to various aspects of the evolution of the Italian Communist Party (PCI) may serve to introduce readers to the phenomenon of European communism west of the Iron Curtain. Here the two key English-language texts are Grant Amyot, *The Italian Communist Left: The Crisis of the Popular Front Strategy* (London: Croom Helm, 1981), and Stephen Gundle, *Between Hollywood and Moscow: The Italian Communists and the Challenge of Mass Culture, 1943–1991* (Durham, NC: Duke University Press, 2000). The two volumes by Nello Ajello, *Intellettuali e PCI 1944/1958* (Bari: Laterza, 1979) and *Il lungo addio: intellettuali e PCI dal 1958 al 1991* (Bari: Laterza, 1997), ably describe the rise and fall of Italian communism as an alternative to the status quo. An early analysis and critique of PCI strategy is Livio Maitan, *Teoria e politica comunista del dopoguerra* (Milan: Schwarz, 1959), written from an orthodox Trotskyist perspective. Sergio Dalmasso, *Il caso 'Manifesto' e il PCI degli anni '60* (Turin: Cric, 1989), draws the outlines of the experience (and expulsion) of the radical reformist current within the PCI, which gave rise to a major newspaper publication surviving as a daily until the present day, *Il Manifesto*. The last major instance of widespread popular belief in the PCI as a liberatory force, its prominent engagement in municipal and regional politics in central and northern Italy in the 1970s, is ably covered by the Swiss authors Max Jäggi, Roger Müller, and Sil Schmid, *Red Bologna* (London: Writers and Readers Publishing Cooperative, 1977).

Still by far the most comprehensive and insightful presentation of the new left from a comparative and transnational perspective remains Massimo Teodori, *Storia delle nuove sinistre in Europa, 1956–1976* (Bologna: Il Mulino, 1976). The first published English-language attempt to cover the new left from a supranational perspective was George Katsiaficas, *The Imagination of the New Left: A Global Analysis of 1968* (Boston: South End Press, 1987). A stimulating early unpublished work which, despite its title, is for all practical purposes a comparative study is Anthonie Paul Marius Lucardie, 'The New Left in the Netherlands (1960–1977): A Critical Study of New Political Ideas and Groups on the Left in the Netherlands with Comparative References to France and Germany', Ph.D. dissertation, Queen's University, Kingston, Ontario, 1980. A recent book-length essay is

Ingrid Gilcher-Holtey, *Die 68er Bewegung: Deutschland, Westeuropa, USA* (Munich: Beck, 2001). An excellent comparison of the West German and American new left is Michael Schmidtke, *Der Aufbruch der jungen Intelligenz: Die 68er Jahre in der Bundesrepublik und in den USA* (Frankfurt: Campus, 2003). All other studies are primarily or exclusively investigations of particular national contexts.

Here are some highly recommended texts for the new left in the United States: Paul Jacobs and Saul Landau (eds.), *The New Radicals: A Report with Documents* (New York: Random, 1966); Maurice Isserman, *If I had a Hammer: The Death of the Old Left and the Birth of the New* (New York: Basic Books, 1987); Wini Breines, *Community and Organisation in the New Left: 1962–1968* (New Brunswick, NJ: Rutgers University Press, 1989); James Miller, *Democracy is in the Streets: From Port Huron to the Siege of Chicago* (Cambridge, Mass.: Harvard University Press, 1994); and Kevin Mattson, *Intellectuals in Action: The Origins of the New Left and Radical Liberalism, 1945–1970* (University Park, Penn.: Pennsylvania State University Press, 2002). For Britain see, above all, Michael Kenny, *The First New Left: British Intellectuals After Stalin* (London: Lawrence & Wishart, 1995); Lin Chun, *The British New Left* (Edinburgh: Edinburgh University Press, 1993); David Widgery (ed.), *The Left in Britain 1956–68* (Harmondsworth: Penguin, 1976), which provides materials on many other aspects of British politics in addition to the new left; and Robin Archer *et al.* (eds.), *Out of Apathy: Voices of the New Left 30 Years on* (London: Verso, 1989). On Mediterranean new left politics, see, for Italy, Silvano Miniati, *PSIUP: 1964–1972. Vita e morte di un partito* (Roma: Edimez, 1981), Attilio Mangano, *L'altra linea: Fortini, Bosio, Montaldi, Panzieri e la Nuova Sinistra* (Catanzaro: Pulano, 1992), Franco Ottaviano, *La rivoluzione nel labirinto. Sinistra e sinistrismo dal 1956 agli anni ottanta*, i. *Critica al revisionismo e nuova sinistra (1956–1976)* (Soveria Mannelli: Rubbettino, 1993), and Paolo Ferrero (ed.), *Raniero Panzieri: Un uomo di frontiera* (Milan: Punto rosso, 2005). For the Spanish new left, operating in the anti-Franco underground, see above all Julio Antonio García Alcalá, *Historia del Felipe (FLP, FOC y ESBA): De Julio Cerón a la Liga Comunista Revolucionaria* (Madrid: Centro de Estudios Políticos y Constitucionales, 2001), and Eduardo G. Rico, *Queríamos la revolución: Crónicas del Felipe* (Barcelona: Flor de Viento, 1998). Charles Hauss, *The New Left in France: The Unified Socialist Party* (Westport, Conn.: Greenwood, 1978), covers the outlines of the evolution of the lively forces gravitating around the PSU. The most informative volume on the plethora of French new left currents and countercurrents remains Jean-François Kesler, *De la gauche dissidente au nouveau Parti socialiste: Les minorités qui ont rénové le P.S.* (Toulouse: Privat, 1990). One of the many monographs on aspects of the French intellectual new left tradition is Philippe Gottraux, *'Socialisme ou Barbarie': Un engagement politique et intellectuel dans la France de l'après-guerre* (Lausanne: Payot, 1997).

The far left tradition is thus far almost exclusively treated in monographs concentrating on one national context only or, more likely, on one specific party-political formation. Here are some of the more informative studies of this type for the all-important Italian case: Daniele Protti, *Cronache di 'nuova sinistra': Dal PSIUP a Democrazia Proletaria* (Milan: Gammalibri, 1979); Diego Giachetti, *Oltre il sessantotto: Prima, durante e dopo il movimento* (Pisa: BFS, 1998); Franco Ottaviano, *La rivoluzione nel labirinto: Sinistra e sinistrismo dal 1956 agli anni ottanta*, ii. *I partiti del sinistrismo (1969–1976)* (Soveria Mannelli: Rubbettino, 1993); three important monographs on one particularly prominent organization: Luigi Bobbio, *Storia di Lotta Continua* (Milan: Feltrinelli, 1988), Aldo Cazzullo, *I ragazzi che volevano fare la rivoluzione: 1968–1978. Storia di Lotta continua*

(Milan: Mondadori, 1998), and Corrado Sannucci, *Lotta Continua: Gli uomini dopo* (Arezzo: Limina, 1999); and finally two English-language volumes, Steve Wright, *Storming Heaven: Class Composition and Struggle in Italian Autonomist Marxism* (London: Pluto, 2002), and the evocative collection of letters to the editor of *Lotta Continua*, the newspaper which survived the demise of the political organization with the same name for several years, Margaret Kunzle (ed.), *Dear Comrades: Readers' Letters to Lotta Continua* (London: Pluto, 1980). For Spain, the two key works are José Manuel Roca (ed.), *El proyecto radical: Auge y decline de la izquierda revolucionaria en España (1964–1992)* (Madrid: Los Libros de la Catarata, 1994), and Consuelo Laíz, *La lucha final: Los partidos de la izquierda radical durante la transicón española* (Madrid: Los Libros de la Catarata, 1995).

The French cauldron of far left politics may be accessed via the two studies by A. Belden Fields, *Trotskyism and Maoism: Theory and Practice in France and the United States* (New York: Praeger, 1988), and Gérard Filoche, *Ces années-là, quand Lionel...* (Paris: Ramsay, 2001). The best of the various books published on specific West German groups is now Michael Steffen, *Geschichten vom Trüffelschwein: Politik und Organisation des Kommunistischen Bundes 1971 bis 1991* (Berlin: Assoziation A, 2003). An early account of the negative experiences within the—in this case West German—far left was the anonymously edited *Wir warn die stärkste der Partein...: Erfahrungsberichte aus der Welt der K-Gruppen* (Berlin: Rotbuch, 1977). The Dutch experience can be best accessed via the case study of the remarkable evolution of an erstwhile hard-Maoist grouping by Kees Slager, *Het geheim van Oss* (Amsterdam: Atlas, 2001), and the comprehensive survey by Antoine Verbij, *Tien rode jaren: Links radicalisme in Nederland 1970–1980* (Amsterdam: Ambo, 2005). The Swiss experience, fragmented along confederal lines, is the subject of Benoît Challand, *La Ligue Marxiste Révolutionnaire en Suisse romande (1969–1980)* (Fribourg: Université de Fribourg, 2000), and Pompeo Macaluso, *Storia del Partito Socialista Autonoma* (Lugano: Dadò, 1997). One example each may suffice for the experiences of Austria, Britain, and the United States: Wilhelm Svoboda, *Sandkastenspiele: Eine Geschichte linker Radikalität in den 70er Jahren* (Vienna: Promedia, 1998); John Callaghan, *The Far Left in British Politics* (Oxford: Basil Blackwell, 1987); and Max Elbaum, *Revolution in the Air: Sixties Radicals Turn to Lenin, Mao and Che* (London: Verso, 2002).

Index

Printed in the United States
131156LV00001BA/67-102/P